Accounting Guide

Brokers and Dealers in Securities

September 1, 2017

1 2 3 4 5 6 7 8 9 0 AAP 1 9 8 7

ISBN 978-1-94549-832-9

Printed in Canada

Preface

> Prepared by the Stockbrokerage and Investment Banking Committee.

(Updated as of September 1, 2017)

About AICPA Accounting Guides

This AICPA Accounting Guide has been developed by the AICPA Stockbrokerage and Investment Banking Committee to assist management in the preparation of their financial statements in conformity with U.S. generally accepted accounting principles (GAAP). The guidance within this publication has no authoritative status.

AICPA Guides may include certain content presented as "Supplement," "Appendix," or "Exhibit." A supplement is a reproduction, in whole or in part, of authoritative guidance originally issued by a standard setting body (including regulatory bodies) and applicable to entities or engagements within the purview of that standard setter, independent of the authoritative status of the applicable AICPA Guide. Both appendixes and exhibits are included for informational purposes and have no authoritative status.

The Financial Reporting Executive Committee (FinREC) is the designated senior committee of the AICPA authorized to speak for the AICPA in the areas of financial accounting and reporting. Conforming changes made to the financial accounting and reporting guidance contained in this guide are approved by the FinREC Chair (or his or her designee). Updates made to the financial accounting and reporting guidance in this guide exceeding that of conforming changes are approved by the affirmative vote of at least two-thirds of the members of FinREC.

This guide does the following:

- Identifies certain requirements set forth in FASB *Accounting Standards Codification*® (ASC).
- Describes FinREC's understanding of prevalent or sole industry practice concerning certain issues. In addition, this guide may indicate that FinREC expresses a preference for the prevalent or sole industry practice, or it may indicate that FinREC expresses a preference for another practice that is not the prevalent or sole industry practice; alternatively, FinREC may express no view on the matter.
- Identifies certain other, but not necessarily all, industry practices concerning certain accounting issues without expressing FinREC's views on them.
- Provides guidance that has been supported by FinREC on the accounting, reporting, or disclosure treatment of transactions or events that are not set forth in FASB ASC.

Accounting guidance for nongovernmental entities included in an AICPA Accounting Guide is a source of nonauthoritative accounting guidance. As discussed later in this preface, FASB ASC is the authoritative source of U.S. accounting and reporting standards for nongovernmental entities, in addition to guidance issued by the SEC.

Recognition

AICPA Senior Committee

Financial Reporting Executive Committee

James Dolinar, *Chair*

The AICPA gratefully acknowledges those members of the AICPA Stockbrokerage and Investment Banking Committee (2016–2017) who reviewed or otherwise contributed to the development of this edition of the guide: Jeffrey Alfano, David Bonnar, Timothy Bridges, Nancy Grimaldi, John Iacobellis, Paul Lameo (former chair), Daniel Palomaki, Karl Ruhry, Keith Wenk, Stephen Zammitti (former chair), and the chair of the expert panel, Christopher Donovan.

In addition to the 2016–2017 expert panel members listed, the AICPA gratefully acknowledges those who reviewed and otherwise contributed to the development of this guide: Amy Altman, Patrick Haisten, Eric Hatch, Jeannine Hyman, Lauren Koster, Michael Macchiaroli, Kathryn Mahoney, Eric McGuinn, Katherine Mohrhauser, Dina Nussbaum, David Shelton, Israel Snow, Ryan Vaz, Stephen (Chip) Verrone, Tim Vintzel, and Elena Zak.

AICPA Staff

Ivory Bare
Lead Manager
Product Management and Development

Irina Portnoy
Senior Manager
Accounting Standards
and
Staff Liaison
AICPA Stockbrokerage and Investment Banking Committee Expert Panel

Guidance Considered in This Edition

This edition of the guide has been modified by the AICPA staff to include certain changes necessary due to the issuance of relevant guidance since the guide was originally issued, and other revisions as deemed appropriate. Relevant guidance issued through September 1, 2017, has been considered in the development of this edition of the guide. However, this guide does not include all accounting, reporting, regulatory, and other requirements applicable to a broker-dealer. This guide is intended to be used in conjunction with all applicable sources of relevant guidance.

Relevant guidance that is issued and effective on or before September 1, 2017, is incorporated directly in the text of this guide. Relevant guidance issued but not yet effective as of September 1, 2017, but becoming effective on or before December 31, 2017, is also presented directly in the text of the guide, but shaded gray and accompanied by a footnote indicating the effective date of the new guidance. The distinct presentation of this content is intended to aid the reader in differentiating content that may not be effective for the reader's purposes (as part of the guide's "dual guidance" treatment of applicable new guidance).

Relevant guidance issued but not yet effective as of the date of the guide and not becoming effective until after December 31, 2017, is referenced in a "guidance update" box; that is, a box that contains summary information on the guidance issued but not yet effective.

In updating this guide, all relevant guidance issued up to and including the following was considered, but not necessarily incorporated, as determined based on applicability:

- FASB Accounting Standards Update (ASU) No. 2017-12, *Derivatives and Hedging (Topic 815): Targeted Improvements to Accounting for Hedging Activities*
- SEC Release No. 33-10385, *Adoption of Updated EDGAR Filer Manual*

FASB ASC Pending Content

Presentation of Pending Content in FASB ASC

Amendments to FASB ASC (issued in the form of ASUs) are initially incorporated into FASB ASC in "pending content" boxes following the paragraphs being amended with links to the transition information. The pending content boxes are meant to provide users with information about how the guidance in a paragraph will change as a result of the new guidance.

Pending content applies to different entities at different times due to varying fiscal year-ends, and because certain guidance may be effective on different dates for public and nonpublic entities. As such, FASB maintains amended guidance in pending content boxes within FASB ASC until the "roll-off" date. Generally, the roll-off date is six months following the latest fiscal year end for which the original guidance being amended could still be applied.

Presentation of FASB ASC Pending Content in AICPA Accounting Guides

Amended FASB ASC guidance that is included in pending content boxes in FASB ASC on September 1, 2017, is referenced as "Pending Content" in this guide. Readers should be aware that "Pending Content" referenced in this guide will eventually be subjected to FASB's "roll-off" process and no longer be labeled as "Pending Content" in FASB ASC (as discussed in the previous paragraph).

Terms Used to Define Professional Requirements in This AICPA Accounting Guide

Any requirements described in this guide are normally referenced to the applicable standards or regulations from which they are derived. Generally, the terms used in this guide describing the professional requirements of the referenced standard setter (for example, the SEC) are the same as those used in the applicable standards or regulations (for example, *must* or *should*). However, where the accounting requirements are derived from FASB ASC, this guide uses *should*, whereas FASB uses *shall*. In its resource document "About the Codification" that accompanies FASB ASC, FASB states that it considers the terms *should* and *shall* to be comparable terms and to represent the same concept—the requirement to apply a standard.

Readers should refer to the applicable standards and regulations for more information on the requirements imposed by the use of the various terms used to define professional requirements in the context of the standards and regulations in which they appear.

Certain exceptions apply to these general rules, particularly in those circumstances in which the guide describes prevailing or preferred industry practices for the application of a standard or regulation. In these circumstances, the applicable senior committee responsible for reviewing the guide's content believes the guidance contained herein is appropriate for the circumstances.

Applicability of PCAOB Standards

Audits of the financial statements of *nonissuer broker-dealers* (those broker-dealers that are not subject to the Sarbanes-Oxley Act of 2002 [SOX], but are subject to the rules of the SEC) and *issuer broker-dealers*, as defined by the SEC (those broker-dealers that are subject to SOX and the rules of the SEC), are conducted in accordance with standards established by the PCAOB, a private sector, not-for-profit corporation created by SOX. The SEC has oversight authority over the PCAOB, including approval of its rules, standards, and budget.

Applicability of Quality Control Standards

QC section 10, *A Firm's System of Quality Control* (AICPA, *Professional Standards*), addresses a CPA firm's responsibilities for its system of quality control for its accounting and auditing practice. A system of quality control consists of policies that a firm establishes and maintains to provide it with reasonable assurance that the firm and its personnel comply with professional standards, as well as applicable legal and regulatory requirements. The policies also provide the firm with reasonable assurance that reports issued by the firm are appropriate in the circumstances.

QC section 10 applies to all CPA firms with respect to engagements in their accounting and auditing practice. In paragraph .13 of QC section 10, an *accounting and auditing practice* is defined as "a practice that performs engagements covered by this section, which are audit, attestation, compilation, review, and any other services for which standards have been promulgated by the AICPA Auditing Standards Board (ASB) or the AICPA Accounting and Review Services Committee (ARSC) under the "General Standards Rule" (ET sec. 1.300.001) or the "Compliance With Standards Rule" (ET sec. 1.310.001) of the AICPA Code of Professional Conduct. Although standards for other engagements may be promulgated by other AICPA technical committees, engagements performed in accordance with those standards are not encompassed in the definition of an *accounting and auditing practice*."

In addition to the provisions of QC section 10, readers should be aware of other sections within AICPA *Professional Standards* that address quality control considerations, including the following provisions that address engagement level quality control matters for various types of engagements that an accounting and auditing practice might perform:

- AU-C section 220, *Quality Control for an Engagement Conducted in Accordance With Generally Accepted Auditing Standards* (AICPA, *Professional Standards*)
- AT-C section 105, *Concepts Common to All Attestation Engagements* (AICPA, *Professional Standards*)
- AR-C section 60, *General Principles for Engagements Performed in Accordance With Statements on Standards for Accounting and Review Services* (AICPA, *Professional Standards*)

Because of the importance of engagement quality, this guide includes appendix D, "Overview of Statements on Quality Control Standards." This appendix summarizes key aspects of the quality control standard. This summarization should be read in conjunction with QC section 10, AU-C section 220, AT-C section 105, AR-C section 60, and the quality control standards issued by the PCAOB, as applicable.

AICPA.org Website

The AICPA encourages you to visit the website at www.aicpa.org, and the Financial Reporting Center website at www.aicpa.org/frc. The Financial Reporting Center supports members in the execution of high-quality financial reporting. Whether you are a financial statement preparer or a member in public practice, this center provides exclusive member-only resources for the entire financial reporting process and provides timely and relevant news, guidance, and examples supporting the financial reporting process. Another important focus of the Financial Reporting Center is keeping those in public practice up to date on issues pertaining to preparation, compilation, review, audit, attestation, and assurance and advisory engagements. Certain content on the AICPA's websites referenced in this guide may be restricted to AICPA members only.

PCAOB Oversight

The Dodd-Frank Wall Street Reform and Consumer Protection Act amended SOX to give the PCAOB full oversight authority over audits of all broker-dealers (including nonissuers), which includes standard setting, inspection, and enforcement. As of the date of this guide, the SEC has approved three rules related to PCAOB oversight. The first is a rule that establishes an interim inspection program related to audits of broker-dealers. The second rule amends PCAOB funding rules to provide for a portion of the accounting support fee (previously assessed on issuers only) to be allocated among a certain class of broker-dealers. See the discussion in chapter 3, "Regulatory Considerations," of this guide for more information. The third rule requires that all audits of broker-dealers, for periods ending on or after June 1, 2014, be performed in accordance with standards issued by the PCAOB.

Applicability of Requirements of SOX

Publicly held companies and other issuers are subject to the provisions of SOX and related SEC regulations for implementing SOX. Their outside auditors are also subject to the provisions of SOX and the rules and standards issued by the PCAOB. Nonissuer broker-dealers are not currently subject to the provisions of SOX.

Purpose and Applicability

This AICPA Accounting Guide has been prepared to assist broker-dealers in preparing financial statements in conformity with GAAP. It is important to note that the content in this guide is directed toward nonissuer broker-dealers.

This guide applies to the preparation of financial statements of entities that are broker-dealers. The activities of broker-dealers are described in chapter 1, "The Securities Industry." Operations of such entities are subject to the rules and regulations of the SEC and other regulatory bodies.

Broker-dealers are subject to regulation under the Securities Exchange Act of 1934. Some broker-dealers are also futures commission merchants for commodity futures and commodity option contracts subject to regulation under the Commodity Exchange Act.

Members of the Financial Industry Regulatory Authority are subject to the rules of that organization, and members of securities exchanges are also subject to the rules of the exchanges of which they are members. Some of these rules, as currently in effect, are discussed in this guide. However, the rules, regulations, practices, and procedures of the securities and commodities futures industries have changed frequently and extensively in recent years. Still, further changes are under consideration as this guide goes to press, and readers should keep abreast of these changes.

Limitations

The guide is intended to highlight significant matters and establish general guidance. It is not intended to provide a comprehensive discussion of all possible matters of significance related to broker-dealers.

Consulting the accounting and financial reporting sections of the guide cannot take the place of a careful reading of specified authoritative literature. Internal controls over financial reporting are discussed in the context of operational controls commonly found at broker-dealers. Although they may correspond to controls that are subject to procedures performed in an audit engagement performed in accordance with PCAOB standards, internal controls over financial reporting are not presented in that context and are not intended to address the considerations of such engagements.

TABLE OF CONTENTS

Chapter 1

The Securities Industry[1]

1.01 The securities industry has played an important role in the growth of global business by providing accessible markets for the initial and secondary offerings, as well as subsequent purchase and sale of securities. The industry has made investment in securities more readily available to the public and provided it with many diverse financial products. Through efficient financial markets, the industry has made it possible for business entities and governmental agencies that need to raise capital to be matched with investors who have funds to invest.

1.02 The securities industry has accomplished its role through a variety of financial products, services, and institutions. Capital formation is achieved through public offerings, private placements, asset securitization, and merchant banking activities. Efficient secondary markets are maintained when securities firms act as agents for customers' securities transactions, trading, and arbitrage activities through a broker and dealer's (broker-dealer's) own accounts, market-making, and designated market maker (formerly known as specialist) activities. The securities industry also aids the risk mitigation process through a variety of transactions, products (such as futures, forwards, swaps, and options), and techniques.

1.03 Many different institutions facilitate the processing of the products and providing of services. The following are some of the key types of institutions that the securities industry comprises:

- Broker-dealers
- The financial markets (exchange markets and over-the-counter [OTC] markets)
- Clearing organizations and depositories
- Transfer agents and registrars
- Qualified custodians
- Regulatory agencies

Broker-Dealers

1.04 Pursuant to the Securities Exchange Act of 1934 (1934 Act), the SEC developed a comprehensive system to regulate broker-dealers and the securities industry in general. As a result, all broker-dealers are subject to regulation by the SEC.

1.05 On July 30, 2013, the SEC amended Rule 17a-5, *Reports to Be Made by Certain Brokers and Dealers*, to require that audits of all broker-dealers' financial statements and supplemental information, as well as the auditor's

---

[1] The Dodd-Frank Wall Street Reform and Consumer Protection Act (Dodd-Frank Act), passed in July 2010, set in motion a multiyear rulemaking process that changes the structure of federal financial regulation and institutes new requirements for a number of industries and market participants. Rulemaking continues in a number of areas. Upon full implementation of its provisions, the act will have a significant impact on the securities industry. In February 2017, the president signed an executive order that sets in motion scaling back some of the provisions of the Dodd-Frank Act. Readers should be alert for further developments.

examination of the compliance report or the auditor's review of the exemption report, be conducted in accordance with PCAOB standards, effective for fiscal years ending on or after June 1, 2014. In conjunction with these changes, the PCAOB issued AS 2701, *Auditing Supplemental Information Accompanying Audited Financial Statements* (AICPA, *PCAOB Standards and Related Rules*), and two attestation standards, Attestation Standard No. 1, *Examination Engagements Regarding Compliance Reports of Brokers and Dealers* and Attestation Standard No. 2, *Review Engagements Regarding Exemption Reports of Brokers and Dealers* (AICPA, *PCAOB Standards and Related Rules*). Additionally, the PCAOB has modified its existing standards to encompass broker-dealers.

1.06 Securities broker-dealers perform various functions within the securities industry. Brokers acting as agents facilitate their customers' purchase and sale of securities and related financial instruments and usually charge commissions. Dealers or traders acting as principals buy and sell for their own accounts from and to customers and other dealers. Dealers typically carry an inventory and make a profit or loss on the spread between bid and asked prices or on markups from dealer prices, or they make a speculative profit or loss on market fluctuations. Many firms are known as broker-dealers because they act in both capacities. The range of their activities can go far beyond those described previously. For example, many broker-dealers provide such financial services as the following:

- Underwriting, or participating in the underwriting of, publicly offered securities
- Assisting in the private placement of securities
- Providing investment research and advice
- Developing new financial products, including derivative products
- Providing a source of market liquidity (market makers and designated market makers) and creating a secondary market for many products
- Providing loans and financings, including equity loans and mortgage loans
- Providing the means for companies to hedge foreign currency, interest rate, credit risk, and other risks
- Accommodating international investing, including U.S. investments in foreign markets and the investment activity of foreign investors in the U.S. markets
- Extending credit to customers who have bought securities on margin and to business entities that need financing for mergers, acquisitions, or leveraged buyouts
- Acting as a depository for securities owned by customers; disbursing to customers dividends and interest received; and informing customers about calls, tenders, and other reorganization activities pertaining to their securities
- Serving in an advisory capacity for public and corporate finance activities (such as mergers and acquisitions and leveraged buyouts) and providing investment and management advisory services to individual and institutional investors (for example, mutual funds, insurance companies, and pensions)

- Offering access to cash sweep products (such as money market funds or FDIC-insured bank deposit programs)
- Providing many other financial services (such as credit cards, checking accounts, and insurance products)

1.07 Many types of broker-dealers exist, and they may be distinguished by the range of activities they perform or the geographical area in which they operate. Full-service broker-dealers do not restrict themselves to particular activities or services. Regional broker-dealers are similar but generally concentrate their activities on a specific geographical area. Retail broker-dealers focus on individuals, whereas institutional broker-dealers are primarily concerned with nonnatural persons (for example, corporations). Introducing broker-dealers "introduce" their customers' business—on an omnibus or a fully disclosed basis—to a clearing broker-dealer. Broker-dealers may clear or carry their own customer trades or do so for an introducing broker. Boutiques or specialty firms, in contrast, engage in only one or a few activities, such as leveraged buyouts, arbitrage, direct private placements, mergers and acquisitions, customer discretionary accounts, or industry-specific research.

Discount Brokers

1.08 On May 1, 1975, fixed commission rates on securities transactions were abolished. With fully negotiated commissions, the discount broker assumed a role in the securities markets. Discount brokers generally charge lower commissions than full-service broker-dealers and provide fewer services. For example, they frequently provide no research support or little, if any, investment advice. Due to technological advances and the growth and popularity of the Internet, the major discount broker-dealers typically have their customers place securities transactions or otherwise manage their brokerage accounts via websites, or mobile devices, rather than through a registered representative.

Investment Bankers

1.09 *Investment bankers* are broker-dealers who assist in bringing new securities to the investing public. The three major functions of investment bankers are origination, underwriting, and distribution. New securities are created during origination, bought by investment bankers during underwriting, and sold to investors during the distribution phase. Investment banking revenues are derived principally from fees for services and price spreads from underwriting securities issues.

1.10 Because new security issuances are complex, many security issuers look to the investment banker for investment advice, information, and assistance. Issuers depend heavily on investment bankers who are financial market specialists to create securities that meet most of the issuers' needs and, simultaneously, are acceptable to investors. For a new issue, the investment banker commonly does the following:

- Advises the issuer on the kind of security, timing of the issuance, pricing, and specific terms that are most acceptable during current financial market conditions
- Prepares and assists in filing a registration statement with the SEC
- Facilitates the investor roadshow to market the issuance
- Arranges for the efficient distribution of the new issue

- Arranges for a number of operational requirements, such as trustees, security indentures, and safekeeping

1.11   Investment banking firms often buy (or underwrite) a new issue or guarantee its sale at a specified price. If the securities are not sold to investors at the offering price, the investment banker may be required to buy the securities for its own account and be subject to market risk until the investment banker is able to distribute or sell the shares to the secondary market. To sell the issue quickly, a syndicate of many firms is often formed for each issue, and the securities are distributed through a large network, reaching many potential investors. Historically, large syndicates, comprising many firms, were formed to create networks for selling issues quickly. Although this process continues for initial public offerings of equity securities, the advent of the shelf registration process for certain debt securities has increased the speed with which these issues are brought to market. As a result, the underwriters that usually make up the underwriting group for distributing these securities are fewer and have larger capital bases.

1.12   Investment bankers also provide advice to institutions on sales, divestitures, mergers, acquisitions, tender offers, privatizations, restructurings, spin-offs, and joint ventures. Investment bankers earn fees for providing these services which are typically contingent upon the closing of a transaction.

1.13   The Jumpstart Our Business Startups Act (JOBS Act) was enacted on April 5, 2012, with the purpose of stimulating the growth of small to midsized companies by making it easier for startup and emerging growth companies to raise capital, by easing various securities regulations, and to meet regulatory reporting requirements, including extending the amount of time that certain new public companies have to begin complying with certain requirements under the Sarbanes-Oxley Act of 2002. Specifically, Section 401 of the JOBS Act adopted amendments to Regulation A which provides an exemption from the registration requirements of the Securities Act of 1933 (the 1933 Act) offerings of up to $50 million of securities annually. See chapter 3, "Regulatory Considerations," for additional information.

1.14   In recent years, the equity underwriting market has experienced fewer issuances because many start-up companies receive multiple rounds of funding prior to a public offering. There are fewer public companies today than there have been over the last two decades, this is largely due to costs associated with regulatory compliance, market volatility, the availability of cheaper funding alternatives, and complex reporting requirements.

Government Securities Dealers

1.15   *U.S. government securities dealers* are a group of dealer firms that underwrite and trade U.S. government and federal agency securities. Certain of these firms are designated by the Federal Reserve Bank of New York as primary dealers in U.S. government securities, and they deal directly with U.S. government fiscal agents (the Federal Reserve Banks) in acquiring new securities issues. These primary dealers serve as a counterparty to the Federal Reserve Bank of New York by participating in auctions of U.S. government debt. Additionally, they make a market in most U.S. government and federal agency securities and, as such, quote bid and ask prices. Primary dealers also provide the Federal Reserve Bank of New York's trading desk with market information and analysis helpful in the formulation and implementation of monetary policy. In addition to complying with the rules and regulations promulgated by the SEC pursuant to the federal securities laws, these broker-dealers are also subject to certain rules and regulations of the Department of the Treasury. See chapter 3 for specific rule provisions relating to government securities dealers.

Designated Market Maker

1.16 A *designated market maker* (formerly known as *specialists*) is a broker-dealer authorized by an exchange to be a party through which all trading on the floor of the exchange in a particular security is transacted. A designated market maker provides for a fair and an orderly market for the selected list of securities it is authorized to trade. The designated market maker must generally be ready to take the other side of a transaction if other buyers or sellers are not available. The designated market maker also maintains a book of limit orders and acts as a broker's broker in executing these limit orders against incoming market orders. With the proliferation of electronic trading, the designated market maker's role has been diminished in recent years.

Clearing Brokers

1.17 A *clearing broker* is a broker-dealer who receives and executes customers' instructions, prepares trade confirmations, settles the money related to the trades, arranges for the book entry (or physical movement) of the securities, and shares responsibility with the introducing brokers for compliance with regulatory requirements. See paragraph 1.52 for a discussion of the delivery of securities.

Carrying Brokers

1.18 A *carrying broker* is a broker-dealer that holds customer accounts for introducing broker-dealers. Typically, this type of firm is also a clearing firm for those introducing firms. A carrying broker-dealer is responsible for performing the customer reserve computation and possession and control requirements of SEC Rule 15c3-3. A carrying broker-dealer may carry customer accounts on an omnibus or a fully-disclosed basis.

Prime Brokers

1.19 *Prime brokerage* is a system developed by full-service broker-dealers to facilitate the clearance and settlement of securities trades for substantial retail and institutional customers who are active market participants. Prime brokerage involves three distinct parties: the prime broker, the executing broker, and the customer. The *prime broker* is the broker-dealer that clears and finances the customer trades executed by one or more executing broker-dealers at the behest of the customer. Prime brokers typically provide services such as securities lending, financing, customized technology, and operational support to hedge funds and other sophisticated investors. In addition, a prime broker may also offer other value-added services such as capital introduction and risk management. Most prime brokerage agreements are executed with hedge funds and separately managed accounts.

Swap Dealers

1.20 Swap dealers act as a counterparty in a swap agreement. Swap dealers are the market makers in the swap market. Swaps are derivative contracts through which two parties exchange financial instruments typically involving cash based on notional amounts. Each cash flow comprises one leg of the swap.

One cash flow is typically fixed while the other is variable. There are various types of swaps including interest rate swaps and credit default swaps. Historically, swaps have been traded in the OTC market between financial institutions in largely unregulated transactions.

1.21 The SEC and Commodity Futures Trading Commission (CFTC) jointly adopted final rules under the Dodd-Frank Wall Street Reform and Consumer Protection Act (Dodd-Frank Act) defining, among other things, the terms *swap dealer* and *security-based swap dealer*. The term *swap dealer* is defined in CFTC Regulation 1.3(ggg) under the Commodity Exchange Act and the SEC defines the term *security-based swap dealer* in SEC Rule 3a71-1 under the 1934 Act. The designation as a swap dealer or a security-based swap dealer within the meaning of the Dodd-Frank Act depends on the types of swap or security-based swap activities in which an institution engages. An institution is considered a swap dealer or a security-based swap dealer, as applicable, if it engages in one or more of the following activities:

- Holding itself out as a swap dealer or security-based swap dealer;
- Making markets in swaps or security-based swaps;
- Regularly entering into swaps or security-based swaps with counterparties in the ordinary course of business for its own account; or
- Engaging in activities that cause oneself to be commonly known in the trade as a dealer or market maker in swaps or security-based swaps.

Introducing Brokers

1.22 An *introducing broker* is a broker-dealer firm that accepts customer orders but elects to clear the orders through another broker for cost efficiencies (for example, not having to perform all the clearance functions on a small volume of business, thereby eliminating many fixed costs). In this arrangement, the introducing broker accepts the customers' orders and the clearing brokers or other parties clear the trades. Either party may initiate the execution of a trade. The clearing broker-dealer processes and settles the customer transactions for the introducing broker and usually maintains detailed customer records. Essentially, the introducing broker is using the back-office processing of the clearing broker-dealer. The commissions received from the transactions are collected by the clearing broker and divided in any manner agreed to by the introducing and clearing broker-dealers and stipulated in written contracts (for example, clearing agreements).

Brokers' Brokers

1.23 A *broker's broker* is a broker-dealer firm that acts as an agent for an undisclosed principal (another broker-dealer) for the purchase and sale of treasury, municipal, and corporate debt securities. These firms do not maintain securities inventories. Brokers' brokers play a significant role in the secondary market as intermediaries for trades between broker-dealers. Brokers' brokers typically provide the bid and ask prices for securities of their client on an undisclosed basis on trading screens of the brokers' broker and then match up buyers and sellers. Brokers' brokers commonly deal in U.S. treasury, municipal, and corporate bond trading businesses for which no exchanges are available. Some brokers' brokers concentrate in certain kinds of securities and act as intermediaries for registered dealers and receive commissions that are usually determined by the size of the transaction.

Bank-Owned Brokers (Section 4k4(e) and Section 20 Brokers)

1.24 A Section 20 broker was established by a bank pursuant to Section 20 of the Glass-Steagall Act of 1933. The Gramm-Leach-Bliley Act of 1999, also known as the Financial Services Modernization Act, repealed Section 20 of the Glass-Steagall Act of 1933 and changed the types of activities that are permissible for bank holding company affiliates and subsidiaries of banks, creating so-called "financial holding companies" that may engage in a broad array of activities. Financial holding company affiliates, as well as direct subsidiaries of banks, may now engage in underwriting, dealing in, or making a market in securities. Broker-dealers of financial holding companies are now subject to the rules pursuant to Section 4k4(e) of the Gramm-Leach-Bliley Act of 1999. The Gramm-Leach-Bliley Act of 1999 affirmed the concept of functional regulation. Federal banking regulators will continue to be primary supervisors of the banking affiliates of financial holding companies, and the SEC and securities self-regulatory organizations will supervise the securities businesses of those entities.

Independent Broker-Dealers

1.25 Independent broker-dealers provide independent financial advisers with front, middle, and back office support in technology, clearing and settlement, compliance services, training, and research. Independent broker-dealers offer its services to financial advisers operating as self-employed business owners and are classified for tax purposes as independent contractors. Independent broker-dealers primarily engage in the sale of packaged products, such as mutual funds, exchange traded funds, variable and fixed insurance products, and real estate investment trusts. In addition to commission-based business, independent broker-dealers also provide a fee-based business under their registered investment advisory platforms.

The Financial Markets

1.26 Financial markets comprise many types of participants, both domestic and foreign, in which securities are bought and sold. International financial markets continue to grow and gain in sophistication. Many financial organizations are involved with international trading strategies to gain the advantages of the global marketplace, as well as different tax policies and trading activities. International trading markets vary depending on the country or community in which the market exists, and international settlement procedures vary depending on the exchange or the local country rules. Some exchanges exhibit more sophisticated or faster trade and settlement characteristics than U.S. exchanges; others trade securities in a negotiated fashion with lengthy settlement periods.

1.27 Financial markets can be categorized according to the kinds of instruments traded (such as futures, options, municipals, equities, and government and corporate debt). Financial markets have primary and secondary market operations. Primary markets provide for the original distribution of new securities. Secondary markets, which consist of exchanges and OTC markets, provide for the resale of securities. In addition, the characteristics of the securities traded may be used to categorize the financial markets. For example, the markets for U.S. Treasury bills, certificates of deposit, federal funds, bankers' acceptances, and commercial paper are commonly referred to as money markets. Money market securities[2] generally have maturities of one year or less, have less credit risk than equivalent long-term securities, and trade in large denominations.

1.28 Financial markets may also be characterized according to whether a party must find the counterparty to a trade and negotiate with that counterparty directly or whether the counterparty is approached through an intermediary. The intermediary may be an agent who conducts a search for a counterparty (either an individual or institution) to be a buyer or seller of a particular security, may complete the transaction by trading with dealers who hold themselves out as willing to buy and sell (such as in OTC markets), or may transact directly against the orders of other potential counterparties by communicating through a single centralized location (exchange markets).

Exchange Market

Floor-Based Exchange

1.29 An *exchange market* is a central meeting place established to facilitate the trading of securities or commodities. A *securities exchange* is an exchange market that provides trading facilities for stocks, bonds, or options. Exchange markets are generally characterized as auction places where bids and offers are directed and executed by brokers or designated market makers.

1.30 Transactions in securities executed on an exchange are normally initiated by a customer communicating with a registered representative (salesperson or account executive) of a broker-dealer to request that a specified number of shares of a particular security be bought or sold at a stated price or the current market price. The order is usually communicated to the order room of the broker-dealer and then to its floor clerk, who is stationed at the exchange that trades the security. Securities transactions executed on an exchange may be in round lots (units of trading, normally 100 shares as specified by the exchange that lists the security) or in odd lots (quantities of less than 1 unit of trading).

1.31 Once the order is conveyed to the floor of the exchange, it is given by the floor clerk to a floor trader, who will attempt to execute it. If the broker-dealer is not a member of the particular exchange, the order is relayed to a correspondent broker who executes the trade on the exchange. Once executed, the details of the transaction (price, quantity, other broker with whom the transaction was consummated, and so forth) are reported back to the order room of the broker-dealer for transmission to the purchase and sales department. A confirmation of the trade is then prepared and sent to the customer.

1.32 With the advent of advanced technology, certain exchanges have provided their members with the facility of direct order entry to designated market makers, in addition to other electronic enhancements to trading.

1.33 In recent years, the equities markets have become fragmented where shares are trading on multiple exchanges and alternative trading venues. For

---

[2] On July 23, 2014, the SEC issued Final Rule Release No. 33-9616, "Money Market Fund Reform; Amendments to Form PF." The rules are aimed at reducing the potential for money market fund "runs" by requiring funds that cater to large institutional investors to abandon their fixed $1 per share price and to float in value like other mutual funds. The rules also allow funds to restrict redemptions during periods of market stress through gating features or penalties. Readers should consult the full text of SEC Final Rule Release No. 33-9616, which can be accessed on the Final Rules page at www.sec.gov.

example, the New York Stock Exchange's (NYSE) share of trading in its listed stocks has declined over the last several years. There are advantages and disadvantages to market fragmentation. The May 2010 "flash crash" demonstrates issues with fragmentation as high frequency traders and complex computer algorithms caused a severe market drop in seconds. There are also advantages, as demonstrated by an outage in July 2015, of more than four hours on the NYSE where orders seamlessly were routed to other trading venues with no discernable negative impact to the market.

Electronic-Based Exchange

1.34 An exchange may also operate through electronic trading platforms and networks to create a virtual marketplace for the purpose of trading securities and other financial instruments. When using an electronic stock exchange for trading, computer networks match buyers and sellers, thus providing an efficient and a fast method for executing trades. This may be especially important for those making a large volume of trades. One example of an electronic stock exchange is NASDAQ.

OTC Market

1.35 Many companies have insufficient shares outstanding, stockholders, or earnings to meet the listing requirements of an exchange or, for other reasons, choose not to be listed. Securities of these companies are traded in the OTC market between dealers who make markets acting as principals or brokers for customers.

1.36 The OTC market is not a location; rather, it is a communications network linking those dealers that make markets in securities generally not listed on exchanges. The OTC market is regulated by the Financial Industry Regulatory Authority (FINRA). An offer to buy or sell an unlisted security is executed by a broker-dealer entering into a transaction with a customer or another broker-dealer that makes a market in that security.

1.37 The broker-dealer may be an OTC market maker and act for its own account (dealer as principal) or for the account of a customer (broker as agent) in a purchase or sale transaction with a customer or another broker-dealer. Acting as a dealer, no commission is charged; instead, the broker-dealer realizes a profit or loss based on the spread between the cost and selling price of the securities. Acting as a broker (agent), a commission is charged.

1.38 The market makers publish quotes for security prices on a bid-and-ask basis (that is, they buy a security at the bid price and sell it at the ask price). The difference between the price for which the dealer is willing to purchase (bid for) the security and the price for which the dealer is willing to sell (ask for) the security is the spread.

1.39 Firm price quotations for OTC equity securities are available from the interdealer quotation systems, such as FINRA's OTC Bulletin Board and OTC Markets Group's OTC Pink.

Third Market

1.40 OTC trading of shares listed on an exchange takes place in the third market by broker-dealers and investors that are not exchange members. Members of an exchange are generally required to execute buy and sell orders in listed securities that are not SEC Rule 19c-3 eligible through that exchange during exchange hours. Rule 19c-3 includes those equity securities that were listed and registered on an exchange on or after April 26, 1979. However, a broker-dealer firm that is not a member of the exchange can make a market in a listed stock in the same way it would make a market in an unlisted stock.

Alternative Trading Venues

1.41   Direct trading of securities between two parties with no broker intermediary takes place in the fourth market. In many cases, both parties involved are institutions. For example, securities may trade on a private placement basis whereby the parties negotiate the terms of the placement. Because limited information may be publicly available, a small group of sophisticated investors generally hold privately placed securities.

Electronic Communication Network

1.42   An *electronic communication network (ECN)*, a type of alternative trading system, is an electronic system that brings buyers and sellers together for the electronic execution of trades. ECNs are required to be registered with the SEC and may be registered as either a dealer or an exchange. Those who subscribe to ECNs (generally, institutional investors, broker-dealers, and market-makers) can place trades directly on the ECN, typically using limit orders. ECNs post orders on their system for other subscribers to view. The ECN will then automatically match orders for execution. If a subscriber wants to buy a stock through an ECN, but there are no sell orders to match the buy order, the order cannot be executed until a matching sell order comes in. If the order is placed through an ECN during regular trading hours, an ECN that cannot find a match may send the order to another market center (for example, the NYSE or NASDAQ) for execution.

1.43   The benefits investors get from trading with an ECN include speed; trading after hours; real-time display of orders (whereas on the NYSE, most investors are limited to viewing only the best bid and ask prices); ability to trade among themselves without having to go through a middleman (smaller spreads, lower commissions, better price executions); and anonymity (which is often important for large trades).

Dark Pools

1.44   A dark pool of liquidity is trading volume or liquidity that is not openly available to the public. The bulk of dark pool trades represent large trades by financial institutions that are offered away from public exchanges so that trades are anonymous. The fragmentation of financial trading venues and electronic trading has allowed dark pools to be created, and they are normally accessed through crossing networks or directly between market participants.

1.45   There are three major types of dark pools. The first is where independent companies set up to offer a unique differentiated basis for trading. The second is where the broker-dealer owns the dark pool and clients of the broker-dealer can interact, most commonly with other clients of the broker (possibly including its own proprietary traders) in conditions of anonymity. The third is where public exchanges, or consortiums of broker-dealers, create their own dark pools to allow their clients the benefits of anonymity and non-display of orders while offering an exchange's resources and infrastructure.

1.46   These systems and strategies typically seek liquidity among open and closed trading venues, such as other alternative trading systems. As such, they are particularly useful for computerized and quantitative strategies. Dark pools have been growing in importance, with dozens of different pools garnering a substantial portion of U.S. equity trading. Dark pools are of various types and can execute trades in multiple ways, such as through negotiation or automatically, throughout the day or at scheduled times.

Clearing Organizations and Depositories

1.47 After orders in securities have been executed, whether on an exchange or in the OTC market, the transactions are compared, cleared, and settled. Comparison occurs when broker-dealers or their agents exchange their trade information (security, number of units, and price) to confirm the existence of a contract and match the buy and sell sides of the trade. *Clearance* is the process of accounting for compared trades in terms of the trading parties' obligations to pay money and deliver securities. *Settlement* is the process of exchanging the money for securities (that is, delivery and payment) that consummates the transaction. In the U.S. equity and corporate markets, settlement has historically occurred three business days after the trade. Under SEC Release No. 34-80295, "Amendment to Securities Transaction Settlement Cycle," the SEC amended Rule 15c6-1(a), *Settlement Cycle Rule*, to shorten the standard settlement cycle for most broker-dealer transactions from three business days after the trade date ("T+3") to two business days after the trade date ("T+2").[3] Trade comparison, clearance, and settlement are aspects of posttrade processing.

1.48 The exchange markets have sponsored central clearing agencies, known as clearing organizations, to assist in the comparison, clearance, and settlement functions. Deliveries and receipts of securities and the related cash settlements are made through these clearing organizations for broker-dealers. The National Securities Clearing Corporation (NSCC), a subsidiary of the Depository Trust & Clearing Corporation (DTCC), is one such U.S. clearing organization. In the OTC market, clearance may be accomplished by a variety of methods, including the buying and selling of broker-dealers' exchange-of-trade tickets directly with one another or through a clearing organization. Introducing broker-dealers operating through clearing brokers settle their transactions through those clearing brokers that in turn, settle the transactions through the clearing organizations. The Options Clearing Corporation and the clearing organizations of the commodity exchanges perform similar functions for options and futures trading. Clearance of securities traded on international markets is accomplished in a variety of ways, ranging from centralized clearing organizations (for example, Euroclear) to business entities whose securities are cleared by major banking organizations.

1.49 Most U.S. government and agency security transactions clear through the use of the book entry safekeeping system maintained by the Federal Reserve Bank of New York. The 12 district Federal Reserve Banks operate a securities transfer system that permits these securities to be transferred between the book entry safekeeping accounts.

1.50 The Fixed Income Clearing Corporation (FICC) provides clearing for fixed income securities, including U.S. Treasury securities and mortgage

---

[3] The effective date of this release was May 30, 2017, and the compliance date was September 5, 2017. Readers are encouraged to consult the full text of the release, available at www.sec.gov/rules/final/2017/34-80295.pdf.

backed securities. FICC was created in 2003 to handle fixed income transaction processing, integrating the Government Securities Clearing Corporation and the Mortgage-Backed Securities Clearing Corporation. Securities transactions processed by the FICC include U.S. Treasury bills, bonds, notes, zero-coupon securities, government agency securities, mortgage-backed securities, and inflation-indexed securities. Participants in this market include mortgage originators, government-sponsored enterprises, registered broker-dealers, institutional investors, investment managers, mutual funds, commercial banks, insurance companies, and other financial institutions.

1.51 Settlement of securities transactions can be complex, especially when there is a large volume of transactions in many securities. To avoid duplicated receipt and delivery of securities, the NSCC uses an electronic netting system known as continuous net settlement (CNS). In CNS, a broker-dealer's purchases and sales in the same security are netted, thus leaving the broker-dealer with one daily net settlement obligation per security. The broker-dealer then settles that obligation with the clearing organization. Unique to CNS, the clearing agency interposes itself between the trading broker-dealers on each trade and guarantees the settlement obligations of each broker-dealer's countertrading party. Thus, the broker-dealer's settlement is with the clearing organization, not the other broker-dealer. Other clearing mechanisms may or may not guarantee settlement. A broker-dealer can settle each day or carry open commitments forward to net against the next day's settlement (hence the continuous nature of CNS).

1.52 Security deliveries in the current U.S. environment are generally by book entry (that is, by electronic debits and credits to a broker-dealer's account) at a securities depository where the securities certificates are immobilized and where broker-dealers hold the certificates in the street name for their customers. Thus, delivery is accomplished without the physical movement of the securities certificates. The securities depositories, which are similar to banks, pursue the business of custodian operations, including holding securities certificates in physical form or maintaining electronic records of book entry securities holdings for their customers, mainly financial institutions.

1.53 One of the major depositories for equities, corporate debt securities, certain eligible mortgage-backed securities, and municipal debt securities is the DTCC and its subsidiaries.

Transfer Agents

1.54 Although many securities issuers use a bank or trust company as their transfer agent, an issuer may use an independent transfer agent or may act as its own transfer agent. There are two basic functions of a transfer agent: the transfer function and the registrar function. A transfer agent may perform one or both of these functions.

1.55 The transfer function includes the canceling of old certificates that are properly presented and endorsed in good deliverable form (which usually includes a signature guarantee), making appropriate adjustments in the issuer's shareholder records, establishing a new account in the name of the new owner, and issuing new certificates in the name of the new owner. Transfer agents also review legal documents to ensure that they are complete and in perfect order before transferring the securities. If the legal documents are incomplete, the transfer agent either will notify the presenter that the documents are incomplete and hold the old certificate and accompanying documentation until the presenter sends the transfer agent the proper documents or will reject the transfer and return the securities.

1.56 For mutual funds, transfer agents enter the amount of securities purchased by a shareholder on the issuer's books and redeem (liquidate) shares upon receipt of the customer's written or wire request. Transfer agents, as part of their transfer function, maintain records of the name and address of each security holder, the amount of securities owned by each security holder, the certificate numbers corresponding to a security holder's position, the issue date of the security certificate, and the cancellation date of the security certificate. Many transfer agents also act as paying agents for cash dividends and the distribution of stock dividends and stock splits.

1.57 A transfer agent performing the registrar function monitors the issuance of securities in an issue with a view toward preventing the unauthorized issuance of securities. The registrar checks to ensure that the issuance of the securities will not cause the authorized number of shares in an issue to be exceeded and that the number of shares represented by the new certificate or certificates corresponds to the number of shares on the canceled ones. After the registrar performs these functions, the registrar countersigns the certificate.

Regulatory Overview

1.58 Regulatory environments differ from country to country, and the freedom of entry into the marketplace likewise varies depending on the local regulation. In the United States, the 1934 Act provides for the regulation of securities transactions after the securities are initially distributed to public investors in an underwriting. The 1934 Act established the SEC that, among other things, is authorized to promulgate and enforce rules governing the regulation of broker-dealers in securities. The SEC developed, pursuant to the 1934 Act, a comprehensive system to regulate broker-dealers. Under the 1934 Act, all broker-dealers are required to be members of self-regulatory organizations, such as FINRA, which performs routine surveillance and monitoring of its members. A similar regulatory framework was established for commodity broker-dealers (that is, futures commission merchants) under the Commodity Futures Trading Commission Act of 1974, which established the CFTC and gave it exclusive jurisdiction over commodity futures matters. The Commodity Futures Modernization Act of 2000 (CFMA) authorized joint regulation by the CFTC and the SEC of security futures products on individual equity issues and on narrow-based indexes of securities. The CFMA created a flexible structure for the regulation of futures trading, codified an agreement between the CFTC and the SEC to repeal the ban on trading single-stock futures, and provided legal certainty for OTC derivatives markets. The CFMA amended the definition of *security* in the 1933 Act and the definitions of *security* and *equity security* in the 1934 Act to include a security future. In April 2002, the SEC amended the definition of *equity security* in rules under the 1933 Act and the 1934 Act to conform them to the statutory definitions with respect to security futures. The Commodity Futures Trading Commission Act of 1974 also authorized the creation of registered futures associations, giving the futures industry the opportunity to create a nationwide, self-regulatory organization. The National Futures Association (NFA), which began operations in 1982, is the self-regulatory organization for the U.S. derivatives industry, including exchange-traded futures, retail off-exchange foreign currency, and OTC derivatives.

1.59 Since its adoption, the 1934 Act has been amended to include virtually all participants in the securities markets and an ever-increasing range of securities-related activities. Originally, the scope of the 1934 Act was limited to the regulation of exchanges, members of exchanges, and trading in securities listed on exchanges. The Maloney Act of 1938 amended the 1934 Act to cover the OTC markets. The Maloney Act of 1938 also established the National Association of Securities Dealers (NASD) (that was subsequently consolidated with NYSE Regulation, Inc. into a single self-regulatory organization: FINRA), which is an independent, non-governmental regulator for all securities firms doing business with the public in the United States.

1.60 In 1975, the 1934 Act was amended to extend the authority of the SEC to include securities transfer agents, clearing organizations, and securities depositories. This amendment also established the Municipal Securities Rulemaking Board that was authorized to prescribe rules regulating the activities of municipal securities broker-dealers. In 1986, the 1934 Act was amended by the Government Securities Act of 1986 to require U.S. government securities broker-dealers to register with the SEC. Under the Government Securities Act of 1986, the SEC has the authority to enforce rules promulgated by the Department of the Treasury that concern U.S. government securities broker-dealers. Thus, the 1934 Act today provides a comprehensive scheme of regulation for virtually all broker-dealers in securities, the exchanges, and the OTC markets, as well as the facilities for clearing and settling transactions among broker-dealers, depositories, transfer agents, and registrars.

1.61 The Securities Investors Protection Corporation (SIPC) was established when Congress enacted the Securities Investor Protection Act of 1970 (SIPA). SIPC is a nonprofit membership corporation designed to protect, up to a specific maximum amount, customers' cash and securities in the custody of a broker-dealer that fails and is liquidated under SIPA. Broker-dealers registered with the SEC, with some limited exceptions, are required to be members of SIPC. The money required to protect customers beyond that which is available from the customer property in the possession of the failed broker-dealer is advanced by SIPC from a fund maintained for that purpose. The sources of money for this fund are assessments collected from SIPC members and interest on the fund's investments in U.S. government securities made with the funds collected. See chapter 3 for more information on the SIPC assessment and related reporting.

1.62 The Department of Labor (DOL) Fiduciary Rule is a new ruling that will be phased in through January 1, 2018. It includes a transition period for the applicability of certain exemptions to the rule extending through January 1, 2018. Readers should be alert for further developments, particularly regarding the effective dates.

1.63 The rule expands the "investment advice fiduciary" definition under the Employee Retirement Income Security Act of 1974 (ERISA). The DOL's definition of a fiduciary demands that advisors act in the best interests of their clients, and to put their clients' interests above their own. The rule requires financial advisors to be free of any potential conflicts of interest, and states that all fees and commissions must be clearly disclosed in dollar form to clients. Fiduciary is a much higher level of accountability than the suitability standard previously required of financial salespersons, such as brokers, planners and insurance agents, who work with retirement plans and accounts. "Suitability" meant that as long as an investment recommendation met a client's defined need and objective, it was deemed appropriate. Now, financial professionals are legally obligated to put their client's best interests first rather than simply finding "suitable" investments.

1.64 Financial advisors who choose to continue working on commission will need to provide clients with a disclosure agreement, called a Best Interest Contract Exemption (BICE), in circumstances where a conflict of interest could exist (such as, the advisor receiving a higher commission or special bonus for selling a certain product). This is to guarantee that the advisor is working unconditionally in the best interest of the client. Additionally, all compensation that is paid to the fiduciary must be clearly documented.

1.65 Covered retirement plans include defined-contribution plans such as 401(k) plans, 403(b) plans, employee stock ownership plans, simplified employee pension (SEP) plans; defined-benefit plans such as pension plans or those that promise a certain payment to the participant as defined by the plan document; and individual retirement accounts (IRAs).

Business Activities

Brokerage

1.66 Broker-dealers can earn commissions by buying or selling securities and commodities on their customers' behalf. Broker-dealers' handling of customers' funds and securities is subject to rules administered by the SEC, the Board of Governors of the Federal Reserve System (Federal Reserve), and the self-regulatory organizations. Although the specific definition of the term *customer* varies in the SEC's rules, SEC Rule 15c3-3 defines customer as "any person from whom or on whose behalf a broker or dealer has received or acquired or holds funds or securities for the account of that person." The rule excludes certain categories of persons from the definition, including broker-dealers, municipal securities dealers, and government securities broker-dealers. It also excludes general partners, directors, and principal officers of the broker-dealer and any other person to the extent that the person has a claim for property or funds which by contract, agreement or understanding, or by operation of law, is part of the capital of the broker-dealer or is subordinated to the claims of creditors of the broker-dealer.

1.67 Broker-dealers regularly finance the transactions of their customers. The initial extension of credit by broker-dealers is governed by Federal Reserve Regulation T (Regulation T) of the Federal Reserve System. Regulation T classifies transactions into specifically defined accounts. Most transactions with customers are done in cash or margin accounts.

1.68 *Cash account.* In a cash account, the customer pays in full within a specified settlement period for any security purchased. Regulation T generally requires cash payment by the customer for the purchase of securities within two business days after settlement date; however, a self-regulatory organization or national securities association may grant an extension of time before payment is required. If the customer does not make timely payment for the securities, Regulation T requires the broker-dealer to promptly cancel or liquidate the transaction. In general, the broker-dealer will hold the customer responsible for any resulting loss.

1.69 If a customer sells securities, the customer must promptly deliver the certificates to the broker-dealer. Either the proceeds of a sale will be credited to the customer's account on the settlement date, or if requested, a check will be mailed to the customer. In general, under SEC Rule 15c3-3, if the broker-dealer does not receive the securities sold within 10 business days of the settlement date, the broker-dealer is required to close the transaction with the customer by purchasing securities of like kind and quantity. Again, the broker-dealer will hold the customer responsible for any resulting loss.

1.70 *Margin accounts.* Under Regulation T, the broker-dealer is required to record the purchase or sale of securities by customers on other-than-immediate cash settlement terms in a margin account. A purchase on margin contemplates a prolonged extension of credit to the customer by the broker-dealer. The maximum amount of initial credit is prescribed by Regulation T. The maximum amount of credit the broker-dealer can extend beyond the initial transaction is prescribed by the rules of the appropriate self-regulatory organization. Customer margin requirements relating to securities futures are prescribed by joint final rules issued by the SEC and the CFTC in August 2002.

1.71 If the amount of equity in the customer's account is below the amount required to cover the initial margin, Regulation T requires the broker-dealer to eliminate the margin deficiency within five calendar days after it was created or increased. When a deficiency arises, the broker-dealer will normally issue a call for margin from the customer.

1.72 The customer can satisfy the margin call by making additional margin deposits of cash or securities. If the customer does not make the deposits within the specified time, including approved extensions of time by a self-regulatory organization or national securities association, Regulation T requires the broker-dealer to liquidate securities sufficient to satisfy the required margin. Broker-dealers also have self-imposed margin requirements that are generally more stringent than the Federal Reserve System or self-regulatory organization requirements.

1.73 *Accounts carried for other brokers.* Clearing brokers maintain the customer accounts of introducing brokers. *Fully disclosed accounts* are accounts of the introducing broker's customers that are carried on the books of a clearing broker. In a fully disclosed account, the introducing broker's customers are treated as if they were the clearing broker's own customers, except that correspondence to customers usually refers to the introducing broker by including a phrase such as "through the courtesy of [*the introducing broker's name*]." The clearing broker maintains the customers' accounts and is usually responsible for collecting the purchase price, the commission, and other fees from the customers. However, the introducing broker generally indemnifies the clearing broker for uncollected amounts from any resulting unsecured accounts of the introducing broker's customers. The clearing broker and the introducing broker enter into a contract that describes the distribution of commissions between brokers.

1.74 In contrast, an *omnibus account* is an account of the introducing broker that is carried on the books of the clearing broker and that represents the sum of the activity of customers of the introducing broker. The introducing broker's customer accounts are carried separately on the books of the introducing broker. For an omnibus account, the introducing broker prepares and sends confirmations and monthly statements to customers, maintains customers' accounts and margin records, and retains most of the responsibility for compliance with regulatory matters.

Firm Trading

1.75 Firm trading (also referred to as proprietary trading) involves a full range of activities whereby broker-dealers may take principal positions for their own accounts. Certain broker-dealers make markets in particular OTC securities by standing ready to buy or sell securities to their customers or other broker-dealers. These broker-dealers often carry an inventory of the securities in which they make a market and are exposed to the market risks inherent in such positions. In addition, these broker-dealers may sell securities short in anticipation of decreases in the price of the securities.

1.76 *Riskless arbitrage.* *Riskless arbitrage* is the simultaneous purchase and sale of the same or an equivalent security in order to profit from price discrepancies. *Convertible arbitrage* is a form of riskless arbitrage that uses convertible securities or warrants versus the underlying equity securities. Broker-dealers can profit from the temporary price differences that exist from the same or similar securities traded in different financial markets. Another kind of basic arbitrage involves purchasing and selling similar securities in like markets.

1.77 *Risk arbitrage.* *Risk arbitrage* is a term used to describe special situations (such as mergers, reorganizations, recapitalizations, tenders for cash, and tenders for securities) in which the arbitrage trader buys or sells securities without fully hedging or offsetting risk, with the intention of realizing a profit at some future period based on the anticipated market movement when the special situation is completed.

1.78 *Program trading.* *Program trading* is a term used to describe the simultaneous buying and selling of a large number of different stocks based on their perceived correlation. Program trading may encompass several index-related trading strategies, including hedging, index arbitrage, and portfolio insurance. Program trades are often accomplished through an exchange's high-speed order system. By using a high-speed order system, program trades can be carried out in a matter of minutes. Program trading enables institutions to make broad changes in their portfolios and thus facilitates index arbitrage. Index arbitrage combines the buying and selling of stocks with offsetting trades in stock index futures or options.

1.79 *Algorithmic trading.* Algorithmic trading, also called automated trading, black-box trading, or algo trading, is the use of electronic platforms for entering trading orders with an algorithm which executes pre-programmed trading instructions whose variables may include timing, price, or quantity of the order, or in many cases the order is initiated electronically, without human intervention. Algorithmic trading is widely used by investment banks, pension funds, mutual funds, and other buy-side (investor-driven) institutional traders, to divide large trades into several smaller trades to manage market impact and risk. Broker-dealers and some hedge funds, provide liquidity to the market, generating and executing orders automatically. A special class of algorithmic trading is high-frequency trading, which is often most profitable during periods of high market volatility.

1.80 *Block trading.* *Block trading* is the acquisition or disposition of large quantities of securities by a broker-dealer to facilitate the execution of buy or sell orders of customers, usually institutions. Block traders locate suitable trading partners and assist the buyer and seller in negotiating the terms of the trade. The broker-dealer's assistance is needed because the inflow of orders to the exchange floor is generally too small to execute the trade in a reasonable period of time, and designated market makers typically do not have sufficient capital to execute such transactions. In addition, designated market makers are not allowed to communicate directly with public buyers and sellers, whereas block traders may communicate with them. If the broker-dealer has negotiated a trade, it is crossed on the exchange (that is, the broker executes two or more matched orders on the exchange).

1.81 *When-issued transactions. When-issued transactions* are contracts to purchase or sell securities only when, as, and if new securities are issued. Broker-dealers enter into such purchase or sale transactions on pending issues of new securities. Trading in when-issued securities normally begins when the U.S. Treasury, a municipality, a state, or some other issuer of securities announces a forthcoming issue. Such transactions are contingent upon the issuance of the securities. Because the exact price and terms of the securities are unknown before the issuance date, trading prior to that date is on a yield basis (that is, based on the yields that buyers expect). The exact terms and price of the security become known on the issuance date, and when-issued trading continues until the settlement date, at which time the securities are delivered and the issuer is paid. When-issued transactions may also arise as a result of underwritings, exchanges, and mergers after preliminary agreement to issue the securities is established but before a date for settlement has been set.

1.82 *To-be-announced (TBA) trades. TBA* is a term used to describe forward mortgage-backed securities trades. The term TBA is derived from the fact that the actual mortgage-backed security that will be delivered to fulfill a TBA trade is not designated at the time the trade is made. The securities are to be announced 48 hours prior to the established trade settlement date.

1.83 *Delayed delivery.* A *delayed delivery transaction* is a transaction in which both parties to the trade agree on a deferred settlement. Delayed delivery transactions are purchases or sales of securities similar in most respects to regular-way transactions (normal settlement) except that, by agreement, the date of consummation or settlement is extended.

1.84 *Hedging.* Hedging instruments and techniques have been developed by broker-dealers to offset or minimize the risk of losses that an enterprise may be exposed to because of the effect of price changes on its assets, liabilities, or future commitments. Hedging instruments and techniques were developed in response to the volatility of interest rates, securities and commodity prices, and foreign exchange rates. These instruments may be used for speculative purposes, as well as hedging. The more common hedging instruments used as risk management tools include futures contracts; forward contracts; options; interest rate caps, floors, and collars; and swaps.

1.85 *Futures and forward contracts. Futures contracts* are standardized contracts traded on organized exchanges to purchase or sell a specified financial instrument or commodity on a future date at a specified price. Financial futures include contracts for debt instruments (interest rate futures), foreign currencies, and stock indexes. Forward contracts are individually negotiated and have economic characteristics similar to those of futures contracts, but they are not traded on an organized exchange, and consequently, they are generally referred to as OTC. *Forward contracts* are contracts for forward placement or delayed delivery of financial instruments or commodities in which one party agrees to buy, and another to sell, a specified security or commodity at a specified price for future delivery.

1.86   Forward contracts and futures contracts both have substantial market risk. A buyer (long position) of a futures contract profits when the value of the underlying financial instrument or commodity increases, whereas a seller (short position) of the futures contract incurs a loss.

1.87   The credit risk associated with a futures contract is generally less than it is for forward contracts because of the protections afforded by the exchange clearing organization system. All futures contracts cleared through a clearing organization are subsequently measured at fair value (see the glossary of this guide), and the financial result is settled daily between the clearing organization and clearing member. Because of this daily settlement, the amount of unsettled credit exposures is limited to the amount owed the clearing member for any one day.

1.88   The clearing organization also has a guarantee fund consisting of cash, securities, and bank guarantees that is contributed to by all clearing member firms. In the event the guarantee funds are insufficient to cover a failed member firm's obligations to the clearing organization system, the clearing organization has additional assessment authority over all the other member firms.

1.89   These protections are intended to permit the clearing organization to fulfill the obligations of any failed clearing member firm to other clearing member firms. However, the exchange clearing organization will not necessarily guarantee the performance or the money balances of the failed member firm with respect to the individual customer accounts of a failed member firm (that is, the clearing organization guarantee is generally limited to the commodities clearing obligations of the failed member firm to the other clearing member firms).

1.90   *Options.* An option contract conveys a right, but not an obligation, to buy or sell a specified number of units of a financial instrument at a specific price per unit within a specified time period. The instrument underlying the option may be a security; futures contract (for example, an interest rate option); commodity; currency; or cash instrument. Options may be bought or sold on organized exchanges or OTC on a principal-to-principal basis or may be individually negotiated. A call option gives the holder the right, but not the obligation, to buy the underlying instrument. A put option gives the holder the right, but not the obligation, to sell the underlying instrument. The price at which the underlying instrument may be bought or sold during the specified period is referred to as the *strike* or *exercise price*. The option buyer (holder) is the party that obtains the right, by paying a premium, to buy (call) or sell (put) an instrument. The option seller (writer) is the party that is obligated to perform if the option is exercised.

1.91   The option buyer's profit potential can be virtually unlimited. The option buyer's loss, however, is limited to the cost of the option (premium paid). Unlike the buyer of an option contract, an option seller may be exposed to large and sometimes unlimited market risk; however, the premiums received by the seller may provide a potentially attractive return.

1.92   After the initial exchange of the premium, the writer of the option is not at risk to a counterparty's default because the buyer is no longer obligated to perform. The buyer of the option, however, is exposed to the writer's ability to perform. The risk of counterparty default can be reduced by trading through an exchange because the clearing organization of the exchange acts as guarantor for the option contracts.

1.93 When an option is exercised depends on the market price versus the strike price, the outlook on how one option will perform in relation to the other before the expiration date, and the kind of option—European or American. A European option is exercisable only at the maturity date of the option, whereas an American option is exercisable at any time during the option period.

1.94 *Caps, floors, and collars.* An *interest rate cap* is a contractual agreement between two counterparties in which the buyer, in return for paying a fee, will receive cash payments from the seller at specified dates if rates go above a specified interest rate level known as the strike rate (cap). An *interest rate floor* is a contractual agreement between two counterparties in which the buyer, in return for paying a fee, will receive cash payments from the seller at specified dates if interest rates go below the strike rate. The cap or floor fee (premium) is generally paid in advance to the seller by the buyer, but it may be paid over the life of the cap or floor agreement. At each settlement date during the term of the cap or floor, the strike rate is compared with the market rate (index rate) to determine whether the seller must make a payment to the buyer. The timing of these payments varies depending on the agreement between the buyer and seller.

1.95 The economic characteristics of caps and floors are analogous to those of a series of European interest rate options. The risks associated with caps and floors are also similar to those of options (that is, they are asymmetrical). The buyer of a cap or floor is protected against adverse interest rate changes (the loss is limited to the premium) while having the ability to profit from favorable changes in interest rates.

1.96 As with an option, the writer of a cap or floor has no risk of counterparty default unless the cap or floor fee (premium) is paid over the life of the cap or floor arrangement. The buyer, in contrast, incurs counterparty credit risk because the third party may not fulfill its obligation.

1.97 The buyer of the interest rate cap can lower the fee paid in advance to the writer by writing a floor (minimum level of a floating rate) on the transaction. If the floating rate goes below the floor, the buyer of the interest rate cap (writer of the floor) has to compensate the counterparty for the difference. An interest rate contract that specifies both a cap and floor for interest rates is referred to as a *collar*.

1.98 *Swap transactions.*[4] *Swaps* are financial transactions in which two counterparties agree to exchange streams of payments over time according to a predetermined formula. Swaps are normally used to transform the market exposure associated with a loan or bond borrowing from one interest rate base (fixed term or floating rate) or currency denomination to another (across markets).

1.99 The typical interest rate swap is an agreement between two parties under which each party agrees to pay the other specified or determinable cash amounts on specified future dates. The cash amounts to be paid by each party

---

[4] In July 2012, the SEC and Commodity Futures Trading Commission jointly adopted and published in the Federal Register new rules and interpretations further defining the terms "swap" and "security-based swap." See Further Definition of "Swap," "Security-Based Swap," and "Security-Based Swap Agreement"; Mixed Swaps; Security-Based Swap Agreement Recordkeeping, 77 FR 48208.

are defined in terms of applying a specified interest rate (either fixed or variable) to a hypothetical principal amount, referred to as the notional principal amount. The interest rate swap does not modify preexisting debt instruments, and no securities actually change hands between the parties.

1.100 Currency swaps are similar to interest rate swaps in that interest streams are exchanged between two counterparties; however, unlike interest rate swaps, they are in two different currencies (either fixed for fixed, fixed for floating, or floating for floating). Further, unlike interest rate swaps, because two different currencies are involved, there is generally an exchange of principal at inception of the agreement and a re-exchange of like principal at maturity.

1.101 The term *currency swap*[5] is also used to describe arrangements in which spot and forward foreign exchange contracts are entered into with the same counterparty (foreign exchange swap). The forward amount exchanged is different from the spot amount because the forward amount includes an interest differential between a fixed rate in one currency and a fixed rate in the other currency. Unlike the currency swaps described in the preceding paragraph in which there is a series of forward exchanges (interest flows), a foreign exchange swap has only one forward exchange.

1.102 In interest rate swaps, there is unlimited market risk and reward to the extent interest rates fluctuate. The fixed-rate receiver loses if interest rates rise, and the fixed-rate payer loses if interest rates fall. There is no market risk in the principal amount of interest rate swaps. The counterparty to a currency swap is exposed to interest rate movements and to foreign exchange risk on the principal and interest.

1.103 The contractual or notional amounts related to interest rate and currency swaps do not indicate the risk of default of the counterparty. Risk of default varies with the financial strength of the counterparties. Further, the amount at risk at a point in time is limited to the unrealized gain and varies with market conditions. Additional credit protection may be provided through the use of an intermediary who guarantees the payment streams by providing a backup letter of credit, collateral, or some other support arrangement. In addition, in 2016 the CFTC adopted final regulations requiring certain swap counterparties to exchange initial margin and variation margin for swap transactions that are not cleared by derivatives clearing organizations. Such exchanges of margin are intended to mitigate the risks resulting from a counterparty default.

1.104 *Asset securitization. Asset securitization* is the process of converting receivables and other assets that are not readily marketable into securities that can be placed and traded in capital markets. Assets that have been securitized include residential mortgages; commercial mortgages; agency securities (including those of Government National Mortgage Association [Ginnie Mae], Federal National Mortgage Association [Fannie Mae], and the Federal Home Loan Mortgage Corporation [Freddie Mac]); consumer receivables (credit card loans and home equity loans); retail installment loans (automobile, recreational vehicle, and mobile home); time-share mortgage loans; trade receivables; insurance-policy-related receivables; leases (equipment, operating, and automobile); student loans; high-yield corporate bonds; and federal assets.

---

[5] See footnote 4.

1.105 Securitization transactions span a wide spectrum. At one extreme are outright sales of assets or interests in assets. At the other extreme are borrowings collateralized by assets. In between are sales of assets with varying degrees of recourse to the seller and nonrecourse borrowings collateralized by assets. Asset-backed securities may be issued through a variety of structures, including pay-through securities; pass-through securities; and commercial paper with multiple classes, differing degrees of subordination, and varying cash flow priorities. The securities are often backed by some form of credit enhancement. Credit enhancement can take the form of letters of credit, third-party guarantees, liquidity facilities, spread accounts, reserve funds, subordinate interests, and overcollateralization.

1.106 In a typical asset securitization transaction, an originator (transferor) transfers assets to a special-purpose entity (SPE), which may also be a variable interest entity (VIE). Beneficial interests in the SPE are sold to investors and the proceeds are used to pay the transferor for the assets transferred. The SPE or VIE might be organized in such a way that the likelihood of its bankruptcy is remote and that the transferred assets are protected from the estate of the transferor in the event of its bankruptcy.

1.107 One type of asset securitization is a *collateralized mortgage obligation,* a mortgage-backed bond that aggregates individual mortgages or mortgage-backed securities into mortgage pools that are separated into different maturity classes, called tranches. Each tranche has unique risk characteristics for paying interest, paying principal, or retaining residual ownership.

1.108 Securitization often allows the holder of assets to raise funds at a lower rate than the cost of general obligation borrowings, to free up capital through off-balance sheet financing, to reduce interest rate and credit risk, to limit loss exposure, and to gain access to nontraditional funding sources.

1.109 Mutual funds, insurance companies, pension funds, banks, thrifts, retail investors, and diverse other foreign and domestic investors participate in the mortgage- and asset-backed securities market. New investment instruments, flexible payment terms, investment-grade credit quality, various degrees of liquidity, and reduced event risk are among the benefits offered by these securities. The market risks affecting these securities include interest rate risk, prepayment risk, and varying degrees of credit risk. Given the multitude of assets and the complexity of securitization structures, an investor must understand both the investment profile and the risks specific to each investment.

1.110 *Credit derivatives. Credit derivative* refers to various instruments and techniques designed to separate and then transfer the credit risk, or the risk of an event of default of a corporate or sovereign borrower, transferring it to an entity other than the lender or debt holder. An unfunded credit derivative is one where credit protection is bought and sold between bilateral counterparties without the buyer having to put up money up front or at any given time during the life of the deal unless an event of default occurs. Usually these contracts are traded pursuant to an International Swaps Dealers Association master agreement. Most credit derivatives of this sort are credit default swaps. When the credit derivative is entered into by a financial institution or a SPE and payments under the credit derivative are funded using securitization techniques, such that a debt obligation is issued by the financial institution or SPE to support these obligations, it is known as a funded credit derivative.

1.111 *International trading.* A number of major broker-dealers have the capabilities for executing purchase and sale orders in securities traded abroad. The recent admission of U.S. broker-dealers to foreign financial markets offers the possibility of 24-hour trading. In addition, many foreign securities are traded by market makers in the United States. Many broker-dealers trade equity securities in the form of American depository receipts (ADRs). An *ADR* is a registered negotiable receipt for shares of a foreign corporation held in custody in the foreign location. Some ADRs are listed on the NYSE, and many others trade in the OTC market.

Investment Banking

1.112 Many broker-dealers are engaged in providing investment banking services to their customers. These services typically include the raising of capital through the public offering or private placement of securities. In addition, these broker-dealers counsel companies in the management of their money and advise companies about corporate structuring opportunities.

1.113 *Public offerings.* Business entities and governmental entities that desire to raise funds through the public sale of securities normally engage securities broker-dealers to underwrite their securities issues. *Underwriting* is the act of distributing a new issue of securities (primary offering) or a large block of issued securities (secondary offering). Underwritings are accomplished on either a firm-commitment or best-efforts basis. The underwriting group for a transaction on a firm-commitment basis agrees to buy the entire security issue from the issuer for a specified price, with the intent to resell the securities to the public at a slightly higher price. The underwriting group for a best-efforts underwriting agrees to sell the issue at a price to be determined, normally with a minimum requirement to complete the underwriting. An underwriting group may also be formed on a standby basis in which there is a commitment to buy the securities if called on.

1.114 Underwriting subjects the broker-dealer to substantial risks. A broker-dealer underwriting securities on a firm-commitment basis is required to buy a portion of the positions offered. This results in the need to finance the unsold portions and assume the market risk of ownership. In addition, the broker-dealer may be held liable to the purchasers of the securities under the 1933 Act. The statute holds all persons (including underwriters) connected with a registration statement responsible for any material misstatements contained in the registration statement. An underwriting also exposes the broker-dealer to the risk that its customers or other group members who had committed to buy the securities being underwritten may refuse to honor the transactions.

1.115 Because the value of a new issue of securities and the liability for successful marketing may be too great for any one dealer, group accounts or syndicates may be formed to spread the risk. In addition, selling groups, which may include broker-dealers other than members of the underwriting group, are sometimes formed to obtain wider distribution of the new issue.

1.116 The liability of the underwriting group may be divided or undivided. If it is divided, each member of the group has a specified maximum liability to buy a certain number of shares of stock or principal amount of bonds. If it is undivided, each member of the underwriting group has a designated percentage liability for unsold securities.

1.117 *Advisory services.* Broker-dealers provide advisory services for which they receive fee income. These may include consulting on mergers and acquisitions, reorganizations, tender offers, leveraged buyouts, conversions, swaps, and the pricing of securities to be issued. Fees for these services are generally determined by the transaction size and are often contingent upon results, which may not be final until after the services are completed. In addition, broker-dealers may earn fees by advising investment company asset managers about mutual fund assets and the distribution and maintenance of mutual fund shares.

1.118 *Private placements.* Broker-dealers may also arrange the private placement of securities by business or government entities. Private placements are usually conducted on a best-efforts, agency basis and, therefore, expose the placement agent to less risk than that associated with the underwriting liability of a public offering. *Private placements* are distributions of securities that do not involve public offerings. Typically, private placements are sold to sophisticated institutional investors and, hence, do not require a registration statement to be filed with the SEC. The securities involved in private placements can be either an initial issuance or a resale of previously issued securities and are generally restricted regarding subsequent resale. For example, they may require registration under state and federal securities laws prior to resale or an opinion of counsel providing an exemption from registration requirements. The company's history, size, stability, and cash needs are factors in determining when the use of a private placement of debt or equity securities might be preferable to registering securities for sale to the public. In many instances, the expertise of the broker-dealer may be essential in analyzing the company's activities and requirements in order to determine the kind of securities to be offered and to assist in structuring the placement to enhance marketability. Because private placements are usually conducted on a best-efforts, agency basis by a broker-dealer, maximum consideration is normally given to locating an investor or a relatively small group of investors whose investment objectives closely parallel the expectations of the issuer.

1.119 The SEC adopted Rule 144A[6] to provide a safe-harbor exemption from the registration requirements of the 1933 Act for the resale of private placements when the resale is made to a qualified institutional buyer. Broker-dealers can qualify as institutional buyers if they own and invest on a discretionary basis at least $10 million in the securities of unaffiliated issuers. Broker-dealers with less than $10 million may buy securities as riskless principals for clients that are themselves qualified institutional buyers.

Financing

1.120 Broker-dealers may finance their activities through the use of bank loans, stock loans, and repurchase agreements (repos). In recent years, stock lending and repos have also evolved into firm trading strategies whereby broker-dealers earn interest spreads on the simultaneous borrowing and lending of funds collateralized by securities. A discussion of some of the activities described as broker-dealer financing activities follows.

---

[6] In July 2013, the SEC issued a final rule which amends SEC Rule 144A. See Release No. 33-9415, *Eliminating the Prohibition Against General Solicitation and General Advertising in Rule 506 and Rule 144A Offerings*. Simultaneously, the SEC issued a proposed rule to further amend the related rules. See Release No. 33-9416, *Amendments to Regulation D, Form D and Rule 156 under the Securities Act*, because of the publication date of this guide this rule has not been finalized. See chapter 3, "Regulatory Considerations," for more information.

1.121 *Bank loans.* One source of financing in the securities industry is bank loans. These loans are callable by the bank and are often collateralized (secured) by securities owned by the broker-dealer or, if used to finance loans to the customer, by customer securities that are not fully paid for. The interest rate charged by banks on these loans is called the *brokers' call rate.* Commercial banks typically provide bank loan financings to broker-dealers on a committed or uncommitted basis depending on the credit strength of the broker-dealer. Bank loans can also be provided on an unsecured basis.

1.122 In addition to the risks faced by all businesses concerning collateralized bank loans, broker-dealers are subject to a unique requirement resulting from regulations governing collateral. SEC Rule 15c3-3 prohibits broker-dealers from utilizing their customers' fully paid or excess margin securities as collateral for bank loans. Federal Reserve Regulations G, T, U, and X of the Federal Reserve system establish the ratio of collateral value to the amount of loans that must be maintained for loans used to finance customer-related activity and firm-related activity. Thus, firms must maintain separate records for customer and firm loans and related collateral.

1.123 *Securities lending agreements.* A *stock loan* is an arrangement in which securities are loaned from one broker-dealer to another in exchange for collateral. Broker-dealers may lend securities to enable a borrowing broker-dealer to make deliveries of securities sold that the borrowing broker-dealer does not have available to deliver on the settlement date. Securities lending can be an effective and efficient means of generating funds for financing broker-dealers' operations. Securities lending is usually conducted through open-ended "loan" agreements that may be terminated on short notice by the lender or borrower. Securities lending is generally collateralized by cash, although securities or letters of credit may also be used as collateral. The nature of these transactions is generally governed by Regulation T and SEC Rule 15c3-3.

1.124 Each stock loan is initially collateralized at a predetermined margin that is slightly in excess of the value of the securities loaned. If the fair value of the security falls below an acceptable level during the time a loan is outstanding, the borrower of the security requests the return of the excess cash collateral. If the value of the security rises, the lender of the security generally requests additional cash collateral to cover potential exposure to credit risk.

1.125 When a stock loan is terminated, the securities are returned to the lender and the collateral or cash to the borrower. Fees (often referred to as rebates) are paid to the cash lender based on the principal amounts outstanding. Such fees are generally calculated at a rate lower than the broker-dealer's call rate, and they fluctuate based on the availability of the particular securities loaned. Some broker-dealers participate in the securities-lending and securities-borrowing market as intermediaries. They conduct a finder or conduit business in which securities are borrowed from one broker-dealer (or other institution) and loaned to another.

1.126 *Repos or reverse repos.* According to the FASB *Accounting Standards Codification* (ASC) glossary, a *repurchase agreement accounted for as a collateralized borrowing (repo agreement)* refers to a transaction in which a seller-borrower of securities sells those securities to a buyer-lender with an agreement to repurchase them at a stated price plus interest at a specified date or in specified circumstances. A repurchase agreement accounted for as a collateralized borrowing is a repo that does not qualify for sale accounting under FASB

ASC 860, *Transfers and Servicing.* The payable under a repurchase agreement accounted for as a collateralized borrowing refers to the amount of the seller-borrower's obligation recognized for the future repurchase of the securities from the buyer-lender.

1.127 A repo may be made on an overnight or a fixed-maturity basis or with an agreement for the seller to buy back the same securities at an open date to be decided by the buyer and seller. Dollar repurchase agreements (also called dollar rolls) are agreements to sell and repurchase substantially the same but not identical securities.

1.128 As defined in the FASB ASC glossary, a *reverse repurchase agreement accounted for as a collateralized borrowing* (also known as a reverse repo) refers to a transaction that is accounted for as a collateralized lending in which a buyer-lender buys securities with an agreement to resell them to the seller-borrower at a stated price plus interest at a specified date or in specified circumstances. The receivable under a reverse repurchase agreement accounted for as a collateralized borrowing refers to the amount due from the seller-borrower for the repurchase of the securities from the buyer-lender.

1.129 The buyer is said to enter into a reverse repo transaction (receiving securities, giving up cash) while the seller enters into a repo transaction (receiving cash, giving up securities). This reciprocal procedure enables the seller to obtain short-term financing while the buyer is able to earn interest on its excess cash and hold securities as collateral. For the buyer, the transaction represents another form of secured lending.

1.130 Government bond dealers that have large inventories to be financed find it advantageous to execute repos with institutional investors because a repurchase transaction usually has a lower interest rate than the interest rate charged by a bank, and they can finance a greater percentage of their collateral. By using repos, buyers are able, with negligible market risk, to earn interest on their balances. The principal risk to the buyer is the creditworthiness of the seller but only if the collateral is in the possession of the seller or if its value has declined substantially. The possession of the collateral is an important determinant of the credit risk of a repo transaction. There are three kinds of custodial arrangements relating to repo transactions: triparty repos, deliver-out repos, and hold-in-custody repos.

1.131 In a triparty repo, an independent institution acting in a custodial capacity enters into a tripartite agreement with the two counterparties to the transaction. This third-party custodian assumes certain responsibilities for safeguarding the interests of both counterparties and is involved in transferring funds and securities between those two parties. In a deliver-out repo, the securities are delivered to the investor or its designated custodial agent, who has no relationship with the repo seller. A hold-in-custody repo is characterized by the repo seller retaining control of the securities and serving simultaneously throughout the transaction not only as principal but also as the investor's custodial agent.

1.132 Some commonly used terms that describe various kinds of repurchase transactions include *overnight repos, term repos,* and *repos to maturity.* Paragraphs 19–21 of FASB ASC 860-10-05 discuss the nature of these terms. Broker-dealers make their profits on the differences between the interest charged on the repos and the interest earned on the reverse repos. See chapter 5, "Accounting Standards," and chapter 6, "Financial Statement Presentation and Classification," for additional information.

Other Activities

1.133 *Commodities.* A commodity may be bought for current delivery or future delivery. Broker-dealers buy and sell commodity contracts for future delivery on the request of their customers or for their own account. In a purchase contract (long position), the buyer agrees to accept a specific commodity that meets a specified quality in a specified month. In a sale contract (short position), the seller agrees to deliver the specified commodity during the designated month.

1.134 Growers, processors, warehouse operators, and other dealers often buy and sell commodity futures for hedging purposes (that is, they transfer the price risk to speculators). Speculators buy and sell commodity futures because of the potential for a large return that could result from the leverage inherent in commodity futures trading. This leverage exists because a commodity contract controls a substantial amount of the commodity, and only a small money payment (margin deposit) is made.

1.135 *Investment company shares.* Established under the Investment Company Act of 1940, *investment companies* are institutions that issue shares representing a portfolio of assets. The sale and redemption of investment company shares are often handled by broker-dealers. The AICPA Audit and Accounting Guide *Investment Companies* provides accounting and auditing guidance relevant to these institutions.

1.136 Broker-dealers may act as agents to offer their customers the opportunity to invest in investment company shares. Brokers act as agents for their customers by placing or redeeming orders with mutual funds. Orders with mutual funds are placed in the customers' names through the shareholders' servicing agent that keeps records of individual share ownership, including additions for the reinvestment of dividends and capital gains. The broker-dealer's financial involvement with mutual funds may be limited to the receipt of commission checks if orders are placed with funds that charge commissions.

1.137 *Unit investment trusts.* A *unit investment trust* (UIT) registered under the Investment Company Act of 1940 is a pool of securities fixed at the date of origination in which an investor holds an interest. Because it is not a managed investment vehicle, a UIT appeals to investors who, though desiring diversification, do not seek active professional investment advice. A UIT differs from a mutual fund in that it has a fixed termination date, roughly corresponding to the maturities of the securities in its portfolio. In addition, a UIT does not have a board of directors and an investment adviser. Rather, it has a trustee (or custodian) who holds the UIT's assets; a sponsor who establishes, promotes, sells, and makes a secondary market in the UIT's units; and an evaluator who periodically values the UIT's portfolio.

1.138 *Exchange traded funds.* An exchange traded fund (ETF) is an investment fund traded on stock exchanges, much like stocks. An ETF holds assets such as stocks, commodities, or bonds, and trades close to its net asset value over the course of the trading day. Most ETFs track an index, such as a stock index or bond index. ETFs may be attractive as investments because of their low costs, tax efficiency, and stock-like features. An ETF combines the valuation feature of a mutual fund or unit investment trust, which can be bought or sold at the end of each trading day for its net asset value, with the tradability feature of a closed-end fund, which trades throughout the trading day at prices that may be more or less than its net asset value. Closed-end funds are not considered to be ETFs, even though they are funds and are traded on an exchange.

1.139 *Foreign exchange.* The trading of currencies and bank deposits denominated in various currencies takes place in the foreign exchange market. The largest dealers in foreign exchange are money center banks. These dealers either arrange transactions between each other (in the interbank market) or place bids and offers through a brokerage system wherein brokers (including a number of securities broker-dealers) will attempt to bring buyers and sellers together for a commission. Currencies are traded in either the spot or forward markets and the futures markets. Spot transactions call for the immediate exchange of currencies (typically a two-day settlement), whereas forward transactions settle at a predetermined future date. The spot and forward markets are utilized primarily by large commercial users and institutional traders, whereas the futures market serves smaller commercial users and speculators.

1.140 *Soft-dollar arrangements.* The FASB ASC glossary defines a *soft-dollar arrangement* as one in which a broker-dealer provides research to a customer in return for trade order flow (a certain volume of trades) from a customer.

1.141 Most soft-dollar arrangements are triangular. In the first corner of the triangle is a money manager who wants to buy research data without writing a check. In the second corner is a broker with whom the money manager, or the money manager's client, trades. The broker uses a part of the commission (soft-dollars) to pay the research firm on behalf of the money manager. In the third corner is the researcher who is paid by the broker and sends the data to the money manager. Since the 1970s, when soft-dollars were first used, some brokers and money managers have used soft-dollars to cover transactions not associated with research. These types of transactions are governed by Section 28(e) of the 1934 Act that allows the paying of a brokerage commission if the manager determines in good faith that the commission is reasonable in relation to the value of the brokerage and research services received.

1.142 *Financial technology.* Also known as "fintech," financial technology is an economic industry composed of companies that use technology to make financial services more efficient. Financial technology companies are generally startups trying to disintermediate incumbent financial systems and challenge traditional corporations that are less reliant on software. Fintech refers to new applications, processes, products or business models in the financial services industry.

1.143 The fintech revolution has also led to the advent of "robo-advisors." Robo-advisors are a class of financial advisers that provide financial advice or portfolio management online with minimal human intervention. They provide digital financial advice based on mathematical rules or algorithms. These algorithms are executed by software and thus financial advice does not require a human advisor. The software utilizes its algorithms to automatically allocate, manage and optimize clients' assets.

1.144 *Equity crowdfunding.* The online offering of private company securities to a group of people for investment is referred to as "equity crowdfunding, crowdinvesting, investment crowdfunding, or crowd equity." Because equity crowdfunding involves investment into a commercial enterprise, it is often subject to securities and financial regulation. Equity crowdfunding is a mechanism that enables broad groups of investors to fund startup companies and small businesses in return for equity. Investors give money to a business and receive ownership of a small piece of that business.

Chapter 2

Broker-Dealer Functions, Books, and Records

Introduction

Overview

2.01   Accounting by broker-dealers for securities transactions is unique in that two sets of books—the general ledger and the securities record (commonly referred to as the stock record)—are maintained. The general ledger is used to record entries reflecting money balances, and the securities record is used to account for security positions.

2.02   This chapter discusses the flow of securities transactions, whether manual or automated, and standard departments and records ordinarily found within a broker-dealer. Many of the records and activities are automated, including the execution, clearance, and settlement of trades and the processing of transactions, balancing, and reconciliations of records both within the broker-dealer and with external entities such as the Depository Trust & Clearing Corporation (DTCC) and its subsidiaries, including the Depository Trust Company (DTC), the National Securities Clearing Corporation (NSCC), and the Fixed Income Clearing Corporation (FICC).

2.03   In addition, external service sources, such as market valuation services, provide information that is incorporated into the automated recordkeeping system. The extent of automation within the industry varies from company to company.

Original Entry Journals

2.04   Original source (trade) data are recorded onto original entry journals. These journals, which are often referred to as blotters, contain the following:

- An itemized daily record of the details for all purchases and sales of securities (by market)
- Receipts and deliveries of securities
- Cash receipts and disbursements
- Other debits and credits, such as listings of floor brokerage receivables or payables, mutual fund commissions earned, and investment counseling fees

2.05   For each transaction, the blotters or related records generally indicate the following:

- The quantity, class, and description of the securities, including the certificate numbers of the securities
- The unit and aggregate purchase or sales price (if any)
- The trade date
- The name of the broker-dealer from which the securities are purchased or received or to which the securities are sold or delivered

2.06 A broker-dealer may keep separate blotters to record different types of transactions. For example, a broker-dealer may keep a clearinghouse blotter to record purchases and sales of cleared securities transacted on an exchange in round lots and several other blotters in which transactions in odd lots, unlisted securities, foreign currencies, bonds, cash receipts and deliveries, and journal entries are recorded. Other types of blotters for special kinds of business include a cash blotter to record cash disbursements and receipts; a receive blotter to record purchases, receipts of securities, and payments of cash; and a deliver blotter to record sales, deliveries of securities, and receipts of cash.

General Ledger

2.07 Broker-dealers maintain general ledgers reflecting their assets, liabilities, revenue, expenses, and capital accounts. The general ledger and related subsidiary ledgers (commonly referred to as daily bookkeeping ledgers) (*a*) provide details relating to all asset, liability, and nominal accounts; (*b*) enable the broker-dealer to prepare a trial balance in order to prepare financial statements showing the broker-dealer's financial position, results of operations, and cash flows; and (*c*) facilitate preparation of required regulatory filings. A description of the general ledger accounts is presented in chapter 6, "Financial Statement Presentation and Classification," of this guide. Those records are also used in preparing required net capital and reserve requirement computations.

Stock Record

2.08 The *stock record* is a double-entry accounting system for shares of stock or principal amounts of debt by security issue. It is a record of accountability reflecting all securities for which the firm has custodial responsibility or proprietary ownership. The stock record should balance the way a general ledger balances: debits and credits are equal in the general ledger; likewise, long positions and short positions should equal in the stock record. See the "Illustrative Stock Record Entries" section of this chapter, which shows how transactions are recorded in the stock record.

2.09 A long position in the stock record indicates ownership of the security or the right of possession. The most common positions on the long side of the stock record are the following:

- Customer (securities owned by customer)
- Firm (securities held in inventory for the broker-dealer's own account and risk)
- Reverse repurchase agreements (also known as resale agreements or reverse repos)
- Fail-to-deliver (securities sold to or through another broker-dealer but not delivered)
- Securities borrowed from another broker-dealer or customer

2.10 A short position in the stock record indicates either the location of the securities or the responsibility of other parties to deliver them to the broker-dealer. Every security owned or held by the broker-dealer should be accounted for by its location. The following list includes the most common short positions:

- *Box.* Securities are physically located at the broker-dealer's own location, typically in the cashier's cage.

- *Vault.* Securities are physically located at the broker-dealer's own location in a secured area or a bank safe deposit box.

- *Depositories.* Securities are on deposit at a depository, such as the DTC (a subsidiary of the DTCC), or a custodian bank.

- *Transfer.* Securities are at a transfer agent being re-registered.

- *Fail-to-receive.* The broker-dealer has purchased securities that have not yet been received.

- *Securities loaned.* Securities have been loaned to another broker-dealer.

- *Customer short.* A customer sold securities, but delivery has not yet been made.

- *Firm short.* The broker-dealer sold a security it does not own.

- *Repurchase agreements* (repos).

- *Bank loan.* Securities are held on deposit at a bank and pledged as collateral for a loan.

2.11 The stock record lists securities by security number, normally by Committee on Uniform Security Identification Procedure (or CUSIP) number or International Securities Identification Number, and, for each securities position, the accounts that are long or short in terms of shares (for stocks and mutual funds); principal amounts (for bonds, treasuries, and other debt securities); or number of contracts (for options). A stock record summary indicating all account positions in the security and an activity list indicating daily changes in the stock record are tabulated daily by the broker-dealer.

2.12 The chart of accounts is the key to reading and understanding the stock record because transactions are recorded by account numbers and quantities. Many accounts can have both securities positions and related money balances. However, certain accounts (such as box, vault, transfer, and depository locations) have only security positions without related money balances.

Regulatory Recordkeeping Requirements

2.13 The basic requirements for preparing and maintaining books and records are described in SEC Rules 17a-3 and 17a-4 under the Securities Exchange Act of 1934 (the 1934 Act). In Rule 17a-3, the SEC specifies the minimum books and records a broker-dealer should make and keep current. They include a complete set of financial accounting books and records, including books of original entry, general and subsidiary ledgers, and the stock record. Rule 17a-3 also sets forth other recordkeeping requirements of broker-dealers. Among other things, Rule 17a-3 states that broker-dealers should maintain a memorandum of each brokerage order and a memorandum for each purchase and sale of securities for its own account, showing the price and, to the extent feasible, the time of execution. The rule also specifies that the broker-dealer should maintain certain records regarding transactions of employees and customers, as well as a periodic trial balance and net capital, reserve formula, and other regulatory computations. Such books and records should be maintained for prescribed periods as set forth in Rule 17a-4.

2.14 In July 2013, the SEC amended Rule 17a-3(a)(23) to impose a new requirement on certain broker-dealers to make and keep current a record documenting the credit, market, and liquidity risk management controls established and maintained by the broker-dealer to assist it in analyzing and managing the risks associated with its business activities. This documentation requirement applies only to broker-dealers that have more than (1) $1,000,000 in aggregate credit items as computed under the customer reserve formula of SEC Rule 15c3-3a, or (2) $20,000,000 in capital, including debt subordinated in accordance with appendix D to SEC Rule 15c3-1. SEC Rule 17a-4(e)(9), as amended, discusses the corresponding records retention requirements.

2.15 Furthermore, in their constitutions and rules, the Financial Industry Regulatory Authority (FINRA)[1] and many securities exchanges prescribe certain books and records that members keep. Depending on the needs of the individual broker-dealer's business, situations may warrant the maintenance of certain additional records not specifically required under the rules of the various regulatory bodies.

Trade Date and Settlement Date

2.16 Prior to computer automation and processing, broker-dealers recorded securities transactions in their trial balances and stock records on the date the securities were due for settlement (settlement date) rather than the date on which the transaction was initiated (trade date). With the advent of automation, many firms now record their proprietary transactions on a trade-date basis, in accordance with accounting principles generally accepted in the United States of America. However, customer records are generally still maintained on a settlement date basis (see the "Trade-Date Versus Settlement-Date Accounting" section of chapter 5, "Accounting Standards," of this guide for further discussion of trade date and settlement-date accounting). During the period between trade-date and settlement date, various operational departments are responsible for clearing or settling trades.

2.17 The time period between trade date and settlement date varies depending on the product and specific transaction. Although any settlement date can be negotiated for any given purchase or sale, the following table provides a reference for the current standardized (regular way) settlement dates by product. Effective September 5, 2017, broker-dealers are required to comply with the amendments to SEC Rule 15c6-1(a). The amended rule prohibits a broker-dealer from effecting or entering into a contract for the purchase or sale of a security that provides for payment of funds and delivery of securities later than T+2, unless otherwise expressly agreed to by the parties at the time of the transaction. The amended rule applies a T+2 settlement cycle to the same securities transactions that were previously covered by the T+3 settlement cycle. These include transactions for stocks, bonds, municipal securities, exchange-traded funds, certain mutual funds, and limited partnerships that trade on an exchange.

---

[1] The Financial Industry Regulatory Authority (FINRA) is the largest nongovernmental regulator for the securities industry in the United States. See the FINRA website at www.finra.org for more information. Also see footnote 3.

Standardized Settlement Dates

Product	Settlement Date
Equity Securities	Two business days after trade date
Corporate Bonds	Two business days after trade date
Municipal Bonds	Two business days after trade date
Exchange-traded Funds	Two business days after trade date
Government Securities	One business day after trade date
Government Agency Securities	Varies depending on product
Futures and Commodities	Same-day settlement
Listed Options (Chicago Board Options Exchange)	One business day after trade date
Money Market Instruments	One business day after trade date
Mutual Funds	Two business days after trade date
Currency Contract Spot	Two business days after trade date

The settlement periods herein refer to the U.S. marketplace. Settlement dates in other countries vary and may not be standardized. Currently, there is an effort to standardize global security settlement periods.

2.18 Trade-date information, which includes proprietary inventory reports used by a broker-dealer's traders, is normally available in the broker-dealer's internal reporting systems. In addition, customer information is used daily by the broker-dealer to determine the amount of margin required for each customer's account. Trade-date information is also important to the operations departments to assist it in settlement and clearance.

Trade Execution

Customer Trades

2.19 *Sales.* The manner in which trades are initiated varies with the type of broker-dealer (that is, full service or discount and online brokerage). The customers of full-service broker-dealers usually have a designated registered representative or salesperson with whom they place buy or sell orders for securities. The registered representative normally resides at one of the broker-dealer's branch offices that are established to serve a strategic geographic area. Buy and sell orders may be based on the registered representative's recommendations (solicited) or may be initiated by the customers (unsolicited). Orders may also be entered by the broker-dealer pursuant to discretionary powers granted by the customer. In any case, the registered representative is responsible for routing an order to the proper operational department so that the order can be executed and processed. For discount and online broker-dealers, orders are generally unsolicited and, in many cases, have been automated to the point that the customer places the order directly into the broker-dealer's system through a personal access code.

2.20 Before initiating an order, the customer determines the following:

- The security
- The trading action to be initiated (buy, sell long, or sell short)

- The number of shares or units to be traded
- The type of order
- The price of the transaction
- The disposition of securities purchased or sold
- The method of payment (cash or margin)
- Other incidental information, such as selling against a prior purchase

2.21 A customer may place many types of orders; the most common are the market order and the limit order. A *market order* is an order to buy or sell a stated amount of a security at the most advantageous price obtainable after the order is received on the exchange floor or in the trading area. A *limit order* is an order to buy or sell a stated amount of a security at a specified price or at a better price if obtainable after the order is received on the exchange floor or in the trading area.

2.22 Exchange trading is normally done in round lots (usually 100 shares), and a bid and offer on a security is usually made for the minimum unit of trading. A customer may accept a partial execution, in units of trading, unless the order is marked "all or none" (AON) or "fill or kill" (FOK). A customer's order to buy or sell is generally transacted as soon as possible after its receipt on the exchange floor or in the broker-dealer's trading area. An order is considered valid only for the day of the order; however, a customer can enter an order as good 'til canceled (GTC) or an open order, which is valid for longer than 1 day until either executed or cancelled. The customer can cancel a GTC order if no action has been taken before the cancellation is received. Customers may enter good-through-the-week and good-through-the-month orders for bonds.

2.23 Customer orders may also be executed by brokers away from an exchange through an electronic communication network (ECN). Institutional customers can execute directly with the ECN. *ECN* is the term used for a type of computer system that facilitates trading of financial products outside of stock exchanges. The primary products that are traded on ECNs are stocks and currencies. ECNs came into existence in 1998 when the SEC authorized their creation. ECNs increase competition among trading firms by lowering transaction costs, giving clients full access to their order books, and offering order matching outside of traditional exchange hours. In order to trade with an ECN, one must be a subscriber or have an account with a broker that provides direct access trading. ECN subscribers can enter orders into the ECN via a custom computer terminal or network protocols. The ECN will then match contra-side orders (that is, a sell order is contra-side to a buy order with the same price and share count) for execution. The ECN will post unmatched orders on the system for other subscribers to view. Generally, the buyer and seller are anonymous, with the trade execution reports listing the ECN as the party.

2.24 When a customer places an order, an order ticket is completed. The ticket includes the following:

- The security description
- The quantity to buy or sell
- The desired price, if specified
- The type of order
- The customer's name and account number
- For sell orders, whether the position is long or short

2.25 The *order ticket* is the broker-dealer's record of the customer's instructions. SEC Rule 17a-3 states that broker-dealers should maintain a record of each brokerage order given or received for the purchase or sale of securities, regardless of whether the order is executed. The record should show the terms and conditions of the order and any modification or cancellation. The order should indicate the customer account for which the order is entered; the time of entry; the execution price; and, if feasible, the time of execution or cancellation. Orders entered by the broker-dealer pursuant to discretionary powers should be designated as discretionary transactions. SEC Rule 17a-3 outlines the information to be recorded on order tickets. A brokerage order ticket should contain the identity of the associated person, if any, responsible for the account and any other person who entered or accepted the order on behalf of the customer and whether it was entered subject to discretionary authority. The brokerage order ticket should also include the time the broker dealer received the customer order. Dealer tickets should include information about any modifications to the order.

2.26 *Order entry.* The completed order ticket is entered into the system, which accepts and reviews the ticket and relays the customer's instructions to the exchange floor or trading desk where it is to be executed. The exchanges have developed systems whereby an order is routed to an automated order matching system depending on its size or price restriction. In addition, some firms have developed internal order matching systems. Once the order has been executed, the transaction is confirmed with the customer. Information concerning executed trades is sent to the purchase and sales (P&S) department, which is responsible for ensuring that system-generated trade confirmations are correct and mailed to customers.

2.27 Orders for over-the-counter (OTC) securities and certain listed securities are generally processed by the trading desk. The trader can either buy or sell the security from the firm's inventory (principal) or can buy from, or sell to, another dealer for the account of the customer (agent). If the trader buys for, or sells from, its own inventory, the price to the customer reflects a dealer spread in lieu of a commission. Alternatively, a trader may initiate an order on the firm's behalf for the benefit of a customer by negotiating the terms with another broker-dealer. This entails agreeing on the price and terms of the trade and executing the transaction, for which the customer is charged a commission.

2.28 SEC Rule 17a-3 states that broker-dealers should maintain records of each purchase and sale of securities, showing the price and, to the extent possible, time of execution, as well as copies of confirmations of all purchases and sales of securities. Records of dealers' quotations or bids or offers made in the course of trading are not required by the rule.

2.29 An executed trades report containing the terms of the executed orders is generated daily to facilitate further processing. Executed trades reflecting the purchase or sale of securities are recorded on a blotter, but they are generally not posted to the firm's general ledger and stock record until the settlement date. Instead, they are held in a pending file and posted on a memo basis to margin records and a bookkeeping journal. Additionally, to bring better price transparency to the fixed income securities market, the Trade Reporting and Compliance Engine (TRACE) was developed by FINRA to facilitate the mandatory reporting of OTC secondary market transactions in eligible fixed income securities. All broker-dealers who are FINRA member firms have an obligation to report transactions in corporate bonds and U.S. Treasury securities to

TRACE under an SEC approved set of rules. The current reporting time frame of eligible fixed income securities transactions is 15 minutes from execution. Additionally, in accordance with FINRA Regulatory Notice 13-19, firms are required to report OTC transactions in equity securities to FINRA as soon as practicable, but no later than 10 seconds following execution. FINRA believes firms should automate their trade processing to the greatest extent possible to provide timely trade information to facilitate best execution for customers.

2.30 *Customer records.* SEC Rule 17a-3 states that broker-dealers should maintain a ledger account or other record for each cash and margin account of every customer, regardless of the frequency of transactions. Transactions in the customer accounts cover both money balances and security positions, with the security transaction and related money generally recorded on the settlement date. Customer accounts should include itemization of the following:

- All purchases and sales
- Securities or commodities received in or delivered out
- Cash receipts and disbursements
- Dividends and interest received or charged
- Other debits and credits

As amended, SEC Rule 17a-3(a)(17) states that broker-dealers should create a customer account record with certain minimum information about each customer. In addition, broker-dealers should furnish account record information to customers on a periodic basis and provide records to regulators when requested.

2.31 A customer may have several different accounts. Cash and margin accounts, which are the most common accounts, require distinction because they are subject to different rules under Federal Reserve Regulation T (Regulation T) of the Board of Governors of the Federal Reserve System and the regulations of various self-regulatory organizations.

2.32 A cash account requires a customer to purchase or sell securities strictly on a cash basis. Cash account purchases are limited by Regulation T to purchases for which sufficient funds are held in the account or in reliance on an agreement that the customer will promptly make full cash payment for the security and that the customer does not contemplate selling the security to make such payment. Cash account sales are similarly limited to sales for which the security is held in the account or in reliance on an agreement that the customer owns the security and will make prompt delivery.

2.33 Under Regulation T, no credit may be extended to a customer with a cash account except for short periods of time between the time an order is executed and the time payment is received from the customer. Full cash payment normally should be made within 5 business days after the date the security is purchased. Assuming a 2-day settlement period,[2] full cash payment should be made no later than 2 business days after the settlement date. However, if an institutional customer purchases a security with the understanding that the security will be delivered promptly and that the full cash payment will be

---

[2] Through SEC Release No. 34-80295, "Amendment to Securities Transaction Settlement Cycle," the SEC amended Rule 15c6-1(a), *Settlement Cycle Rule*, to shorten the standard settlement cycle for most broker-dealer transactions from three business days after the trade date (T+3) to two business days after the trade date (T+2). The effective date of this release was May 30, 2017, and the compliance date was September 5, 2017.

made promptly against such a delivery, meaning a cash-on-delivery or delivery-versus-payment account, the time period for making payment is not to exceed 35 calendar days from the trade date.

2.34 A customer's failure to make timely payment would ordinarily require the prompt cancellation or liquidation of the transaction. The periods of settlement date plus 2 business days and 35 calendar days may be extended for 1 or more limited periods by applying to the broker-dealer's examining authority.

2.35 A margin account allows a customer to buy securities without paying in full. The difference between the purchase price and the amount paid by the customer represents a collateralized loan to the customer on which interest is charged. The margin account provides a record of purchase transactions for which the broker-dealer is expected to extend credit for a portion of the purchase price. The amount of credit extended is subject to the limits prescribed under Regulation T. Commodity Futures Trading Commission (CFTC) Regulations 41.42–41.49 and SEC Rules 400–406 establish margin requirements for securities futures.

2.36 Regulation T establishes the maximum loan value of the securities in the account and requires the broker-dealer to obtain a deposit of cash or securities necessary to meet the initial margin requirement within 2 business days after the settlement date. That 2-day period may be extended for 1 or more limited periods by applying to a national securities exchange or FINRA. Maximum loan values for securities and a listing of marginable securities are prescribed periodically by a supplement to Regulation T. Certain securities exchanges have rules establishing minimum maintenance margin requirements (for example, FINRA Rule 4210).[3] After a purchase of stock on margin, FINRA Rule 4210[4] supplements the requirements of Regulation T by placing maintenance margin requirements on margin accounts. Under this rule, as a general matter, and pertaining to long positions in equity securities, broker-dealers require the account holder to maintain equity in the value of the securities of at least 25 percent. If the equity in the account falls below the required amount, the broker-dealer is required to make a maintenance margin call that requires the customer to deposit more funds or securities in order to maintain the equity at the 25 percent level. The failure of the customer to meet the margin call may result in the liquidation of securities in the account. A broker-dealer may establish initial or maintenance margin requirements that are greater than those required by the rules of the regulatory bodies.

2.37 A *short sale* is a sale of a security that the seller does not own. Before a broker-dealer can execute a short sale for a customer, it must know it can obtain the security. The broker-dealer is expected to borrow the security,

---

[3] Following the consolidation of the National Association Of Securities Dealers and the New York Stock Exchange (NYSE) Member Regulation into FINRA, NASD rules and certain NYSE rules were combined to form the FINRA *Transitional Rulebook*. The incorporated NYSE rules apply only to those members of FINRA who are also members of the NYSE (dual members). FINRA has established a process to develop a new consolidated rulebook that will apply to all FINRA members. Work is continuing on this consolidation of rules. The SEC must approve the rules that will make up the new *Consolidated FINRA Rulebook*. This information is available on the FINRA website at www.finra.org/industry/regulation/finrarules/p038095.

[4] In 2016 the SEC approved amendments to FINRA Rule 4210. For further information regarding the amendments and effective dates, see Regulatory Notice 16-31, available at www.finra.org/sites/default/files/notice_doc_file_ref/regulatory-notice-16-31.pdf.

if necessary, on behalf of the customer for the purpose of satisfying the delivery requirements. Short sales are governed by Regulation SHO–Regulation of Short Sales (Regulation SHO) under the 1934 Act, the margin requirements of Regulation T and the rules of self-regulatory organizations. A short sale account should be used to record transactions when securities are sold short.

2.38   Under Regulation SHO, a broker-dealer must mark all sell orders of any equity security as "long," "short," or "short exempt." In addition, Regulation SHO requires that the trading center establish, maintain, and enforce written policies and procedures reasonably designed to (1) prevent the execution or display of a short sale order of a covered security at a price that is less than or equal to the current national best bid if the price of that covered security decreases by 10 percent or more from the covered security's closing price as determined by the listing market for the covered security as of the end of regular trading hours on the prior day; and (2) impose this short sale price test restriction for the remainder of the day and the following day when a national best bid for the covered security is calculated and disseminated on a current and continuing basis by a plan processor pursuant to an effective national market system plan.

2.39   SEC Rule 15c3-3 requires that if a security is sold, other than in a short sale, and not received from the customer within 10 business days after the settlement date, the broker-dealer should close the transaction by purchasing the related security for the account of the selling customer unless an extension is obtained. Certain municipal bonds and government securities are exempt from this buy-in requirement.

2.40   Naked short selling is prohibited in the United States, as well as other jurisdictions, as a method of driving down share prices. *Naked short selling*, or *naked shorting*, is the practice of short-selling a financial instrument without first borrowing the security or ensuring that the security can be borrowed, as is conventionally done in a short sale. When the seller does not obtain the shares within the required time frame, the result is known as a fail-to-deliver (as described in paragraph 2.09). The transaction generally remains open until the shares are acquired by the seller or the seller's broker, allowing the trade to be settled. In the United States, naked short selling is covered by various SEC regulations that prohibit the practice.

2.41   A statement of the account should be sent to the customer for any month for which there is activity and at least quarterly if positions or cash are held, as required by regulatory bodies. Broker-dealers should send (pursuant to SEC Rule 10b-10) and retain (pursuant to SEC Rule 17a-4) confirmations of all purchases and sales of securities and notifications of all other debits and credits for cash securities or other items for the accounts of customers.

2.42   To facilitate the transfer of customer accounts between broker-dealers, the NSCC (a subsidiary of the DTCC) has developed a system known as the Automated Customer Account Transfer Service (ACATS).

2.43   *Extension of credit.* After a transaction is recorded, the margin department monitors the customer's trade activity and account balance to ensure that payment and delivery are satisfied in accordance with federal, exchange, and firm requirements. The margin department protects the firm by enforcing collection procedures and policies (checking credit status) and by reviewing customer account activity to ensure that the firm complies with the rules and regulations of various regulatory agencies, such as Regulation T and the rules of self-regulatory organizations. The margin department normally does the following:

- Determines initial margin
- Maintains customer accounts
- Controls the extension of credit
- Checks the credit status of customers
- Controls payments from accounts
- Initiates margin calls
- Processes and monitors applications for extensions of time for cash account customers to pay for securities purchased and for margin account customers to meet initial margin requirements
- Issues instructions for moving securities to or from safekeeping or segregation
- Maintains copies of documents pertaining to transactions

2.44 Records maintained by the margin department normally indicate the following on a trade-date basis for each margin customer:

- Market value[5] of the securities
- Money balance of the account
- Margin excess or deficit
- Safekeeping and segregation instructions
- Pending trades
- Special miscellaneous account balance calculated in conformity with Regulation T and the rules of self-regulatory organizations

2.45 The margin department advises other departments when they can complete their responsibilities (for example, when a security delivery or cash payment can be completed). Other records and information that may be maintained by the margin department are the following:

- Standing customer instructions regarding the delivery of securities
- The disposition of cash from the sale of securities
- Standing customer instructions regarding the receipt of dividends and interest
- Guarantees of customers' accounts

2.46 The margin department maintains an account record for each customer and, based on that information, authorizes the cashier's department to make delivery on sales and payments on purchases. The margin department instructs the cashiering department to transfer and deliver securities to customers who have paid in full and want possession of certificates.

2.47 Generally, the margin department computes the amount of money customers should deposit and when it should be deposited. The functions of the margin department relate not only to margin transactions but also cash

---

[5] The terms *market value* and *mark-to-market* are used within this chapter as operational terms. Accordingly, in practice they may not necessarily be synonymous to the terms *fair value* and *subsequently measured at fair value*, which are used within the financial statements in accordance with FASB Accounting Standards Update No. 2012-04, *Technical Corrections and Improvements*.

accounts and cash transactions. For transactions in cash accounts, the margin department ensures that payment is received from the customers on purchases within the regulatory specified time periods.

2.48 For margin and short-sale transactions, the margin department ensures that customers deposit sufficient collateral to meet federal and exchange regulations. The margin department tracks the market value of the collateral; if the value of the collateral falls below firm guidelines or exchange (maintenance) requirements, the customers are required to satisfy the deficiencies. Due to the volatility in securities values, it is essential that up-to-date records be maintained so that the margin department is able to make informed decisions to limit the firm's exposure to losses.

Proprietary Trades

2.49 *Dealer*. Many broker-dealers attempt to profit from firm trading by selling securities at a higher price than what they paid for them. Firm proprietary trading activity can be broadly divided into dealer and positioning strategies.

2.50 With a dealer strategy, the broker-dealer attempts to balance buy and sell transactions with different customers or other broker-dealers and earn the difference between the price paid on the purchase (bid) and the price received on the sale (ask). If a broker-dealer cannot simultaneously execute a buy and corresponding sell, the firm is at risk to market volatility during the time between execution of the purchase and execution of the sale. Hedging strategies are often employed to minimize that risk; however, hedge accounting is permitted only if the requirements of FASB *Accounting Standards Codification* (ASC) 815, *Derivatives and Hedging*, are met.

2.51 Positioning strategies involve the broker-dealer buying and selling securities in anticipation of certain market movements and holding such positions for longer periods than with dealer strategies. If a trader anticipates that a security's price will rise, the trader may take a long position in that security; if a security is expected to decline in value, the trader may take a short position. Positioning strategies are riskier than dealer strategies because the security is held for a longer time. If a trader incorrectly forecasts the market, losses can be incurred.

2.52 *Trader and investor*. Trading desks typically maintain trade date records based on trading strategies that may include different types of instruments. Those records, if not integrated with the accounting department records, should be reconciled periodically to them.

2.53 In addition to marketable securities, broker-dealers may purchase securities for investment that are not readily marketable or whose sale is restricted by the purchase terms. Securities purchased for investment should be designated and recorded separately in the accounts of a broker-dealer to meet the requirements of the IRS because they are purchased with the expectation of future capital gains. The broker-dealer's records should clearly indicate by the close of the day on which an investment security is acquired (floor specialists currently have seven business days) that it is held for investment.

2.54 *Underwriter*. A broker-dealer participating in underwriting activities may act as managing underwriter, comanaging underwriter, or participating underwriter. The managing underwriter is responsible for organizing the other participating underwriters and the selling group. This function is often performed jointly by two or more firms as comanagers. A managing underwriter, in addition to being a participating underwriter, typically negotiates the transaction with the issuer of the security and maintains the records of the underwriting group. A comanager takes part in the negotiations but does not maintain the records of the group.

2.55 Underwritings are either firm commitments or best efforts. In a "firm commitment" underwriting, the underwriter or underwriting group acts as principal and has an open contractual commitment to purchase securities from the issuer and a liability for unsold securities. In a "best efforts" underwriting the underwriter or underwriting group acts as agent and has no open contractual commitment to purchase securities from the issuer or any liability for unsold securities. Publicly offered underwritings are generally on a firm commitment basis. Private offerings of securities may be either on a firm commitment or best efforts basis. The following paragraphs describe a public offering on a firm commitment basis. Rule 15c3-1 and related FINRA interpretations prescribe net capital treatment for open contractual commitments related to the offering of securities.

2.56 Participating underwriters maintain records of each underwriting participation only to the extent they are involved. To spread the risk of an underwriting and facilitate its distribution, the underwriters may sell all or part of the securities directly to the public or a selling group that in turn sells the securities to the public. If an issue is not fully sold, the liability is shared among the participating underwriters through either an undivided or divided arrangement. An *undivided liability* is an arrangement whereby each member of an underwriting syndicate is liable for its proportionate share of unsold securities in the underwriting account regardless of the number of securities it has previously sold. Under divided liability, the member's liability for an underwriting is fixed or definite in amount. Selling groups are not underwriters and have no obligation to sell the securities allocated to them. Accordingly, they are entitled only to a selling concession.

2.57 The managing underwriter maintains the subscription records for the underwriting and receives from the participating underwriters and members of the selling group reports of orders from their customers so that it knows the status of the offering.

2.58 The managing underwriter maintains daily position listings of the entire issue and ascertains the status of securities subscribed to and whether they have been delivered to the participating underwriters. Expenses associated with each underwriting are accumulated in the general ledger in separate deferred expense accounts. That is known as running the books. When the underwriting is completed, the profit or loss on the underwriting is determined and distributed to the participating underwriters.

2.59 The difference between the price to the public and that to the issuer (the gross underwriting spread) represents the underwriters' and selling group's compensation for the risk and cost of selling the issue. The gross underwriting spread is generally apportioned between the underwriters and selling group and consists of a management fee, an underwriting fee, and a selling concession. The underwriters may be entitled to a management fee, an underwriting fee, or both.

2.60 As noted in FASB ASC 940-605-05-1, the *management fee* is the fee paid to the manager or comanagers of the underwriting for services rendered in organizing the syndicate of underwriters and maintaining the records for the distribution. The underwriting fee is paid to the underwriting participants as compensation for the risk assumed through their agreement to buy a specified portion of the issue. It is usually net of the expenses directly associated with the underwriting. The *selling concession* is the fee paid for selling the offering.

Clearance and Settlement

Overview

2.61 Most transactions on securities exchanges and in certain active unlisted securities are cleared and settled through clearing organizations that were established to simplify and expedite the settlement of transactions between member firms. Clearance is facilitated through DTCC's Continuous Net Settlement (CNS) systems that minimize paperwork and the movement of securities and money. This results in one net position in each security (either to deliver or receive) between the broker-dealer and clearing organization. Clearing organizations prepare daily reports for members, showing the net security position (beginning balance less sales and plus purchases, plus receipts, and less deliveries) by security and the net money balance that is due to or from the clearing organization.

2.62 After a trade has been executed, the P&S department enters the trade into the bookkeeping system. Prior to the settlement date, the P&S department determines the amount to be paid or received at settlement. The P&S department determines and maintains records supporting its calculation of the following:

- The contract money (including accrued interest on bonds and other fixed-income securities)
- Commissions
- Taxes
- All other related money amounts

2.63 FASB ASC 940-320-30-1 explains that accrued interest earned on fixed-income securities is computed from the last coupon payment date up to the settlement date. This amount is paid to the seller of the instrument by the purchaser, who then receives the full periodic interest amount on the next coupon payment date.

2.64 The P&S department maintains the records of floor brokerage fees that are due to other broker-dealers who execute orders on the firm's behalf and brokerage fees due from other broker-dealers. Floor brokers employed by the firm may execute trades on behalf of other broker-dealers for which the firm is paid a brokerage fee. Broker-dealers often engage floor brokers who are responsible for executing securities transactions on the exchanges for the account of the broker-dealer.

2.65 As explained in FASB ASC 940-20-25-8, if the floor broker is employed by the broker-dealer, any costs associated with the floor broker's employment are generally reported as employee compensation. Costs paid to independent floor brokers or floor brokers of other firms for trades on behalf of the broker-dealer are generally reported as floor brokerage expense.

Comparison

2.66 Comparison procedures performed by the P&S department vary depending on whether a trade is cleared through a clearing organization, through a clearing bank if it is a government security, or directly with another broker-dealer. After a trade is executed, the terms, conditions, and details of the transaction are compared with those of the clearing organization or other counterparty.

2.67 On the trade date, each member broker-dealer electronically transmits a list of its day's trades to a clearing organization, detailing the following for each trade:

- The quantity of a security bought or sold
- A description of the security
- The contract price
- The identification number of the contra broker-dealer

2.68 These data are sorted by a clearing organization's computerized facility, such as that of the Securities Industry Automation Corporation. To qualify for clearing through a clearing organization's CNS system, a trade must be between two member broker-dealers, and the security must be eligible. Eligible securities are fairly active issues that provide high liquidity. Unless both of these requirements are satisfied, the parties cannot use the clearing facilities' CNS system, and the trades are to be settled directly in the trade-for-trade system or between the individual broker-dealers. Contract sheets itemizing the purchases and sales by broker-dealers are prepared for eligible securities cleared through the clearing organization. These contract sheets contain lists of compared and uncompared trades.

2.69 All trades are compared by the P&S department to verify that all terms and conditions agree before further processing. *Compared trades* are matched transactions in which the information received from both parties agrees. They require no further processing by the P&S department. Uncompared trades contain differences between the information supplied by the contracting broker-dealers, such as discrepancies in prices, quantities, descriptions of issues, or counterparties. All uncompared trades are resolved by the P&S department by the second day following the trade date, or they are settled directly between the broker-dealers (ex-clearing). Clearing organization-cleared trades may be corrected by the broker-dealer at fault by advising the clearing organization to correct the discrepancy. Differences not settled in that way are settled directly between broker-dealers.

2.70 For trades that are not processed through a clearing organization, the P&S department reviews a system-generated broker-to-broker comparison that is sent to the counterparty for verification of all pertinent trade information. If the counterparty agrees with all details of the transaction, the comparison is signed and returned to the P&S department to evidence its acceptance. If the other broker-dealer disagrees with the details of the transaction, any corrections made in the firm's accounting records are recorded to enable proper settlement to occur.

Settlement

2.71 Active securities are those used by the broker-dealer to carry out its daily business and are most typically located in depositories, such as the DTCC, that maintain book entry systems. Active securities include the following:

- Customers' securities not yet paid for

- Securities purchased by customers on margin that collateralize funds advanced by the broker-dealer against the purchase price
- Securities owned by the broker-dealer

2.72 Any active securities maintained on the broker-dealer's premises are referred to as being "in the box."

2.73 A clearing organization delivers securities by transferring securities on deposit at a depository such as the DTCC. The selling (delivering) broker-dealer or clearing organization delivers instructions electronically to the depository to transfer the securities by book entry rather than physical movement. This is known as *clearing through book entry*.

2.74 Money is paid or received daily by the broker-dealer so that the money balance in the account approximates the net market value of the open security positions. Included in the transmittal to the clearing organization are credit lists showing the total dollar amounts due from each of the purchasing broker-dealers.

2.75 The cashiering department is responsible for receipts and deliveries of securities and money and reconciles on a daily basis the money balance due to or from the clearing organization or the depository with the firm's records. After this is accomplished, a check, draft, or other payment method is used to facilitate net money settlement with the respective clearing organization.

2.76 Although most securities are held in book entry form, the procedures used in the handling of physical securities are described in the following paragraphs. Procedures performed relating to such settlement of transactions usually begin on the day prior to the settlement date with the receipt of blotters of trades scheduled to be settled the next business day. Accompanying the blotters are receive and deliver tickets for transactions to be settled directly with other broker-dealers and transactions to be settled through the clearing organization. Physical securities are delivered to the clearing organization with the delivery tickets attached on the settlement date.

2.77 Physical securities received from a selling broker-dealer are counted, verified, matched with the receive ticket, and determined to be in negotiable form. If the delivery is good, a copy of the deliver ticket is authorized for payment, and payment is made.

2.78 For deliveries to be made directly to other broker-dealers, blotters are examined, and requests for the securities needed for delivery are made, usually on the business day before the settlement date. If the securities are not available after all receipts on the day before settlement, the needed security may be borrowed, in which case the stock loan department would be requested to borrow the securities from another broker-dealer. If the securities are on hand, the securities are removed from the box, checked for proper negotiability, and delivered to the purchasing broker-dealer. If the delivery matches the purchasing broker-dealer's receive instructions, the selling broker-dealer receives payment.

2.79 Payment received by the selling broker-dealer is verified for propriety and entered into the cash receipts records. If the purchasing broker-dealer's instructions do not agree with the delivery attempted, the purchasing broker-dealer will DK (don't know) the delivery, which means the broker-dealer does not know the delivery. If the discrepancy is not corrected by the end of the day, the transaction represents a fail-to-receive for the purchasing broker-dealer and a fail-to-deliver for the selling broker-dealer.

2.80 *Fails-to-receive or fails-to-deliver.* As noted in the FASB ASC glossary, a *fail-to-receive* is a securities purchase from another broker-dealer not received from the selling broker-dealer by the close of business on the settlement date. As explained in FASB ASC 940-20-25-5, it is recorded as a liability in the general ledger. As per industry practice, a corresponding entry is recorded for a short position on the stock record.

2.81 As noted in the FASB ASC glossary, a *fail-to-deliver* is a securities sale to another broker-dealer that has not been delivered to the buying broker-dealer by the close of business on the settlement date. As explained in FASB ASC 940-20-25-4, it is recorded as an asset in the receivable account. As per industry practice, a corresponding entry is recorded for a long position on the stock record.

2.82 Most broker-dealers have automatic fail systems that generate pending files containing all unsettled securities after the trade date. As securities are settled, they are removed from the pending files. Any unsettled trades remaining on the day following the settlement date are transferred to fail files. Blotters of all open fails are forwarded to the cashiering department daily to be controlled and monitored.

2.83 Fails are forwarded for entry to the stock record (securities) and general ledger (money). Normally, an updated file of open fails is produced daily. When a fail is cleared (securities having been either received or delivered versus payment), the date of the clearance is noted, and the fail position is cleared from the broker-dealer's records. A non-CNS fail-to-receive position may require the broker-dealer to buy in (see the glossary) the security if the fail is outstanding longer than the time period specified by SEC Rule 15c3-3.

2.84 Broker-dealers generally record fail-to-receive transactions separately from fail-to-deliver transactions for each broker-dealer with whom they execute transactions. The cashiering department is responsible for resolving fails as quickly as possible because of the market risk exposure and financing implications involved. Broker-dealers continuously monitor their fail exposure by contract and counterparty. A broker-dealer has exposure if the contract value exceeds the market value for a fail-to-deliver or if the contract value is less than the market value for a fail-to-receive. Broker-dealers mark their fail positions to market to determine their exposure and calculate any net capital charges pursuant to SEC Rule 15c3-1. In addition to its market risk exposure, a broker-dealer is concerned with securities in its possession that it has failed to deliver because it must then finance its receivables by other means, such as bank loans.

2.85 Broker-dealers clearing transactions through correspondent brokers maintain fail-to-receive and fail-to-deliver records only for transactions that are self-cleared through U.S. correspondent broker-dealers. For transactions with foreign correspondent brokers, a broker-dealer is required to maintain fail records until notified by the foreign correspondent that the transaction has cleared.

2.86 *Depositories.* Depositories provide physical custody and transfer of certain securities, as well as the settlement of securities transactions between broker-dealers without the physical movement of securities. Securities held by depositories may be pledged to banks as collateral for loans without the physical transfer of the securities to the banks.

2.87 Each depository prepares daily reports for member broker-dealers, indicating activity by security, the money balance on deposit, and a statement of the balance of all security positions. Broker-dealers have the responsibility of indicating in their records whether the securities held at a depository are available for clearance and financing activities (that is, as collateral for bank loans) or should be reduced to possession or control, as required by SEC Rule 15c3-3. The status of such securities may be indicated on a stock record or in separate records supporting the total stock record position shown for a depository.

Bookkeeping

2.88 The P&S department's responsibilities include ensuring that trades are entered into the bookkeeping system correctly. If a trade is not properly recorded by the settlement date, the difference is posted to a suspense account until it is resolved (for example, a trade ticket not passed, a one-sided entry processed, or a bad account number used).

2.89 An entry is also made to a P&S suspense account when only one side of a principal-party buy or sell trade ticket is processed. The P&S suspense account item is resolved when the processing of the trade ticket is completed and reflected in the appropriate account. An operations suspense account records unidentified cash receipts and differences in trade billings or cash settlements of trade tickets.

2.90 Debit money balances and short security positions that cannot immediately be identified and cleared are recorded in suspense accounts. They reflect a potential exposure to the firm and should not be netted against like credits and long positions that are also placed in suspense accounts. Any material balances in suspense accounts should be identified and resolved on a timely basis. This suspense account can subject a broker-dealer to off-balance sheet liability risk if the error is resolved against the broker-dealer and the value of the security is also against the broker-dealer.

Specialized Clearance Activities

Mortgage-Backed Securities

2.91 The books and records maintained by broker-dealers in mortgage-backed securities (MBSs) are somewhat unique because of the requirements for recording receipts and payments of MBS principal and interest (P&I), maintaining records of both the original face value and amortized face value of MBSs, recording the allocation of mortgage pools to fulfill sales commitments, and maintaining records for trades for forward settlement when underlying pool numbers have yet to be announced (TBA).

2.92 MBSs or pass-through securities are created when mortgages are pooled together and sold. Payments of P&I on the underlying mortgages are passed through monthly to investors (less certain fees). In some instances, inefficient recordkeeping in registering the owner of an MBS with the paying agent has caused monthly payments of P&I to be forwarded to previous owners, forcing the current owner to submit claim letters to recoup missing P&I funds. The proper recordkeeping of P&I receivables and payables is essential to ensure accurate recording and collection.

2.93 Monthly payments for P&I are calculated using factors; the factor represents the percentages of each pool's original face value still outstanding. With the increasing application of computer technology to MBSs, the P&I problems are being resolved. By interfacing with a principal paydown factor service, a broker-dealer can automatically calculate the monthly accruals for P&I receivables and payables. Broker-dealers can also efficiently track partial payments and nonpayments to ensure recovery of receivables.

2.94 Computerized access to factor tapes also allows the broker-dealer to maintain records of the amortized face value of MBSs more efficiently. The amortized face value of MBSs is necessary to allocate pools properly to fulfill sales commitments, as well as amortize properly the purchased premium or discount.

2.95 A significant amount of MBS trading occurs in TBAs. The broker-dealer maintains accounting subledgers that reflect outstanding TBA buy and sell transactions. TBA transactions can be settled by receiving or delivering pools pursuant to the terms of the trade (within 0.01 percent of the trade amount) or by offsetting the trade through an offsetting TBA purchase or sale. In both cases, accurate subledgers are important to properly calculate the pools received or delivered pursuant to the TBA transactions. Additionally, TBAs have specific margin requirements and net capital treatment.

Government Securities

2.96 Treasury issues (with the exception of registered securities) and many U.S. government agency securities are available in book entry form through the Federal Reserve's book entry system. Only depository institutions (such as commercial banks, savings and loan associations, credit unions, and certain other depositories, as defined in the Monetary Control Act of 1980) can maintain accounts on the system. A depository institution may have several accounts, including clearing safekeeping accounts and trust safekeeping accounts. The book entry system electronically transfers government and agency securities between accounts based on instructions from its members.

2.97 Broker-dealers use members of the system to clear and settle transactions because they do not have direct access to Federal Reserve Wire Network (Fedwire), the Federal Reserve's communication system. The broker-dealer gives instructions to its clearing bank (a member of the Federal Reserve) for the transfer of funds and securities. Broker-dealers that have significant activity can make deliveries electronically through the Federal Reserve member bank by means of a remote access unit, which their clearing bank can supply.

2.98 All primary government securities dealers and some nonprimary government securities dealers are members of a clearing agency known as the Government Securities Division (GSD) of the FICC, which is a subsidiary of the DTCC. Participating government securities dealers use this net settlement system for the clearance and settlement of government securities positions. This net settlement system will net down settlements (including interest) for delivery through the Federal Reserve System. The GSD guarantees all transactions that are already compared between participants. The settlement of transactions for government securities is done using federal funds. Government securities normally settle as regular way trades one business day after the trade date. They can also settle for cash (same day as the trade date) or for any mutually agreed-on settlement date.

Repos and Reverse Repos

2.99 Repos and reverse repos are generally traded on a cash settlement basis (same day as the trade date). Executions for repo transactions are usually completed during the morning hours of a business day to allow time for the adequate processing and clearing of trades. The paperwork and delivery of the securities and funds are accomplished during the afternoon. Most securities transfers and the delivery of funds are settled over Fedwire. As noted previously, for government securities, only members of the Federal Reserve have direct access to Fedwire, so the broker-dealer uses its clearing bank for the transfer of funds and securities for repo transactions. Actual written purchase and sale confirmations are also delivered, when applicable. Depending on the arrangement of the repo transaction, the repo collateral may be delivered (transferred) to the buyer, held in safekeeping in a segregated customer account by the seller, or delivered to the buyer's custodial account at the seller's clearing bank. DTCC's FICC, through GSD, matches and nets repo transactions as part of its netting process for other government securities trading activity.

2.100 Additional securities transfers or delivery of funds may be necessary over Fedwire depending on changes in the market value of the underlying collateral (mark-to-market). Market value changes can necessitate adjustment of the repo transaction, either by repricing or a margin call. In a repricing, the change requires a delivery of funds, whereas a margin call requires a transfer of collateral.

Derivative Securities[6]

2.101 FASB ASC 815 establishes accounting and reporting standards for derivative instruments, including certain derivative instruments embedded in other contracts. Broker-dealers value investments in trading securities and hedges at fair value. This practice is an important one to consider in a review of the provisions of FASB ASC 815. See the "Derivatives" section of chapter 5 of this guide for discussion of FASB ASC 815. Derivative products (such as interest rate and currency swaps, swaptions, caps, and floors) involve certain unique settlement procedures. The settlement of these products does not involve the delivery of physical or book entry securities, but rather only cash exchanges between counterparties based on interest rates and notional or contract accounts. Settlement procedures for interest rate swaps require the monitoring and calculation of the required interest payment for the floating rate cash flow and the calculation of the fixed-rate interest payment for the fixed-rate cash flow. Once these amounts are determined on the interest payment date, the cash payments

---

[6] The Dodd-Frank Act divides regulatory authority over swap agreements between the Commodity Futures Trading Commission (CFTC) and the SEC (with other regulators also having a role, such as the Federal Reserve Board, which has an important role in setting capital and margin for swap entities that are banks). Under the comprehensive framework for regulating swaps and security-based swaps established in Title VII, the CFTC is given regulatory authority over swaps, the SEC is given regulatory authority over security-based swaps, and the commissions shall jointly prescribe such regulations regarding mixed swaps as may be necessary to carry out the purposes of Title VII.10. In addition, the SEC is given antifraud authority over, and access to information from, certain CFTC-regulated entities regarding security-based swap agreements, which are a type of swap related to securities over which the CFTC is given regulatory authority. In July 2012, the SEC issued Release No. 33-9338, *Further Definition of "Swap," "Security-Based Swap," and "Security-Based Swap Agreement;" Mixed Swaps; Security-Based Swap Agreement Recordkeeping*. This final rule further defines the terms *swap, security-based swap,* and *security-based swap agreement* and provides further information on mixed swaps and security-based swap agreement recordkeeping. See the SEC and the CFTC websites for more information on ongoing swap and derivative rulemaking.

are then transmitted to the appropriate counterparty by the method specified in the master swap agreement, such as wire or check. Often, a broker-dealer will have more than one swap agreement with a counterparty. If a master netting agreement is in place, the counterparty may net the interest payments or receipts, and one net cash payment will be made to or from the broker-dealer on the interest payment date. The floating rate cash flow of an interest rate swap is continually updated, as specified under the terms of the swap agreement, to enable the broker-dealer to calculate the interest payment or receipt from the contract and also to calculate unrealized gain or loss on a contract.

2.102 Caps, floors, and swaptions are settled solely for cash and do not require the exchange of physical or book-entry securities. For interest rate caps, upfront payments or premiums are paid to the writer in exchange for the right to receive the excess of a reference interest rate over a given rate. For interest rate floors, premiums are paid to the writer for the right to receive the excess of a given rate over a reference interest rate. The underlying contract is monitored continuously to determine whether the change in the floating rate has triggered the cap or floor. Once triggered, the cash payments or receipts of the amounts in excess of the cap amount and the amounts below the floor amount are calculated. Again, cash payments will be made in accordance with the master swap agreement. On the interest payment date, cash payments or receipts may be netted for counterparties that have a master netting agreement.

2.103 *Swaptions* are options to enter into an interest rate swap at a future date or to cancel an existing swap in the future. Premiums are paid to the writers of swaptions. Upon exercise of the swaption, the same clearance procedures would apply for interest rate swaps, or the swap would terminate with no further cash payment or receipt.

Commodity Futures and Options on Futures

2.104 The underlying commodities in the commodity futures contracts currently traded include grains, soybeans, rice, potatoes, sugar, coffee, and other foodstuffs; cotton; meat products, such as live and feeder cattle, pork bellies and live hogs, and broilers (chickens); precious and other metals, including gold, silver, copper, palladium, and platinum; foreign currencies; and energy products, such as crude oil, heating oil, and leaded and unleaded gasoline. Contracts in financial instruments such as U.S. Treasury bills, bonds and notes, Government National Mortgage Association securities, bank certificates of deposits, and Eurodollars are traded by those who wish to speculate or hedge using various interest rate futures. Also, stock index futures contracts are used for hedging portfolios or speculating against changes in stock market prices. As previously discussed, hedge accounting is permitted only if the requirements of FASB ASC 815 are met.

2.105 Most commodity futures contracts can be settled by taking or making delivery of the actual underlying commodity. Futures on stock market indexes and certain other futures are settled in cash. Exchange-traded options on futures contracts are settled through the delivery of the related futures contract by book entry. Although a futures contract may be settled by delivery, virtually all the commodity futures and option contracts are not settled by delivery, but rather with an offsetting purchase or sale of the same futures or options contract.

2.106 *Clearing organization for settlement of commodity futures and option contracts.* A clearing organization is affiliated with a commodity exchange to clear or match trades executed on that exchange. The clearing organization that comprises clearing members prepares daily settlement reports for each member. The reports show details of the trades cleared and the original margin on futures or premium deposits on options separately for customer and noncustomer trades. The open trades at the close of business each day are marked to market (trade price versus settlement price), resulting in a net cash payment to, or collection from, each clearing member as a result of price changes (that is, gains or losses). The payable or receivable is settled by check, draft, or wire transfer before the market opens on the next business day. In addition, the clearing organization may call on the clearing member for additional original margin. The margin and option premiums deposited at the clearing organizations are kept under the control of these clearing organizations as a guarantee against defaults.

2.107 *Special commodities records.* The CFTC, which regulates activities in futures and options on futures, requires full, complete, and systematic records of all transactions relating to the business. At a minimum, those records include the following:

- Monthly computation of minimum financial requirements
- Daily computations of 1) funds segregated for customers trading on U.S. futures exchanges, 2) funds segregated for customers engaging in cleared swap transactions, and 3) funds held for customers trading on non-U.S. futures exchanges
- Records of all charges and credits in each customer's account and all of the following:
  — Futures and cleared swap transactions executed for such accounts (including the date, price, quantity, market, commodity, and applicable settlement month)
  — Options on futures transactions executed for such accounts (including the date; an indication of whether the transaction involved a put or call; the expiration date; the quantity; the underlying contract for future delivery or underlying physical strike price; and details of the purchase price of the option, including premium, mark-up, commission, and fees)
- Details of securities and property received as margin
- Confirmations to each customer of futures, cleared swaps, and options transactions executed on the customer's behalf
- Purchase and sale statements to each customer for offsetting transactions
- Monthly statements to customers specifying open positions and trade prices, net unrealized profits or losses in all open futures contracts and cleared swaps, the market value of all open options on futures contracts, the ending ledger balance reflected in the customer's account, and details of any securities and property deposited by the customer as margin
- The customer name and address file indicating the principal occupation or business of the customer, signature cards, and risk disclosure statements
- Time-stamped order and execution tickets that include the account identification and order number

- Details of investments of customer funds
- A trade register that is a record for each business day, detailing all futures transactions, cleared swap transactions, and options on futures transactions executed on that day
- The monthly point balance that accrues, or brings to the official closing price or settlement price fixed by the clearing organization, all open contracts of customers as of the last business day of each month or of any regular monthly date selected (however, although CFTC regulations only require a monthly point balance, a firm with strong internal control would be performing this balancing on a daily basis)

2.108 A contract position record is usually maintained on a daily basis and shows a balancing of futures contracts by customer and for the broker-dealer's own account, offset by the position with the carrying broker or clearing organization. These positions are typically compared daily with the clearing organization in a procedure referred to as point balancing.

2.109 Broker-dealers record an accrual for commission income for futures and options on futures transactions on a half-turn basis (see the glossary), although in some instances the round-turn commissions (see the glossary) may be reflected in the customer's account upon entering into the transactions or on the date of the round turn.

Forward Transactions

2.110 *Forward transactions (forwards)* are defined as existing trade commitments with settlement dates subsequent to regular-way trades (see the "Trade-Date Versus Settlement-Date Accounting" section of chapter 5). They may have a time differential of up to one year or more, and are thus traded on a delayed delivery or forward basis. These transactions are normally recorded on memo records (such as a pending or when-issued file) that are confirmed on a regular basis similar to other customer positions that have settled. The accounting for those forward transactions is to recognize the gain or loss on a current basis (that is, by valuing the individual transaction on a current basis). See the "Derivatives" section of chapter 5 for a discussion of FASB ASC 815, which establishes the accounting and reporting standards for derivative instruments and hedging activities.

Municipal Securities

2.111 The clearance and settlement process for municipal securities is very similar to that for equities and corporate bonds. Most securities clear through the NSCC, and issues that are depository eligible normally settle by book entry.

2.112 However, certain factors make the municipal securities market unique. The most significant are the following:

- Municipal securities, other than new issues, settle trade for trade rather than CNS because the Municipal Securities Rulemaking Board (MSRB) prohibits partial settlements.
- MSRB real-time transaction reporting requires brokers, dealers, and municipal securities dealers to report most transactions within 15 minutes of execution.

- MSRB rules limit the buy-in period for aged fails to receive to 90 business days without full cooperation with the contra party. If a buy-in has not been completed within that time, the contra broker-dealer cannot be held liable for any losses incurred.
- Many municipal securities are not depository eligible and, therefore, require physical settlements.
- Because of the tax-exempt status of municipal securities, they are generally not sold short and are not actively loaned or borrowed.

International Securities

2.113 Certain issues are unique to non-U.S. securities that are traded in foreign markets. Each foreign market should be examined separately because of the following characteristics:

- There are custody issues related to the receipt and delivery of securities corresponding to transactions, the collection and payment of dividends and interest, information gathering, and processing with regard to corporate actions. Foreign custody agents must qualify under SEC Rule 17f-4 governing the eligibility of depositories.
- Custody requirements vary by country. Settlement cycles, as well as holiday schedules, are usually different. Other than in the United States, the exchange of shares for money seldom takes place simultaneously. In some clearing environments, the actual delivery of shares takes place more than 24 hours before payment. Therefore, counterparty risk and the process for choosing counterparties are important factors.
- The means of settling transactions in different countries can be dissimilar. Depending on the marketplace, book shares, physical shares (both registered and bearer), issuers' receipts, or transfer agent receipts may be the norm for transfer of ownership.
- Trading in offshore markets may involve the use of corresponding foreign exchange (FX) transactions to convert into the local currency of the foreign market. Such an FX transaction is another contract with its own risks and liabilities.
- Each country has its own unique rules relating to certain exception-type transactions. The issues may be whether short sales are allowed in the trading environment, if a stock loan is a business in that market, and what the regulatory issues relating to contract closeouts are.
- Tax and regulatory issues within a foreign market are additional considerations to review. Issues relating to the withholding of taxes, principal and income repatriation, and proper registrations are important within that market. The U.S. rules as they relate to a U.S. broker-dealer transacting business in the international marketplace are also a variable that affects business. Aged foreign fails are treated differently from domestic fails with respect to net capital charges and buy-ins (see SEC Rules 15c3-1 and 15c3-3).
- Cultural differences, although not a quantitative concept, can at times be a factor in doing business internationally. Issues such as language barriers, differences in work habits, and time-zone differences might be considered.

Options on Securities

2.114 The books and records required to be maintained by a general securities broker-dealer are also required of an options clearing firm under SEC Rules 17a-3 and 17a-4. An order ticket is required for each option transaction and should contain all relevant information, including the type of account (customer, firm, or market maker); whether the transaction is a put or call; whether it is a purchase or sale; the underlying trading unit; the exercise price; the expiration date; the premium per unit; and the purchasing and writing clearing members. In addition, the clearing firm should maintain a separate P&S blotter and a separate position record for all option transactions for itself and its customers or market makers.

2.115 Every clearing broker-dealer is required to furnish the following to its customers:

- Confirmations of each trade showing whether it was a purchase or sale, the underlying trading unit, the exercise price, the expiration month, the number of option contracts, the premium, the commission, the trade date, and the settlement date

- Monthly statements showing all purchases and sales during the month, including all commissions, taxes, interest charges and any other special charges, the ending market value of all long and short positions in the account, and the general account equity

2.116 Listed option trades settle on the next business day. Options Clearing Corporation (OCC) member broker-dealers are required to reconcile all option money and positions on a daily basis. An OCC clearing broker-dealer can exercise a long options contract by notification to the OCC. Exercise notices are assigned by the OCC on a random basis to clearing member firms and are effective the following day. Each assigned clearing member firm is required to allocate assignment notices to proprietary, customer, and market-maker short positions by using established set procedures. The allocation of assignment notices should be either on a random-selection or first-in, first-out basis.

2.117 The OCC issues a daily position report that lists all option activity and ending positions for all accounts carried by the OCC member broker-dealer and the net daily pay or collect amount due to or from the OCC. The OCC also issues a margin report that shows the OCC margin requirement on the aggregate short option positions and exercised contracts for each account carried by the OCC member broker-dealer. Required margin may be paid by cash, check, government securities, common stocks with a market value as specified by the rules, or an irrevocable letter of credit issued by an OCC-approved bank or trust company.

2.118 All OCC member broker-dealers that clear market-maker accounts or floor broker accounts are required to issue an OCC-approved letter of guarantee and a letter of authorization for floor brokers, and such letters are filed with the appropriate exchange. A letter of guarantee provides that the issuing clearing member accepts financial responsibility for all option market-maker transactions guaranteed by the clearing broker-dealer. A letter of authorization provides that the clearing broker-dealer accepts responsibility for the clearance of all option trades by the floor broker.

2.119 OCC member broker-dealers clearing market-maker transactions are required to "haircut" (see the glossary) the market-maker accounts as required by SEC Rule 15c3-1(c)(2)(X). Because the carrying broker-dealer guarantees the market-maker account to the OCC, the carrying broker-dealer is required to reduce its own net capital by the amount the market maker's Rule 15c3-1(c)(2)(X) haircut charges exceed the equity in the account. In addition, SEC Rule 15c3-1 requires that the sum of all market-maker Rule 15c3-1(c)(2)(X) haircut charges not exceed 1,000 percent of the carrying broker-dealer's net capital (the 1,000 percent test).

Reconciliation and Balancing

2.120 Daily cash receipts and disbursements are totaled on the journals or blotters, and the closing balance for each bank account is determined. A summary of the postings is prepared showing the distribution to the control accounts in the general ledger. The summary is agreed with the totals of the various source documents and with related items in the summaries prepared by the receive and deliver departments. In addition to the settlement and cash journal summaries, broker-dealers may prepare an overall summary of cash transactions processed by the cashier's department. Normally, this cash summary sheet contains numerous descriptive categories and columns to which the cash movements are posted. Entries are compiled by summarizing working documents, including blotters, journals, drafts, and other receipt and disbursement forms.

2.121 The securities record department is responsible for monitoring and controlling the recording of all securities movements under the broker-dealer's jurisdiction. The stock record department ensures that longs equal shorts for securities positions and is responsible for correcting all breaks in the securities record, just as the accounting department is responsible for ensuring that debits equal credits for money balances. Uncorrected breaks could cause serious losses to the firm, and accordingly, such items should be monitored, aged, and reported to management daily.

2.122 Securities differences may be caused by inaccurate recordkeeping on the part of a broker-dealer, by an out-of-balance condition in the stock record (a stock record break), or by errors in the receipt and delivery of securities. Such differences are normally disclosed through the automated daily balancing of the stock record, periodic counts of securities on hand, and examination or confirmation of items such as transfers and fails.

2.123 When a security difference is discovered, it should be recorded in a security difference account (a suspense account) pending research concerning the reason for the difference. When the difference is resolved, entries are made clearing the difference position from the stock record. If a short difference is not resolved, SEC Rule 15c3-3 requires the broker-dealer to buy-in the shortages. Subject to legal interpretation concerning ownership, the overages may be sold.

Custody

2.124 Customers' fully paid and excess-margin securities may be kept at a depository (see the following section, "Possession or Control") or in a vault on the broker-dealer's premises. Securities belonging to customers are recorded on the broker-dealer's records so that the real or beneficial owners (customers) can always be identified. The securities record often provides data concerning customer securities required to be held in segregation or safekeeping, which may be shown on the same securities record by using an additional column or memo entry, thus eliminating the need for a separate listing or summary. Customers' certificates may be registered in the broker-dealer's name (segregation) so that the securities can be delivered quickly. Alternatively, if a customer's certificates are registered in the customer's own name (safekeeping), they are nonnegotiable until a stock power is attached, endorsing a change in the beneficial owner, which would then be signature-guaranteed by attachment of an appropriate medallion.

Possession or Control

2.125 Customers' fully paid or excess-margin securities should be reduced to the possession or control of the broker-dealer within the time frame specified in SEC Rule 15c3-3. Permissible control locations include box, segregation, and safekeeping. Safekeeping securities are customers' securities fully paid for and held in custody by the broker-dealer for the accounts of customers. Safekeeping securities are normally registered in the name of the customer. Segregated securities are securities that have been reduced to the possession or control of the broker-dealer for the benefit of customers who have fully paid for them or securities of margin customers in excess of margin requirements. They are registered in the name of the broker-dealer or its nominee. Securities may be held in book-entry or physical form at approved depositories, such as the DTC. Customer and proprietary accounts of broker-dealers (PAB)[7] fully paid and excess margin securities are required to be held in segregated accounts, as specified in SEC Rule 15c3-3.

2.126 Securities usually are transferred to and from possession or control on the basis of instructions prepared by the margin department. The instructions reflect the following:

- The customer's name
- The quantity and description of the security
- The date the instructions were prepared
- The customer's account number

2.127 The ownership of securities that should be reduced to possession or control is usually indicated by means of additional columns or codes in the securities record. Instructions for the segregation or release from segregation of securities are issued by the margin department, frequently through an automated system. These instructions are processed into the broker-dealer's stock record, and total customer segregation requirements are compared with the total quantity of specific securities currently in possession or control. This comparison generates a report to the cashier's department indicating, by issue, the number of shares pending to be placed in segregation by the cashier or the number of shares in excess of requirements that may be removed from segregation by the cashier. The cashier's department carries out the instructions generated by this comparison, which is produced on a daily basis. This system (commonly known as bulk segregation) does not relate certificates to specific customers; as an alternative, some firms may use specific identification for determining their segregation requirements.

---

[7] See chapter 3, "Regulatory Considerations" for further information on proprietary accounts of broker-dealers (PAB) accounts.

2.128 Securities pending safekeeping or segregation (securities designated to be placed in safekeeping or segregation) may be fail-to-receive items, transfer items, out on loan to another broker, or collateral for bank loans. SEC Rule 15c3-3 limits the length of time during which securities can remain in those locations before the broker-dealer should take action to bring the securities into possession and control.

2.129 SEC Rule 15c3-3(b)(5) states that a broker or dealer is required to obtain and thereafter maintain the physical possession or control of securities carried for a PAB account,[8] unless the broker or dealer has provided written notice to the account holder that the securities may be used in the ordinary course of its securities business, and has provided an opportunity for the account holder to object.

Securities Transfer

2.130 The transfer department is responsible for transfers of ownership, registration, and reissuance of securities in different certificate denominations (usually to meet delivery requirements). Securities are generally registered in the name of the firm, unless the customer specifically requests that fully paid securities be registered in his or her name. If the securities are to be registered in the customer's name, the transfer instructions are issued by the margin department.

2.131 The transfer or margin department of a broker-dealer normally prepares securities-transfer instructions containing the following:

- The name in which new certificates are to be registered (and the account number and mailing address if they are to be registered in a customer's name)
- The number of shares or principal amount and description of the securities
- Instructions indicating whether the new certificates are to be sent to the customer or held by the broker-dealer for the customer's account
- Certificate numbers of the securities being transferred

2.132 The instructions from the margin department are recorded, and the security is designated as in transfer on the stock record. The instructions are then kept in an open transfer ticket file, which constitutes the supporting detail for the stock record transfer position. A copy of the instructions is sent to the transfer agent with the securities to be transferred.

2.133 The transfer department sends registered securities to transfer agents to be reregistered in the new owners' names. Transfer agents (often banks) maintain the company's list of owners. The certificates should be endorsed by the registered holder and authorized by a power of attorney. Reregistration may be made in the name of the beneficial owners or a nominee. Registration of certificates has been curtailed through the use of depositories.

2.134 Securities received from transfer are matched against the open transfer instructions, and the completed instructions are used as the basis for removing the open transfer position from the stock record. If the certificates

---

[8] Reverse repurchase agreements discussed in this guide are usually referred to as repurchase agreements by the investment company and banking industries.

are returned, the transfer department records them and returns them to the vault or sends them to the cashier's department for delivery. Those instructions remaining in the transfer department provide the supporting detail for the transfer positions on the stock record.

2.135 The transfer and reorganization departments maintain an aging of open transfer and reorganization items because any item in excess of 40 calendar days for which a confirmation has not been received from the transfer agent should be reported in the broker-dealer's regulatory monthly net capital and weekly reserve computations.

Dividends, Interest, and Reorganization

Dividends and Interest

2.136 The dividend department records distributions receivable on securities (such as cash dividends, stock dividends, rights, splits, and interest on debt instruments) of customers and the broker-dealer. Key dates are the following:

- *The declaration date.* The date a business entity announces the dividend.
- *The record date.* The date that determines who will be paid (stockholders and bondholders who are registered owners on the record date will be paid the distribution).
- *The payable date.* The date of the dividend and interest payment.
- *The ex-dividend date* (or *ex-date*). The date on which securities traded no longer include rights to the upcoming dividend payment (note, the market price generally drops to reflect the amount of the dividend on that date).

2.137 The principal exchange on which a security is listed sets the ex-date for listed stocks; FINRA sets the date for those securities traded in the OTC market. The ex-date is generally two business days before the record date for cash dividends.

2.138 On the dividend or interest record date, the dividend department obtains listings that show the record date holders and locations of each security. The record will indicate how the securities are registered (that is, in the name of the broker-dealer or in the name of another broker-dealer or individual from whom the dividend or interest is claimed).

2.139 To reduce the number of claims, the dividend department usually notifies the cashier's department daily of securities with approaching record dates. The cashier's department checks for securities on hand that are registered in a name other than the broker-dealer's own name and will attempt to deliver such securities to the transfer agent so that the registration may be transferred to the broker-dealer's name as of the record date. Broker-dealers usually use information provided electronically by dividend-reporting services to identify information regarding dividend dates.

2.140 For each cash dividend or interest payment, the dividend department prepares a memo proof to ascertain the total receipts and disbursements that will be processed in comparison with the total long and short positions for a particular security. The dividend department determines which customers' or firm inventory accounts are to be credited or debited on the payable date for the dividend or interest versus the receivable or payable account. Differences between the amounts received and the receivable amounts should be investigated by the dividend department.

2.141 For each stock dividend distribution, the dividend department performs procedures similar to those for cash dividends. Long and short entries to customer and firm accounts are made on the payable date and are offset by entries to stock dividend accounts; the stock dividend accounts are flattened (zeroed out) after the actual securities have been received.

2.142 As noted in FASB ASC 940-20-05-7, the dividend department maintains a record of securities the broker-dealer fails to receive or deliver on the record date. Securities received or delivered against fails that were open on the record date and that are in the name of the delivering broker should be accompanied by due bills. A *due bill* is an official authorization allowing the purchasing broker-dealer to make a legal claim on the selling broker-dealer for a future distribution to which it is entitled. For cash dividends or interest payments, this typically takes the form of a postdated check. It is usually the responsibility of the dividend department to collect or authorize payments for transactions of this nature.

2.143 Broker-dealers should maintain records for each security by individual declaration date and should not net dividends or interest either by security or between dates.

2.144 Amounts received that have not been paid or credited because proper account identification cannot be made are considered to be unclaimed dividends and interest (suspense items) and are normally paid only on receipt of valid claims. Balances remaining in dividends or interest payable accounts may be subject to abandoned property (escheat) laws. Aged dividend or interest receivables should be readily identifiable so that appropriate net capital charges can be computed in accordance with SEC Rule 15c3-1 and that appropriate reserve computation treatment can be applied pursuant to SEC Rule 15c3-3.

Reorganization

2.145 Reorganization transactions result if an entity undergoes a change in its ownership or structure affecting its outstanding securities. A common example of a reorganization transaction is a tender offer on the part of a third party to purchase a company's shares.

2.146 Reorganization transactions may be either voluntary offers or mandatory exchanges. Voluntary offers are processed if the broker-dealer is so instructed by customers who have the option to accept or reject a tender; subscribe to an issuance; exercise options, rights, or warrants; or convert convertibles shares.

2.147 Mandatory exchanges are generally processed for customers on the effective date. They include mergers, splits and reverse splits, "when issued" trading, subscriptions, consolidations, acquisitions, exchanges of convertible securities into common stocks, and certain called securities.

2.148 The reorganization department is responsible for processing securities involving corporate reorganizations. The responsibilities include the following:

- Executing corporate calls for redemption of issues in the custody of the brokerage firm
- Converting securities into common stock on request of their underlying owner
- Exchanging one class of security for another class of the same issuer, pursuant to a reorganization of the business entity
- Exchanging one company's securities for another company's securities or money, pursuant to a merger or an acquisition
- Subscribing for new shares in a company, pursuant to a rights offering
- Transmitting securities to an intended purchaser under terms of a tender offer on specific written instructions from its beneficial owner
- Allocating results to customer accounts on partial tenders

2.149 *Recording customer or proprietary reorganization transactions.* On the effective date of the reorganization, the original security is removed from the customer or proprietary trading account and set up as a long position in the reorganization account. The new security (or cash, in the case of a cash tender) is set up long (credited) in the customer or proprietary trading account and short (debited) to the reorganization account. When the securities or cash are received from the reorganization agent, the reorganization account is flattened (zeroed out).

Collateralized Financing

Stock Loan and Stock Borrow

2.150 Securities not available to be delivered on the settlement date may be borrowed. A stock borrow occurs when a broker-dealer needs a security to deliver against a settling transaction, such as a short sale. A *short sale* is the sale of a security not owned by the firm or a customer. Short sales are often made in anticipation of a market decline or as part of a trading or hedging strategy. As previously discussed, hedge accounting is permitted only if the requirements of FASB ASC 815 are met.

2.151 A broker-dealer also may be involved in a finder's business, whereby securities are borrowed to relend to another broker-dealer, thus allowing the broker-dealer to earn a spread on the transaction. Broker-dealers may also engage in equity securities borrowed transactions solely for financing the positions of another broker-dealer in which the equity securities are initially borrowed without a permitted purpose pursuant to Regulation T Section 220.10(a), and placed in a box location. These transactions, which are referred to as nonpurpose borrows, have regulatory implications that need to be considered in the computation of net capital. Rule 203 of SEC Regulation SHO contains requirements and guidance for broker-dealers related to the long and short sales of equity securities.

2.152 In general, broker-dealers borrow securities to deliver them to another broker-dealer or customer, often leveraging utilities like Loanet (see the glossary) to do so. If the cashiering department needs to borrow securities, it instructs the stock loan department to borrow them. The borrowing broker-dealer is required to deposit cash or other collateral that may be in the form of securities issued or guaranteed by the United States or its agencies, certain certificates of deposit or bankers' acceptances, or irrevocable letters of credit. When the borrowing broker-dealer deposits cash, it receives an interest-like rebate on the amount that was exchanged for the securities. This rebate is negotiated, with the rate usually established by the lender and agreed to by the borrower. If a security is difficult to obtain (that is, hard to borrow), a lower or negative rebate would be acceptable. The borrowing broker-dealer records the transaction as a long on the stock record and as an asset in the general ledger (receivable from the lending broker). The lending broker records a short position on the stock record and a liability in the general ledger. FASB ASC 860, *Transfers and Servicing*, provides specific criteria for determining whether a securities lending transaction is to be accounted for as a sale or secured borrowing and provides an illustration of the latter. Among other matters, FASB ASC 860 provides guidance for recognition and reclassification of collateral and for disclosures relating to securitization transactions and collateral. (See chapter 5 of this guide for a discussion of secured borrowing.)

2.153 For each security borrow or loan position, information may be prepared and retained in the cashiering department to be used as the basis for an out-of-loaned or out-of-borrowed entry and also in the comparison of cashiering department records with the stock record and general ledger for control purposes. The cashiering department records contain details of securities borrowed and loaned transactions, such as the following:

- Date
- Description of the security
- Quantity
- Total amount of the deposit made (securities borrowed) or received (securities loaned)
- Party from whom the securities have been borrowed or to whom they have been loaned

2.154 As with fail-to-receive and fail-to-deliver items, those records provide the supporting details for the stock record borrow and loan security positions, as well as for the general ledger money control of amounts due to and due from others. It is general practice for broker-dealers to adjust the contract value of the securities borrowed and loaned to market value (mark-to-market) on a daily basis.

Bank Loan Financing

2.155 The day-to-day financing needs of a broker-dealer are provided by the treasurer's department, which may negotiate short-term loans from banks or other parties.

2.156 A separate record is generally maintained for each such loan, usually indicating the following:

- The bank's name
- The type of loan (that is, firm, customer, or noncustomer, depending on the collateral pledged)
- The loan amount
- The interest rate

- The quantity, description, and market value of securities used as collateral for the loan

2.157 A separate file for securities used as collateral may be maintained in certain systems. The loan records are the supporting details of the general ledger and the security positions shown on the stock record as bank loan collateral.

2.158 From the reports indicating the collateral loan securities are being recalled from the bank, or additional securities are being sent to the bank, either in substitution for securities recalled or as additional collateral, entries are prepared and entered on the stock record. Separate accounts are generally maintained in the general ledger for each loan, with separate positions maintained in the stock record for the securities collateralizing each loan. Broker-dealers are required to differentiate their bank loans as either firm, customer or nonfirm, or noncustomer as provided in SEC Rules 8c-1 and 15c2-1. This distinction is also required in determining collateral requirements pursuant to federal regulations and determining amounts to report in the reserve formula, as required by SEC Rule 15c3-3. Securities used to collateralize bank loans of customers cannot be fully paid-for or excess-margin securities because such securities are required to be segregated by the broker-dealer.

Reverse Repos and Repos

2.159 Reverse repos are similar to securities-borrowed transactions, except that reverse repos are generally executed with government and government-agency securities. Securities are usually borrowed to make deliveries on short sales, whereas reverse repos are frequently related to investment activities as well as meeting delivery requirements.[9]

2.160 In a reverse repo transaction, a broker-dealer receives securities for a stated price from another party and agrees to sell them to the same party at a later date (*a*) at the same price plus interest at a stated rate or (*b*) at a higher price. The higher price reflects the interest earned on the contract price for the number of days the contract is outstanding.

2.161 The party entering into a reverse repo does not own the securities. Accordingly, the reverse repo is treated as a collateralized receivable rather than an inventory position. The party selling the securities with the commitment to repurchase maintains most incidences of ownership.

2.162 In a repo, a broker-dealer sells securities at a stated price to another broker or a customer and agrees to repurchase an identical security at a later date at the same price plus interest at a stated rate or at a higher price, which reflects the interest on the principal amount borrowed.

2.163 The rights of parties involved in a repo or reverse repo transaction depend on the particular terms and conditions of the transactions that are documented in a written agreement or transaction confirmation. Most firms use a standard agreement developed by the Securities Industry and Financial Markets Association (formerly the Bond Market Association). The use of standardized documentation diminishes uncertainties for such transactions. Written agreements should describe the transaction, the terms and conditions of the contract, and the rights of the parties, including the following:

---

[9] Reverse repurchase agreements discussed in this guide are usually referred to as repurchase agreements by the investment company and banking industries.

- The names of the parties
- The quantity and a description of the securities
- Interest, or the formula for determining interest to be paid or received
- The date and terms of delivery or receipt
- Provisions for marking to market and margin requirements
- The terms of loan or the conditions for return or recall
- The capacity of the parties as principal or agent
- The right and ability of the purchaser of the securities to substitute like securities for repurchase on the repurchase date
- A description of events of default that would permit the purchaser or seller to liquidate or purchase the underlying securities
- A description of the rights of any trustee or custodian who may hold the underlying securities during the life of the agreement
- A description of the party that is to have title to the underlying securities during the term of the agreement
- Timely correction of mark-to-market deficiencies or excesses and a description of the method of computing mark-to-market requirements
- The right of offset

2.164 The accounting records should include details of all securities in repo and reverse repo transactions showing the following:

- Amount of the contract
- Dates of delivery or receipt
- Identification of counterparties
- Dates and amounts of mark to market and dates the securities are to be recalled or returned

Regulatory Considerations

2.165 The general presumption of SEC Rule 17a-3 is that the financial accounting records have accounting integrity, be balanced, have an appropriate audit trail, and be posted currently. The rule does not specify the medium or even format of the records. Instead, it simply specifies the generic records to be made and requires that they be kept current. This generally means that financial and regulatory computations can be made promptly using those records.

2.166 SEC Rule 17a-4 prescribes the period of time that the books and records, as well as certain additional records, should be maintained by the broker-dealer under SEC Rule 17a-3. The rule applies to those records maintained in connection with a broker-dealer's business, not only those required by SEC Rule 17a-3. For example, record retention requirements for correspondence, canceled checks, memorandums, and other records of the broker-dealer's business are included under the rule.

2.167 The records of a broker-dealer are generally required to be maintained for two years in a readily accessible place at the broker-dealer's principal place of business. Thereafter, the length of time the broker-dealer is required to maintain the records varies. Basic accounting records should be kept for six years. Records relating to the terms and conditions of opening and maintaining an account should be kept at least six years after closing the account. Other records (such as corporate charters, partnership agreements, minute books, and stock certificate books) should be kept for the life of the broker-dealer. Certain states and other authorities may have additional requirements for keeping books and records.

2.168 SEC Rule 17a-4 permits the broker-dealer to utilize microfilm or microfiche to preserve the firm's records. Other means, such as electronic files (for example, image processing), have been approved by the SEC as an alternative method of preserving a firm's records, provided certain criteria are met. If records are kept on such media, two copies should be made and kept in separate places to protect against loss. If an outside service bureau or other facility is used by the broker-dealer to prepare the records, the broker-dealer and facility should have an agreement that the facility's records are available to the SEC and self-regulatory organizations.

2.169 A broker-dealer operating as a sole proprietor should maintain records of all assets and liabilities of the proprietor that are not related to the broker-dealer's operation. Such records are necessary for determining whether the broker-dealer has complied with the net capital rule's (SEC Rule 15c3-1) requirement that the excess of personal liabilities over assets not used in the business be treated as a deduction when computing net capital.

2.170 SEC Rule 17a-11 under the 1934 Act requires broker-dealers to notify the SEC and their designated examining authority if certain situations occur or are experienced. The rule also requires notification if certain minimum net capital requirements are not met. With regard to the books and records, the rule requires a broker-dealer that has failed to keep its books and records current as specified under SEC Rule 17a-3, to give notice of this fact immediately; to specify the books and records that have not been made and kept current; and to file a report within 48 hours of the notification stating the steps taken to correct the situation. There are other situations that may require notification under the rules, see chapter 3, "Regulatory Considerations," for further information regarding notification requirements.

2.171 SEC Rule 17a-13 under the 1934 Act requires quarterly securities examinations (including physical securities counts, verifications, and comparisons with the records of the firm) and the recording of differences, as well as appropriate documentation of such procedures.

2.172 The broker-dealer is also required to be in compliance with the net capital rule at all times. At least monthly, a broker-dealer is required to prepare and maintain a record of the proof of money balances for all ledger accounts in the form of trial balances and a record of the computation of aggregate indebtedness (unless the alternative capital computation, which uses aggregate debit items from SEC Rule 15c3-3, is being elected) and net capital under SEC Rule 15c3-1, as of the same date. In addition, SEC Rule 15c3-3 requires that records be maintained of the periodic (weekly or monthly) calculations of aggregate debit and credit items and the deposits required in the special reserve bank account for the exclusive benefit of customers and that compliance with the requirements for maintaining physical possession or control of fully paid and excess-margin securities of customers be documented.

Tax Information Reporting for Certain Customer Transactions

2.173 A broker-dealer is required to file information returns with the IRS for certain customer transactions and to also send the related form(s) to the customer. Examples of the more common returns and of the information they provide include the following:

- *Form 1099-B (broker transactions).*[10] The gross proceeds from the sale of securities conducted by the broker-dealer during the year.
- *Form 1099-INT (interest).* The amount of interest received by the customer from securities held by the broker-dealer during the year.
- *Form 1099-DIV (dividends).* The amount of dividends received by the customer from equity securities held by the broker-dealer during the year.
- *Form 1099-OID (original issue discounts).* The amount of interest accreted on original issue discount securities (and any interest received on original issue discount securities) held by the broker-dealer during the year.
- *Form 1099-R (retirement funds).* The amounts withdrawn during the year from an individual retirement account (IRA) or a pension account that is held at the broker-dealer's firm (the broker-dealer is also required to provide other information about IRA arrangements on Form 5498).
- *Form 1099-MISC (miscellaneous).* The amount of payments in lieu of dividends earned by the customer but not received because the security was placed by the broker-dealer in a stock loan at the customer's request.

2.174 The IRS generally matches information returns filed by the broker-dealer to its database to determine whether the payee's name and taxpayer identification number (TIN) correspond to its records. If there is a mismatch, the IRS notifies the broker-dealer (payor) of this fact. The payor is then required to send a letter to the payee informing him or her of the mismatch and request a Form W-9 be returned within 30 business days of the date of the notification from the IRS. If the payee does not return this W-9, all future reportable payments are subjected to backup withholding. If a payor does not withhold when required to do so, the payor becomes responsible for the tax.

2.175 The IRS has rules regarding what action to take when a payee has provided an incorrect TIN. Certain notices should be sent to the payee. Depending on the situation, the broker-dealer may be required to begin backup

---

[10] IRC Section 6045, as amended, requires that in the case of a covered security, every broker required to report the gross proceeds from the sale of a security under IRC Section 6045(a) must also report the customer's adjusted basis in the security and whether any gain or loss with respect to the security is long term or short term. The reporting is typically done on IRS Form 1099-B. Form 1099-B instructions contain information about a covered security and the additional information required to be reported.

In addition, a broker (and certain other persons that transfer custody of a covered security to a receiving broker) must furnish to the receiving broker a written statement that allows the receiving broker to satisfy the basis reporting requirements. The required statement must be furnished to the receiving broker within 15 days after the date of the transfer. Information regarding this requirement can also be found in Form 1099-B instructions.

withholding and continue backup withholding until notified by either the IRS or the Social Security Administration to stop. Once again, failure to withhold when required to do so will result in the payor being held responsible for the tax. Publication 1281, *Backup Withholding for Missing and Incorrect Name/TIN(s)*, is available on the IRS website and contains information and forms related to backup withholding.

2.176 The IRS requires broker-dealers to file Financial Crimes Enforcement Network (FinCEN) Form 104, *Currency Transaction Report* (formerly Form 4879), for customer deposits, withdrawals, exchanges of currency, or other payments or transfers by, through, or to the broker-dealer if they involve a transaction in currency of more than $10,000. In addition, FinCEN Form 101, *Suspicious Activity Report by the Securities and Futures Industries*, should be filed to report suspicious activity. The instructions to FinCEN Form 101 outline when and under what circumstances a form should be filed.

Illustrative Stock Record Entries

2.177 All stock record entries are recorded on a security-by-security basis on the settlement date. Trade date information is maintained on other files of the broker-dealer. Although not common, some firms maintain their stock record on a trade date basis.

1. Customer A buys 100 shares of ABC at $20 per share. Note that the entry assumes the securities are not received on the settlement date.

Stock Record	(Quantity)	General Ledger	($)
Long—Customer A	100	Dr. Customer A	2,000
Short—Fail-to-Receive	100	Cr. Fail-to-Receive	2,000

2. Customer A pays $2,000 for the securities.

Stock Record	(Quantity)	General Ledger	($)
No entry needed		Dr. Cash	2,000
		Cr. Customer A	2,000

3. Because the 100 shares of ABC have not been received, the firm borrows 100 shares of ABC.

Stock Record	(Quantity)	General Ledger	($)
Long—Stock Borrow	100	Dr. Stock Borrow	2,000
Short—DTC	100	Cr. Cash	2,000

4. The security failed to receive is now received at the DTC.

Stock Record	(Quantity)	General Ledger	($)
Long—Fail-to-Receive	100	Dr. Fail-to-Receive	2,000
Short—DTC	100	Cr. Cash	2,000

5. Instead of being returned, the stock borrow was loaned.

Stock Record	(Quantity)	General Ledger	($)
Long—DTC	100	Dr. Cash	2,000
Short—Stock Loan	100	Cr. Stock Loan	2,000

6. Customer B sold 200 shares of DEF at $30 per share. Note that the entry assumes the securities were in transfer and, therefore, not delivered on the settlement date.

Stock Record	(Quantity)	General Ledger	($)
Long—Fail-to-Deliver	200	Dr. Fail-to-Deliver	6,000
Short—Customer B	200	Cr. Customer B	6,000

7. DEF was delivered through the DTC.

Stock Record	(Quantity)	General Ledger	($)
Long—DTC	200	Dr. Cash	6,000
Short—Fail-to-Deliver	200	Cr. Fail-to-Deliver	6,000

8. The stock record is balanced against the DTC, and it was noted that the firm shows 200 more shares of DEF than does the DTC statement.

Stock Record	(Quantity)	General Ledger	($)
Long—DTC	200	No entry needed	
Short—Suspense	200		

9. In addition, the firm's reconciliation showed that the DTC sent the firm a check for $3,500 when the firm's records showed a receivable of $5,000.

Stock Record	(Quantity)	General Ledger	($)
No entry needed		Dr. Cash	3,500
		Dr. Suspense DTC	1,500
		Cr. Receivable from DTC	5,000

10. The firm decides to buy 5,000 shares of GHI at $2 per share for its inventory.

Stock Record	(Quantity)	General Ledger	($)
Long—Firm Inventory	5,000	Dr. Firm Inventory	10,000
Short—Box or DTC	5,000	Cr. Cash or DTC	10,000

11. The firm decides to repo Treasury bills held at the DTC with a face value of $10 million. Note that the entry assumes delivery of the security and that the market value of the securities is the same as the face amount.

Stock Record	(Quantity)	General Ledger	($)
Long—DTC	10,000,000	Dr. Cash	10,000,000
Short—REPO	10,000,000	Cr. Securities Sold under agreements to repurchase	10,000,000

Chapter 3

Regulatory Considerations[1]

3.01 Pursuant to the Securities Exchange Act of 1934 (the 1934 Act), the SEC developed a comprehensive system to regulate broker-dealers and the securities industry in general. As a result, all broker-dealers are subject to regulation by the SEC.

3.02 The audit and reporting requirements for securities broker-dealers are regulated by SEC Rule 17a-5 under the 1934 Act. Such requirements for broker-dealers that are also commodities brokers, known as CFTC-registered futures commission merchants (FCMs) or CFTC-registered introducing brokers (IBs) are regulated by Regulation 1.16 of the Commodity Exchange Act, whereas the requirements for registered broker-dealers in U.S. government securities are regulated by Section 405.2 of the regulations pursuant to Section 15C of the 1934 Act. Those rules are listed in the "Commodities Brokers" section of this chapter.

3.03 The Dodd-Frank Wall Street Reform and Consumer Protection Act (Dodd-Frank Act), signed into law by the president on July 21, 2010, called for a number of regulatory changes related to the securities industry. In February 2017, the president signed an executive order that sets in motion scaling back some of the provisions of the Dodd-Frank Act. Readers should be alert for further developments.

3.04 One of the provisions of this act amended the Sarbanes-Oxley Act of 2002 (SOX) to give the PCAOB full oversight authority over audits of all broker-dealers, including nonissuer broker-dealers. The Dodd-Frank Act included a provision that audits of broker-dealers, including nonissuer broker-dealers, be performed in accordance with PCAOB auditing standards. The SEC finalized amendments to SEC Rule 17a-5, through Release No. 34-70073, *Broker-Dealer Reports*, on July 30, 2013 which require PCAOB auditing and attestation standards be applied to the annual reporting for all broker-dealers effective for fiscal year ends on or after June 1, 2014.[2] Before undertaking the audit of a broker-dealer in securities, the auditor should obtain an understanding of regulatory factors. This generally includes reading the applicable standards and rules in order to have an understanding of the prescribed scope of the audit and the related reporting requirements.

Applicable Rules

3.05 SEC Rule 17a-5(f)(2) requires the auditor to be designated by the broker-dealer, in writing, to the SEC and the designated examining authority,

---

[1] Guidance in this chapter should not replace a full understanding of the rules and interpretations issued by all applicable regulatory agencies.

[2] For further information see the two frequently asked questions (FAQs) that were released by the SEC, the first in March 2014, *Frequently Asked Questions Concerning the Amendments to Certain Broker-Dealer Financial Responsibility Rules*, and the second in April 2014, *Frequently Asked Questions Concerning the July 30, 2013 Amendments to the Broker-Dealer Financial Reporting Rule*. Both are available at www.sec.gov/divisions/marketreg/mrfaq.htm.

such as the Financial Industry Regulatory Authority (FINRA)[3] or a securities exchange, of which the broker-dealer is a member.

3.06 SEC Rule 15c3-5, "Risk Management Controls for Brokers or Dealers with Market Access," requires broker-dealers with access to trading securities directly on an exchange or alternative trading system (ATS), including those providing sponsored or direct market access to customers or other persons, and broker-dealer operators of an ATS that provide access to trading securities directly on their ATS to a person other than a broker-dealer, to establish, document, and maintain a system of risk management controls and supervisory procedures.[4] On April 15, 2014, the SEC issued an FAQ, *Responses to Frequently Asked Questions Concerning Risk Management Controls for Brokers or Dealers with Market Access*, which is available at www.sec.gov/divisions/marketreg/faq-15c-5-risk-management-controls-bd.htm. For more information, see section "SEC Rule 15c3-5, 'Risk Management Controls for Brokers or Dealers with Market Access'" of this chapter.

3.07 The primary rules under the 1934 Act and other regulations that are applicable to the audits of broker-dealers in securities are as follows:[5]

- Rules 8c-1 and 15c2-1, "Hypothecation of Customers' Securities"
- Rule 15a-6, "Exemption of Certain Foreign Brokers or Dealers"[6]
- Rule 15c3-1, "Net Capital Requirements for Brokers or Dealers"
- Rule 15c3-1(e), "Notice Provisions Relating to Limitations on the Withdrawal of Equity Capital"
- Rule 15c3-3, "Customer Protection—Reserves and Custody of Securities"
- Rule 15c3-5, "Risk Management Controls for Brokers or Dealers with Market Access"
- Rule 17a-3, "Records to Be Made by Certain Exchange Members, Brokers, and Dealers"
- Rule 17a-4, "Records to Be Preserved by Certain Exchange Members, Brokers, and Dealers"

---

[3] For additional information see Financial Industry Regulatory Authority (FINRA) Regulatory Notice 14-39, *New Template Available on FINRA Firm Gateway for Compliance with SEA Rule 17a-5(f)(2) (Statement Regarding Independent Public Accountant)*.

[4] On November 19, 2014, the SEC issued Final Rule 34-73639, *Regulation Systems Compliance and Integrity*. The amendments include the addition of Regulation Systems Compliance and Integrity (Regulation SCI) under the Securities Exchange Act of 1934 (the 1934 Act) and conforming amendments to Regulation ATS under the Exchange Act. Regulation SCI will apply to certain self-regulatory organizations (including registered clearing agencies), alternative trading systems (ATSs), plan processors, and exempt clearing agencies (collectively, SCI entities), and will require these SCI entities to comply with requirements with respect to the automated systems central to the performance of their regulated activities. The full release is available on the SEC website at www.sec.gov/rules/final/2014/34-73639.pdf.

[5] Paragraphs 3.184–.185 provide additional discussion of rules adopted under the Securities Exchange Act of 1934 (1934 Act) for over-the-counter (OTC) derivatives dealers who register with the SEC under a limited regulatory structure rather than under the usual broker-dealer regulatory regime of Section 15(b) of the 1934 Act. Also, see paragraph 3.184 for a listing of rules under Title 17, *Commodity and Securities Exchanges* U.S. *Code of Federal Regulations* Chapter IV, that are applicable specifically to government securities broker-dealers.

[6] For further information, see the FAQ that was released by the SEC on March 21, 2013, *Frequently Asked Questions Regarding Rule 15a-6 and Foreign Broker-Dealers*. The FAQ is available at www.sec.gov/divisions/marketreg/mrfaq.htm.

- Rule 17a-5, "Reports to Be Made by Certain Brokers and Dealers"
- Rule 17a-11, "Notification Provisions for Brokers and Dealers"
- Rule 17a-13, "Quarterly Security Counts to Be Made by Certain Exchange Members, Brokers, and Dealers"
- Rule 17h-1T, "Risk Assessment Recordkeeping Requirements for Associated Persons of Brokers and Dealers"
- Rule 17h-2T, "Risk Assessment Reporting Requirements for Brokers and Dealers"
- Rule 17Ad-17, "Lost Securityholders and Unresponsive Payees"
- Rule 17Ad-22, "Clearing Agency Standards"
- SEC 17-248–Subpart C, "Regulation S-ID: Identity Theft Red Flags" (Regulation S-ID)
- SEC Rule 506 of Regulation D and Rule 144A
- Federal Reserve Regulation T (Regulation T) of the Board of Governors of the Federal Reserve System
- Account Statement Rule (for example, FINRA Manual—the National Association of Securities Dealers (NASD) Rule 2340, "Customer Account Statements" or equivalent rules of the designated examining authority)
- For broker-dealers that are also CFTC-registered FCMs and CFTC-registered IBs, Commodity Futures Trading Commission (CFTC) Regulations 1.10–1.32, 5.6–5.14, 22.2–22.7, and 30.7, as applicable (see paragraph 3.182 and the CFTC website at www.cftc.gov for more information)
- For broker-dealers that are also registered as investment advisers under the Investment Advisers Act of 1940 (see also, section "Additional Requirements for Registered Investment Advisers" of this chapter)

3.08 A general familiarity with the rules of the various regulatory bodies, the SEC, FINRA,[7] National Futures Association (NFA), the U.S. Department of the Treasury (Treasury Department), and the CFTC if the broker-dealer is also registered as an FCM or IB will be helpful in understanding the relationships among the rules.[8]

---

[7] Following the consolidation of the National Association of Securities Dealers (NASD) and the New York Stock Exchange (NYSE) Member Regulation into FINRA, NASD rules and certain NYSE rules were combined to form the FINRA Transitional Rulebook. The incorporated NYSE rules apply only to those members of FINRA that are also members of the NYSE (dual members). FINRA has established a process to develop a new consolidated rulebook that will apply to all FINRA members. Work is continuing on this consolidation of rules. The SEC must approve the rules that will make up the new Consolidated FINRA Rulebook. This information is available on the FINRA website at www.finra.org/industry/regulation/finrarules/p038095.

[8] Each year, FINRA publishes an *Annual Regulatory and Examination Priorities Letter* to highlight new and existing areas of significance to its regulatory programs. The information in the letter represents FINRA's current assessment of certain key industry issues. The annual letters can be found on the FINRA website at www.finra.org/industry/regulation/guidance/communicationstofirms/p122861.

The SEC Office of Compliance Inspections and Examinations (OCIE) also publishes annual examination priorities. These "Priorities Memos" can be found on the SEC OCIE website at www.sec.gov/ocie.

Interpretations of Rules

3.09 Published interpretations of certain rules of the regulatory bodies[9] may be found in the following reference materials:

- Financial and Operational Combined Uniform Single (FOCUS) report forms (Form X-17A-5 Part II and Part IIA) and their general instructions, which include line item references to specific rules. These forms can be accessed at www.sec.gov/about/forms/secforms.htm.

- SEC interpretative releases (1934 Act series) and published interpretative and no action letters, which can be accessed at www.sec.gov/divisions/marketreg/mr-noaction.shtml.

- Treasury Department interpretations, which can be accessed at www.federalreserve.gov/boarddocs/legalint/.

- CFTC interpretations and advisories, which can be accessed at www.cftc.gov/lawregulation/cftcstaffletters/advisories/index.htm.

- NFA interpretive notices, which can be accessed at https://www.nfa.futures.org/rulebook/index.aspx.

- FINRA manual and regulatory notices, which can be accessed at https://www.finra.org/industry/notices.

- FINRA interpretive guidance regarding the financial responsibility rules can be accessed at www.finra.org/Industry/Regulation/Guidance/FOR/index.htm.

- Interpretative instructions distributed to their respective memberships by other self-regulatory organizations.

- Published securities services (Commerce Clearing House, Prentice-Hall, and *Securities Regulation and Law Report*).

3.10 The auditor may inquire whether the broker-dealer has requested and received specific interpretations or "No Action Letters" from any regulatory agency since the prior audit. This information will assist the auditor in giving the issue appropriate consideration regarding their effect, if any, on the financial statements of the broker-dealer being audited.

Explanation of Significant SEC Financial Responsibility Rules

SEC Rule 15c3-3, "Customer Protection—Reserves and Custody of Securities"

3.11 The Customer Protection Rule is designed to accomplish the following purposes:

- To ensure that customers' funds held by broker-dealers, including funds derived through the lending, hypothecation, and other permissible uses of customers' securities, are used "in safe areas of

---

[9] Appendix A, "Information Sources," of this guide contains contact information for many of the organizations listed here.

the broker-dealers' business related to serving its customers," or otherwise deposited into a reserve account

- To require brokerage firms promptly to obtain and thereafter maintain possession or control of all fully paid securities and excess-margin securities carried for the accounts of customers

- To effectuate a separation of the brokerage operation from that of dealer activities such as underwriting and trading

- To ensure that broker-dealers keep more current records. In this regard, the rule requires daily determination that securities which need to be protected are in adequate control locations and frequent computations of the customer reserve requirement

- To move the entire securities industry into a more efficient mode of operation prohibiting securities from being kept in unacceptable locations

- To require broker-dealers to operate conservatively by way of limiting the expansion of their business through the use of customers' funds

- To continue the program of improving broker-dealer financial responsibility

- To improve the protection of customers in connection with the liquidation of broker-dealers by definition of specifically identifiable property pursuant to the Securities Investor Protection Act of 1970

3.12 Those objectives are accomplished through the two main sections of the rule that provide for (*a*) the requirement that the broker-dealer obtain and maintain possession or control of fully paid and excess-margin customer securities and (*b*) the reserve formula computations and the maintenance of a "Special Reserve Bank Account for the Exclusive Benefit of Customers" and/or "Special Reserve Bank Account for Brokers and Dealers."

3.13 Due to their emphasis on safeguarding customer assets, regulators have consistently taken a stringent enforcement approach to SEC Rule 15c3-3, closely scrutinizing any apparent differences between broker-dealer practices occurring at the computation date and those occurring on a day-to-day basis. Stringent enforcement has included significant fines, public censure, and the banning of officers from the security business for periods of time. Accordingly, broker-dealers often retain an additional amount, or "cushion," in the reserve accounts.

3.14 The term *PAB account*, as defined in SEC Rule 15c3-3(a)(16), is a proprietary securities account of a broker or dealer (which includes a foreign broker or dealer, or foreign bank acting as a broker or dealer) other than delivery-versus-payment or a receipt-versus-payment account and does not include an account that has been subordinated to the claims of creditors of the carrying broker or dealer.

3.15 Under the financial responsibility rules, there is no requirement that PAB account owners (for example, introducing broker-dealers) obtain a written agreement from the carrying firm indicating that it will perform the PAB reserve computation to receive allowable asset treatment under SEC Rule 15c3-1 for proprietary assets held at a carrying broker. SEC Rule 15c3-3 requires the carrying firm to perform the PAB reserve computation, if applicable. See exhibit

6-9 of chapter 6, "Financial Statement Presentation and Classification," of this guide for illustrative examples of the supplementary information required to be filed with the financial statements.

3.16 The restrictions on the use of customers' funds and securities and the requirement that securities be brought promptly under physical possession or control are designed to protect customer assets in the event that a broker-dealer is liquidated. SEC Rule 15c3-3 also acts as a control over the unwarranted expansion of a broker-dealer's business by prohibiting the use of customers' funds and customer-derived funds in other aspects of the broker-dealer's business, such as underwriting, trading, and travel and entertainment.

3.17 SEC Rule 15c3-3 offers further customer protection by requiring, under certain circumstances, a broker-dealer to increase the amount of its cash and/or qualified securities reserve under the formula as a result of undelivered securities (fails and short sales) related to customer positions, aged receivables, security positions that cannot be located or verified, and unresolved security and money differences. Reserve increases related to the latter two conditions are intended to spur improvements in operational practices and controls.

3.18 Under SEC Rule 15c3-3, the term *customer* is defined as any person from whom, or on whose behalf, a broker-dealer has received, has acquired, or holds funds or securities for the account of that person. It does not include the following:

- Broker-dealers
- Municipal securities dealer or a government securities broker or government securities dealer
- General partner, managing member of a limited liability company, or director or principal officer of the broker or dealer
- A counterparty who has delivered collateral to an over-the-counter (OTC) derivatives dealer who registers with the SEC under a limited regulatory structure, as discussed in paragraph 3.184, pursuant to a transaction in an eligible OTC derivative instrument or pursuant to the OTC derivatives dealer's cash management securities activities or ancillary portfolio management securities activities, and who has received certain prominent written notices from the OTC derivatives dealer
- Any person, to the extent they have a claim on property or funds that by contract, agreement, or law are part of the capital or subordinated debt of the broker-dealer

3.19 The following broker-dealer accounts are also considered customer accounts:

- A special omnibus account in compliance with Regulation T
- A special custody account for the exclusive benefit of customers in compliance with SEC Rule 15c3-3(c)(7)
- A special custody account for accommodation transfers for the exclusive benefit of customers in compliance with SEC Rule 15c3-3(c)(7)

3.20 *Possession or control.* The SEC requires broker-dealers carrying accounts of customers and PAB to promptly obtain and thereafter maintain the physical possession or control of fully paid-for securities and excess-margin securities carried for the account of customers and PAB, as applicable. *Fully paid-for securities* are defined to include all securities carried for the account of a customer in a *special cash account*, as defined in Regulation T, as well as certain equity securities within the meaning of Regulation T held in a customer margin account.

3.21 The rule defines *excess-margin securities* as those customer securities carried in a customer's general or special accounts (referred to in SEC Rule 15c3-3 as margin accounts), as defined in Regulation T, having a market value[10] in excess of 140 percent of the total of the debit balances in the customer's margin account(s).

3.22 There are two exceptions to the possession or control requirements as found in SEC Rule 15c3-3:

a. A temporary business lag between the time when a security is required to be in the possession or control of the broker-dealer and the time it is taken into physical possession or control is one exception. The broker-dealer must show it is making a timely and good faith effort to establish prompt physical possession or control.

b. The broker-dealer borrows from its customers fully paid or excess-margin securities that it is required to have in possession or control and enters into a written securities borrowing agreement with the customer setting forth the compensation for the securities borrowing, the rights or liabilities of the parties, and the identity of the securities borrowed at the time of the borrowing. The agreement should also specify that upon the execution or at least by the close of the business day of the securities borrowing, the broker-dealer is to provide the customer with certain qualified collateral at least equal to the market value of the securities borrowed and must mark the securities borrowed to the market not less than daily. The agreement should also contain a prominent notice that the provisions of the Securities Investor Protection Act of 1970 may not protect the customer with respect to the securities loaned.

3.23 *Possession or control requirements.* The broker-dealer should perform the following procedures daily to comply with the rule's possession or control requirements:

- Determine which customer securities are fully paid for or are excess margin.
- Identify which fully paid and excess-margin securities are in physical possession or control.
- Take appropriate action to obtain proper possession or control of fully paid or excess-margin securities not already in physical possession or control.

3.24 For cash accounts, the broker-dealer should specifically identify customer payments to security purchases and segregate securities when the securities have been paid for.

---

[10] The terms *market value* and *mark-to-market* are used within this chapter as operational terms; accordingly, in practice they may not necessarily be synonymous to the terms *fair value* and *subsequently measured at fair value*, which are used within the financial statements in accordance with FASB Accounting Standards Update No. 2012-04, *Technical Corrections and Improvements*.

3.25   The time at which instructions (lockups) should be issued to the cashiering function to acquire possession or control on the purchase of securities by customers is on or before the business day following the settlement date or the business day following the actual date of receipt of payment, whichever is later.

3.26   The time at which instructions (releases) may be issued to the cashiering function to release from possession or control on sales of securities by customers is not earlier than the morning of business on settlement date minus one business day, which is deemed to allow adequate time for processing securities for pending deliveries. Such securities cannot be used for securities loans or bank loans.

3.27   Most broker-dealers have fully computerized the task of determining segregation requirements. These systems determine the quantity of fully paid or excess-margin securities in each customer's account as of the close of business each day. These systems generally use memo fields on the stock record to show the amount of securities that should be segregated.

3.28   The broker-dealer should determine, by customer, the amount of each security that should be segregated. The broker-dealer should then determine the total securities to be segregated. Securities are considered to be under the control of the broker-dealer if they are held

     a.   in the custody or control of a clearing corporation or depository.

     b.   in the custody or control of a bank (as defined in Section 3(a)(6) of the 1934 Act), provided that the delivery of such securities does not require payment, and the bank acknowledges that it, or another party through it, cannot impose a lien or claim on such securities. See item (*c*) regarding foreign depositories because it may apply to U.S.-based banks holding customer foreign securities.

     c.   in the custody of a foreign depository, foreign clearing agency, or foreign custodian bank as designated by the SEC. This may be problematic due to the use by the designated domestic or foreign custodian of subcustodians, over which the former has no control.

     d.   in transfer for less than 40 calendar days or, if beyond 40 days, confirmed as being in transfer (the securities are the subject of bona fide items of transfer).

     e.   in transit for five business days or less between the offices of a broker-dealer (for example, between the main and branch offices).

     f.   in a special omnibus account carried for the account of any customer by another broker-dealer and carried in the name of the broker-dealer in compliance with Regulation T (such securities are considered in control to the extent the broker-dealer has instructed the carrying broker-dealer to maintain physical possession or control of them free of any charge, lien, or other claim in favor of the carrying firm).

3.29   Some common examples of fully paid or excess-margin securities that are not considered to be in a broker-dealer's physical possession or control include the following:

- Securities collateralizing bank loans
- Securities loaned to other broker-dealers

- Securities failed to receive
- Stock dividend receivables, stock splits or receivables

3.30 *Special reserve bank account for the exclusive benefit of customers and PAB accounts.* As required by SEC Rule 15c3-3, every broker-dealer, unless otherwise exempt, should maintain a "Special Reserve Bank Account for the Exclusive Benefit of Customers" and a "Special Reserve Bank Account for Brokers and Dealers" separate from all other bank accounts of the broker-dealer. In the reserve bank accounts, the broker-dealer should at all times maintain, through deposits made therein, cash or qualified securities, or both, in an amount not less than the amount computed under the rule's reserve formula. Rule 15c3-3 prohibits the broker-dealer from maintaining cash deposits in the reserve accounts if the bank is affiliated and limits the amount of cash that can be deposited in nonaffiliated bank accounts to 15 percent of the bank's equity capital as reported by the bank in its most recent Reports of Condition and Income (Call Report) or any successor form the bank is required to file by its appropriate Federal banking agency.

3.31 *Reserve formula computations.* Exhibit A of SEC Rule 15c3-3 provides a detailed formula for determining the customer and PAB reserve bank account requirements. The rule requires the reserve to be calculated as the excess of customer-related credits over customer-related debits. The formula is intended to limit the broker-dealer's use of customer funds and encompasses receivables from and payables to customers, as well as transactions that involve customer securities. The computation is limited solely to customer-related debits and credits, with a few exceptions and adjustments (such as aged differences and receivables). In the "Notes Regarding The PAB Reserve Bank Account Computation" section of SEC Rule 15c3-3, a specific note is included which indicates that broker-dealers should use the formula prescribed in exhibit A of that rule for computing the PAB reserve requirement by substituting the term "PAB accounts" where references to "accounts," "customer accounts," or "customers" appear.

3.32 In addition, SEC Rule 15c3-3 stipulates the designated times for performing the computations. The time frames may need to be adjusted when the broker-dealer is located outside of the time zone that its normal home office (main headquarter) is in. See Interpretation No. 99-5 issued from the SEC to the New York Stock Exchange (NYSE) in May 1999. The designated times are as follows:

- For broker-dealers required to make weekly computations, the computations should be made as of each week's end and at month's end (that is, the last business day of the week or month), with necessary deposits made no later than one hour after the opening of banks on the second business day after the computation date. The computation is not required for the week's end following a computation at month's end.

- Monthly computations should be made only if the broker-dealer does not have aggregate indebtedness in excess of 800 percent of net capital and has less than $1 million in customer credits. Deposits are also due no later than 1 hour after the opening of banks on the second business day after the computation date.

3.33 In conjunction with its annual year-end reporting, a broker-dealer that does not make a claim of exemption from SEC Rule 15c3-3 throughout the most recent fiscal year is required to make certain assertions, in a compliance report, regarding Internal Controls Over Compliance related to the possession or control requirements and Internal Controls Over Compliance and specific compliance with the reserve elements of the Customer Protection Rule. The broker-dealer's auditor is required to perform an examination of the assertions in the compliance report, following PCAOB standards, and issue a report based on that examination. See paragraph 3.152 for further discussion.

3.34 *Bank sweep products.* Broker-dealers that carry customer accounts may offer bank sweep programs as a means to place customer funds in an account subject to Federal Deposit Insurance Corporation (FDIC) coverage while earning interest on those funds. Although broker-dealers may assert that customer funds are better protected, regulators have questioned the large interest rate spreads obtained by broker-dealers in such arrangements, the nature and extent of disclosure that the broker-dealers provide their customers regarding the interest rate differential, and whether the arrangements are structured such that the broker-dealers have satisfactorily given up possession of the customer funds.

3.35 In a *sweep program*, customer funds are transferred out of a broker-dealer customer account to a money market fund or an interest-bearing account for the customer at a bank often affiliated with the broker-dealer. Broker-dealers that offer sweep programs in which customer funds leave the broker-dealer and are held for any period of time by a party other than the bank must address critical issues relating to customer protection and net capital requirements. Customer credit balances that leave the broker-dealer and are not immediately reinvested in an FDIC-protected account may be deemed to be included as a credit in the computation of SEC Rule 15c3-3 (customer reserve). In addition, any receivable on the broker-dealer's books resulting from a sweep may be deemed to be a nonallowable asset in the computation of SEC Rule 15c3-1 (net capital).

3.36 The financial responsibility rules require written affirmative consent from customers and certain required disclosures to those customers who participate in sweep programs. Refer to SEC Release No. 34-70072, *Financial Responsibility Rules for Broker-Dealers,* for further information on amendments to SEC Rule 15c3-3 related to the use of sweep programs.

3.37 *Broker-dealers claiming exemption from SEC Rule 15c3-3.* Certain broker-dealers operate completely pursuant to the exemptive provisions of Rule 15c3-3. In doing so, the broker-dealer is not required to comply with the remaining provisions of that rule, such as computations of amounts required to be on deposit in the "Special Reserve Bank Account for the Exclusive Benefits of Its Customers," possession or control requirements, and the related record-keeping. The detailed requirements to be met in order to qualify for this exemption are described in paragraph (k) of Rule 15c3-3 and need to be considered in connection with the rule in its entirety.

3.38 In conjunction with its annual year-end reporting, a broker-dealer that claims an exemption from SEC Rule 15c3-3 throughout the most recent fiscal year, is required to make certain assertions, in an exemption report, regarding its claim of exemption and any instances of identified exceptions based on its claim. The broker-dealer's auditor is required to perform a review of the assertions in the exemption report, following PCAOB standards, and issue a report based on that review. See paragraph 3.153 for further discussion. As discussed in footnote 20, broker-dealer financial statements that are filed with the SEC must be certified by a PCAOB registered public accounting firm. The term *independent auditor*, as used in this guide, assumes the firm is registered with PCAOB, as required. See paragraph 3.117 of this chapter for additional information regarding independence of the accountant.

3.39 In reporting on a broker-dealer exempt from SEC Rule 15c3-3, the supplemental schedule(s) titled "Computation for Determination of Reserve Requirements Under Rule 15c3-3" and "Information for Possession or Control Requirements Under Rule 15c3-3" are still required, but such computations and information are not applicable. In lieu of the computations and information, management should include a statement indicating the section under which exemption is claimed.

3.40 *Notification requirements.* All broker-dealers are required to make certain notifications to the regulators if instances of noncompliance exist. In addition, a carrying broker-dealer is required to make a notification to the regulators if a material weakness (as defined by SEC Rule 17a-5) exists. A *material weakness* [11] is defined with respect to the compliance report, therefore notification requirements to regulatory bodies regarding material weaknesses only apply to carrying broker-dealers. If, during the course of the audit, the auditor determines that the broker-dealer is not in compliance with SEC Rule 15c3-3 or that a material weakness (as defined by SEC Rule 17a-5) exists, the auditor should immediately consider the notification requirements under SEC Rules 17a-5 and 17a-11 pertaining to noncompliance or material weakness (as defined by SEC Rule 17a-5). See paragraph 3.111 for further discussion.

SEC Rule 15c3-1, "Net Capital Requirements for Brokers or Dealers"

3.41 SEC Rule 15c3-1, "Net Capital Requirements for Brokers or Dealers," was adopted under the 1934 Act in order to create a uniform capital requirement for all registered broker-dealers and to ensure the liquidity of broker-dealers.

3.42 The net capital rule requires broker-dealers to maintain minimum levels of liquid assets to support the volume and risk exposures of the businesses in which they are engaged. This is accomplished through the following mechanisms:

- The broker-dealer's regulatory capital (U.S. GAAP equity plus qualified subordinated indebtedness and other potential add-backs, as outlined in the rule) is reduced to give effect to the elements of market, credit, or operational risk inherent in the business in which the broker-dealer currently is engaged.

- The minimum capital the broker-dealer is required to maintain pursuant to SEC Rule 15c3-1(a) is established on the basis of the greater of either (*a*) the amount of the broker-dealer's aggregate indebtedness (that is, the broker-dealer's obligations payable in cash, with limited exceptions) or (*b*) the level of customer-related

---

[11] A *material weakness*, as defined in SEC Rule 17a-5, is a deficiency, or a combination of deficiencies, in Internal Control Over Compliance such that there is a reasonable possibility that noncompliance with SEC Rule 15c3-1 or SEC Rule 15c3-3(e) will not be prevented or detected on a timely basis or that noncompliance to a material extent with SEC Rule 15c3-3, except for paragraph (e), SEC Rule17a-13, or any Account Statement Rule will not be prevented or detected on a timely basis.

receivables (aggregate debit items) computed pursuant to SEC Rule 15c3-3 (the alternative standard), and a minimum amount based on the broker-dealer's business activities. Pursuant to SEC Rule 15c3-1(a)(ii), a broker-dealer may elect to be subject to the alternative standard rather than the basic standard by notifying its designated examining authority in writing.

If the broker-dealer is also registered with the CFTC as an FCM or IB, it must also always be in compliance with the CFTC regulations, specifically CFTC Regulation 1.17(a)(1). Broker-dealers that are subject to both SEC and CFTC minimum net capital requirements should always maintain net capital equal to the greater of the two regulatory requirements. The CFTC adopted a risk-based capital requirement for FCMs effective September 30, 2004, but the SEC has not yet revised Rule 15c3-1(a)(1)(iii) to reference and reflect this change.

3.43   In each case, the level of capital is established to ensure that, in the event of liquidation, the broker-dealer is maintaining sufficient capital for the payments of (*a*) its obligations to customers and other broker-dealers and (*b*) compensation to employees retained to wind up the firm's affairs.

3.44   By monitoring the maintenance of liquid assets in excess of the minimum requirements, the SEC and relevant designated examining authority are in a position to take action to protect customers prior to the time when the broker-dealer's assets would be insufficient to satisfy customers' claims in the event of liquidation.

3.45   A designated examining authority utilizes the capital rules to provide an early warning of any broker-dealer that may be at risk of not having sufficient capital to stay in operation. Under those rules and various designated examining authority regulations, broker-dealers should restrict the growth of their business if their regulatory capital fails to meet certain minimums set by the designated examining authority, reduce the size of current operations if capital falls to a point below other minimums set by the designated examining authority, and ultimately liquidate if the regulatory minimums are not met. Obviously, it is the intent of the designated examining authority to identify potential problems early and correct them.

3.46   Although the broker-dealer is required to maintain sufficient net capital at all times, the SEC requires all registered broker-dealers to calculate net capital on a periodic basis in order for the designated examining authority and broker-dealer to ensure that the broker-dealer has adequate liquid assets in the event of sudden adverse business conditions and to maintain compliance with the rule at all times. *Net capital* is the broker-dealer's net worth reduced by illiquid (nonallowable) assets, certain operational capital charges, and potential adverse fluctuations in the value of securities inventory ("haircuts").

3.47   There are two main components to the net capital computation: determination of net capital (as described in paragraphs 3.52–.53) and comparison with aggregate indebtedness or alternative percentage requirements.

3.48   Under the aggregate indebtedness standard, the broker-dealer's net capital requirement is equal to 6 2/3 percent of its aggregate indebtedness. A broker-dealer is not permitted to allow its aggregate indebtedness to exceed 15 times its net capital (or 8 times its net capital for 12 months after commencing business as a broker or dealer). If the ratio of aggregate indebtedness to adjusted net capital exceeds 15 to 1, the broker-dealer is prohibited from engaging in any securities transactions. If the ratio exceeds 12 to 1, the broker-dealer may be required to reduce its business. If it exceeds 10 to 1, the broker-dealer may be prohibited from expanding its business.

3.49 As set forth in SEC Rule 15c3-1, a broker-dealer may elect to compute its net capital requirements under the alternative standard. Whereas the aggregate indebtedness approach is a measure of the risk the broker-dealer imposes on its creditors (the extent of its financial leverage), the alternative standard is a measure of the credit risk exposure the broker-dealer has to its customers. The minimum net capital percentage required under the alternative standard is 2 percent of the aggregate customer debits carried by the broker-dealer and includable in the customer reserve formula. Such debits result almost entirely from customer margin transactions (that is, from customers borrowing from the broker-dealer to purchase securities).

3.50 The aggregate indebtedness and alternative standards are one measure of a broker-dealer's net capital requirement; the other measure is the minimum net capital amount required as a result of the broker-dealer's securities activity. A broker-dealer's net capital requirement is the higher of the selected standard or minimum level. For example, if a broker-dealer engages in proprietary trading[12] and selects the aggregate indebtedness standard, its net capital requirement is the greater of 6 2/3 percent of its aggregate indebtedness or $100,000.

3.51 Percentage requirements also restrict the withdrawal of equity capital and the repayment of subordinated obligations and the making of any unsecured advance or loan to a stockholder, a partner, a sole proprietor, an employee, or an affiliate.

3.52 *Computation of net capital.* The net capital of a broker-dealer is equal to its net worth adjusted by certain additions and deductions. The additions include the following:

- Certain liabilities approved by the examining authorities that have been subordinated to the claims of general creditors. The extent to which these liabilities may be included in capital is subject to limitations. Standardized subordination, secured demand note, and secured demand note collateral agreements are available from FINRA, and all executed agreements must be approved by the broker-dealer's designated self-regulatory organization before they qualify for capital purposes. A subordination agreement[13] should meet the following requirements:

    — Be written

    — Have a minimum term of one year

    — Be for a specific dollar amount

---

[12] On December 10, 2013, the SEC issued final rule BHCA-1, *Prohibitions and Restrictions on Proprietary Trading and Certain Interests in, and Relationships with, Hedge Funds and Private Equity Funds,* as mandated by Section 619 of the Dodd-Frank Act (commonly referred to as the Volcker Rule). The rule prohibits banking entities from proprietary trading; acquiring or retaining any equity, partnership, or other ownership interest in a hedge fund or private equity fund; and sponsoring a hedge fund or private equity fund. Proprietary trading consists of transactions made by an entity that affect the entity's own account but not the accounts of its clients. Note that the Volcker Rule contains an exception for certain market making-related activities.

[13] For more information, see the specific requirements contained in the debt-equity requirements of SEC Rule 15c3-1 and appendix D of SEC Rule 15c3-1.

— Effectively subordinate the lender's right to prior payment of all claims of present and future creditors

— Give the broker-dealer the right to deposit any cash proceeds in its own name in any bank, as well as the right to pledge or hypothecate securities without notice

— Include certain prepayment restrictions

— Suspend the repayment or maturity obligation if, after giving effect to the obligation, the aggregate indebtedness of the broker-dealer would exceed 1,200 percent of its net capital or its net capital would be less than 5 percent of aggregate debits if the alternative standard were used

- Certain discretionary liabilities, such as a noncontractual bonus accrual that is not a fixed payable as of the computation date, is a common type of discretionary liability that may, if certain criteria are satisfied, be added back to total equity.

- Deferred income tax liabilities resulting from the recognition for tax purposes of unrealized income or appreciation related to long inventory, investment positions, or assets that are nonallowable for net capital; deferred income tax liabilities related to intangible assets recognized in a business acquisition and deferred income tax benefits resulting from the recognition for tax purposes of unrealized losses or depreciation related to long inventory or investment positions, but only up to the extent of recognized income tax liabilities. Please see the specific requirements contained in SEC Rule 15c3-1 and related interpretations.

3.53 Broker-dealers are required to deduct items in the net capital computation to take into account market and liquidity risks. The deductions are in the following basic forms:

- *Nonallowable assets.* These are recognized assets that do not meet liquidity tests or have been defined as nonallowable by SEC Rule 15c3-1. In general, *nonallowable assets* are assets not readily convertible into cash. Examples of the most frequently encountered nonallowable assets are fixed assets, securities not readily marketable, unsecured receivables (certain receivables are allowable for the first 30 days), deficits in customer accounts, good-faith deposits, prepaid expenses, exchange memberships, and intangibles. Broker-dealers that retain cash or securities at their carrying broker-dealer should treat such assets as allowable, unless the account has been subordinated to the claims of creditors of the carrying broker-dealer.

- *Other deductions and charges.* In general, these items are operational in nature and may involve off-balance sheet risk. These items include, for example, aged fails to deliver, over- or under-collateralized secured lending positions, and security count differences.

- *Haircuts on proprietary positions and commitments.* "Haircuts" are percentage deductions that are designed to take into account market and portfolio risk exposures on proprietary positions and commitments. They apply to marketable securities only. An additional charge may also be required when the broker-dealer holds a significant concentration in individual proprietary positions. An OTC derivatives dealer who registers with the SEC under a limited regulatory structure, as discussed in paragraph 3.184, may apply to the SEC for authorization to compute capital charges for market and credit risk pursuant to appendix F of SEC Rule 15c3-1 in lieu of computing securities haircuts pursuant to Rule 15c3-1(c)(2)(vi).

- *Temporary capital contributions.* If a capital contribution is governed by an agreement that provides the investor with the option to withdraw the capital or it is intended to be withdrawn within a period of one year of its contribution, the amount must be subtracted from net worth.

3.54 *Computation of aggregate indebtedness.* SEC Rule 15c3-1 states that aggregate indebtedness consists of the total money liabilities of a broker-dealer arising in connection with any transaction whatsoever and includes, among other things, money borrowed, money payable against securities loaned and securities failed to receive, the market value of securities borrowed to the extent to which no equivalent value is paid or credited, customers' and noncustomers' free credit balances, credit balances in customers' and noncustomers' accounts having short positions in securities, equities in customers' and noncustomers' future commodities accounts, and credit balances in customers' and noncustomers' commodities accounts. There are a number of specific exceptions, primarily related to circumstances in which the liability is collateralized or offset by a related proprietary position.

3.55 *Expense-sharing agreements.* Many broker-dealers enter into what is generally referred to as an expense-sharing agreement with their parent or an affiliated company. The parent or affiliate is usually not registered as a broker-dealer and, accordingly, may not be a regulated entity. In certain instances, a parent or an affiliate has established a broker-dealer to conduct limited or specialized securities activities that are coincidental or tangential to the operations of the parent or affiliate. In other instances, the parent or affiliate will have limited operations and will conduct separate financial activities using funds obtained from the broker-dealer's operations. In either case, the broker-dealer and parent or affiliate are likely to incur common costs, such as rent, and, as a result, devise an arrangement to allocate or assign direct or general (or both) overhead costs between them and specify which party will settle the related obligations. Thus, such an arrangement will deal with both cost recognition and payment responsibility.

3.56 In interpretations related to Rule 15c3-1, the SEC Division of Trading and Markets staff have stated that, for the purpose of computing net capital, broker-dealers are required to recognize costs on their books and records in accordance with accounting principles generally accepted in the United States of America (GAAP) (that is, costs need to be recognized as incurred and in amounts related to the broker-dealer's economic obligations). Because regulatory financial reports submitted by broker-dealers seemed to indicate a number of deviations from this standard, the Division of Trading and Markets staff issued an interpretative letter on July 11, 2003, addressing situations when another party assumes responsibility for payment of a broker-dealer's expenses.

3.57 The interpretive letter is designed to provide guidance for broker-dealers, such that when computing net capital, broker-dealers would reflect all costs for which they are in any way obligated to pay either contractually or constructively; that is, the broker-dealer serves as the immediate or ongoing source of funds for paying a vendor or creditor, which has a contractual arrangement with the parent or affiliate. Further, in the interpretive letter the Division of Trading and Markets aims to proscribe cost assignment, other than through the use of a reasonable, consistently applied and well-documented allocation process. The interpretive letter presumes that if another party reflects in its financial statements the costs of services or goods benefiting or consumed by the broker-dealer, any amounts the broker-dealer remits to this party represent a reimbursement of all or a portion of such costs and the broker-dealer must reflect the remittance as a liability from the date that the "related" costs were incurred. In October 2003, NASD published Notice to Members 03-63, which provides additional guidance regarding the interpretive letter, discusses the technical issues in greater detail, and includes related examples. (The interpretive letter can be found at www.sec.gov/divisions/marketreg/mr-noaction/macchiaroli071103.pdf, and NASD Notice to Members 03-63 is available on FINRA's website.)

3.58 In addition, the financial responsibility rules further address issues related to certain liabilities or expenses assumed by third parties, and codified such requirements into SEC Rule 15c3-1. Specifically, an expense of the broker-dealer assumed by a third-party will be considered a liability for net capital purposes unless the broker-dealer can demonstrate that the third party has adequate resources independent of the broker-dealer to pay the liability or expense. Broker-dealers can continue to rely on the guidance provided through the NASD Notice to Members 03-63 in complying with the financial responsibility rules.

3.59 In conjunction with its annual year-end reporting, a broker-dealer that does not make a claim of exemption from SEC Rule 15c3-3 throughout the most recent fiscal year is required to make certain assertions, in a compliance report, regarding Internal Controls Over Compliance and specific compliance with the Net Capital Requirements for Brokers or Dealers Rule. The auditor is required to perform an examination of the assertions in the compliance report, following PCAOB standards, and issue a report based on that examination. See paragraph 3.152 for further discussion.

3.60 *Notification requirements.* All broker-dealers are required to make certain notifications to the regulators if instances of noncompliance exist. In addition, a carrying broker-dealer is required to make a notification to the regulators if a material weakness (as defined by SEC Rule 17a-5) exists. If, during the course of the audit, the auditor determines that the broker-dealer is not in compliance with SEC Rule 15c3-1 or that a material weakness (as defined by SEC Rule 17a-5) exists, the auditor should immediately consider the notification requirements under SEC Rules 17a-5(h) and 17a-11 pertaining to noncompliance or material weakness (as defined by SEC Rule 17a-5). *Material weakness*[14] is defined with respect to the compliance report, notification requirements to regulatory bodies regarding material weakness only apply to carrying broker-dealers. See paragraph 3.111 for further discussion. Carrying and clearing brokers also should consider the notification requirements in FINRA Rule 4120.

---

[14] See footnote 11.

SEC Rule 15c3-1(e), "Notice Provisions Relating to the Limitations on the Withdrawal of Equity Capital"

3.61 Because of concerns that cash or other liquid assets generated in the broker-dealer's business could be removed to support financial obligations of the broker-dealer's parent or affiliates, SEC Rule 15c3-1(e) is intended to prevent controlling persons from making material withdrawals of liquid assets from a broker-dealer without first notifying its designated examining authority.

3.62 Broker-dealers are subject to notifications of, or limitations on, capital withdrawals that reduce the excess net capital by various percentages, as discussed in SEC Rule 15c3-1(e), or are deemed by the SEC or its designated examining authority, to inhibit the ability to sustain the current business activities or meet the financial obligations of the broker-dealer. It is inappropriate for broker-dealers to record withdrawals of equity capital or capital distributions as an expense, a receivable, or an investment.

3.63 Broker-dealers are required to notify the SEC and their designated examining authority (for example, FINRA)

    a. 2 days in advance of any withdrawal, which, when aggregated with withdrawals made during the preceding 30 days, exceeds 30 percent of the broker-dealers' excess net capital, and

    b. 2 days following any such withdrawal, which, when aggregated with withdrawals made during the preceding 30 days, exceeds 20 percent of the broker-dealers' excess net capital.

3.64 SEC Rule 15c3-1(e) precludes any withdrawal if it results in the broker-dealer having unacceptably low levels of net capital relative to the nature of its business activities. For example, the rule prohibits a withdrawal that would result in the broker-dealer's net capital amounting to less than 25 percent of its total market risk deductions (haircuts). Specific withdrawal limitations are enumerated in SEC Rule 15c3-1(e)(2). Also, the SEC could prohibit any withdrawal for 20 days if the SEC concluded that the withdrawal would impair the financial integrity of the broker-dealer or affect the broker-dealer's ability to repay customers' claims and liabilities.

3.65 Paragraph (1) of FINRA Rule 4110(c) requires a member firm to obtain written approval from FINRA prior to withdrawal of capital, which was contributed within the preceding 12 months. Paragraph (2) of FINRA Rule 4110(c) applies solely to member firms that carry accounts or otherwise clear transactions. Such firms must first obtain written approval from FINRA prior to withdrawal of liquid assets if such withdrawal, when aggregated with withdrawals occurring over the preceding 35 days, exceeds 10 percent of the firm's excess net capital. For more information, see Regulatory Notice 09-71 on FINRA's website.

SEC Rule 17a-13, "Quarterly Security Counts to Be Made by Certain Exchange Members, Brokers, and Dealers"[15]

3.66 SEC Rule 17a-13 requires that the examination, count, verification, and comparison be made or supervised by persons whose regular duties do not

---

[15] See the discussion beginning in paragraph 3.172 for additional requirements for broker-dealers that are also registered investment advisers.

require them to have direct responsibility for the proper care and protection of the securities or for the making or preservation of the books and records.

3.67 Under SEC Rule 17a-13 of the 1934 Act, most broker-dealers are required to conduct a securities count at least once in each calendar quarter. The rule requires that at least once in each calendar quarter, but not more than four months or less than two months apart, all positions in each security should be accounted for simultaneously, although not all securities are required to be accounted for at the same time. The procedures performed by the broker-dealer would include the following:

- Physically examine and count all securities held.

- Account for all securities in transfer, in transit, pledged, loaned, borrowed, deposited, failed to receive and failed to deliver, subject to repurchase agreements (repos) or reverse repos, or otherwise subject to the broker-dealer's control or direction but not in its physical possession, by examining and comparing the supporting detail records with the appropriate ledger control accounts.

- Verify (through confirmation or other form of outside documentation) all securities in transfer, in transit, pledged, loaned, borrowed, deposited, failed to receive and failed to deliver, subject to repo and reverse repo, or otherwise subject to the broker-dealer's control or direction but not in its physical possession, if such securities have been in such status for longer than 30 days.

- Compare the results of the count and verification with the broker-dealer's records.

- Record in the books and records all unresolved differences resulting from the count and verification (setting forth the security involved and the date of comparison) in a security count difference account no later than seven business days after the date of each securities examination count and verification. This securities difference account is then considered in determining the applicable deduction from net capital.

3.68 The examination, count, verification, and comparison may be made as of a certain date or on a cyclical basis covering all securities. Cyclical counts enable the broker-dealer to perform the preceding procedures on specific groups of securities at different time intervals.

3.69 For broker-dealers subject to FINRA rules, paragraph (b) of FINRA Rule 4522 requires that each carrying or clearing member subject to SEC Rule 17a-13 make more frequent counts, examinations, verifications, comparisons, and entries when prudent business practice would so require. Further, each such carrying or clearing member is required to receive position statements monthly with respect to securities held by clearing corporations, other organizations, or custodians and, at such time, reconcile all such securities and money balances by comparison of the clearing corporations' or custodians' position statements to the member's books and records. The carrying or clearing member must promptly report any differences to the contra organization, and both the contra organization and member firm must promptly resolve the differences. When there is a higher volume of activity, the rule provides that good business practice may require a more frequent exchange of statements and performance of reconciliations. Differences from such verifications that are unresolved for seven days, must be recorded to a "Difference" account and reflected in the net capital and customer reserve computations as required.

3.70 In conjunction with its annual year-end reporting, a broker-dealer that does not make a claim of exemption from SEC Rule 15c3-3 throughout the most recent fiscal year is required to make certain assertions, in a compliance report, regarding Internal Controls Over Compliance related to SEC Rule 17a-13 (Quarterly Security Counts to Be Made by Certain Exchange Members, Brokers, and Dealers Rule). The auditor is required to perform an examination of the assertions in the compliance report, following PCAOB standards, and issue a report based on that examination. See paragraph 3.152 for further discussion.

SEC Rule 17a-3, "Records to Be Made by Certain Exchange Members, Brokers, and Dealers"

3.71 SEC Rule 17a-3 requires parties to construct and keep current certain books and records. It requires broker-dealers with more than: (1) $1,000,000 in aggregate credit items as computed under SEC Rule 15c3-3a or (2) $20,000,000 in capital (which includes debt subordinated in accordance appendix D to SEC Rule 15c3-1) to document the credit, market, and liquidity risk management controls that are established and maintained to address risks associated with its business activities. For a further discussion of this rule, refer to chapter 2, "Broker-Dealer Functions, Books, and Records," of this guide.

SEC Rule 17a-4, "Records to Be Preserved by Certain Exchange Members, Brokers, and Dealers"

3.72 SEC Rule 17a-4 establishes time requirements for the retention of the books and records constructed pursuant to SEC Rule 17a-3. (For a further discussion of this rule, refer to chapter 2 of this guide.)

Regulation T and Maintenance Margin

3.73 Regulation T has been promulgated by the Board of Governors of the Federal Reserve System by authority of the 1934 Act. Regulation T establishes the rules and regulations applicable to the extension of credit to customers and to related transactions. For a customer to enter securities transactions, he or she should open either a cash account or margin account.

3.74 Section 8 of Regulation T governs cash accounts. This type of account was created by Regulation T for those transactions in which the broker-dealer is not extending credit to the customer. The broker-dealer may purchase for (as agent), or sell to (as principal), a customer any security, provided that either (*a*) funds sufficient for the purpose are already in the cash account, or (*b*) the purchase or sale is in reliance on an agreement accepted by the creditor in good faith that the customer will promptly make full cash payment before selling and does not contemplate selling the security prior to such payment.

3.75 If full cash payment is not made within five business days after the trade date of the purchase, the broker-dealer should cancel or liquidate the transaction or request an extension of time from FINRA or an applicable exchange. Extensions of the payment date are normally granted when both the broker-dealer and customer are acting in good faith, and the circumstances are viewed as warranting such action.

3.76 A margin account is used to record transactions that result in the customer borrowing money from the broker-dealer. The customer agrees to pay a certain percentage of the purchase price, and the broker-dealer will lend the balance. Extensions of credit by broker-dealers are subject to Regulation T.

3.77 If a customer purchases securities on margin, the security should remain under the control of the broker-dealer. A customer generally signs a hypothecation agreement with the broker-dealer at the time the margin account is opened. This agreement allows the broker-dealer to hypothecate the securities, pledging them as collateral for money borrowed on a customer bank loan or loaning them to other broker-dealers.

3.78 In a margin account, the broker-dealer holds the customer's securities as collateral in readily negotiable form, thus enabling the broker-dealer to liquidate the securities if the customer fails to maintain a proper level of margin. A *margin transaction* is an open-ended collateralized loan, with the amount of collateral the customer is required to deposit prescribed by Regulation T. The customer may leave the loan open as long as the broker-dealer remains satisfied with the condition of the account. If the value of the securities in the customer's account appreciates above the Regulation T margin requirement, the broker-dealer can extend to the customer additional credit (referred to as Regulation T excess). The customer may then either withdraw the excess from the account or use it to meet the requirements on additional purchases.

3.79 FINRA, applicable exchanges, and broker-dealers themselves may set margin requirements that are higher than those specified in Regulation T. For example, FINRA establishes minimum maintenance margin requirements and more specific initial margin requirements than provided for in Regulation T for certain security positions (such as debt securities) and creditor relationships (such as broker-dealer extending credit to another broker-dealer). FINRA Rule 4210, *Margin Requirements*,[16] sets forth minimum equity requirements that must be maintained in margin accounts. In addition, many broker-dealers maintain "house" margin requirements (both initial and maintenance) that are higher than those established by FINRA.

Account Statement Rule(s)

3.80 Designated examining authorities have rules that require broker-dealers to send account statements to customers of the broker-dealer. One such rule is FINRA Rule 2340, *Customer Account Statements*. The rule outlines the requirements for applicability, frequency of delivery, contents of the account statements, and relevant definitions.

3.81 In conjunction with its annual year-end reporting, a broker-dealer that does not make a claim of exemption from SEC Rule 15c3-3 throughout the most recent fiscal year is required to make certain assertions, in a compliance report, regarding Internal Controls Over Compliance related to any rule of the designated examining authority of the broker-dealer that requires account statements to be sent to customers of the broker-dealer. The auditor is required to perform an examination of the assertions in the compliance report, following PCAOB standards, and issue a report based on that examination. See paragraph 3.152 for further discussion.

---

[16] In 2016 the SEC approved amendments to FINRA Rule 4210, *Margin Requirements*. For further information regarding the amendments and effective dates, see Regulatory Notice 16-31, available at www.finra.org/sites/default/files/notice_doc_file_ref/regulatory-notice-16-31.pdf.

SEC Rules and CFTC Regulations Governing Customer Margin for Transactions in Security Futures

3.82 The Commodity Futures Modernization Act of 2000 (CFMA) (see chapter 1, "The Securities Industry," of this guide) provides for the issuance of rules governing customer margin for transactions in security futures. Specifically, the CFMA directed the Federal Reserve Board to prescribe rules establishing initial and maintenance customer margin requirements. SEC Rules 400–406 and CFTC Regulations 41.42–.49 were issued in August 2002 establishing margin requirements for security futures pursuant to joint authority delegated by the Federal Reserve Board.

SEC Rules 17h-1T and 17h-2T

3.83 SEC Rules 17h-1T and 17h-2T require broker-dealers to maintain and preserve records and other information related to the associated persons of a broker-dealer and to provide reports to the SEC regarding financial activities of affiliates that could have a material effect on the financial or operational condition of the broker-dealer. Broker-dealers that do not clear customer accounts or are exempt from SEC Rule 15c3-3 and that have less than $20 million in capital, including subordinated debt, are not required to comply with these rules.

3.84 SEC Rules 17h-1T and 17h-2T use the term *material associated person* (MAP). Determination of whether an affiliate or other associated person is a MAP requires consideration of the following:

- The legal relationship between the parties
- The financing arrangements of the broker-dealer and the associated person and the degree to which they are financially dependent on each other
- The degree to which the broker-dealer or its customers rely on the associated person for operational support or service
- The level of risk present in the activities of the associated person
- The extent to which the associated person has the authority or ability to cause a withdrawal of capital from the broker-dealer

3.85 The information to be filed for each MAP on a quarterly basis on or with Form 17-H and for which records should be maintained in a readily accessible place for three years includes the following:

- Financial information
- Firm inventory amounts
- Off-balance sheet items
- Unsecured credit extensions
- Current debt
- Summaries of real estate activities

3.86 Certain of these disclosures are required for amounts over a materiality threshold. This amount is the greater of $100 million, 10 percent of the broker-dealer's tentative net capital, or 10 percent of the MAP's tangible net worth. Special exemptions exist regarding the information filed for MAPs that are subject to supervision by other regulatory agencies, such as a federal banking agency or a state insurance commission. In these cases, the broker-dealer

is allowed to satisfy the filing requirements by submitting certain reports filed
for the MAP with its primary regulator.

SEC Rule 17Ad-17, "Lost Securityholders and Unresponsive Payees"

3.87 SEC Rule 17Ad-17 was originally issued in 1997 to address situations in which recordkeeping transfer agents have lost contact with securityholders. The rule requires such transfer agents to exercise reasonable care to
obtain the correct addresses of these "lost securityholders" and to conduct certain database searches to locate them. At that time, the SEC noted that such
loss of contact can be harmful to securityholders because they no longer receive
corporate communications or the interest and dividend payments to which they
may be entitled. Additionally, the securities and any related interest and dividend payments to which the securityholders may be entitled are often placed
at risk of being deemed abandoned under operation of state escheatment laws.
This loss of contact most frequently results from (*a*) failure of a securityholder
to notify the transfer agent of his correct address after relocating; or (*b*) failure
of the estate of a deceased securityholder to notify the transfer agent of the
death of the securityholder and the name and address of the trustee or administrator for the estate.

3.88 The Dodd-Frank Act added a requirement for the SEC to revise Rule
17Ad-17 to extend to brokers and dealers the rule's requirement that recordkeeping transfer agents search for "lost securityholders," as defined in SEC
Rule 17Ad-17(b)(2). To comply with this requirement, the SEC issued Release
No. 34-68668 in January 2013. SEC Rule 17Ad-17(a)(1) requires that every
broker or dealer that has customer security accounts that include accounts of
lost securityholders should exercise reasonable care to ascertain the correct addresses of such securityholders. To meet this requirement, the broker or dealer
should conduct two database searches using at least one information database
service. The search should be conducted using the taxpayer identification number or name, if a search based on the taxpayer identification number is not
reasonably likely to locate the securityholder. Such database searches must
be conducted without charge to a lost securityholder and with the following
frequency:

- Between 3 and 12 months of such securityholder becoming a lost
  securityholder
- Between 6 and 12 months after the first search for such lost securityholder

3.89 SEC Rule 17Ad-17(a)(2) states that a transfer agent, broker, or dealer
may not use a search method or service to establish contact with lost securityholders that results in a charge to a lost securityholder prior to completing the
searches set forth in SEC Rule 17Ad-17(a)(1).

3.90 SEC Rule 17Ad-17(a)(3) outlines the circumstances in which a transfer agent, broker, or dealer is not required to conduct the searches set forth in
SEC Rule 17Ad-17(a)(1).

3.91 SEC Rule 17Ad-17(c) discusses the requirements for brokers or dealers when a securityholder is an "unresponsive payee." A securityholder should
be considered an unresponsive payee if a check is sent from the paying agent
to the securityholder and the check is not negotiated before the earlier of the
paying agent's sending of the next regularly scheduled check or the elapsing of

6 months (or 180 days) after the sending of the original nonnegotiated check. A securityholder should no longer be considered an unresponsive payee when the securityholder negotiates the check or checks that caused the securityholder to be considered an unresponsive payee.

3.92 In accordance with SEC Rule 17Ad-17(c)(1), the paying agent must provide a single written notification to each unresponsive payee no later than 7 months (or 210 days) after the sending of any not yet negotiated check to inform the unresponsive payee that a check was sent and that it has not yet been negotiated. SEC Rule 17Ad-17 also (*a*) provides an exclusion for paying agents from the notification requirements when the value of the not yet negotiated check is less than $25; and (*b*) adds a provision to make clear that the notification requirements imposed on paying agents shall have no effect on state escheatment laws.

SEC Rule 17Ad-22, "Clearing Agency Standards"

3.93 SEC Rule 17Ad-22 establishes minimum requirements regarding how registered clearing agencies must maintain effective risk management procedures and controls as well as meet the statutory requirements under the 1934 Act on an ongoing basis. Each registered clearing agency should establish, implement, maintain, and enforce written policies and procedures reasonably designed to meet the criteria outlined in SEC Rule 17Ad-22(d), as applicable. Additionally, a registered clearing agency that performs central counterparty services should establish, implement, maintain, and enforce written policies and procedures reasonably designed to meet the criteria outlined in SEC Rule 17Ad-22(b).

3.94 SEC Rule 17Ad-22(c) states that (1) each fiscal quarter (based on calculations made as of the last business day of the clearing agency's fiscal quarter), or at any time upon SEC request, a registered clearing agency that performs central counterparty services should calculate and maintain a record, in accordance with SEC Rule 17a-1, of the financial and qualifying liquid resources necessary to meet the requirements, as applicable, of Sections (b)(3) and (e)(7) of SEC Rule 17Ad-22, and sufficient documentation to explain the methodology it uses to compute such financial resources or qualifying liquid resources requirement; and (2) within 60 days after the end of its fiscal year, each registered clearing agency should post on its website its annual audited financial statements. Such financial statements should

- include, for the clearing agency and its subsidiaries, consolidated balance sheets as of the end of the two most recent fiscal years and statements of income, changes in stockholders' equity and other comprehensive income and cash flows for each of the two most recent fiscal years;

- be prepared in accordance with GAAP, except that for a clearing agency that is a corporation or other organization incorporated or organized under the laws of any foreign country, the consolidated financial statements may be prepared in accordance with GAAP or International Financial Reporting Standards as issued by the International Accounting Standards Board;

- be audited in accordance with standards of the PCAOB by a registered public accounting firm that is qualified and independent in accordance with Section 2-01, "Qualifications of Accountants," of SEC Regulation S-X; and

- include a report of the registered public accounting firm that complies with Section 2-02, "Accountants' Reports and Attestation Reports," of SEC Regulation S-X.

SEC Rule 17-248—Subpart C, "Regulation S-ID: Identity Theft Red Flags"

3.95 In accordance with the rulemaking mandated by the Dodd-Frank Act, in April 2013 the SEC added Subpart C "Regulation S-ID: Identity Theft Red Flags" to SEC Rule 17-248, at the same time the CFTC added Subpart C "Identity Theft Red Flags" to CFTC Regulation 17-162. The following are the two main provisions addressed:

- Financial institutions and creditors[17] are required to develop and implement a written identity theft prevention program designed to detect, prevent, and mitigate identity theft in connection with certain existing accounts or the opening of new accounts. The program must be appropriate to the size and complexity of the financial institution or creditor and the nature and scope of its activities. The rules include guidelines to assist entities in the formulation and maintenance of programs that would satisfy the requirements of the rules.
- Special requirements for any credit and debit card issuers are subject to the commissions' respective enforcement authorities to assess the validity of notifications of changes of address under certain circumstances.

SEC Rule 506 of Regulation D and SEC Rule 144A

3.96 In July 2013, the SEC amended Rule 506 of Regulation D and Rule 144A under the Securities Act of 1933 to implement Section 201(a) of the Jumpstart Our Business Startups Act. The amendment to SEC Rule 506 permits an issuer to engage in general solicitation or general advertising in offering and selling securities pursuant to SEC Rule 506, provided that all purchasers of the securities are accredited investors and the issuer takes reasonable steps to verify that such purchasers are accredited investors. The amendment to SEC Rule 506 also included a nonexclusive list of methods that issuers may use to satisfy the verification requirement for purchasers who are natural persons. The amendment to SEC Rule 144A provides that securities may be offered pursuant to SEC Rule 144A to persons other than qualified institutional buyers, provided that the securities are sold only to persons that the seller and any person acting on behalf of the seller reasonably believe are qualified institutional buyers. Form D was also amended to require issuers to indicate whether they are relying on the provision that permits general solicitation or general advertising in a SEC Rule 506 offering.

3.97 To implement Section 926 of the Dodd-Frank Act, the SEC amended SEC Rule 506 to disqualify issuers and other market participants from relying

---

[17] *Financial institution* or *creditor*, as defined in the Fair Credit Reporting Act (Title 15 *U.S. Code* [USC] Part 1681), is (*a*) a broker, dealer, or any other person that is registered or required to be registered under the 1934 Act, (*b*) an investment company that is registered or required to be registered under the Investment Company Act of 1940 that has elected to be regulated as a business development company under that act, or that operates as an employees' securities company under that act, or (*c*) an investment adviser that is registered or required to be registered under the Investment Advisers Act of 1940.

on SEC Rule 506 if "felons and other 'bad actors'" are participating in the SEC Rule 506 offering. Paragraph (d) of SEC Rule 506 provides guidance on the bad actor disqualification.

SEC Rule 15c3-5, "Risk Management Controls for Brokers or Dealers with Market Access"[18]

3.98 SEC Rule 15c3-5 addresses the risks that can arise as a result of the automated, rapid electronic trading strategies that exist in the current marketplace. Rule 15c3-5 eliminated the practice known as "naked access" that allowed high-speed traders and others to buy and sell stocks on exchanges using a broker's computer code without requiring the trades to filter through the broker's systems or undergo any pretrade checks. Rule 15c3-5 is applicable to broker-dealers with access to trading securities by virtue of being an exchange member, an ATS subscriber, or an ATS operator with nonbroker-dealer subscribers.

3.99 SEC Rule 15c3-5 requires broker-dealers with access to trading securities directly on an exchange or ATS, including those providing sponsored or direct market access to customers or other persons, and broker-dealer operators of an ATS that provide access to trading securities directly on their ATS to a person other than a broker-dealer to establish, document, and maintain a system of risk management controls and supervisory procedures designed to systematically limit the financial exposure of the broker-dealer that could arise as a result of market access and to ensure compliance with all regulatory requirements that are applicable in connection with market access. The controls and supervisory procedures must be reasonably designed to

- prevent the entry of orders that exceed appropriate preset credit or capital thresholds or that appear to be erroneous.
- prevent the entry of orders unless there has been compliance with all regulatory requirements that must be satisfied on a preorder entry basis.
- prevent orders that the broker-dealer or customer is restricted from trading.
- restrict market access technology and systems to authorized persons.
- assure appropriate surveillance personnel receive immediate post-trade execution reports.

3.100 A broker-dealer is required to preserve a copy of its supervisory procedures and a written description of its risk management controls as part of its books and records in a manner consistent with SEC Rule 17a-4(e)(7). The financial and regulatory risk management controls and supervisory procedures required by SEC Rule 15c3-5 must be under the direct and exclusive control of the broker-dealer with market access, with limited exceptions as found in Rule 15c3-5(d)(1). In addition, a broker-dealer is required to establish, document, and maintain a system of regularly reviewing the effectiveness of the risk management controls and supervisory procedures and for promptly addressing any issues. The CEO (or equivalent) of the broker-dealer is required to annually certify that the risk management controls and supervisory procedures comply with Rule 15c3-5 and that the regular review has been conducted.

---

[18] See footnote 4.

The certification is required to be preserved by the broker-dealer as part of its books and records.

3.101 On April 15, 2014, the SEC issued an FAQ, *Responses to Frequently Asked Questions Concerning Risk Management Controls for Brokers or Dealers with Market Access*, which is available at www.sec.gov/divisions/marketreg/faq-15c-5-risk-management-controls-bd.htm.

SEC Rule 17a-5, "Reports to Be Made by Certain Brokers and Dealers"

3.102 SEC Rule 17a-5 describes the objectives of an audit of a broker-dealer's financial statements and supplemental information. Specifically, the audit should be made in accordance with PCAOB standards.[19] In accordance with the requirements in SEC Rule 17a-5(g), the audit should include all procedures necessary under the circumstances to enable the independent public accountant to express an opinion on the statement of financial condition; results of operations; cash flows; and the supplemental information in the "Computation of Net Capital under Rule 15c3-1, the Computation for Determination of Reserve Requirements for Brokers or Dealers under Exhibit A of Rule 15c3-3, and Information Relating to the Possession or Control Requirements Under Rule 15c3-3." See exhibit 6-9 of chapter 6 of this guide for illustrative examples of the supplementary information required to be filed with the financial statements.

3.103 In addition to the audited financial statements, broker-dealers are required to file a compliance report or an exemption report annually. An independent auditor will be required to examine the broker-dealer's compliance report relating to specific financial responsibility rules or review the statements regarding the broker-dealer's claim of exemption from SEC Rule 15c3-3, pursuant to PCAOB standards. (The internal control report formerly required by SEC Rule 17a-5(g) has been eliminated.)

3.104 *Compliance Report.* The rules require a broker-dealer that did not claim exemption from Rule 15c3-3 throughout the most recent fiscal year to prepare and file an annual report on compliance, and Internal Control Over Compliance, with certain financial responsibility rules, specifically the Net Capital Rule (SEC Rule 15c3-1), Customer Protection Rule (SEC Rule 15c3-3), Quarterly Security Counts to Be Made by Certain Exchange Members, Brokers, and Dealers Rule (SEC Rule 17a-13), and Account Statement Rules of the designated examining authority. The compliance report must include statements as to whether:

a. The broker-dealer has established and maintained Internal Control Over Compliance

b. The Internal Control Over Compliance of the broker-dealer was effective during the most recent fiscal year

c. The Internal Control Over Compliance of the broker-dealer was effective as of the end of the most recent fiscal year

d. The broker-dealer was in compliance with Rule 15c3-1 and paragraph (e) of Rule 15c3-3 as of the end of the most recent fiscal year

---

[19] See paragraph 3.04.

e. The information the broker-dealer used to state whether it was in compliance with Rule 15c3-1 and paragraph (e) of Rule 15c3-3 was derived from the books and records of the broker-dealer

3.105 If applicable, the compliance report must also describe (*a*) each identified material weakness (as defined by SEC Rule 17a-5) in the Internal Control Over Compliance during the most recent fiscal year, and (*b*) any instance of noncompliance with Rule 15c3-1 or Rule 15c3-3(e) as of the end of the most recent fiscal year.

3.106 *Noncompliance.* For SEC Rules 15c3-1 and 15c3-3(e) noncompliance is described as an instance that would trigger notification requirements pursuant to SEC Rules 15c3-1, 15c3-3, or 17a-11. For SEC Rules 17a-13 and 15c3-3, with the exception of 15c3-3(e), and those self-regulatory organizations and designated examining authority rules governing account statements, noncompliance "to a material extent" is described as an instance of noncompliance where the overall assessment requires judgment based on the facts and circumstances.

3.107 *Internal Controls Over Compliance. Internal Control Over Compliance* is defined in the rule as internal controls that have the objective of providing the broker or dealer with reasonable assurance that noncompliance with the financial responsibility rules will be prevented or detected on a timely basis.

3.108 *Material weakness. Material weakness*, as defined by SEC Rule 17a-5, is a deficiency, or combination of deficiencies, in the broker-dealer's Internal Control Over Compliance such that there is a reasonable possibility that noncompliance with Rule 15c3-1 or Rule 15c3-3(e) will not be prevented or detected on a timely basis, or that noncompliance to a material extent with Rule 15c3-3, except for 15c3-3(e), Rule 17a-13 or any Account Statement Rule will not be prevented or detected on a timely basis.

3.109 *Exemption report.* The rules require a broker-dealer that claims an exemption from SEC Rule 15c3-3 throughout the most recent fiscal year to file an annual exemption report. The exemption report includes statements made to the "best knowledge and belief of the broker-dealer," where the broker-dealer:

a. Identifies the provisions in SEC Rule 15c3-3(k) under which the broker-dealer claimed an exemption

b. Indicates it has met the identified exemption provision throughout the most recent fiscal year without exception or that it met the identified exemption provisions in SEC Rule 15c3-3(k) throughout the year except as described in the exemption report, and

c. If applicable, identifies each exception and briefly describes the nature of each exception and the approximate date(s) on which the exception existed.

3.110 The SEC issued two FAQs, the first on March 6, 2014, *Frequently Asked Questions Concerning the Amendments to Certain Broker-Dealer Financial Responsibility Rules*, and the second on April 4, 2014, *Frequently Asked Questions Concerning the July 30, 2013 Amendments to the Broker-Dealer Financial Reporting Rule*, both are available at www.sec.gov/divisions/marketreg/mrfaq.htm.

3.111 The auditor's responsibility with respect to noncompliance or material weakness (as defined by SEC Rule 17a-5) is described in SEC Rule 17a-5(h) and includes requirements for the auditor to contact the SEC if he or she is aware that the broker-dealer failed to make appropriate notification about the existence of noncompliance and material weaknesses (as defined by SEC Rule 17a-5). The following is paraphrased from SEC Rule 17a-5(h):

- If, during the course of the audit or interim work, the independent public accountant determines that the broker-dealer is not in compliance with SEC Rule 15c3-1, SEC Rule 15c3-3, or SEC Rule 17a-13 or the Account Statement Rules of the designated examining authority or that a material weakness (as defined by SEC Rule 17a-5) exists, the independent public accountant must immediately notify the CFO of the broker-dealer. If the notice from the accountant to the CFO concerns an instance of noncompliance that would require a broker-dealer to provide a notification under SEC Rules 15c3-1, 15c3-3, or 17a-11, or if the notice concerns a material weakness (as defined by SEC Rule 17a-5), the broker-dealer must provide a notification in accordance with Rules 15c3-1, 15c3-3, or 17a-11, as applicable, within one business day and provide a copy of the notification to the independent public accountant.

- If the accountant fails to receive such notice from the broker-dealer within one business day or if the accountant disagrees with the statements contained in the notice of the broker-dealer, the accountant shall have a responsibility to inform the SEC and designated examining authority by report of noncompliance or material weakness (as defined by SEC Rule 17a-5) within one business day thereafter as set forth in SEC Rule 17a-11. Such report from the accountant shall, if the broker-dealer failed to file a notice, describe any instances of noncompliance or any material weaknesses (as defined by SEC Rule 17a-5) found to exist. If the broker-dealer filed a notice, the accountant shall file a report detailing the aspects, if any, of the broker-dealer's notice with which the accountant does not agree.

3.112 SEC Rule 17a-5 also contains rules relating to the qualification, designation, independence, and replacement of public accountants who audit the financial statements of broker-dealers.

3.113 *Qualification of accountant.*[20] The SEC does not recognize any person as a CPA who is not duly registered and in good standing as such under the laws of his or her place of residence or principal office. The SEC also does not recognize any person as a public accountant who is not in good standing and entitled to practice as such under the laws of his or her place of residence or principal office.

3.114 *Designation of accountant.* SEC Rule 17a-5 also requires every broker-dealer that is required (by Rule 17a-5(d)) to file an annual report of financial statements to also file, by no later than December 10 of each year a statement with the SEC's principal office in Washington, D.C.; with the regional office of the SEC for the region in which its principal place of business

---

[20] Although the Sarbanes-Oxley Act of 2002 (SOX) is directed at *issuers* (as defined by SOX) and their auditors, nonissuer broker-dealers also come under the scope of certain provisions of SOX because Section 205(c)(2) of SOX amended *Commerce and Trade*, USC 15, Section 78q of the 1934 Act to require all broker-dealers (both issuer and nonissuer) to be audited by a public accounting firm registered with the PCAOB. For fiscal years ending after December 31, 2008, financial statements of nonissuer broker-dealers must be certified by a PCAOB-registered public accounting firm.

is located; and with the principal office of the designated examining authority for such broker-dealer indicating the existence of an agreement dated no later than December 1 with an independent public accountant covering a contractual commitment to conduct the broker-dealer's annual audit during the following calendar year. The agreement may be of a continuing nature, providing for successive yearly audits, in which case no further filing is required. However, if the agreement is for a single audit, or if the continuing agreement previously filed has been terminated or amended, a new statement must be filed by the required date.

3.115 The notice filed with the SEC should be headed "Notice Pursuant to Statement Regarding Independent Public Accountant Under Rule 17a-5(f)(2)" and should contain the following information and representations:

- The name, address, telephone number, and registration number of the broker-dealer
- The name, address, and telephone number of the independent public accountant
- The date of the fiscal year of the annual reports of the broker-dealer for the year covered by the engagement
- Whether the engagement is for a single year or is of a continuing nature
- A representation that the independent public accountant has been engaged to audit the annual financial statements, footnotes, and supplemental information, as well as prepare a compliance examination report or exemption review report
- A representation that the broker-dealer allows the regulators access to audit documentation and allows the independent public accountant to discuss findings with the regulators (this representation is not applicable for a broker-dealer that neither clears nor carries customer accounts)

3.116 Any broker-dealer that is exempted from the requirement to file an annual audited report of financial statements should nevertheless file the notice and indicate the date as of which the unaudited report will be prepared. Every newly registered broker-dealer should file the notice designating its accountant within 30 days following the effective date of its registration as a broker-dealer.

3.117 *Independence of accountant.* SEC Rule 17a-5 requires that the provisions set forth in SEC Rules 2-01(b) and (c) of Regulation S-X be adhered to when determining whether the accountant is deemed to be independent. In May 2014, the AICPA and the Center for Audit Quality jointly issued a Member Alert, (available at www.thecaq.org/docs/alerts/caq-broker-and-dealer-alert-2014-06.pdf?sfvrsn=2) which discusses, amongst other things, SEC and PCAOB independence considerations for broker-dealers and their independent accountant.

3.118 In January 2003, the SEC adopted amendments to its requirements regarding auditor independence to enhance the independence of accountants who audit and review financial statements and prepare attestation reports filed with the SEC. Auditors of nonissuer broker-dealers are restricted from performing those services specifically excluded by SOX and are expected to comply with all other SEC independence rules, including those that prohibit bookkeeping and the preparation of financial statements for nonissuer broker-dealers. SEC answers to frequently asked questions regarding the independence rules can be found at www.sec.gov/info/accountants/ocafaqaudind121304.htm.

3.119 *Replacement of accountant.* A broker-dealer is also required to file a notice with the SEC's principal office in Washington, D.C.; the SEC regional office for the region in which the broker-dealer's principal place of business is located; and the principal office of the designated examining authority for such broker-dealer no more than 15 business days after any of the following:

- The broker-dealer has notified the accountant whose opinion covered the most recent financial statements filed under SEC Rule 17a-5(d) that his or her services will not be used in future engagements.

- The broker-dealer has notified an accountant who was engaged to give an opinion covering the financial statements to be filed under SEC Rule 17a-5(d) that the engagement has been terminated.

- An accountant has notified the broker-dealer that he or she would not continue under an engagement to give an opinion covering the financial statements to be filed under SEC Rule 17a-5(d).

- A new accountant has been engaged to give an opinion covering the financial statements to be filed under SEC Rule 17a-5(d) without any notice of termination having been given to or by the previously engaged accountant.

3.120 SEC Rule 17a-5(f)(3) requires the notice to state the date of notification of the termination of the engagement (or notification of the engagement of the new accountant, as applicable) and to state the details of any problems that existed during the 24 months (or the period of the engagement, if less) preceding such termination or new engagement relating to any matter of accounting principles or practices, financial statement disclosure, auditing scope or procedure, or compliance with applicable SEC rules and that, if not resolved to the satisfaction of the former accountant, would have caused him or her to make reference to them in connection with his or her report on the subject matter of the problems. The problems required to be reported include both those resolved to the former accountant's satisfaction and those not resolved to the former accountant's satisfaction. Such problems would include those that occur at the decision-making level (that is, between the broker-dealer's principal financial officers and the accounting firm's personnel responsible for rendering its report).

3.121 The notice should state whether the accountant's report on the financial statements for any of the past two years contained an adverse opinion or a disclaimer of opinion or was modified concerning uncertainties, audit scope, or accounting principles. The notice should also describe the nature of each such adverse opinion, disclaimer of opinion, or qualification. The broker-dealer should also request the former accountant to furnish the broker-dealer with a letter that is addressed to the SEC that states whether he or she agrees with the statements contained in the notice of the broker-dealer and, if not, states the respects in which he or she does not agree. The broker-dealer should file three copies of the notice and the accountant's letter, one copy of which should be manually signed by the sole proprietor (or a general partner or a duly authorized corporate officer, as appropriate) and by the accountant, respectively.

3.122 Broker-dealers that are dually registered as FCMs or IBs must comply with both SEC and CFTC regulations.

Anti-money Laundering Regulations[21]

3.123 The Uniting and Strengthening America by Providing Appropriate Tools Required to Intercept and Obstruct Terrorism Act of 2001 (USA PATRIOT ACT) requires broker-dealers to implement certain recordkeeping and reporting requirements. They should also establish an anti-money laundering (AML) program that, at a minimum, contains the following components: development of internal policies, procedures, and controls; designation of a compliance officer; an ongoing employee training program; and an independent audit function to test programs.

3.124 Broker-dealers are required to establish, document, and maintain a written customer identification program (CIP). This program should be appropriate for the firm's size and business; be part of the firm's AML compliance program; and, at a minimum, should contain the following four elements: establishing identity verification procedures; maintaining records related to CIP; determining whether a customer appears on any designated list of terrorists or terrorist organizations; and providing customers with notice that information is being obtained to verify their identities. The CIP rule provides that, under certain defined circumstances, broker-dealers may rely on the performance of another financial institution to fulfill some or all the requirements of the broker-dealer's CIP.

3.125 Among other things, these rules require that firms independently test their AML programs. The independent tests should occur on an annual basis for most firms.[22] Many broker-dealers are concerned about the independent testing requirement and its impact on their auditors' independence. It would be proper for the auditor of the broker-dealer to perform testing of an AML program if it is done in accordance with attestation standards. It can be performed as an agreed-upon procedure or an attestation of management assertions, which would retain auditor independence. However, when performing certain functions under a consulting services agreement, such as generating working papers or reports for FINRA or the NYSE to review, the SEC staff believes this would be considered a management function and, therefore, would impair the auditor's independence. Firms may use internal staff as long as they are independent from the AML program itself and have the knowledge they need to effectively evaluate a firm's AML system. Training internal staff and establishing procedures to ensure their independence can be expensive. Therefore, some firms may find it more cost effective to use a qualified outside party. Some small firms have coordinated with other small firms to hire an outside auditor at a reduced group rate. FINRA Rule 3310, *Anti-Money Laundering Compliance Program*, is substantially the same as the former NASD Rule 3011; however, this rule, as adopted, eliminates the independent testing exception that was in the related NASD rule.

---

[21] The SEC has available on its website an anti-money laundering (AML) source tool for broker-dealers. It is a compilation of key AML laws, rules, and guidance applicable to broker-dealers. The tool organizes the key AML compliance materials and provides related source information. It can be accessed at www.sec.gov/about/offices/ocie/amlsourcetool.htm.

[22] As noted in question 1 of FINRA AML frequently asked questions, as found on the FINRA website at www.finra.org, if the firm does not execute transactions with customers or otherwise hold customer accounts or act as an introducing broker with respect to customer accounts, the independent testing is required every two years.

Reporting Requirements

3.126 Each broker-dealer reports periodically to its designated examining authority in a prescribed format: the FOCUS report. Under the rules, broker-dealers are required to file at the end of each calendar quarter a part II or IIA FOCUS report (although many broker-dealers are required to file at the end of each month). The FOCUS report requires financial information that presents the financial position and results of operations in conformity with GAAP, as well as certain regulatory computations.

3.127 The FOCUS report (Form X-17A-5) comprises the following parts:

- *Part I.* A monthly report of selected summarized financial and operational data filed by broker-dealers that carry customer securities accounts or clear securities transactions. (Examining authorities may require other broker-dealers to file part I on a monthly basis.)

- *Part II.* A report of general purpose financial information that presents the financial position and results of operations, supplemental schedules, and operational data and is filed each calendar quarter by broker-dealers that file part I.

- *Part IIA.* A quarterly report of financial information that presents the financial position and results of operations, supplemental schedules, and operational data filed by broker-dealers that do not carry customer securities accounts or clear securities transactions.

- *Part IIB.* A quarterly report made by OTC derivatives dealers who register with the SEC under a limited regulatory structure, as discussed in paragraph 3.184, that includes statements of financial condition and income, computation of net capital and net capital required, capital withdrawals, and other schedules of financial and operational data.

- *Part III.* A facing page required as part of all FOCUS filings that contains overall information regarding the filing.

- *Schedule I.* Annual supplementary schedules reflecting certain economic and statistical data of broker-dealers on a calendar-year basis.

Note that there are other forms that are applicable for firms that compute capital in accordance with appendix E of the Net Capital Rule.

3.128 In certain cases, such as when a broker-dealer exceeds certain parameters of financial and operational conditions, the designated examining authority may require the broker-dealer to file part II or IIA monthly or weekly. In addition, audited financial statements are required to be filed on a fiscal- or calendar-year basis as of a date selected by the broker-dealer. The annual audit for subsequent years should be as of the same date unless the SEC issues prior approval for a change of the broker-dealer's fiscal year.

3.129 SEC Rule 17a-5 defines *fiscal year* as the broker-dealer's fiscal year for reporting purposes; the fiscal year is not necessarily the same as the tax year. For purposes of defining a time period such as fiscal or calendar quarter, the last Friday or last business day of such period is acceptable.

3.130 If the broker-dealer selects a date for the annual audited financial statements that does not coincide with the end of a calendar quarter, an additional unaudited part II or IIA of the FOCUS report should be filed by the broker-dealer as of the date of the annual audit (an exemption from this additional filing may be obtained if the fiscal year approximates the calendar year).

3.131 SEC Rule 13h-1 requires a *large trader*, defined as a person whose transactions in national market system securities equal or exceed 2 million shares or $20 million during any calendar day or 20 million shares or $200 million during any calendar month, to identify itself to the SEC and make certain disclosures on Form 13H. In addition, the rule imposes additional requirements on registered broker-dealers related to recordkeeping, reporting, and monitoring with respect to large traders.

Consolidation of Subsidiaries

3.132 Appendix C of SEC Rule 15c3-1 requires a broker-dealer to consolidate the financial accounts of any subsidiary or affiliate for which the broker-dealer guarantees, endorses, or assumes its obligations or liabilities. Whereas consolidation would be reflected on a line-by-line basis in the broker-dealer's audited financial statements, the SEC requires equity investment presentation in broker-dealer FOCUS financial statements (that is, in the broker-dealer's FOCUS financial statements the broker-dealer's ownership in the subsidiary or affiliate would be reflected as a one-line investment adjusted for the broker-dealer's share of that entity's profit or loss).

3.133 The effect of consolidating any subsidiary or affiliate may result in an increase of the broker-dealer's net capital or a decrease of its minimum net capital requirement under SEC Rule 15c3-1(a). In that circumstance, in order for the consolidation to be permitted for the purpose of computing net capital, the broker-dealer must meet the other requirements of paragraph (b)(2) of appendix C of the rule and obtain an opinion from legal counsel as of the date of the financial statements (such opinion should be renewed annually) that the net assets of the subsidiary can be liquidated and distributed to the broker-dealer within 30 calendar days. See appendix C of the rule for more details. In no event can a broker-dealer rely on a consolidation of any subsidiary or affiliate to meet its minimum net capital requirement.

3.134 If a broker-dealer guarantees the payment of the financial obligation of a parent, an affiliate, or a subsidiary or is otherwise defined as a primary obligor of such obligation, the broker-dealer must include the current amount of the financial obligation as a reduction in net worth in computing its net capital. Further, if a broker-dealer's assets are included contractually as collateral for the financial obligation of another party, the carrying value of the broker-dealer's allowable assets equal to the amount of the payment obligation are considered encumbered by the SEC and are rendered nonallowable for net capital purposes. Such nonallowable treatment would not occur if the collateral relates to equity interests in the broker-dealer as opposed to the broker-dealer's assets.

Form Custody

3.135 Pursuant to SEC Rule 17a-5(a)(5), all broker-dealers are required to file an unaudited form which provides information on whether a broker-dealer maintains custody of customer and noncustomer assets, and, if so, how the assets are maintained. The requirement to file Form Custody began for the period ended December 31, 2013, and is due within 17 business days after each calendar quarter end, as well as the fiscal year end date if it does not co-incide with a calendar quarter end. Additional information is available in the two FAQs that were issued by the SEC regarding the amendments, issued in 2013, to their rules. Both are available at www.sec.gov/divisions/marketreg/mrfaq.htm.

Other Periodic Reporting

3.136 FINRA Rule 4524, "Supplemental FOCUS Information," requires each member broker-dealer, as designated by FINRA, to file such additional financial or operational schedules or reports as FINRA may deem necessary or appropriate for the protection of investors or in the public interest as a supplement to the FOCUS Report. Additional schedules, each with specific frequency and due dates, include

- Supplemental Statement of Income (SSOI), as a supplement to the Statement of Income (Loss) page of the FOCUS Report.

- Supplemental Schedule for Derivatives and Other Off-Balance Sheet Items (OBS) that generally applies to carrying or clearing firms but also applies to certain non-carrying or non-clearing firms that have significant amounts of off-balance sheet obligations.[23]

- Supplemental Inventory Schedule (SIS) that details inventory positions as of the end of the FOCUS reporting period.

The Annual Audited Financial Report[24]

3.137 SEC Rule 17a-5 requires broker-dealers to file an annual report containing audited financial statements and supplemental information. Under the rule, certain types of broker-dealers need not file an annual report, while certain others must file a report but it need not be audited. However, these two exceptions apply to very narrow classes of broker-dealers. The first exception only applies to specialists, market-makers, and floor brokers that are members of a national securities exchange, limit their securities business solely to transactions with other members of the exchange, and do not carry margin accounts, credit balances, or securities for customers. The second exception only applies to broker dealers (1) that limit their securities business to acting solely as an agent for a single issuer in soliciting subscriptions for the issuer's securities, and that do not carry customer accounts, or (2) that limit their securities business to buying and selling evidences of indebtedness secured by a mortgage, deed of trust or other lien on real estate or leasehold interests, and that do not carry margin accounts, credit balances, or securities for customers. SEC Rule 17a-12 requires OTC derivatives dealers to file audited annual financial statements.

3.138 The annual audited report should consist of a facing page, a table of contents (report checklist), an oath or affirmation, and the following annual audited financial statements with appropriate footnotes:

- Statement of financial condition

---

[23] Refer to FINRA Regulatory Notice 16-11 "SEC Approves Expanded Application of Supplemental Schedule for Derivatives and Other Off-Balance Sheet Items," available at www.finra.org/industry/notices/16-11.

[24] Information regarding FINRA's rules for the application for an extension of time to file the annual audit is available at www.finra.org/industry/annual-audit-extension-time-request-policy.

- Statement of income (loss)
- Statement of cash flows

3.139 In addition, SEC Rule 17a-5 requires that the annual audited financial statements also include a statement of changes in stockholders', partners', or sole proprietor's equity, and a statement of changes in liabilities subordinated to claims of general creditors.

3.140 The contents of each of the annual audited financial statements are discussed in chapter 6 and illustrations are presented in the final section of that chapter. Broker-dealers that have issued securities to the public may also be subject to the disclosure rules that apply to publicly held companies. Such rules require that comprehensive financial information (including statements of income and cash flows) be disseminated to stockholders.

3.141 The annual audited financial statements should also contain the following supplementary schedules, required by SEC Rule 17a-5 and Regulation 1.10(d)(2) of the CFTC, as applicable:

- Computation of net capital and required net capital under SEC Rule 15c3-1.
- Computation for determination of reserve requirements under exhibit A of SEC Rule 15c3-3 (customer).
- Computation for determination of reserve requirements under exhibit A of SEC Rule 15c3-3 (Proprietary Account of Broker Dealers or PAB).
- Information relating to the possession or control requirements under Rule 15c3-3.
- For broker-dealers that are also registered as FCMs, a schedule of segregation requirements and funds in segregation for broker-dealers with customers trading on U.S. commodity exchanges, as well as a schedule of secured amounts and funds held in separate accounts for customers trading on non-U.S. commodity exchanges, and the statement of cleared swaps customer segregation requirements and funds in cleared swaps accounts.
- Reconciliations (including appropriate explanations) of material differences, if any, between the following:
  - The broker-dealer's computation of net capital under Rule 15c3-1 included in the most recent unaudited FOCUS filing.
  - The broker-dealer's computation for determination of the reserve requirements under exhibit A of Rule 15c3-3 included in the most recent unaudited FOCUS filing.
  - The schedule of segregation requirements and funds in segregation included in the most recent unaudited FOCUS filing.
  - The corresponding computations made by the broker-dealer included in the supplemental information of the audited financial statements. As permitted under the SEC Letter to the NYSE dated April 24, 1987, if a broker-dealer files an amended FOCUS report that contains the reconciliation and explanation of material differences

between the amended report and the original report, the supplemental schedule(s) may be reconciled with the amended FOCUS report and would include a statement about whether any material differences are shown in the amendment.

If there are no material differences, a statement that a reconciliation is not necessary pursuant to Rule 17a-5(d)(4) should be made.

3.142 Copies of the annual audited financial statements of the broker-dealer, together with the report of the independent auditor and either a compliance report (and Compliance Examination Report) or an exemption report (and exemption review report), should be filed with the SEC's principal office[25] in Washington, D.C. and with the regional SEC office for the region in which the broker-dealer has its principal place of business. It is also necessary to provide copies to the designated examining authority[26] for the broker-dealer; to the self-regulatory organizations of which the broker-dealer is a member, to the Securities Investor Protection Corporation (SIPC) if the broker-dealer is a member;[27] and in certain circumstances, to many of the states in which the broker-dealer is registered.

3.143 The report must be filed (received by the SEC) within 60 calendar days after the date of the financial statements. If the broker-dealer cannot meet this deadline without undue hardship, an application for an extension of time may be filed with the principal office of their designated examining authority.

3.144 For government securities broker-dealers, similar financial statements should be filed with the SEC within 60 calendar days after the date of the financial statements and for broker-dealers that are also FCMs or IBs, they should be filed simultaneously with the CFTC.

3.145 All annual audited financial statements that are filed with the SEC are treated as public documents unless the broker-dealer makes separate filings of the reports. If the broker-dealer requests confidential treatment of other than the statement of financial condition (not available for public inspection), the statement of financial condition is required to be bound separately from the balance of the statements. The balance of the annual audited financial statements must be bound separately or placed in a separate package and each page

---

[25] Broker-dealers can voluntarily file their annual reports electronically (in lieu of filing reports in hardcopy). For more information, refer to "Electronic Filing of Broker-Dealer Annual Reports" at www.sec.gov/divisions/marketreg/electronic-filing-broker-dealer-annual-reports.htm.

In January 2017, the SEC announced a simplified process for electronic filing of broker-dealer annual reports with the SEC. For more information, refer to the no-action letter dated January 27, 2017, available at www.sec.gov/divisions/marketreg/mr-noaction/2017/finra-012717-electronic-filing-annual-reports.pdf.

[26] As found in Regulatory Notice 11-46, *Annual Audit Reports*, dated October 2011, FINRA has revised the process by which member firms submit the annual audited financial statements required pursuant to SEC Rule 17a-5(d). Firms whose designated examining authority is FINRA are required to submit their annual audit report in electronic form for annual audit reports with a fiscal year end on or after September 30, 2011. Firms must also submit the oath and affirmation electronically and maintain the oath and affirmation page with an original manual signature as part of their books and records in accordance with SEC Rule 17a-4(a). Further information can be found at www.finra.org.

[27] In August 2017, Securities Investor Protection Corporation (SIPC) issued a letter to its members which states "through an arrangement with FINRA, all members that file annual reports with their designated examining authority through the FINRA Firm Gateway on and after September 1, 2017, will use the FINRA Firm Gateway to also file their annual reports with SIPC. SIPC will no longer accept annual reports by any other means. After September 1, 2017 SIPC will deem any annual report received other than through the FINRA Firm Gateway as not having been filed with SIPC." For more information, see www.sipc.org/media/letter-to-members-re-finra-gateway.pdf.

should be stamped "confidential." The public and nonpublic portions of the financial statements must be filed separately in the format required in order for the nonpublic portion of the financial statements to be treated as such.

3.146 The filing with the various exchanges of which the broker-dealer is a member should include both (a) the complete annual audited report filed with the SEC and the CFTC on a confidential basis and (b) the additional filing made with the SEC and the CFTC as a public document.

3.147 Under CFTC Regulation 1.10(g), the following portions of audited and unaudited financial reports filed by FCMs and introducing brokers (IBs) with the CFTC will be considered public information and made available to the public upon request:

- The amount of the FCM's or IB's adjusted net capital, the amount of its minimum net capital requirement under CFTC Regulation 1.17, and the amount of its adjusted net capital in excess of its minimum net capital requirement
- The following statements and footnote disclosures:
  - The Statement of Financial Condition in FCM and IB certified annual financial reports but not such statements in their unaudited financial reports
  - The Statements of Segregation Requirements and Funds in Segregation for customers trading on U.S. commodity exchanges and for customers' dealer options accounts (only FCMs file these statements)
  - The Statement of Secured Amounts and Funds held in Separate Accounts for foreign futures and foreign options customers in accordance with CFTC Regulation 30.7 (only FCMs file this statement)
  - The independent accountant's opinion filed with FCM and IB certified annual financial reports
  - The list, if any, in audited or unaudited FCM financial reports of their "guaranteed IBs"

3.148 As a matter of administrative convenience, the FCM or IB may submit with its certified annual financial report an additional copy that has been marked "public" and contains only the information that is publicly available upon request under CFTC Regulation 1.10(g). The CFTC will not, however, process any petitions for confidential treatment of any part of the audited or unaudited financial reports filed by FCMs and IBs. In accordance with the Freedom of Information Act, the Government in the Sunshine Act, and Parts 145 and 147 of CFTC regulations, all portions of such financial reports will be treated as nonpublic except for those portions specified as publicly available in Regulation 1.10(g).

3.149 Under provisions of the Freedom of Information Act, the CFTC may disclose to third parties portions of the nonpublic information in the report under the following circumstances:

- In connection with matters in litigation
- In connection with CFTC investigations

- When the information is furnished to regulatory, self-regulatory, and law enforcement agencies to assist them in meeting responsibilities assigned to them by law
- In other circumstances in which withholding of such information appears unwarranted

3.150 Pursuant to CFTC Regulation 1.10(g)(5), the independent public accountant's opinion on the public portion of an FCM's financial report filing will be deemed public information.

3.151 Pursuant to CFTC Regulations 145.5(d)(1)(viii) and 145.5(h), the independent public accountant's supplemental report on material inadequacies filed under CFTC Regulation 1.16(c)(5) will be deemed nonpublic information.

Filings Concurrent With the Annual Audited Financial Report

Compliance or Exemption Report Required by SEC Rule 17a-5

3.152 *Compliance report.* For a broker-dealer that does not make a claim of exemption from SEC Rule 15c3-3 throughout the most recent fiscal year, concurrent with the filing of the annual audited financial report, the broker-dealer files a compliance report. The compliance report should be accompanied by an examination report issued by the independent auditor.

3.153 *Exemption report.* For a broker-dealer that claims an exemption from SEC Rule 15c3-3 throughout the most recent fiscal year, concurrent with the filing of the annual audited financial report, the broker-dealer files an exemption report. This exemption report should be accompanied by a review report issued by the independent auditor.

3.154 During the course of the audit, if the independent auditor determines that an instance of noncompliance with the financial responsibility rules or material weakness (as defined by SEC Rule 17a-5) exists, he or she should immediately call it to the attention of the CFO of the broker-dealer, who then has the responsibility of informing the SEC within one business day. If this notification does not occur, the auditor has the responsibility of informing the SEC. See paragraph 3.111 for further discussion.

Report to State Regulatory Agencies

3.155 Other filings may be required by various state regulatory agencies. The auditor should obtain through inquiry of the client, management's determination of all the states in which the annual audited report or portions thereof are required to be filed. Some jurisdictions (including California, Connecticut, and others) require a specific form of oath or affirmation to accompany the annual audited report. Others may require the filing of a statement of financial condition only, not the supplemental report on internal control structure, and others may not require any financial statement filings.

Financial Statements to Be Furnished to Customers of Securities Broker-Dealers

3.156 Unless the broker-dealer is exempt by reason of SEC rules, a statement of financial condition with appropriate notes, including the amount of net capital and required net capital pursuant to SEC Rule 15c3-1 (the Net Capital

Requirements for Brokers or Dealers rule), is required to be mailed semiannually to all customers (as defined in the rule) carried by the broker-dealer.

3.157 The rule requiring that the statement of financial condition be furnished to customers also provides that certain notices be given to each customer concurrently with the statement of financial condition being furnished. These notices advise the customer of the availability at specified locations of (*a*) the latest audited statement of financial condition filed pursuant to SEC Rule 17a-5 (meaning the public report filed concurrently with the annual audited report) and (*b*) notification if the auditor had commented on any material weaknesses in connection with the most recent annual audited report.

3.158 The audited statement of financial condition is required to be sent to customers within 105 days after the date of the financial statements. This statement should be consistent with the statement filed as a public document. An extension of time may be requested from the SEC.

3.159 Broker-dealers are also required by the SEC to furnish each customer with an unaudited statement of financial condition dated 6 months after the date of the audited financial statements. The unaudited statement should conform to the audited statement with respect to presentation and disclosure requirements and should be furnished within 65 days of the statement date.

3.160 SEC Rule 17a-5 contains a conditional exemption from the rule's requirement that a broker-dealer that carries customer accounts send its full statement of financial condition and certain other financial information to each of its customers twice per year. Paragraph (c)(5) of the rule provides that the broker-dealer can send its customers summary information regarding its net capital, as long as it also provides customers with a toll-free number to call for a free copy of its full statement of financial condition, makes its full statement of financial condition available to customers over the Internet, and meets other specified requirements.

3.161 In view of the notification requirements and definitions of material weakness and noncompliance in SEC Rule 17a-5, careful consideration should be given to determining that the suggestions for improving organization, procedures, or efficiency that are included in reports to management upon completion of the audit are not reportable under SEC Rule 17a-5.

Other Reports

Reports on Securities Investor Protection Corporation Assessment

3.162 Broker-dealers registered with the SEC, with some limited exceptions, are required to be members of the SIPC.[28] The SIPC imposes an assessment upon members to maintain its fund and to repay any borrowings by the SIPC. For a number of years, the assessment on members was a flat rate of $150.[29] In March 2009, the SIPC determined that the SIPC fund balance would likely remain less than $1 billion for a period of 6 months or more. Therefore, beginning April 1, 2009, the SIPC reinstituted an assessment rate of 1 quarter of 1 percent (or .0025) per annum of the net operating revenues from the

---

[28] See the discussion in chapter 1, "The Securities Industry," for more information on the SIPC.

[29] The Dodd-Frank Act amended the Securities Investor Protection Act in several areas. Two areas pertain to the SIPC assessment imposed on broker-dealers. See the SIPC website at www.sipc.org/for-members for more information and for the SIPC-7 form.

securities business, without regard to any minimum assessment. At its meeting in September 2016, SIPC's board of directors determined the assessment rate for 2017 would be .0015 of net operating revenue, beginning on January 1, 2017. SIPC has issued two letters regarding the member assessment, both are available at www.sipc.org/for-members/assessment-rate. Specific forms and instructions were created for broker-dealers with fiscal year-ends prior to December 31, 2017, that address the assessment rate change. SIPC assessment forms and payments are due semiannually based on the member's fiscal year-end.

3.163 Membership in the SIPC is automatic upon SEC registration for a broker-dealer, with three exceptions. The SIPC members' website notes that persons registered as a broker-dealer only because it effects transactions in security futures products on a registered exchange are excluded from SIPC membership. In addition, broker-dealers whose business is exclusively the distribution of shares of mutual funds, the sale of variable annuities, the business of insurance, or the business of furnishing investment advice to investment companies or insurance company separate accounts are excluded from membership in the SIPC. Finally, those broker-dealers whose principal place of business, in the determination of the SIPC, is outside the United States and its territories are excluded from membership.

3.164 As approved by the SEC in March 2016, SIPC Rule 600, *Rules Relating to Supplemental Report of SIPC Membership*, requires that a registered broker-dealer file a report, covered by an independent accountants' report, supplemental to the annual audited statement report concerning the status of the broker-dealer's membership in SIPC. This requirement applies to broker-dealers who are not exempt from the audit requirement of SEC Rule 17a-5 and whose gross revenues are in excess of $500,000. The general assessment reconciliation form (SIPC-7) should be submitted only to SIPC (effective March 31, 2016) no later than 60 days after fiscal year-end. The supplemental report should cover the SIPC annual general assessment reconciliation or exclusion from membership forms (SIPC-3) and should include certain procedures specified in SIPC Rule 600.[30]

Reports on Agreed-Upon Procedures for Distributions

3.165 Broker-dealers distribute securities of government-sponsored entities. In connection with those activities, government-sponsored entities may require that broker-dealers have their auditors issue reports on agreed-upon procedures concerning compliance with selling-agreement covenants.

PCAOB Accounting Support Fee

3.166 In order to fund the activities of the PCAOB, SOX provided that funds to cover its annual budget (less registration and annual fees paid by public accounting firms) would be collected from issuers based on each issuer's relative average monthly equity market capitalization. This amount collected is referred to as an accounting support fee.

3.167 As previously discussed, the Dodd-Frank Act amended SOX to grant the PCAOB oversight authority with respect to audits of registered

---

[30] SIPC maintains Member FAQs which include questions and answers regarding SIPC forms, membership, and how and where to file reports. The FAQs can be found at www.sipc.org/for-members/member-faqs.

broker-dealers. To provide funds for the PCAOB's oversight of these audits, the Dodd-Frank Act further amended SOX to require the PCAOB to allocate a portion of the accounting support fee to be collected among broker-dealers, or classes of broker-dealers, based on their relative net capital.

3.168 In order to comply with the provisions of the Dodd-Frank Act, amendments to the PCAOB funding rules[31] were made to

- establish classes of broker-dealers.
- describe the methods of allocating the appropriate portion of the accounting support fee to each broker-dealer within each class.
- address the collection of the assessed share of the broker-dealer accounting support fee.

3.169 The accounting support fee has been divided into an issuer accounting support fee and a broker-dealer accounting support fee. Affiliated entities may be allocated separate shares of both the issuer and broker-dealer accounting support fee.

3.170 The broker-dealer accounting support fee assessed is based on the average tentative net capital reported at the end of the calendar quarters during the previous calendar year. *Tentative net capital* is defined in the PCAOB amendment to have the same meaning as that term has in SEC Rule 15c3-1(c)(15). Two classes of broker-dealers have been established:

- Those with average quarterly tentative net capital greater than $5 million
- Those with average quarterly tentative net capital less than or equal to $5 million or those broker-dealers not filing audited financial statements pursuant to an SEC rule or other action of the SEC or its staff

3.171 The total accounting support fee to be allocated to broker-dealers will be determined each year by the PCAOB and will be allocated to broker-dealers with tentative net capital greater than $5 million based on the broker-dealer's proportional share of the total tentative net capital of that class of broker-dealers. The second class of broker-dealers, which includes those with tentative net capital below the $5 million threshold, will be allocated a share of the broker-dealer accounting support fee of zero under current rules. Assigning a broker-dealer a share of the accounting support fee equal to zero when its tentative net capital is less than $5 million does not affect the board's oversight of the audits of that broker-dealer. See the PCAOB website for more information on the assessment and collection of the broker-dealer accounting support fee.

Additional Requirements for Registered Investment Advisers

3.172 The Investment Advisers Act of 1940 provides for the registration and regulation of most persons who render investment advice to individuals or institutions for compensation. Under Section 2(a)(20) of the Investment Company Act of 1940, an *investment adviser* is a company providing investment

---

[31] For more information see PCAOB Release No. 2011-002 at http://pcaobus.org/Rules/Rulemaking/Docket033/PCAOB_Release_2011-002_Rules.pdf.

advice, research, and often administrative and similar services for a contractually agreed-on fee, based on a percentage of net assets.

3.173 A broker-dealer who is also a registered investment adviser (also known as a dual-registered entity) may be subject to significant requirements as found in Rule 206(4)-2 of the Investment Advisers Act of 1940. Paragraph (a)(4) of Rule 206(4)-2 requires that all registered investment advisers (or an investment adviser required to register) who have custody of client funds or securities, as defined, have an independent public accountant that is registered with, and subject to, inspection by the PCAOB, conduct an examination on a surprise basis once every calendar year. The surprise examination requirement applies even when assets are maintained by an independent qualified custodian. This surprise examination is conducted under AT-C section 315, *Compliance Attestation* (AICPA, *Professional Standards*).

3.174 The independent public accountant must also file a certificate on Form ADV-E with the SEC within 120 days of the time chosen for the surprise examination by the independent public accountant stating that it has examined the funds and securities and describing the nature and extent of the examination. The independent accountant, upon finding any material discrepancies during the course of the examination, should notify the SEC within one business day of the finding by means of a facsimile transmission or email, followed by first class mail, directed to the attention of the Director of the Office of Compliance Inspections and Examinations. See Rule 206(4)-2(a)(4)(ii) under the Investment Advisers Act of 1940. For purposes of the surprise examination, a *material discrepancy* is material noncompliance with the provisions of either Rule 206(4)-2 or Rule 204-2(b) under the Investment Advisers Act of 1940. Instructions from the SEC for sending independent accountant notification of material discrepancies found during annual surprise examination can be found at www.sec.gov/about/offices/ocie/awc-instructions.htm.

3.175 The SEC has released frequently asked questions about the custody rule that can be located at www.sec.gov/divisions/investment/custody_faq_030510.htm.

3.176 The rule defines *custody* to mean an investment adviser or its related person holding, directly or indirectly, client funds or securities or having any authority to obtain possession of them. Rule 206(4)-2(d)(2) provides that an adviser will not be deemed to have custody of client assets held with a qualified custodian that is a related person of the adviser if the adviser does not provide advice with respect to such assets. Note that custody does not equate to serving as a qualified custodian under the rule. Custody includes possession of client funds or securities (but not of checks drawn by clients and made payable to third parties) unless the investment adviser receives them inadvertently and returns them to the sender promptly but in any case within three business days of receiving them.

- any arrangement (including a general power of attorney) under which the investment adviser is authorized or permitted to withdraw client funds or securities maintained with a custodian upon the investment adviser's instruction to the custodian.

- any capacity (such as general partner of a limited partnership, managing member of a limited liability company or a comparable position for another type of pooled investment vehicle, or trustee of a trust) that gives the investment adviser or his or her supervised person legal ownership of, or access to, client funds or securities.

3.177 A *qualified custodian* is defined by the rule as (*a*) a *bank*, as defined in Section 202(a)(2) of the Investment Advisers Act of 1940, or a *savings association*, as defined in Section 3(b)(1) of the Federal Deposit Insurance Act, that has deposits insured by the FDIC under the Federal Deposit Insurance Act; (*b*) a broker-dealer registered under Section 15(b)(1) of the 1934 Act holding the client assets in customer accounts; (*c*) an FCM registered under Section 4f(a) of the Commodity Exchange Act holding the client assets in customer accounts, but only with respect to clients' funds and security futures, or other securities incidental to transactions in contracts for the purchase or sale of a commodity for future delivery and options thereon; and (*d*) a foreign financial institution that customarily holds financial assets for its customers, provided that the foreign financial institution keeps the advisory clients' assets in customer accounts segregated from its proprietary assets. Additionally, *related person* is defined in the rule as any person, directly or indirectly, controlling or controlled by the investment adviser, and any person who is under common control with the investment adviser.

3.178 Rule 206(4)-2 requires that a qualified custodian maintain client funds and securities in a separate account for each client under that client's name or in accounts that contain only the clients' funds and securities under the adviser's name as agent or trustee for the clients. Notice to clients must be provided when an account is opened (and following any changes) with a qualified custodian on their behalf that details the qualified custodian's name, address, and the manner in which the funds or securities are maintained. The investment adviser must also have a reasonable basis, after due inquiry, for believing that the qualified custodian sends an account statement, at least quarterly, to each of the investment advisers' clients for which it maintains funds or securities. See Rule 206(4)-2(b) under the Investment Advisers Act of 1940 for more information and exceptions to these requirements for shares of mutual funds, certain privately offered securities, fee deductions, limited partnerships subject to annual audit, registered investment companies, and certain related persons.

3.179 Additionally, if the broker-dealer who is a registered investment adviser, or its related person, maintains client funds or securities as a qualified custodian in connection with advisory services provided to clients, Rule 206(4)-2(a)(6) requires that such investment adviser must at least once each calendar year obtain or receive from its related person a written internal control report related to its, or its affiliates' custodial services, including the safeguarding of funds and securities, which includes an opinion from an independent public accountant that is registered with, and subject to regular inspection by, the PCAOB. A broker-dealer may be able to use the compliance examination report that is required pursuant to SEC Rule 17a-5 to satisfy this internal control report requirement.[32]

3.180 This requirement could also be satisfied with a type 2 SOC 1® report[33] (formerly known as a type 2 SAS No. 70 report) or an examination

---

[32] See footnote 2.

[33] This guide refers to this type of report prepared under AT-C section 320, *Reporting on an Examination of Controls at a Service Organization Relevant to User Entities' Internal Control Over Financial Reporting* (AICPA, *Professional Standards*), as a SOC 1 report.

on internal control conducted in accordance with AT-C section 320, *Reporting on an Examination of Controls at a Service Organization Relevant to User Entities' Internal Control Over Financial Reporting* (AICPA, *Professional Standards*). Also, see question XIII.3 of the SEC's "Staff Responses to Questions About the Custody Rule," available at the "Frequently Asked Questions" section of the SEC website. This internal control report must include an opinion on whether controls have been placed in operation as of a specific date and are suitably designed and operating effectively to meet control objectives relating to custodial services, including the safeguarding of funds and securities held by either the investment adviser or its related person on behalf of the advisory clients during the year. The accountant must also verify that the funds and securities are reconciled to a custodian (for example, the Depository Trust and Clearing Corporation) other than the investment adviser or its related person. The accountant's tests of the custodian's reconciliation should include either direct confirmation, on a test basis, with unaffiliated custodians or other procedures designed to verify that the data used in the reconciliations performed by the qualified custodian is obtained from unaffiliated custodians and is unaltered. Refer to the AICPA Audit and Accounting Guide *Investment Companies* for more information on guidance related to investment advisers and for example illustrative reports required for broker-dealers that are registered as investment advisers under the act. Example illustrative reports are also posted on the AICPA website in the "Industry Expert Panels—Investment Company" section at www.aicpa.org/InterestAreas/FRC/IndustryInsights/Pages/Expert_Panel_Investment_Companies.aspx.

Rules Applicable to Broker-Dealers in Commodities and U.S. Government Securities

3.181 The following are the primary regulations under the Commodity Exchange Act[34] and rules under the Government Securities Act of 1986 that are currently applicable to the audit of broker-dealers in commodities and government securities.

Commodities Brokers[35]

3.182 Certain sections of the Commodity Exchange Act and CFTC regulations have been, or are in the process of, being revised, as required by the

---

[34] The Dodd-Frank Act amended the Commodity Exchange Act such that a person, including a broker-dealer, for which there is a federal regulatory agency (such as the CFTC and the SEC, among others), should not enter into or offer to enter into certain foreign exchange transactions (commonly referred to as retail forex transactions) with a person who is not an *eligible contract participant*, as defined by the act, except pursuant to a rule or regulation of a federal regulatory agency allowing the transaction under terms it prescribes. The transactions include an agreement, a contract, or a transaction in foreign currency that is a contract of sale of a commodity for future delivery (or an option on such a contract) or an option (other than an option executed or traded on a national securities exchange registered pursuant to Section 6(a) of the 1934 Act). In July 2013, the SEC issued Final Rule 34-69964, *Retail Foreign Exchange Transactions*, which allows a registered broker-dealer to engage in retail forex business until July 31, 2016, provided that the broker-dealer complies with the 1934 Act rules and the rules of the self-regulatory organizations of which it is a member. The SEC adopted this rule, SEC Rule 15b12-1, substantially in the form previously adopted as an interim final temporary rule. The rule expired on July 31, 2016.

[35] Further information regarding regulatory considerations for entities that are registered with the CFTC is included in "Regulatory Considerations for Entities Registered with the Commodity Futures Trading Commission," as issued by the AICPA on November 1, 2015, available at www.aicpa.org/InterestAreas/FRC/IndustryInsights/DownloadableDocuments/BRD/CFTC_Reg_Considerations.pdf.

Dodd-Frank Act or in response to recent industry developments. An FCM is generally defined by CFTC regulations as an entity that solicits or accepts orders from customers for the purchase or sale of any commodity for future delivery or a swap and accepts funds from such customers to margin or secure such transactions. CFTC regulations generally define an IB as an entity that solicits or accepts customer orders for the purchase or sale of any commodity for future delivery or a swap. The main differences between an FCM and an IB are that the IB is prohibited from carrying customer funds. In addition, the capital requirements for FCMs are substantially greater than the capital requirements for an IB due to their different market roles. As of the date of this guide, the sections of the Commodity Exchange Act and CFTC regulations applicable to FCMs, with certain regulations also applicable to IBs, are as follows:

- Section 4d(a)(2), "Segregation requirements"
- Section 4d(f), "Cleared swaps customer collateral"
- Section 4f(b), "Minimum financial requirements"
- Part 1 (Title 17 U.S. *Code of Federal Regulations* [CFR] Ch 1 Part 1—General Regulations Under the Commodity Exchange Act) including the following:

    — Regulation 1.10, "Financial reports of futures commission merchants and introducing brokers"

    — Regulation 1.11, "Risk management program for futures commission merchants"

    — Regulation 1.12, "Maintenance of minimum financial requirements by futures commission merchants and introducing brokers"

    — Regulation 1.14, "Risk assessment recordkeeping requirements for futures commission merchants"

    — Regulation 1.15, "Risk assessment reporting requirements for futures commission merchants"

    — Regulation 1.16, "Qualifications and reports of accountants"

    — Regulation 1.17, "Minimum financial requirements for futures commission merchants and introducing brokers" (also see NFA financial requirements)

    — Regulation 1.18, "Records for and relating to financial reporting and monthly computation by futures commission merchants and introducing brokers"

    — Regulations 1.20–1.30, collectively titled "Customers' Money, Securities, and Property"

    — Regulations 1.31–1.37, collectively titled "Recordkeeping"

    — Regulation 1.49, "Denomination of customer funds and location of depositories"

- Part 22 (17 CFR Ch 1 Part 22), Cleared Swaps
- Part 23 (17 CFR Ch 1 Part 23), Swap Dealers and Major Swap Participants

- Part 30 (17 CFR Ch 1 Part 30—Foreign Futures and Foreign Options Transactions), including Regulation 30.7, *Treatment of foreign futures or foreign options secured amount*
- Part 32 (17 CFR Ch 1 Part 32), Regulation of Commodity Option Transactions
- Part 140 (17 CFR Ch 1 Part 140), Organization, Functions, and Procedures of the Commission

Government Securities Broker-Dealers

3.183 The following are applicable to government securities broker-dealers under 17 CFR Chapter IV:

- Part 402, "Financial Responsibility"
- Part 403, "Protection of Customer Securities and Balances"
- Part 404, "Recordkeeping and Preservation of Records"
- Part 405, "Reports and Audit"

OTC Derivatives Dealers

3.184 An alternative regulatory framework has been created for OTC derivatives dealers.[36] The rules establish a special class of broker-dealers who may choose to register with the SEC under a limited regulatory structure. An OTC derivatives dealer's securities activities are limited to (*a*) engaging in dealer activities in *eligible OTC derivative instruments*, as defined in Rule 3b-13, that are securities; (*b*) issuing and reacquiring securities that are issued by the dealer, including warrants or securities, hybrid securities, and structured notes; (*c*) engaging in cash management securities activities as set out in Rule 3b-14; (*d*) engaging in *ancillary portfolio management securities activities*, as defined in Rule 3b-15; and (*e*) engaging in such other securities activities that the SEC designates by order.

3.185 The rules and rule amendments tailor capital, margin, and other broker-dealer regulatory requirements to OTC derivatives dealers. These tailored requirements include an alternative net capital regime, exemptions from certain provisions of the 1934 Act, and modified rules governing recordkeeping and reporting, substantially the same as for fully regulated broker-dealers, but tailored to the business of OTC derivatives dealers. New rules adopted under the 1934 Act include Rules 3b-12, 3b-13, 3b-14, 3b-15, 11a1-6, 15a-1, 15b9-2, 15c3-4, 17a-12, 36a1-1, and 36a1-2. Various 1934 Act rules have been amended, and Form X-17A-5 was revised.

Swap Dealers and Swaps Marketplace Participants

3.186 In 2010, Congress passed legislation tasking the SEC and CFTC with creating a regulatory regime to govern this multitrillion dollar market. The Dodd-Frank Act assigned the CFTC responsibility for "swaps" and the SEC responsibility for a portion of the market known as "security-based swaps,"

---

[36] The Dodd-Frank Act includes provisions related to the OTC derivatives market that will significantly change the regulatory framework of that market. Rulemaking to implement these provisions is ongoing as of the date of this guide. In February 2017, the president signed an executive order that sets in motion scaling back some of the provisions of the Dodd-Frank Act. Readers should be alert for further developments.

which include, for example, swaps based on a security, such as a stock or a bond, or a credit default swap. This regulatory regime is intended to make this market more transparent, efficient and accessible. The rules and regulations developed by both the CFTC and SEC include, but are not limited to, registration, capital and margin requirements, as well as recordkeeping and reporting requirements.[37]

Annual Compliance Certification

3.187 FINRA Rule 3130, *Annual Certification of Compliance and Supervisory Processes*, requires members to designate a chief compliance officer (CCO) and have the CEO or equivalent officer certify annually that the member has in place processes to establish, maintain, review, test, and modify written compliance policies and written supervisory procedures reasonably designed to achieve compliance with applicable FINRA rules, Municipal Securities Rulemaking Board rules, and federal securities laws and regulations, and that the CEO has conducted 1 or more meetings with the CCO in the preceding 12 months to discuss such processes. Additional information is available on the FINRA website at http://finra.complinet.com/en/display/display_main.html?rbid=2403&element_id=6286.

3.188 FCMs that are regulated by a U.S. prudential regulator or that are also in some capacity registrants of the SEC must also have a designated CCO under CFTC Regulation 3.3, and that person must also be a listed principal of the firm. In addition, FCMs are required to file a CCO Annual Report. Introducing brokers, commodity pool operators, and commodity trading adviser members are not required to have a designated CCO. However, if the firm appoints a person as a CCO then the person must be a listed principal of the firm.

---

[37] For more information regarding swaps rulemaking, refer to the CFTC (www.cftc.gov/LawRegulation/DoddFrankAct/index.htm) and SEC (www.sec.gov/rules/rulemaking-index.shtml) websites.

Chapter 4

Internal Control

Introduction

4.01 Internal control is not one event or circumstance, but a dynamic, iterative, and integrated process. It is not a one-time task because the impact of an entity's internal and external activities is not static but is continually changing. The entity's policies reflect management or board statements of what should be done to effect internal control. These statements may be explicitly stated in management communication or implied through management actions and decisions.

4.02 The Committee of Sponsoring Organizations of the Treadway Commission (COSO) defines *internal control* as a process, effected by an entity's board of directors, management, and other personnel, designed to provide reasonable assurance regarding the achievement of objectives relating to operations, reporting, and compliance.

4.03 In May 2013, COSO published an update to the 1992 *Internal Control—Integrated Framework* (the framework). The updates became necessary due to the increasing complexity of businesses since the original framework was published. The changes were intended to make the framework easier for management to use while, at the same time, allowing management to meet the entity's financial and operations goals. The discussion of internal control in this guide recognizes the definition and description of internal control contained in the framework.

4.04 The following are the five components and seventeen underlying principles of internal control from the framework:

    a. *The control environment.* Sets the tone of an organization, influencing the control consciousness of its people. It is the foundation for all other components of internal control, providing discipline and structure.

        (1) Demonstrates commitment to integrity and ethical values

        (2) Exercises oversight responsibility

        (3) Establishes structure, authority and responsibility

        (4) Demonstrates commitment to competence

        (5) Enforces accountability

    b. *Risk assessment.* The entity's process for identifying and analyzing relevant risks to achievement of its objectives, forming a basis for determining how the risks should be managed.

        (6) Specifies suitable objectives

        (7) Identifies and analyzes risk

        (8) Assesses fraud risk

        (9) Identifies and analyzes significant change

    c. *Control activities.* The policies and procedures that help ensure that management directives are carried out.

        (10) Selects and develops control activities

    (11) Selects and develops general controls over technology

    (12) Deploys through policies and procedures

d. *Information and communication.* These systems support the identification, capture, and exchange of information in a form and time frame that enable people to carry out their responsibilities.

    (13) Uses relevant information

    (14) Communicates internally

    (15) Communicates externally

e. *Monitoring activities.* A process that assesses the quality of internal control performance over time. This is accomplished through ongoing evaluations, separate evaluations, or some combination of the two.

    (16) Conducts ongoing and/or separate evaluations

    (17) Evaluates and communicates deficiencies

4.05 An effective system of internal control provides reasonable assurance regarding the achievement of an entity's objectives. Because internal control is relevant both to the entity and its subsidiaries, an effective system of internal control may relate to a specific part of the organizational structure. An effective system of internal control reduces, to an acceptable level, the risk of not achieving an objective relating to one or more categories. It requires that

- each of the five components of internal control and relevant principles are present and functioning, and
- the five components are operating together in an integrated manner.

4.06 When a major deficiency exists with respect to the presence and functioning of a component, or relevant principle, or in terms of the components operating together, the organization cannot conclude that it has met the requirements for an effective system of internal control.

The Control Environment

4.07 The control environment sets the tone of an organization, influencing the control consciousness of its people. It is the foundation for all other components of internal control, providing discipline and structure. The principles of the control environment are as follows:

- The organization demonstrates a commitment to integrity and ethical values.
- The board of directors demonstrates independence from management and exercises oversight of the development and performance of internal control.
- Management establishes, with board oversight, structures, reporting lines, and appropriate authorities and responsibilities in the pursuit of objectives.
- The organization demonstrates a commitment to attract, develop, and retain competent individuals in alignment with objectives.
- The organization holds individuals accountable for their internal control responsibilities in the pursuit of objectives.

4.08 The control environment comprises the conditions under which the broker-dealer's information and communication system, the risk assessment process, monitoring, and control activities are designed, implemented, and function.

4.09 The control environment represents the collective effect of various factors on the overall effectiveness of the broker-dealer's internal control. These factors include the following:

- Management's personal characteristics, philosophy, and operating style and their commitment to accurate financial reporting have a significant influence on the control environment, particularly if management is dominated by one or a few individuals. A positive tone at the top is an important prerequisite for accurate and complete financial reporting. In a broker-dealer, compliance and control over legal matters and regulatory compliance are important indicators of the overall philosophy held by senior management. Management's approach to taking and monitoring business risks and its commitment to accurate financial reporting are other indications of the tone at the top. Management's commitment to accurate financial reporting may influence the activities of employees throughout the organization. Likewise, the types of activities that a broker-dealer engages in (securities they sell, revenue streams they generate, and the like), as well as the amount of risk management is willing to take, affect the operating style. For example, the following business activities may affect management's operating style:

  — Carrying customer accounts and clearing trades

  — Introducing customers to clearing brokers and managing customer funds

  — Investment banking and private placements

  — Market makers

- The external business and regulatory environment requires management to establish and maintain effective internal control in a broker-dealer. For example, examinations by self-regulatory bodies and their enforcement powers, as well as review of compliance reports by the SEC and other governmental bodies, require management of broker-dealers to establish effective controls. In addition, regulatory minimum books and records requirements mandate that certain control activities be in place and documented. Additionally, Financial Industry Regulatory Authority (FINRA) rules require every broker-dealer to establish and maintain a system to supervise the activities of personnel, including developing and maintaining a set of supervisory control procedures that will reasonably ensure compliance with FINRA and SEC rules and regulations. The supervisory procedures are required to be written and annually certified by the broker-dealer. A broker-dealer's written supervisory procedures and related annual certification may provide valuable summary information about the broker-dealer's compliance controls.

- Management's commitment to designing and maintaining reliable accounting and stock record systems has a significant influence on the control environment. A low level of management concern about acceptable business practices, as well as deficiencies in controls, may lead a broker-dealer's employees either to adopt a similarly low level of concern or attempt to take advantage of deficient controls. The reliability of information systems and the effectiveness of controls may be impaired as a result. Personnel policies may enhance or inhibit the competence and continuity of the broker-dealer's employees. An inadequate or incompetent staff that is unable to process transactions and perform control activities may lead to a reduction in the reliability of information systems and the effectiveness of controls. Management's commitment could be indicated through the broker-dealer's policies with respect to:

  — Systems security (including logical access and change management controls)

  — Trading limits

  — Sales practices

  — Hiring and training practices

- Management's ability to control the business also influences the control environment. In addition, the responsibilities of those charged with governance are of considerable importance, including the independence of the directors, their ability to evaluate the actions of management, and whether there is a group of those charged with governance that understands the entity's business transactions and evaluates whether the financial statements are presented fairly in accordance with accounting principles generally accepted in the United States of America (GAAP). The control environment will generally be stronger when those charged with governance take an active role in overseeing a broker-dealer's accounting and financial reporting practices, as well as those practices regarding the prevention of illegal acts and compliance with laws and regulations. The broker-dealer's management demonstrates control of the business through:

  — The broker-dealer's organizational and governance structures

  — The methods used by the broker-dealer in assigning authority and responsibility

  — The ability of the broker-dealer's management to supervise and monitor operations effectively

  — The methods used by senior management to monitor and control the effectiveness of the accounting system and controls

Risk Assessment for Financial Reporting Purposes

4.10   A broker-dealer's risk assessment for financial reporting purposes is its identification, analysis, and management of risks relevant to the preparation of financial statements that are fairly presented in conformity with GAAP. For example, risk assessment may address how the broker-dealer considers the possibility of unrecorded transactions or identifies and analyzes significant estimates recorded in the financial statements. Risks relevant to reliable financial reporting also relate to specific events or transactions. Risks relevant to financial reporting include external and internal events and circumstances that may occur and adversely affect a broker-dealer's ability to initiate, authorize, record, process, and report financial data consistent with the assertions of management in the financial statements. The purpose of a broker-dealer's risk assessment is to identify, analyze, and manage risks that affect the broker-dealer's objectives. The principles of risk assessment are as follows:

- The organization specifies objectives with sufficient clarity to enable the identification and assessment of risks relating to objectives.

- The organization identifies risks to the achievement of its objectives across the entity and analyzes risks as a basis for determining how the risks should be managed.

- The organization considers the potential for fraud in assessing risks to the achievement of objectives.

- The organization identifies and assesses changes that could significantly impact the system of internal control.

4.11 Once risks are identified, management considers their significance and the likelihood of their occurrence, and decides upon actions to manage them. Management may initiate plans, programs, or actions to address specific risks, or they may decide to accept a risk because of cost or other considerations. Risks can arise or change due to circumstances such as the following:

- *Changes in operating environment.* Changes in the operating environment can result in changes in competitive pressures and significantly different risks.

- *Changes in regulatory environment.* Changes to regulations around net capital, protection of customer assets, and financial reporting requirements can create new risks related to regulatory compliance.

- *New personnel.* New personnel may have a different focus on or understanding of internal control.

- *New or revamped information systems.* Significant and rapid changes in information systems can change the risk relating to internal control.

- *Rapid growth.* Significant and rapid expansion of operations can strain controls and increase the risk of a breakdown in controls.

- *New technology.* Incorporating new technologies into operating processes or information systems may change the risk associated with internal control.

- *New business models, products, or activities.* Entering into business areas or transactions with which a broker-dealer has little experience may introduce new risks associated with internal control.

- *Corporate restructurings*. Restructurings may be accompanied by staff reductions and changes in supervision and segregation of duties that may change the risk associated with internal control.

- *Expanded foreign operations*. The expansion or acquisition of foreign operations carries new and often unique risks that may affect internal control (for example, additional or changed risks from foreign currency transactions).

- *New accounting pronouncements*. Adoption of new accounting principles or changing accounting principles may affect risks in preparing financial statements.

- *Changes in economic conditions*. Changes in economic conditions can increase manipulation of earnings and inappropriate management override of internal control.

4.12 Broker-dealers devote a significant amount of time and resources toward the identification, quantification, analysis, and control of risk. A broker-dealer's control and monitoring activities are concerned with mitigating business risks and exposures. Risk refers to the likelihood that a loss might occur, whereas exposure refers to an amount (or other element) at risk. The decision to incur business risk rests with the broker-dealer's management. The following is an overview of the major risks and exposures facing a broker-dealer.

4.13 *Operational risk*. Operational risk arises in processing broker-dealer transactions. Exposure can be created by a failure to either process transactions properly or safeguard securities adequately. If operational risk is properly managed, other risks will be mitigated. In viewing operational exposure, it is important to look at the broad exposure within particular accounts, such as suspense accounts, difference accounts, reconciling items (for any accounts), and aged transfers and fails. For instance, within a particular suspense account, the exposure is frequently not the net balance in the account. A more accurate view of exposure is to identify debit-only items (no related security positions), short-fair-value-only items (no related money balance), debit money with long fair value, and credit money with short fair value. By viewing each of those items separately, it is easier to understand the total exposure.

4.14 *Credit risk*. Credit risk refers to potential losses arising from the failure of another party to perform according to the terms of a contract (counterparty default).

4.15 Credit risk can be customer- or broker-related, or related to financial instrument inventory. The exposure to the broker-dealer is for the amount of extended credit that is not fully collateralized. Therefore, obtaining adequate collateral from the counterparty could help minimize credit risk. An extension of credit can result in any of the following transactions: margin transactions, cash transactions prior to settlement, stock borrows and resale agreements, swaps, futures, forwards, options, and similar items. Broker-dealers will usually have credit committees that set limits for total credit lines, exposure, and collateral requirements for any particular counterparty. Broker-dealers with over $20 million in capital or $1 million of customer credit items must have formally documented policies, procedures or controls over credit risk.

4.16 *Market risk*. Market risk refers to potential losses from fluctuations in market prices that may make a financial instrument less valuable or more onerous. A change in market price may occur (for example, for interest-bearing financial instruments) because of changes in general interest rates (interest rate risk), changes in the relationship between general and specific market interest rates (an aspect of credit risk), or changes in the rates of exchange between currencies (foreign exchange risk). Broker-dealers may have risk committees that establish trading limits in order to manage market risk. Broker-dealers with over $20 million in capital or $1 million of customer credit items must have formally documented policies, procedures or controls over market risk.

4.17 *Litigation risk.* Litigation risk refers to the risk of losses resulting from lawsuits and the cost of defending against such claims. Lawsuits can arise from the various aspects of the broker-dealer's business. Areas of particular concern include underwriting activities, employment matters, and the maintenance of customer accounts. Broker-dealers can help mitigate litigation risk in many ways, including the following:

- Establishing policies regarding a code of professional conduct, the employer's responsibilities, and due diligence and establishing a system to monitor compliance with such policies

- Establishing a compliance function to review the activities of the sales departments and branch office operations

4.18 *Regulatory risk.* Regulatory risk refers to potential losses that might arise for failing to comply with applicable statutes, regulations, and rules. Broker-dealers operate in a highly regulated industry that requires close attention to compliance matters. Not only may such matters affect a broker-dealer's reputation and growth, but noncompliance may also lead to fines, limitation on activities the broker-dealer is allowed to carry out, or even the suspension or revocation of the broker-dealer's registration.

4.19 *Liquidity and funding risk.* Liquidity and funding risk refers to a broker-dealer's ability to secure funding to satisfy its settlement or other obligations. Market and other factors may affect the broker-dealer's ability to secure funding to satisfy its obligations. Understanding and evaluating this issue, especially in a highly competitive or unstable market, is important in assessing the going-concern assumption. Broker-dealers with over $20 million in capital or $1 million of customer credit items must have formally documented policies, procedures or controls over liquidity risk.

Control Activities

4.20 *Control activities* serve as a mechanism for managing and achieving a broker-dealer's objectives. Control activities support one or more operations, reporting, and compliance objectives. The principles of control activities are as follows:

- The organization selects and develops control activities that contribute to the mitigation of risks to the achievement of objectives to acceptable levels.

- The organization selects and develops general control activities over technology to support the achievement of objectives.

- The organization deploys control activities through policies that establish what is expected and procedures that put policies into action.

4.21 Control activities, whether automated or manual, support all the components of internal control and are particularly aligned with the risk assessment component at various organizational and functional levels. Each entity has its own set of objectives and implementation approaches. Each control activity is designed to accomplish a specific control objective for relevant business processes, information technology, and locations where control activities are needed. Control activities need to be designed in a way to ensure that duties are divided and segregated to reduce the risk of error or inappropriate or fraudulent actions. Control activities that directly support the actions to mitigate transaction processing risks usually include the following:

- *Authorizations and approvals.* Control activities intended to reasonably ensure that transactions are valid and approved before they are executed and recorded.

- *Verification.* Control activities designed to reasonably ensure that two or more items match with each other and are consistent with a respective policy.

- *Physical controls.* Control activities that are designed to protect against unauthorized acquisition, use, or disposal of assets, including customer-related assets.

- *Controls over standing data.* Control activities intended to reasonably ensure that master files supporting business processes (for example, price, positions, and location) are populated, updated, and maintained.

- *Reconciliations.* Control activities designed to reasonably ensure that books and records agree with external and internal records.

- *Supervisory controls.* Control activities intended to reasonably ensure that other transaction control activities are being performed completely, accurately, and in accordance with policies and procedures.

4.22 The reliability of technology within business processes, including automated controls, depends on the selection, development and deployment of general control activities over technology which include control activities over the technology infrastructure, security management, and technology acquisition, development, and maintenance.

4.23 Many of the activities of broker-dealers are unique and require comprehensive policies and procedures. Policies and procedures help to ensure that management directives are carried out and necessary actions are taken to address risks to the achievement of the broker-dealer's objectives. Policies and procedures are communicated either orally or in writing. They establish clear responsibility and accountability of management and personnel for specific control activities. Policies and procedures typically reflect the following:

- Timeliness of a control activity

- Competency and authority of personnel assigned to perform a control activity

- Applicability of corrective actions based on investigation results

- Periodic reassessment of control activities for continued relevance and effectiveness

Information and Communication

4.24 An information system consists of infrastructure (physical and hardware components), software, people, procedures (manual and automated), and data. Infrastructure and software will be absent or have less significance in systems that are exclusively or primarily manual. Many information systems, particularly within the financial services industry, make extensive use of IT. Communication involves providing an understanding of individual roles and responsibilities pertaining to internal control over financial reporting. It includes the extent to which personnel understand how their activities in the financial reporting information system relate to the work of others and the means of reporting exceptions to an appropriate higher level within the broker-dealer. Open communication channels help ensure that exceptions are reported and acted on. The principles of the information and communication system are as follows:

- The organization obtains or generates and uses relevant, quality information to support the functioning of internal control.

- The organization internally communicates information, including objectives and responsibilities for internal control, necessary to support the functioning of internal control.

- The organization communicates with external parties regarding matters affecting the functioning of internal control.

4.25 The information system relevant to financial reporting objectives, which includes the accounting system, consists of the procedures, whether IT or manual, and records established to initiate, authorize, record, process, and report the broker-dealer's transactions (as well as events and conditions) and to maintain accountability for the related assets, liabilities, and equity. Transactions may be initiated manually or automatically by programmed procedures. Authorization includes the process of approving transactions by the appropriate level of management. Recording includes identifying and capturing the relevant information for transactions or events. Processing includes functions such as edit and validation, calculation, measurement, valuation, summarization, and reconciliation, whether performed by IT or manual procedures. Reporting relates to the preparation of financial reports, as well as other information, in electronic or printed format that the entity uses in measuring and reviewing the entity's financial performance and in other functions. The accuracy and completeness of system-generated information affects management's ability to make appropriate decisions in managing and controlling the broker-dealer's activities and to prepare reliable financial reports. Accordingly, an information system encompasses methods and records that

- identify and record all valid transactions.

- describe, on a timely basis, the transactions in sufficient detail to permit proper classification of transactions for financial reporting.

- measure the value of transactions in a manner that permits recording their proper monetary value in the financial statements.

- determine the time period in which transactions occurred to permit recording of transactions in the proper accounting period.

- present properly the transactions and related disclosures in the financial statements.

4.26 Communication can take the form of policy manuals, accounting and financial reporting manuals, and memoranda. Communication also can be made electronically, orally, and through the actions of management.

Information and Communication Control Activities

4.27 Application controls apply to the processing of individual applications. Accordingly, application controls relate to the use of IT to initiate, authorize, record, process, and report transactions or other financial data. These controls help ensure that transactions occurred, are authorized, and are completely and accurately recorded and processed.

4.28 Application controls may be performed by IT or individuals. When application controls are performed by people interacting with IT, they may be referred to as user controls. The effectiveness of user controls, such as reviews of computer-produced exception reports or other information produced by IT, may depend on the accuracy and completeness of the information produced.

4.29 General controls are policies and procedures that relate to many applications and support the effective functioning of application controls by helping ensure the continued proper operation of information systems. General controls commonly include controls over data center and network operations; system software acquisition and maintenance; access security; and application system acquisition, development, and maintenance.

4.30 The use of IT affects the way that control activities are implemented. For example, when IT is used in an information system, segregation of duties often is achieved by implementing security controls.

Monitoring Activities

4.31 *Monitoring* is a process that assesses the quality of an entity's internal control performance over time. It involves assessing the design and operation of controls on a timely basis and taking necessary corrective actions. The COSO principles of control monitoring are as follows:

- The organization selects, develops, and performs ongoing and/or separate evaluations to ascertain whether the components of internal control are present and functioning.

- The organization evaluates and communicates internal control deficiencies in a timely manner to those parties responsible for taking corrective action, including senior management and the board of directors, as appropriate.

4.32 The frequency with which controls are assessed depends on the significance of the risks being controlled and the importance of a particular control in reducing the risks. Higher priority risks generally will require more frequent assessment. Similarly, those controls most critical to reducing a given risk will tend to be assessed more often.

4.33 Ongoing monitoring activities are built into the normal recurring activities of a broker-dealer and include regular management and supervisory activities, comparisons, reconciliations, and other actions personnel take in performing their duties. Managers at divisional and corporate levels are in touch with operations and may question reports that differ significantly from their knowledge of operations. Usually, some combination of ongoing monitoring and separate evaluations will together ensure that internal control maintains its effectiveness over time.

4.34 In many broker-dealers, internal auditors or personnel performing similar functions contribute to the monitoring of the broker-dealer's activities through separate evaluations. They regularly provide information about the functioning of internal control, focusing considerable attention on evaluating the design and operation of internal control. They communicate information about strengths and weaknesses and recommendations for improving internal control.

4.35 Monitoring activities may include using information from communications from external parties. Customers implicitly corroborate transaction data by paying their amount owed or complaining about their charges. In addition, regulators may communicate with the broker-dealer concerning matters that affect the functioning of internal control (for example, communications regarding examinations by self-regulatory organizations). Also, management may consider communications relating to internal control from external auditors in performing monitoring activities.

4.36 In many entities, much of the information used in monitoring may be produced by the entity's information system. If management assumes that data used for monitoring are accurate and complete without having a basis for that assumption, errors may exist in the information, potentially leading management to incorrect conclusions resulting from the entity's monitoring activities.

Broker-Dealer Control and Monitoring Activities

4.37 Control and monitoring activities are generally present in the functions of a broker-dealer. Management uses such activities to mitigate business risk. This guide discusses only those control and monitoring activities that are unique to broker-dealers. The absence of any of these specific control activities is not indicative of a deficiency in internal control; however, a deficiency in internal control may exist if the overall control objective is not met.

4.38 The discussion of control and monitoring activities in this part of the chapter is from management's perspective. Management of all broker-dealers has a responsibility to establish and maintain adequate internal control over financial reporting and to comply with specific rules addressing financial responsibility and recordkeeping.

4.39 Security transactions may be processed, recorded, and monitored by different departments within the broker-dealer. Even though this discussion addresses specific broker-dealer control and monitoring activities, the presentation is general in nature and does not necessarily reflect the actual operations or departments of every broker-dealer. Control and monitoring activities performed by persons with appropriate segregation of duties provides the strongest control environment.

4.40 In many small introducing broker-dealers, individuals play several roles, including having conflicting duties that would ideally be segregated. Some mitigating factors may include

- the types of functions outsourced to third parties (for example, securities clearance, customer statement generation, financial reporting, Financial and Operations Principal [FINOP] functions, and the like),

- the owners' participation as management in the daily activities of the broker-dealer,
- a detailed review of financial performance compared to budget,
- a detailed review of the general ledger by an individual independent of recording transactions, and
- having one individual responsible for recording transactions while another individual independently receives bank and clearing broker statements that are reconciled or compared to the general ledger.

Sales and Compliance

4.41 *New accounts.* Control and monitoring activities for opening and maintaining new accounts are essential for broker-dealers. The opening of new accounts is primarily the responsibility of customer service centers and branch offices. Control and monitoring activities are designed to ensure that recorded transactions are valid, complete, and properly authorized. Broker-dealers follow various procedures (some of which are required by regulatory authorities), such as the following:

- Approving new accounts by appropriately licensed personnel and ensuring that the account file contains documentation concerning the essential facts pertaining to each customer. For instance, if the customer is a corporation, the file indicates that the person from whom the orders are accepted is duly authorized by the corporation to act on its behalf. Rules requiring such documentation, as well as related account supervision activities, are referred to as the "know-your-customer" rules. Special documentation may also be required for other accounts, such as for all customers who wish to trade options or customers who are nonresident aliens.

- Ensuring customer files contain signed copies of IRS Form W-9 and, for non-U.S. citizens, IRS Form W-8.

- Ensuring margin customers sign agreements, referred to as hypothecation agreements, that authorize the broker-dealer to use customers' securities that are not fully paid for. Broker-dealers may finance unpaid balances by borrowing money from banks or other broker-dealers, and use customer securities as collateral to the extent permissible.

- Requiring that all accounts be in the name of the customer, unless the broker-dealer has received a written statement signed by the customer attesting to his or her ownership of an account in any other name, symbol, or number.

- Mailing letters to customers requesting confirmation after being notified of changes in addresses. Some broker-dealers mail confirmation requests to the customers' last known and current addresses.

- Mailing or electronically transmitting, as appropriate, customer statements periodically (at least quarterly, or monthly if there is any activity) unless a customer has requested in writing—and a designated official has approved the request—that the statements not be mailed.

- Requiring written authorization from each customer for whom the broker-dealer carries a discretionary account, receiving the approval (from a designated person who does not exercise discretionary authority) for every trade in the discretionary account, and mailing an advice to the discretionary account customer on the date each trade is executed.

- Identifying the accounts of partners, officers, and employees and their known relatives so that transactions in such accounts can be reviewed by designated personnel.

- Obtaining written approval from another broker-dealer for opening an account of an employee of that broker-dealer.

- Ensuring policies and procedures exist and function to comply with the requirements of the Uniting and Strengthening America by Providing Appropriate Tools Required to Intercept and Obstruct Terrorism Act of 2001 (USA PATRIOT Act).

- Accurately capturing all unique customer data attributes in the broker-dealer's client reference data master files, which will serve as the source for key downstream processing.

4.42 *Order entry.* The primary objectives of the order department are to ensure that all authorized orders are directed to the proper marketplace, executed, and accurately recorded. Customer orders generate accounting entries that affect the following financial statement accounts:

- Receivables from, and payables to, customers
- Firm inventory
- Receivables from, and payables to, other broker-dealers and clearing organizations
- Principal transactions income
- Commission income and expense
- Interest income and expense on margin transactions
- Cash

4.43 Some of the control and monitoring activities typically associated with the order department include the following:

- Assigning a number to orders when placed and accounting for all order numbers.

- Reviewing the open order file, by supervisory personnel.

- Comparing trade data recorded on the customer confirmation with the order form prepared by the order department and registered representative before mailing it to the customer.

- Requiring that the execution price of an order be confirmed by the order department to the registered representative, and by the registered representative to the customer shortly after placing the order. Lack of confirmation of execution usually initiates inquiry by the registered representative or customer.

- Including a check digit in the customer account number on order forms.

- Segregating and not processing orders lacking required information, such as an invalid contra broker-dealer number.

- Verifying completed order forms.

- Not processing limit orders if the execution price is not within predetermined market limits.

- Using order forms that provide for the entry of all relevant information about an order to be processed.

- Time-stamping orders when they are placed, when they are transmitted to exchanges or trading rooms, and upon notice of execution. Disputes regarding prices can be resolved based on the time the order was placed and executed.

- Requiring orders, other than those automatically executed, to be initiated by a registered representative, placed by the order desk, executed by a trader, and confirmed by a clerk.

- Reviewing exception reports to resolve quantity and price differences.

4.44 *Sales compliance.* The compliance department is responsible for ensuring that the broker-dealer's sales activities are conducted in accordance with applicable laws and regulations. Some of the control and monitoring activities typically associated with and in connection with regulatory rules requiring adequate supervision of the sales compliance function include the following:

- Monitoring and reviewing transactions in customer accounts for suitability, particularly with respect to discretionary accounts.

- Documenting and investigating customer complaints.

- Requiring sales representatives to be registered in accordance with applicable regulations.

- Monitoring and reviewing transactions in employee accounts.

- Requiring a cash transaction reporting form to be completed for all receipts of funds, in conformity with anti-money laundering rules and regulations, including the Bank Secrecy Act.

- Reviewing proprietary transactions to identify transactions that may violate prohibitions on insider trading or represent manipulative and deceptive practices.

- Monitoring and actively reviewing closed accounts or inactive accounts.

- Generating and then reviewing exception reports that highlight unusual activity.

- Reviewing sales and advertising literature to ensure compliance with federal and state securities laws, as well as various regulations of self-regulatory bodies.

- Reviewing initial public offerings to customers to ensure that the securities offered are registered in accordance with the Securities Act of 1933 and in accordance with state Blue-Sky laws.

Clearance

4.45 *Purchases and sales.* The purchase and sales (P&S) department processes customer and proprietary orders and is responsible for the following:

- Recording P&S transactions if that is not done automatically through the order entry process.
- Preparing confirmations of securities transactions.
- Comparing transactions with other broker-dealers and clearing organizations and computing commissions, taxes, and other fees.

4.46 Some of the control and monitoring activities typically associated with the P&S department include the following:

- Comparing the total number of orders entered with the total number of orders on the trade date blotter, and reconciling any differences (for instance, canceled trades, limit orders not executed, and rejects).
- Comparing all transactions cleared through clearing organizations with clearing organization contract sheets or electronically through IT interfaces (including electronic communications networks), and comparing all broker-to-broker transactions with confirmations received from the contra broker-dealer.
- Aggregating the adjustments between trade date blotters (such as T/D+1 and T/D+2) on a daily basis, and using them to reconcile those blotters.
- Tracing all totals on the settlement blotters to the general ledger.
- Prohibiting P&S personnel from obtaining access to customer accounts, stock records, margin records, the cashier's department, and the mailing department through systems or other processes.
- Comparing order tickets on a test basis with entries on the trade date blotter, and recomputing commissions, taxes, and other fees.
- Balancing principal transactions with customers internally against the firm trading accounts with exceptions promptly entered into the suspense file and investigated.
- Balancing presettlement customer and streetside transactions daily, to ensure that balance entries are posted to the general ledger and stock record.
- Reviewing, aging, and reporting to appropriate officials concerning open P&S suspense items because suspended trades represent potential fails, "don't knows," unknown inventory positions, or financing costs on a periodic basis (preferably daily).
- Agreeing amounts and account distributions on the settlement blotter to general ledger entries.
- Summarizing on exception reports and actively reviewing "as of" transactions and "canceled and corrected" transactions.
- Mailing trade confirmations to customers, generally before settlement date, and reporting any misstatements noted by customers.

Securities Settlement

4.47 *Receive and deliver.* All receipts and deliveries of securities and money are handled by the receive-and-deliver section of the cashier's department. This is either performed physically or by electronic book entry. Some of the control and monitoring activities typically associated with the receive-and-deliver function include the following:

- Monitoring real-time and overnight batch process matching with clearing organizations to identify any securities due for settlement that cannot be settled.

- Ensuring end-of-day cash and securities movements agree to the clearing organizations for continuous net settlement accounts.

- Periodically reviewing operations suspense items to determine the propriety of receivables or payables carried in the account.

- Receiving or delivering securities only if they are supported by written instructions prepared by another department or workstation.

- Electronic imaging of securities received and delivered to resolve any differences between broker-dealers.

- Examining for negotiability (that is, properly endorsed, signed, guaranteed, or otherwise papered) and for completeness (that is, coupons and warrants) securities received before they are placed in the active box or vault.

- Recording the certificate numbers of securities received.

- Authorizing certain designated employees to execute or guarantee assignments.

- Maintaining control over the facsimile signature devices used.

- Designating an employee who does not handle securities or cash to determine that payment is received when securities are delivered against payment.

- Bonding all employees who handle securities and money.

- Balancing daily movements of securities and assigning responsibility for the clearance of out-of-balance positions to specific individuals who have no other duties related to any other aspects of securities processing.

- Investigating and resolving securities positions (and related ledger amounts) in suspense accounts on a timely basis.

- Ensuring that due bills for dividends are identified and recorded with the receipt or delivery of securities.

- Periodically comparing the details of fails to receive and fails to deliver with the stock record, in accordance with SEC Rule 17a-13, and agreeing the respective amounts receivable or payable to the related general ledger control accounts.

- Maintaining aging schedules of fail-to-receive and fail-to-deliver transactions currently, following up on aged fail transactions and sending confirmations as needed, initiating buy-ins in accordance with various regulatory rules, and analyzing aged fails for regulatory purposes.

- Periodically reviewing operations suspense items to determine the propriety of receivables or payables carried in the account.

- Comparing suspense items with underlying trade tickets or other records and reviewing the propriety of the subsequent clearance of suspense items.

4.48 *Extension of credit.* The margin department, also called the credit department, monitors the extension of credit to customers. Some of the control and monitoring activities over transactions with customers that are typically associated with the margin department include the following:

- Establishing procedures to ensure compliance with the requirements of Federal Reserve Regulation T (Regulation T) of the Board of Governors of the Federal Reserve System, including cash, margin, and other accounts, as well as maintenance margin (FINRA Rule 4210) requirements.

- Implementing a system designed to prevent violations of Regulation T and similar regulations addressing the extension and maintenance of credit, including the prompt issuance of Regulation T calls and maintenance calls, and prompt follow-up action in the event that calls are not met.

- Implementing a system to set and monitor "house" margin requirements that are higher than those established by regulatory authorities if it is considered necessary for the protection of the broker-dealer.

- Performing credit investigations before transacting business with a customer and before establishing credit limits.

- Obtaining signed margin agreements before trading in a margin account can occur.

- Disbursing cash and delivering securities only upon written authorization of the appropriate personnel.

- Requiring the authorization of margin department personnel before paying funds or withdrawing securities from customers' accounts.

- Prohibiting margin clerks from initiating entries to customer accounts and from having contact with customers' securities, remittances, or disbursements.

- Assigning responsibility for monitoring customer accounts to specific employees who are rotated onto other duties periodically.

- Reviewing margin records periodically (by an employee who has no duties in connection with them) to determine that the minimum margin requirements of the firm are being maintained.

- Reviewing customer accounts on a regular basis to ensure sufficient margin exists to meet "house" and regulatory requirements. When accounts are determined to be undermargined, requesting additional collateral from the customer to properly secure the account.

- Promptly reporting to management on customers' undermargined accounts and unsecured or partly secured accounts for purposes of evaluation concerning collectibility.

- Delegating duties appropriately and rotating the duties of personnel in key control areas.

- Accepting securities received from a customer that are registered in a name other than the customer's only if proof of ownership is provided.

- Permitting only designated employees to make entries to customer accounts and requiring that two employees approve

changes to customer account files. Limiting the types of transactions (such as cash receipts, cash disbursements, securities receipts and deliveries, or adjustments) that an employee can initiate.

- Establishing procedures to ensure compliance with the requirements of SEC Rules 400–406 and Commodity Futures Trading
Commission Regulations 41.42–41.49 governing customer margin
for transactions in security futures.

- Reviewing securities underlying receivables and payables regularly concerning their valuation.

Custody[1]

4.49 *Cashiering.* The cashiering department is responsible for the custody,
safekeeping, and segregation of securities, either in the firm vault or at depositories. Some of the control and monitoring activities typically associated with
the custody function include the following:

- Agreeing results of security counts, and verifications to the stock
record with any differences noted, in accordance with Rule 17a-13,
and following to a conclusion.

- Agreeing daily, and reconciling at least monthly, the details of
transactions for accounts carried by other broker-dealers (such as
omnibus accounts) and resolving any differences.

- Reconciling the securities held at depositories to the stock record
daily.

- Balancing, on a daily basis, customer accounts with the stock
record and general ledger control accounts, as well as with margin
department records.

- Identifying and segregating worthless and restricted securities.

- Confirming securities, counting securities, or both, once each calendar quarter and comparing the results to the books and records,
as required under SEC Rule 17a-13. SEC Rule 17a-13 requires
that certain broker-dealers, at least once in each calendar quarter,
physically examine and count all securities held and account for
all other securities that are subject to the broker-dealer's control
or direction and are not in its physical possession. The counting
and verification of securities is required to be performed by, or supervised by, personnel that do not have daily responsibility for the
securities.

- Noting, in the records of the broker-dealer, customers' fully paid
and excess margin securities as securities required to be in its
physical possession or control in accordance with SEC Rule 15c3-
3, maintaining records of customers' fully paid and excess margin
securities not in the broker-dealer's possession or control, determining the location of such securities and initiating action to bring
them into possession or control within the time frames set forth
in the rule.

---

[1] A broker-dealer that is also a registered investment adviser is subject to additional requirements related to custody. See the "Additional Requirements for Registered Investment Advisers" section in chapter 3, "Regulatory Considerations," of this guide.

- Maintaining securities that are on the premises in a fireproof vault.
- Maintaining physical controls over securities on hand by restricting access to areas containing securities to authorized employees and by always keeping the cage and vault doors locked.
- Using dual controls over access to securities.
- Limiting the number of employees who have access to physical securities.
- Periodically electronically imaging securities on hand for use in researching any misstatements.
- Conducting surprise counts of securities on hand.

4.50 *Securities transfer.* The transfer department is responsible for the transfer of ownership and the registration and reissuance of securities. The following are some of the control and monitoring activities typically associated with the transfer department:

- Recording transfer instructions in a memo field on the stock record.
- Matching securities received back from the transfer agent against open transfer instructions.
- Maintaining and reporting, for management and regulatory purposes, the aging of open transfer items.
- Periodically confirming aged open transfer items with the transfer agent.

Dividends, Interest, and Reorganization

4.51 *Dividends and interest.* The dividend department normally monitors dividends declared by business entities, monitors the collection (and payment, if the broker-dealer is short) of dividends, records interest and dividends on securities owned by the firm or its customers, and credits customer and firm accounts with their dividends and interest. The following are some of the control and monitoring activities typically associated with the processing of dividends and interest:

- Receiving information regarding dividend declarations, pending coupon payments, factor changes, and other corporate actions electronically from independent dividend-reporting services.
- Manually reviewing input dividend information separately.
- Obtaining information regarding bond interest coupon dates when new issues are recorded on the securities master file.
- Automatically creating on the record date a dividend file that identifies all long and short security positions in each issue for which a dividend has been declared from an extract of the stock record (commonly referred to as a *take-off sheet*).
- Crediting, through an automated process on the payment date, all entries to customer, noncustomer, and processing accounts.
- Recording in the suspense account and having the dividend department investigate differences between money received and the receivable amount or between money paid and the payable amount.

- Following up with paying agents or depositories holding the firm's and its customers' securities in street name for payments.

- Routinely aging receivables and payables and long and short stock dividends for exposure and for regulatory and escheatment purposes, and reporting them to management.

- Agreeing customer elections as recorded in the dividend system or offline file to supporting documentation, for dividends that may be paid in either cash or shares at the discretion of the customer.

4.52 *Reorganizations.* The reorganization department is responsible for the processing of securities involving corporate reorganizations, consolidations, subscriptions, and exchanges. Some of the control and monitoring activities typically associated with reorganization departments include the following:

- Receiving information regarding pending reorganization transactions electronically from independent reporting services.

- Manually reviewing input reorganization information separately.

- Controlling physical movements of securities subject to pending reorganizations by processing them through the appropriate reorganization accounts.

- Balancing all reorganization transactions on a security-by-security basis.

- Periodically recording and confirming money receivable or securities at agents with any differences entered into a suspense account and investigated.

- Agreeing customer elections as recorded in the reorganization system or offline file to supporting documentation for reorganizations in which a vote, election, or other matter is at the discretion of the customer.

To-Be-Announced Securities

4.53 Broker-dealers often obtain and sell the rights to mortgage-backed securities that have not yet been issued. These to-be-announced (TBA) transactions are unique operationally because they have certain characteristics of both a security and a derivative. Some of the control and monitoring activities that are typically associated with such securities include the following:

- Establishing and monitoring a standardized strategy for allocating TBAs to specified pools.

- Analyzing and monitoring securities received in incoming pools.

- Properly recording unallocated TBAs as fails.

- Ensuring that the allocation of TBAs to pools is efficient, adequately validated, and properly recorded.

- Ensuring that complete and correct factor updates are received on a timely basis.

- Obtaining principal and interest information (including factors) from external sources (especially for derivatives) and ensuring that the validated information is updated on the appropriate systems on a timely basis.

Principal Transactions

4.54 *Firm trading*. Many broker-dealers buy and sell securities and over-the-counter (OTC) derivatives in their capacity as dealers and as part of various positioning strategies that attempt to generate profits by anticipating future market movements. These dealer and positioning strategies are collectively referred to as firm trading. Given the volatility of the financial markets, proper control and monitoring activities over firm trading activities are critical. Some of the control and monitoring activities that are typically associated with firm trading generally include the following:

- Monitoring the internal testing and review of high-frequency trading algorithms prior to implementation.
- Establishing and monitoring overall position limits, as well as separate limits for each trader and product.
- Comparing trade tickets to the daily transaction information recorded on the firm's books and records.
- Time stamping or electronic monitoring of trade tickets at the time a transaction is received and executed.
- Reviewing cancel and correction trade ticket adjustments.
- Sending trade confirmations to each counterparty.
- Reviewing and verifying all confirmations received from counterparties.
- Reviewing suppressed trades and aged trade confirmations.
- Daily monitoring positions and trading gains and losses by each trader on a trade-date basis.
- Independently calculating and reconciling trading desk records, which are maintained on a trade-date basis, to the accounting department records on a daily basis.
- Periodically, independently reviewing the fair value of firm trading positions (see paragraph 4.56 for further details).
- Reviewing, at an appropriate management level, reports of all aged positions.
- Reviewing, at an appropriate management level, reports of position concentrations.
- Recording traders' phone conversations with counterparties.
- Reviewing the automated comparison of settled positions on the firm inventory system versus positions on the stock record on a daily basis.
- Balancing principal transactions conducted with the broker-dealer's customers on a daily basis.
- Reviewing the pending trades file.
- Performing reconciliations between the front-end trading systems and the general ledger.

4.55 *Underwriting*. A broker-dealer may act as a manager, co-manager, or syndicate member in the underwriting of public or private offerings of securities. Many of the control and monitoring activities related to firm trading also serve as control and monitoring activities over underwriting activities. Some additional control and monitoring activities typically associated with the underwriting function include the following:

- Maintaining the subscription records for the underwriting, and receiving from members of the buying and selling groups reports of orders from their customers, so that the managing underwriter knows the status of the offering at all times.

- Separately accounting for the revenue and expenses of the syndicate.

- Aging and separately maintaining on a deal-by-deal basis amounts receivable or payable that are recorded on the broker-dealer's books pursuant to an underwriting.

4.56 *Reporting fair value.* Management is responsible for having controls in place in order to adequately determine the fair value of securities held on a day-to-day basis and at the end of a reporting period. Some of the control and monitoring activities typically associated with calculating and reporting the fair value of financial instruments include the following:

- Employing personnel who are involved in the determination of fair value and are experienced with the products and pricing methodologies used.

- Establishing and maintaining a pricing validation group that is independent from the front office, which reviews securities valuation by comparing pricing or other input data from multiple sources, reviews valuations based on established tolerances, analyzes day-to-day movements in valuation for unusual activity, and evaluates stale data.

- Establishing and maintaining a model validation group for securities held by broker-dealers that are complex or for which there is limited market data available. The model validation group supervisor performs a review of significant inputs and other parameters, and is independent from the front office.

- Ensuring policies and procedures are in place to review and approve new valuation models, or changes to existing valuation models.

- Periodically revalidating outputs of valuation models to ensure the models still function as intended.

- Reporting results of independent pricing and model verifications to senior management and financial reporting departments for review.

- Periodically reconciling automated data feeds to source data.

- Monitoring credit events or other market trends that may indicate a change in previous fair value calculations.

- Periodically analyzing unrealized gains and losses for unusual activity.

- Performing an independent analysis of the classification of securities as level 1, 2, or 3 within the fair value hierarchy based on a verification of the observability of pricing inputs. See FASB *Accounting Standards Codification* (ASC) 820, *Fair Value Measurement.*

OTC Derivative Transactions[2]

4.57 Many broker-dealers enter into derivative transactions in their capacity as dealers and as part of various strategies. Some of the control and monitoring activities that are typically associated with such transactions include the following:

- Providing training to staff with respect to systems used to process derivatives, as well as technical updates on the processing of, and accounting for, new products.
- Hiring staff that is experienced with the various types of products processed and ensuring that such staff is supervised by experienced individuals.
- Reviewing the systems used to process and account for derivative transactions in order to ensure that they are operating as intended.
- Reviewing the system selected to process derivative transactions to ensure it is able to handle the current and projected volume of business.
- Ensuring that systems or technical personnel are capable of supporting the current system and augmenting features of the system as needed.
- Developing a contingency plan in the event the system breaks down.
- Restricting access to the system by using codes and passwords.
- Obtaining and maintaining signed contracts for each derivative transaction, as well as maintaining a list of outstanding unsigned contracts.
- Reviewing master netting agreements and the presentation of netted transactions to ensure that they comply with requirements of FASB ASC 210, *Balance Sheet*.
- Reviewing files periodically to validate that they include correspondence from counterparties regarding payment instructions, amounts to be paid or received, modifications to current contracts, and notifications of early terminations and final payments.
- Separating the functions of inputting derivative transactions into the system and verifying the accuracy of the input.
- Separating such functions as monitoring, calculating, and processing of payments and receipts.
- Ensuring that the execution of derivative transactions and the monitoring of counterparty credit quality and counterparty exposure limits are performed by separate individuals.
- Establishing and maintaining formal policies concerning hedging strategies.[3]

---

[2] Title VII of the Dodd-Frank Wall Street Reform and Consumer Protection Act (Dodd-Frank Act) requires the SEC to work with other regulators, the Commodity Futures Trading Commission in particular, to write rules that result in a reorganization of the over-the-counter derivatives market. The rulemaking required to implement the Dodd-Frank Act provisions in this area is extensive, and work is continuing by regulators.

[3] Hedge accounting is permitted only if the requirements of FASB *Accounting Standards Codification* 815, *Derivatives and Hedging*, are met.

- Restricting control and maintenance over legal documentation.

- Performing reconciliations between cash disbursements and receipts, systems calculations, and correspondence from counterparties.

- Performing the valuation of the derivatives portfolio frequently and consistently obtaining from reliable sources the market data used to value the portfolio on each valuation date (see paragraph 4.56 for further details). Limiting access to models used to value positions and reviewing changes made to those models. The valuation process and the verification of this process are performed by individuals who are independent of the traders.

- Analyzing the changes in the portfolio's valuation into the following separate components:

  — Market fluctuations.

  — Accretion.

  — Swap payments and receipts.

  — Maturations and terminations.

  — New transactions.

- Reconciling traders' estimates of profit and loss to the portfolio valuation system.

Commissions

4.58 Many broker-dealers earn commissions and fees from executing and clearing client transactions on stocks, bonds, options, and futures markets. Some of the control and monitoring activities that are typically associated with such transactions include the following:

- Sending statements to customers that provide account information (for example, statement period, account number, customer contact information, clearing firm and contact information, summary of the client holdings, recent market value of client holdings, income [gains and losses], fees charged, account activity [trading activity, movement of money or securities, and the beginning and ending balance for the statement period], margin, and other portfolio level detail), and reconciling or investigating any variances identified by the customer.

- Mailing trade confirmations to customers and reporting any misstatements noted by customers.

- Maintaining and reviewing a customer complaint log.

- Maintaining an approved commission rates table, including approvals for any subsequent changes made to such tables.

- Reviewing commission rates in excess of commission rate tables.

Collateralized Financings

4.59 *Stock loan and stock borrow.* Stock loan and borrow transactions generally result from the need for one broker-dealer to borrow securities to make delivery to another broker-dealer or customer for a security that the broker-dealer does not have in its possession. At large broker-dealers, the stock loan department has responsibility for entering into and monitoring such transactions, as well as processing the "recall" of the securities as directed by the lender. Some of the control and monitoring activities typically associated with stock loan and stock borrow activities include the following:

- Reviewing counterparties for creditworthiness and obtaining master trade agreements and credit approval for counterparties before entering into a stock loan or stock borrow transaction.
- Establishing approved transaction limits by counterparty.
- Calculating those securities in excess of SEC Rule 15c3-3 possession or control requirements as available to be loaned for any given day. Recalling those securities in deficits within the time frames required.
- Obtaining physical possession or control of all collateral, and reconciling it to signed agreements.
- Ensuring that stock borrows are made in accordance with the requirements of Regulation T.
- Subsequently measuring at fair value all collateral daily and, if a deficit (within established guidelines) exists, obtaining additional collateral from the counterparty.
- Reconciling the stock loan and stock borrow subsidiary ledgers to the stock record (positions) and general ledger (contract amounts) daily. Out of balances are recorded as suspense items and researched immediately.
- Confirming securities borrowed and loaned periodically, on a basis that, at a minimum, complies with SEC Rule 17a-13 regarding the quarterly verification of securities.
- Confirming key contract terms (for example, underlying security, quantity, price, and rate) for each stock loan or stock borrow transaction.
- Listing transactions with unusually high or low rebate terms on an exception report for review by management.
- Obtaining and reviewing the SOC 1 report of third party vendors that are involved in securities lending transactions and addressing all user control considerations and any control issues that are identified.

4.60 *Repos and reverse repos.* A *repurchase agreement* (repo) is the sale of securities along with an agreement to purchase the securities at a specified price at a later, specified date. Repo agreements are typically entered into to finance positions in government and government-agency securities. A *reverse repurchase agreement* (reverse repo) is the purchase of securities along with an agreement to sell the securities at a specified price at a later, specified date. Repos and reverse repos, similar to stock loan and stock borrow transactions, respectively, feature a provider of collateral and a lender of cash. Control and monitoring activities typically associated with repo and reverse repo agreements include the following:

- Reviewing counterparties for creditworthiness and obtaining master trade agreements and credit approval for counterparties before entering into a repo or reverse repo transaction.
- Establishing position and credit limits by counterparty.

- Reviewing net presentation of offsetting transactions to ensure that it complies with the requirements of FASB ASC 210-20-45.

- Subsequently measuring at fair value all collateral daily, and if a deficit (within established guidelines) exists, obtaining additional collateral from the counterparty.

- Reconciling the repo and reverse repo subsidiary ledgers to the stock record (positions) and general ledger (contract amounts) daily. Out of balances are recorded as suspense items and re-searched immediately.

- Periodically confirming transactions on a basis that, at a mini-mum, complies with SEC Rule 17a-13 regarding quarterly verifi-cation of securities.

- Listing transactions with unusually high or low interest terms on an exception report for review by management.

4.61 *Bank loan financing.* A broker-dealer may finance its proprietary or customer activity through collateralized bank loans. Such loans are generally negotiated separately with each bank. Some of the control and monitoring ac-tivities typically associated with bank loan financing include the following:

- Ensuring that customer, noncustomer, and firm bank loans are separately maintained and that procedures are in place to prevent commingling of collateral.

- Maintaining separate accounts in the general ledger for each loan, with separate positions being maintained on the stock record for the securities collateralizing each loan.

- Ensuring that securities used to collateralize bank loans for cus-tomers are not fully paid or excess-margin securities because such securities are required to be segregated pursuant to SEC Rule 15c3-3 possession or control requirements.

- Periodically confirming bank loan collateral on a basis that, at a minimum, complies with SEC Rule 17a-13 regarding the quar-terly verification of securities.

Period End Financial Reporting

4.62 In addition to periodic financial reporting on Financial and Oper-ational Combined Uniform Single (FOCUS) reporting, broker-dealers are re-quired to prepare annual financial statements including required disclosures. Management is responsible for preparing complete and accurate financial statements in accordance with the applicable financial reporting framework. Control and monitoring activities typically associated with the period-end fi-nancial reporting process include the following:

- Ensuring period-end close procedures, including recurring adjust-ments and consolidation procedures, are established and approved by management and documented. Reviewing and comparing the procedures performed and adjustments made to those at previous period ends.

- Reconciling general ledger accounts to source systems and sub-ledgers by personnel other than those making the entries. Identi-fying, researching, and resolving any variances from the expecta-tions, if necessary.

- Appropriately configuring the general ledger system for posting and closing periods, and preventing the period-end close if incomplete or erroneous transactions are detected.

- Reconciling the subledger or stock record, or both, to key external parties, including banks and depositories.

- Reviewing automated reconciliations performed by the system for completeness and accuracy.

- Review of periodic business analyses on performance and other metrics that are prepared using source system data, and researching and appropriately responding to any unexpected findings.

- Reviewing and approving manual journal entries, consolidation entries, and any entries that are recorded directly to the financial statements.

SEC Requirements for Management's Report on Internal Control Over Financial Reporting for Issuers

4.63 SEC Rule 13a-15(f) defines *internal control over financial reporting* as a process designed by, or under the supervision of, the (company's) principal executive and principal financial officers, or persons performing similar functions, and effected by the registrant's board of directors, management, and other personnel to provide reasonable assurance regarding the reliability of financial reporting and the preparation of financial statements for external purposes in accordance with GAAP and includes those policies and procedures that

a. pertain to the maintenance of records that, in reasonable detail, accurately and fairly reflect the transactions and dispositions of the assets of the company;

b. provide reasonable assurance that transactions are recorded as necessary to permit preparation of financial statements in accordance with GAAP, and that receipts and expenditures of the company are being made only in accordance with authorizations of management and directors of the company; and

c. provide reasonable assurance regarding prevention or timely detection of unauthorized acquisition, use, or disposition of the company's assets that could have a material effect on the financial statements.

4.64 As directed by Section 404 of the Sarbanes-Oxley Act of 2002 (SOX), in 2003, the SEC adopted final rules requiring companies subject to the reporting requirements of the Securities Exchange Act of 1934 (the 1934 Act), other than registered investment companies, to include in their annual reports a report of management on the company's internal control over financial reporting. The SEC rules clarify that management's assessment and report is limited to internal control over financial reporting. Management is not required to consider other aspects of control, such as controls pertaining to operations or compliance with laws and regulations. The SEC's definition of *internal control* encompasses the COSO definition, but the SEC does not mandate that the entity use the COSO framework as its criteria for evaluating effectiveness; however, the company must disclose which framework it uses to evaluate internal controls. See the SEC website at www.sec.gov/rules/final/33-8238.htm for the full text of the regulation.

4.65   This requirement is applicable to issuer broker-dealers, whereas non-issuer broker-dealers are not required to include in their annual reports a management report on the company's internal control over financial reporting. However, for broker-dealers that are subsidiaries of public companies (issuers), auditors may perform additional procedures to be able to report on the consolidated entity's financial statements and internal control in accordance with the SEC requirements and PCAOB standards.

4.66   A company that is an accelerated filer or a large accelerated filer, as defined in Rule 12b-2, is required to comply with the SEC rules regarding Section 404(b) of SOX that includes providing an auditor's attestation report on internal control over financial reporting in its annual report. Section 989G of the Dodd-Frank Wall Street Reform and Consumer Protection Act (Dodd-Frank Act) contains a provision that permanently exempts nonaccelerated filers (those filers that do not meet the definition of an accelerated filer or a large accelerated filer) from complying with Section 404(b) of SOX. In 2010, the SEC aligned its regulations with Section 989G of the Dodd-Frank Act, thereby permanently exempting nonaccelerated filers from the provisions of Section 404(b) of SOX.

Annual Reporting Requirements for Issuers

4.67   In accordance with SEC rules, item 9A, "Controls and Procedures," of the company's annual report on Form 10-K must include the following:

a. *Management's Annual Report on Internal Control Over Financial Reporting.* This report on the company's internal control over financial reporting should contain

   i. a statement of management's responsibilities for establishing and maintaining adequate internal control over financial reporting.

   ii. a statement identifying the framework used by management to evaluate the effectiveness of the company's internal control over financial reporting.

   iii. management's assessment of the effectiveness of the company's internal control over financial reporting as of the end of the most recent fiscal year, including a statement concerning whether internal control over financial reporting is effective. This discussion should include disclosure of any material weakness in the company's internal control over financial reporting identified by management. Management is not permitted to conclude that the registrant's internal control over financial reporting is effective if there are one or more material weaknesses in the company's internal control over financial reporting.

   iv. a statement that the registered public accounting firm that audited the financial statements included in the annual report has issued an attestation report on management's assessment of the registrant's internal control over financial reporting.

b. *Attestation Report of the Registered Public Accounting Firm.* This is the registered public accounting firm's attestation report on management's assessment of the company's internal control over financial reporting.

c. *Changes in Internal Control Over Financial Reporting.* This report should disclose any change in the company's internal control over financial reporting that has materially affected or is reasonably likely to materially affect the company's internal control over financial reporting.

Quarterly Reporting Requirements for Issuers

4.68 The SEC rules also require management to evaluate any change in the entity's internal control that occurred during a fiscal quarter and that has materially affected, or is reasonably likely to materially affect, the entity's internal control over financial reporting.

4.69 Additionally, management is required to evaluate the effectiveness of the entity's *disclosure controls and procedures and issue a report concerning their effectiveness on a quarterly basis.* With these rules, the SEC introduced a new term, *disclosure controls and procedures,* as defined in SEC Rule 13a-15(d), that is different from *internal controls over financial reporting* and much broader.

4.70 As defined, *disclosure controls and procedures* encompass the controls over all material financial *and nonfinancial information* in the 1934 Act reports. This definition refers to information disclosed outside the financial statements. Information that would fall under this definition that may *not* be part of an entity's internal control over financial reporting might include, for example, disclosures related to the signing of a significant contract, changes in a strategic relationship, management compensation, or legal proceedings.

Chapter 5

Accounting Standards

FASB *Accounting Standards Codification* (ASC) 606, *Revenue from Contracts with Customers*[1]

The "Pending Content" that links to FASB ASC 606-10-65-1, is effective for annual reporting periods beginning after December 15, 2017, including interim reporting periods within that reporting period, for a public business entity, a not-for-profit entity that has issued, or is a conduit bond obligor for, securities that are traded, listed, or quoted on an exchange or an over-the-counter market, and an employee benefit plan that files or furnishes financial statements with or to the SEC. Earlier application is permitted only as of annual reporting periods beginning after December 15, 2016, including interim reporting periods within that reporting period.

For other entities, FASB ASC 606 is effective for annual reporting periods beginning after December 15, 2018, and interim periods within annual periods beginning after December 15, 2019. Other entities may elect to adopt the standard earlier, however, only as of either

- an annual reporting period beginning after December 15, 2016, including interim periods within that reporting period, or

- an annual reporting period beginning after December 15, 2016, and interim periods within annual periods beginning one year after the annual reporting period in which an entity first applies the "Pending Content" that links to FASB ASC 606-10-65-1.

FASB ASC 606 provides a framework for revenue recognition and supersedes or amends several of the revenue recognition requirements in FASB ASC 605, *Revenue Recognition*, as well as guidance within the 900 series of industry-specific topics, including FASB ASC 940, *Financial Services—Brokers and Dealers*. The standard applies to any entity that either enters into contracts with customers to transfer goods or services or enters into contracts for the transfer of nonfinancial assets unless those contracts are within the scope of other standards (for example, insurance or lease contracts).

Readers are encouraged to consult the full text of FASB ASC 606 on FASB's website at www.fasb.org.

The AICPA has formed 16 industry task forces to assist in developing a new accounting guide on revenue recognition that will provide helpful

---

[1] At the July 20, 2017 meeting of the Emerging Issues Task Force, the SEC staff announced that it would not object to elections by certain public business entities to use the non-public business entities effective dates for the sole purpose of adopting FASB *Accounting Standards Codification* (ASC) 606, *Revenue from Contracts with Customers*, and FASB ASC 842, *Leases*. The staff announcement makes clear that the ability to use non-public business entities effective dates for adopting these new standards is limited to the subset of public business entities "that otherwise would not meet the definition of a public business entity except for a requirement to include or inclusion of its financial statements or financial information in another entity's filings with the SEC." Generally, this election would not be applicable to broker-dealers, however, readers should consult with their regulators and auditors if they believe it is.

hints and illustrative examples for how to apply the new standard. Revenue recognition implementation issues identified by the Brokers and Dealers in Securities Revenue Recognition Task Force are available for informal comment, after review by the AICPA Financial Reporting Executive Committee, at www.aicpa.org/interestareas/frc/accountingfinancialreporting/revenuerecognition/pages/rrtf-brokerdealer.aspx. Readers are encouraged to submit comments to revreccomments@aicpa.org.

As of the date of this publication, nine accounting implementation issues specific to the broker-dealer industry have been identified. Of the nine identified issues, three issues have been finalized and incorporated in the 2017 AICPA Audit and Accounting Guide *Revenue Recognition*. These finalized issues include:

- Considerations for broker-dealers in applying the guidance in FASB ASC 606 to trade-based commission income earned by providing trade facilitation, execution, clearance and settlement, custody, and trade administration services to its customers

- Whether the trade execution performance obligation is satisfied on the trade date or the settlement date

- Considerations for broker-dealers in applying the guidance in FASB ASC 606 when costs are incurred to obtain a contract to provide advisory services to a customer

- Clarification that the recognition of realized and unrealized gains and losses on proprietary transactions involving the purchase and sale of financial instruments and interest and dividend income on financial instrument contracts held by broker dealers are excluded from the scope of FASB ASC 606

For more information, see appendix E, "The New Revenue Recognition Standard: FASB ASC 606," of this guide.

© Update 5-1 *Accounting and Reporting*: Recognition and Measurement of Financial Assets and Financial Liabilities

FASB Accounting Standards Update (ASU) No. 2016-01, *Financial Instruments—Overall (Subtopic 825-10) Recognition and Measurement of Financial Assets and Financial Liabilities*, issued in January 2016, is effective for public entities for fiscal years beginning after December 15, 2017, and interim periods within those fiscal years. Early adoption is not permitted by public business entities; however, the ASU provides for early adoption of certain specified amendments upon issuance as of the beginning of the fiscal year of adoption.

For all other entities, including not-for-profit entities and employee benefit plans within the scope of the FASB ASC 960 through FASB ASC 965 topics for plan accounting, the amendments are effective for fiscal years beginning after December 15, 2018, and interim periods within fiscal years ending after December 15, 2019. Early adoption is permitted by entities other than public business entities as of the fiscal years beginning after December 15, 2017 and interim periods within those fiscal years.

FASB ASU No. 2016-01 amends guidance for recognition, measurement, presentation, and disclosure of financial instruments.

This edition of the guide has not been updated to reflect changes as a result of this ASU, however, this chapter will be updated in a future edition to reflect the amendments in this ASU, particularly an amendment that requires an entity to present separately in other comprehensive income the portion of the total change in the fair value of a liability that results from a change in the instrument-specific credit risk for financial liabilities that the entity has elected to measure at fair value in accordance with the fair value option.

Readers are encouraged to consult the full text of the ASU on FASB's website at www.fasb.org. For more information on FASB ASU No. 2016-01, see appendix G, "Accounting for Financial Instruments," of this guide.

ⓒ Update 5-2 FASB ASU No. 2016-02, *Leases (Topic 842)*[2]

FASB ASU No. 2016-02, issued in February 2016, is effective for fiscal years beginning after December 15, 2018, including interim periods within those fiscal years, for any of the following: 1) a public business entity; 2) a not-for-profit entity that has issued, or is a conduit bond obligor for, securities that are traded, listed, or quoted on an exchange or an over the-counter market; or 3) an employee benefit plan that files financial statements with the SEC.

For all other entities, the amendments in this ASU are effective for fiscal years beginning after December 15, 2019, and interim periods within fiscal years beginning after December 15, 2020.

Early application of the amendments in this ASU is permitted for all entities.

Readers are encouraged to consult the full text of this ASU on FASB's website at www.fasb.org.

This edition of the guide has not been updated to reflect changes as a result of this ASU, however, this chapter will be updated in a future edition. For more information on FASB ASU No. 2016-02, see appendix F, " The New Leases Standard: FASB ASU No. 2016-02," of this guide.

ⓒ Update 5-3 FASB ASU No. 2016-13, *Financial Instruments—Credit Losses (Topic 326): Measurement of Credit Losses on Financial Instruments*

FASB ASU No. 2016-13 was issued in June 2016. For public business entities that are SEC filers, the amendments in this ASU are effective for fiscal years beginning after December 15, 2019, including interim periods within those fiscal years. For all other public business entities, the amendments in this ASU are effective for fiscal years beginning after December 15, 2020, including interim periods within those fiscal years.

For all other entities, including not-for-profit entities and employee benefit plans within the scope of FASB ASC 960, *Plan Accounting—Defined Benefit Pension Plans*, through FASB ASC 965, *Plan Accounting—Health and Welfare Benefit Plans*, on plan accounting, the amendments in this ASU are effective for fiscal years beginning after December 15, 2020, and interim periods within fiscal years beginning after December 15, 2021.

---

[2] See footnote 1.

All entities may adopt the amendments in this ASU earlier as of the fiscal years beginning after December 15, 2018, including interim periods within those fiscal years. See FASB ASU No. 2016-13 for additional information regarding the effective date of this ASU.

This edition of the guide has not been updated to reflect changes as a result of this ASU, however, this chapter will be updated in a future edition. Readers are encouraged to consult the full text of this ASU on FASB's website at www.fasb.org.

© **Update 5-4 FASB ASU No. 2017-12,** *Derivatives and Hedging (Topic 815): Targeted Improvements to Accounting for Hedging Activities*

FASB ASU No. 2017-12 was issued in August 2017. For public business entities, the amendments in this ASU are effective for fiscal years beginning after December 15, 2018, and interim periods within those fiscal years. For all other entities, the amendments are effective for fiscal years beginning after December 15, 2019, and interim periods beginning after December 15, 2020.

Early application is permitted in any interim period after issuance of the ASU. All transition requirements and elections should be applied to hedging relationships existing (that is, hedging relationships in which the hedging instrument has not expired, been sold, terminated, or exercised or the entity has not removed the designation of the hedging relationship) on the date of adoption. The effect of adoption should be reflected as of the beginning of the fiscal year of adoption (that is, the initial application date).

This edition of the guide has not been updated to reflect changes as a result of this ASU, however, this chapter will be updated in a future edition. Readers are encouraged to consult the full text of this ASU on FASB's website atwww.fasb.org.

5.01 Accounting principles generally accepted in the United States of America (GAAP) apply to broker-dealers in the same manner as they apply to other industries; however, certain activities of broker-dealers' operations are unique. It is the purpose of this chapter to identify and discuss the accounting treatment for certain of those unique activities that are engaged in by broker-dealers. New broker-dealer activities may develop that will require accounting guidance to reflect their economic substance. The accounting principles that apply to the specific activities addressed in this chapter can be applied to other activities that are similar to those discussed. Broker-dealers also prepare regulatory reports and supplemental information, in addition to financial statements. Accounting and reporting requirements under GAAP may differ from broker-dealer regulatory accounting and reporting requirements stipulated by the SEC and other regulatory organizations. (See chapter 3, "Regulatory Considerations," of this guide.) In addition, the financial reporting practices and recording of transactions discussed in this chapter may differ significantly from the tax basis of reporting.

Accounting Model

5.02 A broker-dealer accounts for inventory and derivative positions (such as futures, forwards, swaps, and options) at fair value. Most other assets, such as fixed assets, accounts receivable, securities borrowed, securities purchased under agreements to resell (known as resale or reverse repurchase agreements [reverse repos]), and exchange memberships owned, are reported at historical cost or the fair value of collateral to be returned. Obligations for short inventory positions are reported at fair value.

5.03 Per FASB ASC 940-20-30-2, liabilities related to broker-dealer operations, such as fails to receive and securities sold under agreements to repurchase (known as repurchase agreements [repos]), are recorded at contract amounts or the fair value of collateral to be returned.

5.04 Fair value is measured by management using the guidance provided in FASB ASC 820, *Fair Value Measurement*, and is usually determined for accounting purposes as of the close of trading on the principal exchange or market on which the financial instruments are traded.

5.05 FASB ASC 820 defines *fair value* (see the "Definition of Fair Value" section of this chapter), establishes a framework for measuring fair value, and requires certain disclosures about fair value measurement. The following paragraphs summarize FASB ASC 820 but are not intended as a substitute for reviewing FASB ASC 820 in its entirety.

Definition of *Fair Value*

5.06 FASB ASC 820-10-20 defines *fair value* as the price that would be received to sell an asset or paid to transfer a liability in an orderly transaction between market participants at the measurement date. FASB ASC 820-10-35-5 states that a fair value measurement assumes that the transaction to sell the asset or transfer the liability takes place either in the principal market for the asset or liability or, in the absence of a principal market, in the most advantageous market for the asset or liability. The FASB ASC glossary defines the *principal market* as the market with the greatest volume and level of activity for the asset or liability. The reporting entity must have access to the principal (or most advantageous) market at the measurement date. Because different entities with different activities may have access to different markets, the principal or most advantageous market for the same asset or liability might be different for different entities (and business within those entities). The principal market (and, thus, market participants) should be considered from the perspective of the reporting entity, thereby allowing for differences between and among entities with different activities.

5.07 FASB ASC 820-10-05-1B notes that fair value is a market-based measurement, not an entity-specific measurement. For some assets and liabilities, observable market transactions or market information might be available, but, for others, that information might not be available. However, the objective of a fair value measurement in both cases is the same, to estimate the price at which an orderly transaction to sell the asset or transfer the liability would take place between market participants at the measurement date under current market conditions (that is, an exit price at the measurement date from the perspective of a market participant that holds the asset or owes the liability). Conceptually, entry prices and exit prices are different. However, FASB ASC 820-10-30-3 explains that, in many cases, at initial recognition, the transaction price will equal fair value (for example, when the transaction takes place in the market in which the asset would be sold).

5.08 Paragraphs 9B–9C of FASB ASC 820-10-35 provide that the price should not be adjusted for transaction costs. Transaction costs do not include transportation costs. If location is a characteristic of the asset (for example, for a commodity), the price should be adjusted for the costs, if any, that would be incurred to transport the asset from its current location to its principal (or most advantageous) market.

Application of Fair Value Measurement to Liabilities and Instruments Classified in a Reporting Entity's Shareholders' Equity

5.09   Certain broker-dealer liabilities, such as securities sold, not yet purchased, are carried at fair value. According to FASB ASC 820-10-35-16, a fair value measurement assumes that a financial or nonfinancial liability or an instrument classified in a reporting entity's shareholders' equity is transferred to a market participant at the measurement date. The transfer of a liability or an instrument classified in a reporting entity's shareholders' equity assumes the following:

- A liability would remain outstanding and the market participant transferee would be required to fulfill the obligation. The liability would not be settled with the counterparty or otherwise extinguished on the measurement date.

- An instrument classified in a reporting entity's shareholders' equity would remain outstanding and the market participant transferee would take on the rights and responsibilities associated with the instrument. The instrument would not be canceled or otherwise extinguished at the measurement date.

5.10   FASB ASC 820-10-35-16A states that even when there is no observable market to provide pricing information about the transfer of a liability or an instrument classified in a reporting entity's shareholders' equity (for example, because contractual or other legal restrictions prevent the transfer of such items), there might be an observable market for such items if they are held by other parties as assets (for example, a corporate bond or a call option on a reporting entity's shares). In all cases, a reporting entity should maximize the use of relevant observable inputs and minimize the use of unobservable inputs to meet the objective of a fair value measurement. See paragraphs 16D–16L of FASB ASC 820-10-35 for additional guidance regarding measuring the fair value of liabilities and instruments classified in a reporting entity's shareholders' equity.

5.11   Paragraphs 17–18A of FASB ASC 820-10-35 provide that the fair value of a liability reflects the effect of nonperformance risk. Nonperformance risk includes, but may not be limited to, a reporting entity's own credit risk. Nonperformance risk is assumed to be the same before and after the transfer of the liability. When measuring the fair value of a liability, a reporting entity should take into account the effect of its credit risk (credit standing) and any other factors that might influence the likelihood that the obligation will or will not be fulfilled. See paragraphs 17–18A of FASB ASC 820-10-35 for additional guidance.

Valuation Techniques

5.12   A reporting entity should use valuation techniques that are appropriate in the circumstances and for which sufficient data are available to measure fair value, maximizing the use of relevant observable inputs and minimizing the use of unobservable inputs. Three widely used valuation approaches are the market approach, cost approach, and income approach. The main aspects of valuation techniques consistent with those approaches are summarized in paragraphs 3A–3G of FASB ASC 820-10-55. An entity should use valuation techniques consistent with one or more of these approaches to measure fair value:

- The market approach uses prices and other relevant information generated by market transactions involving identical or comparable assets, liabilities, or a group of assets and liabilities, such as a business. Valuation techniques consistent with the market approach include matrix pricing and those that use market multiples derived from a set of comparables.

- The cost approach reflects the amount that would be required currently to replace the service capacity of an asset (often referred to as current replacement cost). From the perspective of a market participant seller, the price that would be received for the asset is based on the cost to a market participant buyer to acquire or construct a substitute asset of comparable utility, adjusted for obsolescence.

- The income approach converts future amounts (for example, cash flows or income and expenses) to a single current (that is, discounted) amount. When the income approach is used, the fair value measurement reflects current market expectations about those future amounts. Valuation techniques consistent with the income approach include present value techniques, option-pricing models, and the multiperiod excess earnings method. Paragraphs 4–20 of FASB ASC 820-10-55 provide guidance for using present value techniques.

5.13 FASB ASC 820-10-35-24B notes that, in some cases, a single valuation technique will be appropriate (for example, when valuing an asset or a liability using quoted prices in an active market for identical assets or liabilities). In other cases, multiple valuation techniques will be appropriate (for example, that might be the case when valuing a reporting unit). If multiple valuation techniques are used to measure fair value, the results (that is, respective indications of fair value) should be evaluated, considering the reasonableness of the range of values indicated by those results. Beginning with the "Pending Content" in paragraph 35 of FASB ASC 820-10-55, there are two cases provided that illustrate the use of multiple valuation techniques. A fair value measurement is the point within that range that is most representative of fair value in the circumstances.

5.14 Paragraphs 25–26 of FASB ASC 820-10-35 explain that valuation techniques used to measure fair value should be applied consistently. However, a change in a valuation technique or its application is appropriate if the change results in a measurement that is equally or more representative of fair value in the circumstances. Revisions resulting from such a change in valuation technique or its application should be accounted for as a change in accounting estimate in accordance with the provisions of FASB ASC 250, *Accounting Changes and Error Corrections*.

Inputs to Valuation Techniques

5.15 FASB ASC 820-10-35-36 notes that valuation techniques used to measure fair value should maximize the use of relevant observable inputs and minimize the use of unobservable inputs. Markets in which inputs might be observable for some assets and liabilities (for example, financial instruments) include, for example, exchange markets, dealer markets, brokered markets, and principal-to-principal markets.

5.16 A reporting entity should select inputs that are consistent with the characteristics of the asset or liability that market participants would take into account in a transaction for the asset or liability. In some cases, those characteristics result in the application of an adjustment, such as a premium or discount (for example, a control premium or noncontrolling interest discount). However, a fair value measurement should not incorporate a premium or discount that is inconsistent with the unit of account in the guidance that requires or permits the fair value measurement. Premiums or discounts that reflect size as a characteristic of the reporting entity's holding (blockage factor) rather than as a characteristic of the asset or liability (for example, a control premium when measuring the fair value of a controlling interest) are not permitted in a fair value measurement. In all cases, if there is a quoted price in an active market (that is, a level 1 input) for an asset or a liability, a reporting entity should use that quoted price without adjustment when measuring fair value, except as specified in FASB ASC 820-10-35-41C.

Application to Financial Assets and Financial Liabilities With Offsetting Positions in Market Risks or Counterparty Credit Risk

5.17 Generally, the unit of account for a financial instrument is the individual financial instrument. A reporting entity should apply adjustments that are consistent with that unit of account, which generally does not include adjustments due to the size of the reporting entity's position.

5.18 FASB ASC 820-10-35-18D permits an exception when a reporting entity manages a group of financial assets and financial liabilities on the basis of its net exposure to either market risks or credit risk. When the criteria in FASB ASC 820-10-35-18E are met, the exception permits a reporting entity to measure the fair value of a group of financial assets and financial liabilities on the basis of the price that would be received to sell a net long position (that is, an asset) or to transfer a net short position (that is, a liability) in an orderly transaction between market participants at the measurement date under current market conditions. FASB ASC 820-10-35-18G states that a reporting entity should make an accounting policy decision about whether to elect to use the exception in FASB ASC 820-10-35-18D. If a reporting entity elects to use the exception, it should disclose that fact.

5.19 When a reporting entity elects to use the exception in FASB ASC 820-10-35-18D, the unit of account becomes the net open risk position. The reporting entity may apply adjustments, including adjustments due to the size of the net open risk position, consistent with market participant assumptions and in accordance with the unit of account. See the "Inputs to Valuation Techniques" section of this chapter for more information.

Inputs Based on Bid and Ask Prices

5.20 FASB ASC 820-10-35-36C states that if an asset or a liability measured at fair value has a bid price and an ask price (for example, an input from a dealer market), the price within the bid-ask spread that is most representative of fair value in the circumstances should be used to measure fair value, regardless of where the input is categorized within the fair value hierarchy (that is, level 1, 2, or 3). The use of bid prices for asset positions and ask prices for liability positions is permitted but not required. GAAP, as stated in FASB ASC 820-10-35-36D, does not preclude the use of mid-market pricing or other pricing conventions that are used by market participants as a practical expedient for fair value measurements within a bid-ask spread. For example, paragraphs 25–26 of FASB ASC 820-10-35 apply to a change from the use of mid-market pricing or other pricing conventions to another valuation technique. In addition, the disclosure requirements in FASB ASC 820-10-50-2bbb apply to such changes.

Present Value Techniques

5.21 Paragraphs 5–20 of FASB ASC 820-10-55 describe the use of present value techniques to measure fair value. Those paragraphs neither prescribe the use of a single specific present value technique nor limit the use of present value techniques to measure fair value to the techniques discussed therein. *Present value* (that is, an application of the income approach) is a tool used to link future amounts to a present amount using a discount rate. A fair value measurement of an asset or a liability using a present value technique captures all of the following elements from the perspective of market participants at the measurement date:

- An estimate of future cash flows for the asset or liability being measured.

- Expectations about possible variations in the amount and timing of the cash flows representing the uncertainty inherent in the cash flows.

- The time value of money, represented by the rate on risk-free monetary assets that have maturity dates or durations that coincide with the period covered by the cash flows and pose neither uncertainty in timing nor risk of default to the holder (that is, a risk-free interest rate). For present value computations denominated in nominal U.S. dollars, the yield curve for U.S. Treasury securities determines the appropriate risk-free interest rate.

- The price for bearing the uncertainty inherent in the cash flows (that is, a risk premium).

- Other factors that market participants would take into account in the circumstances.

- For a liability, the nonperformance risk relating to that liability, including the reporting entity's (obligor's) own credit risk.

5.22 FASB ASC 820-10-55-6 provides the general principles that govern any present value technique, as follows:

- Cash flows and discount rates should reflect assumptions that market participants would use when pricing the asset or liability.

- Cash flows and discount rates should take into account only the factors attributable to the asset or liability being measured.

- To avoid double counting or omitting the effects of risk factors, discount rates should reflect assumptions that are consistent with those inherent in the cash flows. For example, a discount rate that reflects the uncertainty in expectations about future defaults is appropriate if using the contractual cash flows of a loan but is not appropriate if using a technique that already reflects assumptions about the uncertainty in future defaults.

- Assumptions about cash flows and discount rates should be internally consistent. For example, nominal cash flows (that include the effects of inflation) should be discounted at a rate that includes the effects of inflation.

- Discount rates should be consistent with the underlying economic factors of the currency in which the cash flows are denominated.

5.23 FASB ASC 820-10-55-9 describes how present value techniques differ in how they adjust for risk and in the type of cash flows they use. For example, the discount rate adjustment technique uses a risk-adjusted discount rate and contractual, promised, or most likely cash flows. In contrast, method 1 of the expected present value technique uses risk-adjusted expected cash flows and a risk-free rate. Method 2 of the expected present value technique uses expected cash flows that are not risk adjusted and a discount rate adjusted to include the risk premium that market participants require. The traditional present value technique and two methods of expected present value techniques are discussed more fully in FASB ASC 820-10-55.

5.24 This guide includes guidance about measuring assets and liabilities using traditional present value techniques. That guidance is not intended to suggest that the income approach is the only one of the three approaches that is appropriate in the circumstances, nor is it intended to suggest that the traditional present value technique described in the guide is preferred over other present value techniques.

The Fair Value Hierarchy

5.25 As noted in FASB ASC 820-10-35-37, the fair value hierarchy categorizes into three levels the inputs to valuation techniques used to measure fair value. The fair value hierarchy gives the highest priority to quoted prices (unadjusted) in active markets for identical assets or liabilities and the lowest priority to unobservable inputs. The three levels are

- level 1 inputs (paragraphs 40–46 of FASB ASC 820-10-35). *Level 1 inputs* are quoted prices (unadjusted) in active markets for identical assets or liabilities that the reporting entity can access at the measurement date. An *active market*, as defined in the FASB ASC glossary, is a market in which transactions for the asset or liability take place with sufficient frequency and volume to provide pricing information on an ongoing basis. FASB ASC 820-10-35-41 notes that a quoted price in an active market provides the most reliable evidence of fair value and should be used without adjustment to measure fair value whenever available, except as specified in FASB ASC 820-10-35-41C. If the reporting entity holds a position in a single asset or liability (including a position comprising a large number of identical assets or liabilities) and the asset or liability is traded in an active market, the fair value of the asset or liability should be measured within level 1 as the product of the quoted price for the individual asset or liability and the quantity held by the reporting entity. This is the case even if a market's normal daily trading volume is not sufficient to absorb the quantity held and placing orders to sell the position in a single transaction might affect the quoted price.

- level 2 inputs (paragraphs 47–51 of FASB ASC 820-10-35). *Level 2 inputs* are inputs other than quoted prices included within level 1 that are observable for the asset or liability, either directly or indirectly. If the asset or liability has a specified (contractual) term, a level 2 input must be observable for substantially the full term of the asset or liability. FASB ASC 820-10-35-48 provides examples of inputs considered to be level 2 inputs. Adjustments to level 2 inputs will vary depending on factors (noted in FASB ASC 820-10-35-50) specific to the asset or liability. An adjustment to a level 2 input that is significant to the entire measurement might result in a fair value measurement categorized within level 3 of the fair value hierarchy if the adjustment uses significant unobservable inputs. See FASB ASC 820-10-55-21 for examples of level 2 inputs.

- level 3 inputs (paragraphs 52–54A of FASB ASC 820-10-35). *Level 3 inputs* are unobservable inputs for the asset or liability. Unobservable inputs should be used to measure fair value to the extent that relevant observable inputs are not available, thereby allowing for situations in which there is little, if any, market activity for the asset or liability at the measurement date. However, the fair value measurement objective remains the same (that is, an exit price from the perspective of a market participant that holds the asset or owes the liability). Therefore, unobservable inputs should reflect the assumptions that market participants would use when pricing the asset or liability, including assumptions about risk. Assumptions about risk include the risk inherent in a particular valuation technique used to measure fair value (such as a pricing model) and the risk inherent in inputs to the valuation technique. A measurement that does not include an adjustment for risk would not represent a fair value measurement if market participants would include one when pricing the asset or liability. Unobservable inputs should be developed using the best information available in the circumstances, which might include the entity's own data. In developing unobservable inputs, a reporting entity may begin with its own data, but it should adjust those data if reasonably available information indicates that other market participants would use different data, or there is something particular to the reporting entity that is not available to other market participants. A reporting entity need not undertake exhaustive efforts to obtain information about market participant assumptions; however, information about market participant assumptions that is reasonably available should be taken into account. See FASB ASC 820-10-55-22 for examples of level 3 inputs.

5.26 As explained in FASB ASC 820-10-35-37A, in some cases, the inputs used to measure the fair value of an asset or a liability might be categorized within different levels of the fair value hierarchy. In those cases, the fair value measurement is categorized in its entirety in the same level of the fair value hierarchy as the lowest level input that is significant to the entire measurement. Adjustments to arrive at measurements based on fair value, such as costs to sell when measuring fair value less costs to sell, should not be taken into account when determining the level of the fair value hierarchy within which a fair value measurement is categorized.

5.27 As discussed in FASB ASC 820-10-35-38, the availability of relevant inputs and their relative subjectivity might affect the selection of appropriate valuation techniques. However, the fair value hierarchy prioritizes the inputs to valuation techniques, not the valuation techniques used to measure fair value. For example, a fair value measurement developed using a present value technique might be categorized within level 2 or level 3, depending on the inputs that are significant to the entire measurement and the level of the fair value hierarchy within which those inputs are categorized.

5.28 A fair value measurement is for a particular asset or liability; therefore, when measuring fair value, a reporting entity should take into account the characteristics of the asset or liability if market participants would take those characteristics into account when pricing the asset or liability at the measurement date. Such characteristics include the condition and location of the asset or restriction, if any, on the sale or use of the asset. As stated in FASB ASC 820-10-35-2C, the effect on the measurement arising from a particular characteristic will differ depending on how that characteristic would be taken into account by market participants. Example 6 in paragraphs 51–55 of FASB ASC 820-10-55 explains that when the restriction is a characteristic of the asset and, therefore, would transfer to a market participant, the fair value of the asset would be adjusted to reflect the effect of the restriction.

Fair Value Measurements of Investments in Certain Entities That Calculate Net Asset Value per Share (or Its Equivalent)

5.29 Paragraphs 59–62 of FASB ASC 820-10-35 contain guidance that permits the use of a practical expedient, with appropriate disclosures, when measuring the fair value of an alternative investment that does not have a readily determinable fair value. According to FASB ASC 820-10-15-4, this guidance applies only to an investment that meets both of the following criteria as of the reporting entity's measurement date:

a. The investment does not have a readily determinable fair value.[3]

b. The investment is in an investment company within the scope of FASB ASC 946, *Financial Services—Investment Companies*, or is an investment in a real estate fund for which it is industry practice to measure investment assets at fair value on a recurring basis and to issue financial statements that are consistent with the measurement principles in FASB ASC 946.

Examples of investments to which this guidance applies may include hedge funds, private equity funds, real estate funds, venture capital funds, offshore fund vehicles, and funds of funds.

---

[3] FASB ASC 820-10-15-5 notes that the FASB ASC glossary definition of *readily determinable fair value* indicates that an equity security would have a readily determinable fair value if any one of three conditions is met. One of those conditions is that sales prices or bid-and-asked quotations are currently available on a securities exchange registered with the SEC or in the over-the-counter (OTC) market, provided that those prices or quotations for the OTC market are publicly reported by NASDAQ or by OTC Markets Group Inc. The definition notes that restricted stock meets that definition if the restriction expires within one year. If an investment otherwise would have a readily determinable fair value, except that the investment has a restriction expiring in more than one year, the reporting entity should not apply paragraphs 59–62 of FASB ASC 820-10-35 and "Pending Content" in FASB ASC 820-10-50-6A to the investment.

5.30 FASB ASC 820-10-35-60 explains that if the net asset value per share of the investment obtained from the investee is not as of the reporting entity's measurement date or is not calculated in a manner consistent with the measurement principles of FASB ASC 946, the reporting entity should consider whether an adjustment to the most recent net asset value per share is necessary.

5.31 "Pending Content" in FASB ASC 820-10-35-54B[4] states that an investment within the scope of paragraphs 4–5 of FASB ASC 820-10-15 for which fair value is measured using net asset value per share (or its equivalent, for example member units or an ownership interest in partners' capital to which a proportionate share of net assets is attributed) as a practical expedient, as described in FASB ASC 820-10-35-59, should not be categorized within the fair value hierarchy. In addition, the disclosure requirements in the "Pending Content" in FASB ASC 820-10-50-2 do not apply to that investment. Disclosures required for an investment for which fair value is measured using net asset value per share (or its equivalent) as a practical expedient are described in the "Pending Content" in FASB ASC 820-10-50-6A. Although the investment is not categorized within the fair value hierarchy, a reporting entity should provide the amount measured using the net asset value per share (or its equivalent) practical expedient to permit reconciliation of the fair value of investments included in the fair value hierarchy to the line items presented in the statement of financial position in accordance with FASB ASC 820-10-50-2B.

5.32 FASB ASC 820-10-35-61 states that the reporting entity should decide on an investment-by-investment basis whether to apply the practical expedient and should apply that practical expedient consistently to the fair value measurement of the reporting entity's entire position in a particular investment, unless it is probable at the measurement date that the reporting entity will sell a portion of an investment at an amount different from net asset value per share (or its equivalent), as described in FASB ASC 820-10-35-62. In those situations, the reporting entity should account for the portion of the investment that is being sold in accordance with FASB ASC 820-10 and should not apply the practical expedient discussed in FASB ASC 820-10-35-59.

Fair Value Determination When the Volume or Level of Activity Has Significantly Decreased

5.33 Paragraphs 54C–54H of FASB ASC 820-10-35 clarify the application of FASB ASC 820 in determining fair value when the volume or level of activity for an asset or a liability has significantly decreased. Guidance is also included in identifying transactions that are not orderly. In addition, paragraphs 90–98 of FASB ASC 820-10-55, including "Pending Content," include illustrations on the application of this guidance.

---

[4] FASB Accounting Standards Update (ASU) No. 2015-07, *Fair Value Measurement (Topic 820): Disclosures for Investments in Certain Entities That Calculate Net Asset Value per Share (or Its Equivalent) (a consensus of the Emerging Issues Task Force)*, was issued in May 2015. The amendments in this ASU are effective for public business entities for fiscal years beginning after December 15, 2015, and interim periods within those fiscal years. For all other entities, the amendments in this ASU are effective for fiscal years beginning after December 15, 2016, and interim periods within those fiscal years. A reporting entity should apply the amendments retrospectively to all periods presented. The retrospective approach requires that an investment for which fair value is measured using the net asset value per share practical expedient be removed from the fair value hierarchy in all periods presented in an entity's financial statements. Earlier application is permitted. Readers are encouraged to read the full text of the ASU, available at www.fasb.org. Readers should apply the appropriate guidance based on their facts and circumstances.

5.34 FASB ASC 820-10-35-54C lists a number of factors that should be evaluated to determine whether there has been a significant decrease in the volume or level of activity for the asset or liability (or similar assets or liabilities) when compared with normal market activity. If the reporting entity concludes that there has been a significant decrease in the volume or level of activity for the asset or liability in relation to normal market conditions, further analysis of the transactions or quoted prices is needed to determine whether an adjustment to the transactions or quoted prices is necessary. In certain circumstances such adjustments may be significant to the fair value measurement in its entirety. Note that a decrease in the volume or level of activity on its own does not necessarily indicate that a transaction price or quoted price does not represent fair value or that a transaction in that market is not orderly.

5.35 FASB ASC 820 does not prescribe a methodology for making significant adjustments to transactions or quoted prices. Regardless of the valuation technique used, a reporting entity should include appropriate risk adjustments, including a risk premium reflecting the amount that market participants would demand as compensation for the uncertainty inherent in the cash flows of an asset or a liability. FASB ASC 820-10-35-54F notes that if there has been a significant decrease in the volume or level of activity for the asset or liability, a change in valuation technique or the use of multiple valuation techniques may be appropriate. When weighting indications of fair value resulting from the use of multiple valuation techniques, a reporting entity should consider the reasonableness of the range of fair value measurements. The objective is to determine the point within the range that is most representative of fair value under current market conditions.

5.36 Even when there has been a significant decrease in the volume or level of activity for the asset or liability, the objective of a fair value measurement remains the same. *Fair value* is the price that would be received to sell an asset or paid to transfer a liability in an orderly transaction between market participants at the measurement date under current market conditions. FASB ASC 820-10-35-54H states that estimating the price at which market participants would be willing to enter into a transaction at the measurement date under current market conditions if there has been a significant decrease in the volume or level of activity for the asset or liability depends on the facts and circumstances at the measurement date and requires judgment. A reporting entity's intention to hold the asset or to settle or otherwise fulfill the liability is not relevant when measuring fair value because fair value is a market-based measurement, not an entity-specific measurement.

5.37 According to FASB ASC 820-10-35-54I, a reporting entity should evaluate the circumstances to determine whether, on the weight of the evidence available, the transaction is orderly. The determination of whether a transaction is orderly (or is not orderly) is more difficult if there has been a significant decrease in the volume or level of activity for the asset or liability in relation to normal market activity for the asset or liability. In such circumstances, it is not appropriate to conclude that all transactions in that market are not orderly (that is, forced liquidations or distress sales). Circumstances that may indicate that a transaction is not orderly and guidance that should be considered in the determination are found in FASB ASC 820-10-35-54I. FASB ASC 820-10-35-54J notes the factors a reporting entity should consider when measuring fair value or estimating market risk premiums. An entity does not need to undertake exhaustive efforts to determine whether a transaction is orderly, but it should not ignore information that is reasonably available. When a reporting entity is a party to a transaction, it is presumed to have sufficient information to conclude whether a transaction is orderly.

Fair Value Option

© Update 5-5 *Accounting and Reporting*: Recognition and Measurement of Financial Assets and Financial Liabilities

FASB ASU No. 2016-01, issued in January 2016, is effective for public entities for fiscal years beginning after December 15, 2017, and interim periods within those fiscal years. Early adoption is not permitted by public business entities; however, the ASU provides for early adoption of certain specified amendments upon issuance as of the beginning of the fiscal year of adoption.

For all other entities, including not-for-profit entities and employee benefit plans within the scope of the FASB ASC 960 through FASB ASC 965 topics for plan accounting, the amendments are effective for fiscal years beginning after December 15, 2018 and interim periods within fiscal years ending after December 15, 2019. Early adoption is permitted by entities other than public business entities as of the fiscal years beginning after December 15, 2017, and interim periods within those fiscal years.

FASB ASU No. 2016-01 amends guidance for recognition, measurement, presentation, and disclosure of financial instruments.

This edition of the guide has not been updated to reflect changes as a result of this ASU, however, the following section will be updated in a future edition to reflect the amendments in this ASU, particularly an amendment that requires an entity to present separately in other comprehensive income the portion of the total change in the fair value of a liability that results from a change in the instrument-specific credit risk for financial liabilities that the entity has elected to measure at fair value in accordance with the fair value option.

Readers are encouraged to consult the full text of the ASU on FASB's website at www.fasb.org. For more information on FASB ASU No. 2016-01, see appendix G of this guide.

5.38 FASB ASC 825, *Financial Instruments*, creates a fair value option under which an entity may irrevocably elect fair value as the initial and subsequent measure for many financial instruments and certain other items, with changes in fair value recognized in the statement of activities as those changes occur. An election is made on an instrument-by-instrument basis (with certain exceptions) on its election date. Generally, this is when an instrument is initially recognized in the financial statements. See FASB ASC 825-10-25-4 for information on election dates for specific eligible items that are other than when the instrument is initially recognized in the financial statements. The fair value option need not be applied to all identical items, except as required by FASB ASC 825-10-25-5. FASB ASC 825-10-15-4 notes that recognized financial assets and financial liabilities are eligible, except those specifically listed. (See the following paragraph for those items excluded from the election.) In addition to the eligible financial instruments, certain other items are eligible for the election such as firm commitments for financial instruments and certain nonfinancial contracts. FASB ASC 825-10-35-4 explains that an entity should report unrealized gains and losses on items for which the fair value option has been elected in earnings at each subsequent reporting date.

5.39 FASB ASC 825-10-15-5 lists those instruments that are not eligible for the fair value option. Specifically excluded from eligibility is an investment in a subsidiary that the entity is required to consolidate; an interest in a variable interest entity (VIE) that the entity is required to consolidate; employer's and plan's obligations for pension benefits; other postretirement benefits (including health care and life insurance benefits); postemployment benefits and deferred compensation arrangements (or assets representing overfunded positions in those plans); financial assets and liabilities recognized under leases (this does not apply to a guarantee of a third-party lease obligation or a contingent obligation arising from a cancelled lease); deposit liabilities of depository institutions; and financial instruments that are, in whole or part, classified by the issuer as a component of shareholders' equity (including temporary equity).

5.40 FASB ASC 825-10-45 and 825-10-50 also include presentation and disclosure requirements designed to facilitate comparisons between entities that choose different measurement attributes for similar types of assets and liabilities. Paragraphs 1–2 of FASB ASC 825-10-45 state that entities should report assets and liabilities that are measured using the fair value option in a manner that separates those reported fair values from the carrying amounts of similar assets and liabilities measured using another measurement attribute. To accomplish that, an entity should either (*a*) present the aggregate carrying amount for both fair value and non-fair-value items on a single line, with the fair value amount parenthetically disclosed or (*b*) present separate lines for the fair value carrying amounts and the non-fair-value carrying amounts. As discussed in FASB ASC 825-10-25-3, upfront costs and fees, such as debt issue costs, may not be deferred for items for which the fair value option has been elected.

Additional Fair Value Considerations

Financial Instruments Listed on a Recognized Exchange

5.41 Ordinarily, management values a financial instrument traded on a recognized exchange (NASDAQ, for example) based on quotations of completed transactions. This is consistent with the guidance in FASB ASC 820. A financial instrument traded on a recognized exchange on the valuation date is usually valued at the last quoted sales price. Such prices are published daily. In the case of a financial instrument listed on more than one recognized exchange, the financial instrument is valued at the last quoted sales price on the exchange on which the financial instrument is principally traded. A financial instrument traded primarily on foreign exchanges is valued at the U.S. dollar equivalent, generally at the closing sales price on the principal exchange where it is traded.

5.42 Paragraphs 5–6A of FASB ASC 820-10-35 state that in the absence of a principal market, the most advantageous market is used. In either case, the principal (or most advantageous) market should be considered from the perspective of the reporting entity, thereby allowing for differences between and among entities with different activities. If there is a principal market for the asset or liability, the fair value measurement should represent the price in that market (whether that price is directly observable or estimated using another valuation technique), even if the price in a different market is potentially more advantageous at the measurement date.

5.43 The FASB ASC glossary defines *level 1 inputs* as quoted prices (unadjusted) in active markets for identical assets or liabilities that the reporting entity has the ability to access at the measurement date. FASB ASC 820-10-35-41 states that a quoted price in an active market provides the most reliable evidence of fair value and should be used without adjustment to measure fair value whenever available, except as specified in FASB ASC 820-10-35-41C. In the event that a market price is not representative of fair value due to significant events that occur after the close of the market but before the measurement date, the entity should establish and consistently apply a policy for identifying those events that might affect fair value measurement.

5.44 Broker-dealers generally value their portfolios at the time of the close of trading on the principal exchange on which the financial instruments are traded. Related financial instruments may be traded in tandem (for example, as part of an arbitrage-trading strategy whose profitability is determined by the relative value of the financial instruments). It is appropriate to review the prices occurring on different exchanges or in different markets for all the individual financial instruments in the trading strategy at a given time in order to assign the proper value to all securities encompassed in that financial strategy.

5.45 According to FASB ASC 820-10-35-24, a reporting entity should use valuation techniques that are appropriate in the circumstances and for which sufficient data are available to measure fair value, maximizing the use of relevant observable inputs and minimizing the use of unobservable inputs. See the "Valuation Techniques" section of this chapter.

Financial Instruments Not Listed on a Recognized Exchange but Having a Readily Available Market Price

5.46 Nonexchange-traded financial instruments are often traded in over-the-counter (OTC) markets by dealers or other intermediaries from whom market prices are obtainable. Quotations are available from various sources for many financial instruments traded regularly in the OTC market. Those sources include the financial press, various quotation and financial reporting services, and individual market makers.

5.47 Financial instruments not listed on a recognized exchange are more likely to be valued using level 2 or level 3 inputs (as opposed to level 1 inputs). If there is a limited amount of trading activity for a financial instrument (that is, if the instrument is thinly traded), the reliability of the market quotation and other market information (for example, volume data) should be evaluated by management. In instances when the fair value, as determined by management, is higher than or lower than the market quotation for a similar, but not identical, financial instrument, the financial instruments should be valued at such fair value. See the "The Fair Value Hierarchy" section of this chapter for more information on the three levels of inputs to valuation techniques.

5.48 Paragraphs 50–51 of FASB ASC 820-10-35 explain that adjustments to level 2 inputs will vary depending on factors specific to the asset or liability. Those factors include the condition or location of the asset or liability, the extent to which the inputs relate to items that are comparable to the asset or liability (including those factors discussed in FASB ASC 820-10-35-16D), and the volume or level of activity in the markets within which the inputs are observed.

A significant adjustment to a level 2 fair value measurement might result in a fair value measurement categorized within level 3 of the fair value hierarchy if the adjustment uses significant unobservable inputs.

Financial Instruments Not Having a Readily Available Market Price

5.49 A broker-dealer may have to determine the fair values of financial instruments for which there are no readily available price quotations or for which readily available price quotations are unreliable. These price quotations may be deemed unreliable because of a variety of reasons. For example, the financial instruments may have restrictions associated with them (such as not being registered), or the entity may have been forced to sell due to financial difficulties. In such cases, it may be appropriate for these financial instruments to be valued at fair value using level 3 inputs, as found in FASB ASC 820. See the "Fair Value Determination When the Volume or Level of Activity Has Significantly Decreased" section of this chapter.

5.50 As noted in the FASB ASC glossary, *level 3 inputs* are unobservable inputs for the asset or liability. According to FASB ASC 820-10-35-53, unobservable inputs are used to measure fair value to the extent that relevant observable inputs are not available. Unobservable inputs should reflect the assumptions that market participants would use when pricing the asset or liability, including assumptions about risk. See the "The Fair Value Hierarchy" section of this chapter.

5.51 Management of the reporting entity should take into consideration all indications of value that are reasonably available in determining the fair value assigned to a particular financial instrument. The information considered and the basis for the decision should be documented. This guide does not purport to delineate all factors that may be considered.

5.52 As noted in FASB ASC 940-820-30-1, the following is a list of certain factors that have been taken into consideration by broker-dealers as part of the determination of fair value:[5]

- Financial standing of the issuer
- Business and financial plan of the issuer
- Cost at date of purchase
- The liquidity of the market (see the "Inputs to Valuation Techniques" section of this chapter for considerations regarding this factor)
- Contractual restrictions on salability
- Pending public offering with respect to the financial instrument
- Pending reorganization activity affecting the financial instrument (such as merger proposals, tender offers, debt restructurings, and conversions)
- Reported prices and the extent of public trading in similar financial instruments of the issuer or comparable entities

---

[5] The SEC's *Codification of Financial Reporting Policies* provides guidance on the factors to be considered and the methods used to value securities for which market quotations are not readily available. FASB ASC 820-10-35 also provides guidance on the valuation of financial instruments for which market quotations are not readily available.

- Ability of the issuer to obtain needed financing
- Changes in the economic conditions affecting the issuer
- A recent purchase or sale of a security of the entity
- Pricing by other dealers in similar securities

5.53 Management may use a variety of methods to assist in determining the valuation of a financial instrument. These methods include analogy to reliable quotations of similar financial instruments, pricing models, matrix pricing, and other formula-based pricing methods. These methodologies incorporate factors for which published market data may be available. For instance, the mathematical technique known as matrix pricing may be used to determine the values based on market data available with respect to the issue and similar issues without exclusive reliance on issuer-specific quoted market prices. FASB ASC 820-10-35-41C notes that matrix pricing is an alternative pricing method that renders the fair value measurement a lower-level measurement.

5.54 Pricing methods may also be based on a multiple of earnings or a discount (or, less frequently, a premium) from market of a similar, freely traded security; on a yield to maturity with respect to debt issues; or on a combination of these and other methods. In addition, with respect to derivative products, other factors (such as volatility, anticipated future interest rates, and term to maturity) should be considered. If such methods are used, management should continuously review the appropriateness of such methods to satisfy themselves that the resulting valuations are fair and in compliance with FASB ASC 820.

Trade-Date Versus Settlement-Date Accounting

5.55 Broker-dealers execute a wide variety of transactions in financial instruments for their own accounts (proprietary transactions, also referred to as principal transactions) or on behalf of customers (agency transactions). The transactions usually involve at least two important dates:

> **trade date.** The date on which an agreement (an executory contract) is entered into, setting forth the important aspects of the transaction (such as a description of the instruments, quantity, price, delivery terms, and so forth).

> **settlement date.** The date on which the financial instrument is required to be delivered to the purchaser and consideration paid. Depending on the particular transaction, the settlement date could be as early as the same day as the trade date or as far away as months (and sometimes more than one year) after the trade date.

5.56 The settlement date is generally established by convention or regulations of the market in which the transaction is executed (for instance, regular-way trades executed on the floor of a stock exchange); for certain types of transactions, the settlement date is based on the terms agreed to by the parties (for instance, forward transactions).

5.57 Although the terms for each type of transaction may differ in many respects, they tend to have the following two major aspects in common:

> a. On the trade date, the purchaser assumes the risks and rewards of further changes in the value of the underlying financial instrument.

> b. On the settlement date, the seller is required to deliver and the purchaser is required to pay for, the financial instrument.

Proprietary and Principal Transactions

5.58 As explained in FASB ASC 940-320-25-1, the statement of financial condition should reflect all regular-way trades on an accrual or a trade-date basis. Risk, benefits, and economic potentials are created and conveyed at the trade date (that is, the inception of the contract), which is when the major terms have been agreed to by the parties. In order to properly reflect the economic effects of purchase and sale transactions for financial instruments (that is, to reflect the assumption of the risks and rewards resulting from changes in the value of financial instruments), broker-dealers should account for the changes in value relating to all proprietary and principal transactions on a trade-date basis.

5.59 For example, as stated in FASB ASC 940-320-25-2, if the broker-dealer purchased financial instruments for its own account on the date of the statement of financial condition, the transaction should be reflected in the broker-dealer's inventory with a corresponding credit to net receivable or payable for unsettled regular-way trades. Per the FASB ASC glossary, regular-way trades include the following: (*a*) all transactions in exchange-traded financial instruments that are expected to settle within the standard settlement cycle of that exchange (for example, three days for U.S. securities exchanges)[6] and (*b*) all transactions in cash-market-traded financial instruments that are expected to settle within the time frame prevalent or traditional for each specific instrument (for example, for U.S. government securities, one or two days).

5.60 For physical commodities (such as lumber, crude oil, and precious metals), the prevalent trade practice for recording such transactions should be followed, which is typically when title passes.

5.61 As noted in FASB ASC 940-320-05-4, the risk of nonperformance of regular-way settling trades is minimal, given the following: (*a*) they are fully collateralized on the trade date; (*b*) the period of time between trade date and settlement date is reasonably short; and (*c*) most equity, U.S. government, and mortgage-backed agency securities are affirmed by both parties to the trade and settle net through a clearing entity. Accordingly, FASB ASC 940-20-45-3 states that payables and receivables arising from these unsettled regular-way transactions may be recorded net in an account titled "Net Receivable (or Payable) for Unsettled Regular-Way Trades."

5.62 Contracts that are defined as derivative instruments according to FASB ASC 815, *Derivatives and Hedging*, should be measured at fair value, in accordance with FASB ASC 820, and recognized in the statement of financial condition as either assets or liabilities, depending on the rights or obligations under the contracts. The fair values of these contracts or of accrued receivables or payables arising from the contracts may be offset only if the provisions of FASB ASC 210-20-45 or FASB ASC 845-10-45 are met.

5.63 Certain other contracts are also recognized in the financial statements of broker-dealers on a trade-date basis. The fair values of unsettled delayed-delivery and to-be-announced securities trades should be based on

---

[6] Through SEC Release No. 34-80295, "Amendment to Securities Transaction Settlement Cycle," the SEC amended Rule 15c6-1(a), *Settlement Cycle Rule*, to shorten the standard settlement cycle for most broker-dealer transactions from three business days after the trade date (T+3) to two business days after the trade date (T+2). The effective date of this release was May 30, 2017, and the compliance date was September 5, 2017.

prices for forward-settling trades. For example, a foreign-exchange forward contract may call for a party to deliver two million U.S. dollars in exchange for two million British pounds sterling at a specified future date. Under current reporting practice, the party would not record a receivable for the British pounds sterling or a payable for the U.S. dollars. Rather, a net amount reflecting the fair value of the position would be reported in the statement of financial condition. Such contracts frequently meet the definition of a derivative under FASB ASC 815.

5.64 Per FASB ASC 940-320-25-2, if the exchange does not occur on the contracted settlement date (referred to as a fail-to-receive or fail-to-deliver), these transactions should be recognized on the statement of financial condition as fails to deliver or fails to receive. See chapter 2, "Broker-Dealer Functions, Books, and Records," for more information on fails-to-receive and fails-to-deliver.

5.65 The receivables and payables resulting from these failed transactions may be netted for financial statement reporting purposes to the extent the provisions of FASB ASC 210-20 are met.

Agency Transactions

5.66 Unlike a principal transaction in which the broker-dealer is the counterparty to the transaction with the customer and, thus, would have the securities transactions flow through its inventory because it is acting in a dealer capacity, in an agency transaction, the broker-dealer is simply a middleman between two counterparties, and thus, the securities transaction does not flow through its inventory because it is acting in a broker capacity.

5.67 FASB ASC 940-20-25-1 explains that transactions executed by broker-dealers as agents for customers are not reflected in the statement of financial condition of the broker-dealer unless the transaction fails to settle on the contracted settlement date. Because the broker-dealer typically delivers cash or financial instruments on behalf of the customer, if the customer fails on the settlement date, the broker-dealer is required to record the transaction (for example, as a fail-to-receive from customer, payable to customer, or stock borrowed or loaned on behalf of customer).

5.68 In accordance with FASB ASC 940-20-25-2, for securities purchased, commissions should be recorded as a receivable from customers; for securities sold, commissions should be recorded as reductions in the payable to customers. The commission income and related expenses are accrued by the broker-dealer on the trade date because substantially all the efforts in generating the commissions have been completed.

Statement of Financial Condition Considerations

Due From, and Due to, Other Broker-Dealers and Clearing Entities

5.69 Amounts due from, and due to, other broker-dealers and clearing entities may arise from the following:

- Net receivables or payables arising from unsettled regular-way transactions
- Securities borrowed and loaned

- Failed settlement transactions
- Clearing entity balances
- Collateral paid or received on derivative transactions
- Commissions
- Deposits

5.70 Balances arising from the foregoing, with the exception of the net payable or receivable arising from unsettled transactions, are reported gross on the statement of financial condition, unless the provisions of FASB ASC 210-20 are met. For example, a broker-dealer may report on a net basis payables and receivables associated with clearing through a clearing entity that provides for and guarantees net settlement balances because the criteria of FASB ASC 210-20 are met. FASB ASC 210-20-45-9 discusses the nature of support required for an assertion in financial statements that a right of setoff is enforceable at law.

Transfers of Financial Assets

5.71 As noted in FASB ASC 860-10-05-4, transfers of financial assets often occur in which the transferor has some continuing involvement either with the assets transferred or the transferee. This situation raises issues about the circumstances under which a transfer should be considered a sale of financial assets rather than a secured borrowing and how transferees and transferors should account for such transactions. FASB ASC 860, *Transfers and Servicing*, establishes accounting and reporting standards for transfers and servicing of financial assets, including sales of financial assets, secured borrowings and collateral, and servicing assets and liabilities.

5.72 Broker-dealers enter into a variety of transactions that may be required to be accounted for either as sales of securities or secured borrowings,[7] depending on the terms of the particular transaction. These include securities borrowing and lending transactions, repo and reverse repo agreements, and dollar repurchase agreements (dollar rolls).

5.73 Securities lending transactions are documented as loans of securities in which the borrower of securities generally is required to provide collateral, commonly cash but sometimes other securities or standby letters of credit, to the lender of securities. The collateral provided will have a value slightly higher than that of the securities borrowed. If the collateral is cash, the lender of securities typically earns a return by investing that cash at rates higher than the rate paid or rebated to the borrower. If the collateral is other than cash, the lender of securities typically receives a fee.

5.74 Repo and reverse repo agreements are structured such that they are documented legally as sales or purchases of securities with forward purchase or sales contracts. In a repo agreement, a security is sold with an agreement to repurchase the security from the buyer; in a reverse repo agreement, a security is purchased with an agreement to resell the security to the seller-lender at a stated price plus interest at a specific date or in specified circumstances.[8] In general, most repo and reverse repo agreements are accounted for as financings, disregarding the legal form of the agreement.

---

[7] *Secured borrowings*, as that term is used in FASB ASC 860, *Transfers and Servicing*, are also sometimes referred to as collateralized financings.

[8] In certain industries, the terminology is reversed.

5.75 The FASB ASC glossary defines *dollar roll repurchase agreements* (dollar rolls) as agreements to sell and repurchase similar but not identical securities. The securities sold and repurchased are usually of the same issuer. Dollar rolls differ from regular repurchase agreements in that the securities sold and repurchased have all of the following characteristics:

a. They are represented by different certificates.

b. They are collateralized by different but similar mortgage pools (for example, conforming single-family residential mortgages).

c. They generally have different principal amounts.

Fixed coupon and yield maintenance dollar agreements comprise the most common agreement variations. In a fixed coupon agreement, the seller and buyer agree that delivery will be made with securities having the same stated interest rate as the interest rate stated on the securities sold. In a yield maintenance agreement, the parties agree that delivery will be made with securities that will provide the seller a yield that is specified in the agreement.

Sale Treatment of Transferred Assets[9]

5.76 FASB ASC 860-10-40 sets forth the conditions required to be met in order to treat the transfer of financial assets as a sale. There are a number of factors to consider when determining when and how to account for transfers of financial assets. One factor is whether the transferee would be consolidated by the transferor. Another key factor in determining if the transaction is a sale (and, therefore, derecognized from the statement of financial position) is determining whether the transferor has surrendered control over the transferred financial assets.

5.77 As noted in FASB ASC 860-10-40-5, a transfer of an entire financial asset, a group of entire financial assets, or a participating interest[10] in an entire financial asset in which the transferor (including its consolidated affiliates included in the financial statements being presented) has surrendered control over those financial assets should be accounted for as a sale if and only if all of the following conditions are met:

a. The transferred assets have been isolated from the transferor—put presumptively beyond the reach of the transferor and its creditors, even in bankruptcy or other receivership (see paragraphs 7–14 of FASB ASC 860-10-40).

b. Each transferee (or each third-party holder of beneficial interests)[11] has the right to pledge or exchange the assets (or beneficial interests) it received, and no transferor-imposed condition constrains the transferee (or third-party holder of the beneficial interest) from taking advantage of its right to pledge or exchange and, through that constraint, provides more than a trivial benefit to the transferor (see paragraphs 15–21 of FASB ASC 860-10-40). If the transferor and its agents have no continuing involvement with the transferred financial assets, the condition is met.

---

[9] Refer to FASB ASC 860 for complete information.

[10] *Participating interest* is defined in FASB ASC 860-10-40-6A.

[11] Third-party beneficial interest is applicable if the transferee is an entity whose sole purpose is to engage in securitization or asset-backed financing activities, and that entity is constrained from pledging or exchanging the assets it receives.

    c. The transferor (or its consolidated affiliates included in the financial statements being presented or its agents) does not maintain effective control over the transferred assets or third-party beneficial interests related to those transferred assets. Effective control includes, but is not limited to

        i. an agreement that both entitles and obligates the transferor to repurchase or redeem the transferred financial assets before their maturity (see paragraphs 23–25 of FASB ASC 860-10-40);

        ii. an agreement, other than through a cleanup call, that provides the transferor with both the unilateral ability to cause the holder to return specific assets and a more than trivial benefit attributable to that ability (see paragraphs 28–39 of FASB ASC 860-10-40); or

        iii. an agreement that permits the transferee to require the transferor to repurchase the transferred financial assets at a price that is so favorable to the transferee that it is probable the transferee will require the transferor to repurchase them (see FASB ASC 860-10-55-42D).

5.78 FASB ASC 860-20 provides derecognition guidance related to transfers of financial assets that meet the criteria for a sale.

Secured Borrowings

5.79 FASB ASC 860-30 provides guidance related to transfers of financial assets[12] that are accounted for as secured borrowings with a transfer of collateral. This guidance applies to transactions in which cash is obtained in exchange for financial assets with an obligation to enter into an opposite exchange at a later date, including repurchase agreements, dollar rolls, and securities lending transactions. FASB ASC 860-30-25-2 notes that the transferor and transferee should account for a transfer as a secured borrowing with a pledge of collateral in either of the following circumstances:

- If a transfer of an entire financial asset, a group of entire financial assets, or a participating interest in an entire financial asset does not meet the conditions for a sale in FASB ASC 860-10-40-5

- If a transfer of a portion of an entire financial asset does not meet the definition of a *participating interest*

In either of these circumstances, the transferor should continue to report the transferred financial asset on its statement of financial condition with no change in the asset's measurement (for example, its basis of accounting).

5.80 Repurchase agreements and securities lending transactions are required to be evaluated under each of the conditions for derecognition in accordance with FASB ASC 860-10-40-5. FASB ASC 860-10-55-51 states that repurchase agreements and securities lending transactions that do not meet

---

[12] Some of the items subject to this guidance are financial instruments. For guidance on matters related broadly to all financial instruments, including the fair value option, see FASB ASC 825, *Financial Instruments.*

all the conditions in FASB ASC 860-10-40-5 should be treated as secured borrowings.

5.81 Many repurchase agreements and securities lending transactions are accompanied by an agreement that both entitles and obligates the transferor to repurchase or redeem transferred financial assets from the transferee before the maturity date of the transferred assets which maintains the transferor's effective control over those assets under FASB ASC 860-10-40-5(c)(1), provided that all the conditions in FASB ASC 860-10-40-24[13] are met. Those transactions should be accounted for as secured borrowings in which either cash or securities received as collateral that the holder is permitted, by contract or by custom, to sell or repledge is considered the amount borrowed. In a securities lending transaction, the securities loaned are considered pledged as collateral against the cash borrowed and therefore reclassified as pledged, separately from other assets not so encumbered, as set forth in FASB ASC 860-30-25-5(a).

5.82 Paragraphs 5A and 24A of FASB ASC 860-10-40 state that a repo-to-maturity transaction, referring to a repurchase of the same (or substantially the same) financial asset, should be accounted for as a secured borrowing as if the transferor maintains effective control, notwithstanding the characteristics discussed in paragraphs 24–24A of FASB ASC 860-10-40.

5.83 FASB ASC 860-30-25-5 states that the accounting for noncash collateral by the obligor (or debtor) and the secured party depends on whether the secured party has the right to sell or repledge the collateral and whether the debtor has defaulted. As noted in FASB ASC 860-30-25-4, in certain cases, cash collateral should be derecognized by the payer (obligor) and recognized by the recipient (secured party) as proceeds of either a sale or borrowing, rather than as collateral. FASB ASC 860-30 provides additional guidance on accounting for collateral.

5.84 FASB ASC 860-30-25-8 states that the transferor of securities being loaned accounts for cash received in the same way whether the transfer is accounted for as a sale or secured borrowing. Cash collateral or securities received as collateral that a securities lender is permitted to sell or repledge are the proceeds of a borrowing secured by them. The cash received should be recognized as the transferor's asset—as should investments made with that cash, even if made by agents or in pools with other securities lenders—along with the obligation to return the cash. If securities that may be sold or repledged are received, the transferor of the securities being loaned accounts for those securities in the same way as it would account for cash received.

5.85 Balances arising from securities lending transactions that are accounted for as secured borrowings are reported gross on the statement of financial condition. Securities-borrowed and securities-loaned transactions do not typically have explicit settlement dates, which is an indication that the reporting party does not intend to setoff. Therefore, those type transactions do not typically meet the conditions for a right of setoff found in FASB ASC 210-20-45-1. Balances arising from repo transactions accounted for as collateralized borrowings should be reported gross in the statement of financial condition, unless all the provisions of FASB ASC 210-20-45-11 are met. FASB ASC 210-20-45-11 may be applied only to repo and reverse repo transactions.

---

[13] See paragraph 5.77.

Exchange Memberships Owned or Contributed

5.86 As discussed in FASB ASC 940-340-25-1, the accounting for exchange memberships depends on the rights they convey and the reasons they are held as assets, as follows:

     a.   *Intangible asset.* An exchange membership should be accounted for as an intangible asset in accordance with FASB ASC 350-10 if it represents only the right to conduct business on an exchange. Such memberships may have finite or indefinite lives based on the terms of the arrangement and the estimated life of the membership.

     b.   *Ownership interest in the exchange.* An exchange membership should be accounted for as an ownership interest in the exchange if the exchange membership represents (i) both an ownership interest and the right to conduct business on the exchange, which are owned by a broker-dealer and held for operating purposes, or (ii) an ownership interest, which must be held by a broker-dealer to conduct business on the exchange. (In accordance with FASB ASC 940-340-30-1 and 940-340-35-1, an ownership interest in the exchange should be accounted for initially and subsequently at cost or a lesser amount if there is an other-than-temporary impairment in value.)

     c.   *Contributed interest.* A membership may be considered to be an asset of the broker-dealer if its use has been contributed to the broker-dealer under a formal or informal subordination agreement. An exchange membership contributed for the use of the broker-dealer and subordinated to claims of general creditors should be accounted for as a contributed interest and a liability subordinated to claims of general creditors.

In accordance with FASB ASC 940-340-30-2 and 940-340-35-2, an exchange membership recognized as a contributed interest should be recorded initially and subsequently at fair value with an equal and offsetting amount recorded for the subordinated liability.

Suspense Accounts

5.87 FASB ASC 940-20-05-8 notes that because of the number of transactions that take place when trades are cleared for the broker-dealer or its customers, unreconciled differences and trading errors occur. A broker-dealer often has several suspense accounts to facilitate the identification and resolution of differences. Per FASB ASC 940-20-25-6, unreconciled differences are recorded at the amount of the transaction with an appropriate valuation account until a determination of the cause of the differences is made and the differences are resolved. Trading errors are recorded in the broker-dealer's error suspense account until they are resolved. FASB ASC 940-20-35-2 further states that the underlying securities are subsequently measured at fair value, and the gain or loss is recognized in income.

Derivatives

5.88 FASB ASC 815 establishes accounting and reporting standards for derivative instruments, including certain derivative instruments embedded in other contracts (collectively referred to as derivatives), and for hedging activities.

5.89 FASB ASC 815-10-15-83 states that a derivative instrument is a financial instrument or other contract with all three of the following characteristics:

a. It has (i) one or more underlyings and (ii) one or more notional amounts[14] or payment provisions or both. Those terms determine the amount of the settlement(s), and, in some cases, whether a settlement is required.

b. It requires no initial net investment or an initial net investment that is smaller than would be required for other types of contracts that would be expected to have a similar response to changes in market factors.

c. Its terms implicitly or explicitly require or permit net settlement, it can readily be settled net by a means outside the contract, or it provides for delivery of an asset that puts the recipient in a position not substantially different from net settlement.

As noted in FASB ASC 815-10-15-71, notwithstanding the previously mentioned characteristics, loan commitments that relate to the origination of mortgage loans that will be held for sale, should be accounted for as derivative instruments by the issuer of the loan commitment (that is, the potential lender). FASB ASC 815-10-15-69 provides a scope exception for the accounting for certain loan commitments. To the extent that a loan commitment is inventory, a broker-dealer would account for it at fair value.

5.90 When recognizing certain loan commitments, SEC Staff Accounting Bulletin (SAB) No. 109 amends and replaces Section DD of Topic 5. This SAB provides interpretive guidance and emphasizes certain disclosure requirements that may be relevant in the context of mortgage banking activities.

5.91 Broker-dealers enter into derivative transactions to deal, to take proprietary positions, to effect economic hedges of instruments in other trading portfolios, to execute arbitrage strategies, or to hedge long-term debt or long-dated resale and repurchase transactions.

5.92 FASB ASC 815-10-05-4 requires that an entity recognize all derivatives as either assets or liabilities in the statement of financial condition and measure those instruments at fair value. If certain conditions are met, a derivative may be specifically designated as (a) a hedge of the exposure to changes in the fair value of a recognized asset or liability or of an unrecognized firm commitment that is attributable to a particular risk (referred to as a fair value hedge); (b) a hedge of the exposure to variability in the cash flows of a recognized asset or liability or of a forecasted transaction, that is attributable to a particular risk (referred to as a cash flow hedge); or (c) a hedge of the foreign currency exposure of a net investment in a foreign operation, an unrecognized firm commitment, an available-for-sale security, or a forecasted transaction.

5.93 As noted in FASB ASC 815-10-35-2, the accounting for changes in the fair value of a derivative instrument (that is, gains and losses) depends on whether it has been designated and qualifies as part of a hedging relationship and, if so, on the reason for holding it. The gain or loss on a derivative instrument not designated as a hedging instrument should be recognized currently

---

[14] *Notional amount* is the number of units specified in the contract (for example, shares, bushels, or other unit). Sometimes other names are used for the term notional. For example, the notional amount is called a "face amount" in some contracts.

in earnings, except as noted in FASB ASC 815-10-35-3. See FASB ASC 815-20 for guidance on the accounting for the gain or loss on a derivative instrument that is designated as a hedging instrument.

5.94 Derivatives entered into by dealers in connection with their dealing activities should be carried at fair value with resultant gains and losses reported currently in income. Quoted market prices provide the most reliable fair value for derivatives traded on a recognized exchange. Fair value for derivatives not traded on a recognized exchange is generally considered to be the value that could be realized through termination or assignment of the derivative. Common valuation methodologies for an interest rate swap incorporate a comparison of the yield of the swap with the current treasury security yield curve and swap to treasury spread quotations or the current swap yield curve. The swap yield curve is derived from quoted swap rates. Dealer bid and offer quotes are generally available for basic interest rate swaps involving counterparties whose securities are investment grade. Factors that could influence the valuation of an individual derivative include the counterparty's credit standing and the complexity of the derivative. If those factors differ from those basic factors underlying the quote, an adjustment to the quoted price should be considered.

5.95 In determining a derivative's value, consideration should be given to recognizing and providing for credit and liquidity risk and the operational and administrative costs associated with the management of derivative portfolios. The methods for determining the amount of credit risk and operational costs may differ among dealers.

5.96 FASB ASC 815-15-25-4 explains that an entity that initially recognizes a hybrid financial instrument that would otherwise be required to be separated into a host contract and derivative instrument may irrevocably elect to initially and subsequently measure that hybrid financial instrument in its entirety at fair value (with changes in fair value recognized in earnings). The financial instrument should be evaluated to determine that it has an embedded derivative requiring bifurcation before the instrument can become a candidate for the fair value election. FASB ASC 815-15-25-5 states that the recognized hybrid financial instrument could be an asset or a liability and it could be acquired or issued by the entity. Also, the fair value election may be made on an instrument-by-instrument basis at the inception of the hybrid instrument (or upon a remeasurement event) and should be supported by concurrent documentation or a preexisting documented policy for automatic election. For more information see the guidance in FASB ASC 815-15.

5.97 FASB ASC 815-10-50 provides guidance regarding the disclosures required in the notes to financial statements as related to derivatives. Note that in some cases, the disclosures required for derivatives relate to disclosures that appear on the face of the financial statements. See chapter 6, "Financial Statement Presentation and Classification," for information on disclosures related to derivative instruments.

Conditional Transactions

5.98 FASB ASC 940-20-25-7 notes that certain transactions (for example, those for when-issued securities) are, by their nature, conditional (that is, their completion is dependent on the occurrence of a future event or events). For those conditional transactions in which completion is assured beyond a reasonable doubt, the recognition of the transactions and related profit and loss should be the same as for unconditional transactions. For those conditional transactions in which completion is not assured beyond a reasonable doubt, only fair value losses should be recognized, whereas fair value gains should be deferred. As noted in FASB ASC 940-20-35-1, fair value gains that have been deferred under FASB ASC 940-20-25-7 should be recognized when the uncertainty is eliminated. For the scope application of FASB ASC 815 to contracts for the purchase or sale of when-issued securities or other securities that do not yet exist, see FASB ASC 815-10-15-15. (See also the "Derivatives" section of this chapter for a discussion of FASB ASC 815.)

Leveraged Buyouts and Bridge Loans

5.99 As noted in FASB ASC 940-325-05-1, a broker-dealer may make investments in the form of equity or provide financing to another entity in connection with financial-restructuring transactions. These investments may take many forms, including a direct investment or an investment in an entity (sometimes referred to as a bridge entity) that is established for the purpose of accumulating funds from several sources sufficient to make the investment. FASB ASC 940-325-30-1 and 940-325-35-1 state that investments in the form of equity or financing provided to another entity in connection with financial-restructuring transactions should be initially and subsequently measured at fair value. As stated in FASB ASC 940-810-45-1, a majority-owned entity that is not in the scope of the "Variable Interest Entity" subsection of FASB ASC 810-10-15 and in which a parent has a controlling financial interest, should not be consolidated if the parent is a broker dealer, and control is likely to be temporary.

Asset Securitizations [15]

5.100 The complexity of securitized products has increased significantly because of the nature of underlying collateral, the complexity of the structure (for example, residual tranches and interest- and principal-only strips), and the depth of markets. Such factors have affected the accounting and valuation of those products. Broker-dealers may acquire, either through market purchases or the underwriting process, securities arising from asset securitizations. Those securities should be valued at fair value in accordance with the guidelines discussed previously.

5.101 FASB ASC 860-50-30-1 states that an entity should initially measure all separately recognized servicing assets and servicing liabilities at fair value. FASB ASC 860-50-35-1 permits, but does not require, the subsequent measurement of separately recognized servicing assets and servicing liabilities at fair value.

5.102 An entity that uses derivative instruments to mitigate the risks inherent in servicing assets and servicing liabilities is required to account for those derivative instruments at fair value. An entity can elect subsequent fair value measurement to account for its separately recognized servicing assets

---

[15] FASB ASU No. 2015-02, *Consolidation (Topic 810)—Amendments to the Consolidation Analysis*, was issued in February 2015. The amendments are effective for public business entities for fiscal years, and for interim periods within those fiscal years, beginning after December 15, 2015. For all other entities, the amendments are effective for fiscal years beginning after December 15, 2016, and for interim periods within fiscal years beginning after December 15, 2017. Additional effective date information is available in the ASU. A reporting entity also may apply the amendments retrospectively. Readers are encouraged to read the full text of the ASU, available at www.fasb.org. Readers should apply the appropriate guidance based on their facts and circumstances.

and servicing liabilities. By electing that option, an entity may simplify its accounting because that option permits income statement recognition of the potential offsetting changes in fair value of those servicing assets and servicing liabilities and derivative instruments in the same accounting period.

5.103   In addition, certain securities that arise from asset securitizations may raise issues about whether the underlying legal entity should be consolidated by the broker-dealer. FASB ASC 860 provides guidance on the securitization of financial assets held by broker-dealers and for other transfers of financial assets involving special purpose entities. In a typical asset securitization transaction, a company transfers assets to a special-purpose vehicle (SPV) or VIE in exchange for cash or securities issued by the SPV or the VIE. Securitization vehicles need to be evaluated under FASB ASC 810, *Consolidation*, to determine if the broker-dealer is the primary beneficiary of the VIE and, therefore, should consolidate the VIE or if the broker-dealer holds a significant variable interest in the VIE and should make the appropriate disclosures.

Variable Interest Entities [16]

5.104   FASB ASC 810 addresses consolidation by business entities of VIEs with certain characteristics.[17] A *VIE*, as defined by the FASB ASC glossary, is a legal entity subject to consolidation according to the provisions of the "Variable Interest Entity" subsections of FASB ASC 810-10. FASB ASC 810 addresses certain entities in which equity investors do not have the characteristics of a controlling financial interest or do not have sufficient equity at risk for the entity to finance its activities without additional subordinated financial support from other parties. FASB ASC 810-10-50 includes disclosure requirements.

Soft-Dollar Arrangements

5.105   According to the FASB ASC glossary, *soft-dollar arrangements* are arrangements in which a broker-dealer provides research to a customer in return for trade order flow (a certain volume of trades) from that customer. As noted in FASB ASC 940-20-05-4, these arrangements generate commission income for the broker-dealer. Many of these agreements are oral, and the value of the research to be provided is typically based on a percentage of commission income. Soft-dollar customers are typically institutional investors or money managers. Soft-dollar research may be generated either internally by the broker-dealer or purchased by the broker-dealer from a third party.

5.106   Since the 1970s, when soft-dollars were first used, some broker-dealers and money managers have used soft-dollars to cover transactions or expenses not associated with research. These types of transactions are governed by Section 28(e) of the Securities Exchange Act of 1934, which allows the paying of a brokerage commission if the manager determines in good faith

---

[16] See footnote 15.

[17] FASB ASU No. 2014-13, *Consolidation (Topic 810)—Measuring the Financial Assets and the Financial Liabilities of a Consolidated Collateralized Financing Entity (a consensus of the FASB Emerging Issues Task Force)*, was issued in August 2014. The amendments in this ASU are effective for public business entities for annual periods, and interim periods within those annual periods, beginning after December 15, 2015. For entities other than public business entities, the amendments in this ASU are effective for annual periods ending after December 15, 2016, and interim periods beginning after December 15, 2016. Early adoption is permitted as of the beginning of an annual period. Additional effective date information is available in the ASU. Readers are encouraged to read the full text of the ASU, available at www.fasb.org. Readers should apply the appropriate guidance based on their facts and circumstances.

that the commission is reasonable in relation to the value of the brokerage and research services provided.

5.107 In 2006, the SEC published final interpretative guidance (Release No. 34-54165, *Commission Guidance Regarding Client Commission Practices Under Section 28(e) of the Securities Exchange Act of 1934*) regarding the "soft-dollar" safe harbor of Section 28(e) of the Securities Exchange Act of 1934. The release more clearly defines the boundaries of permissible "research" and "brokerage" products under the safe harbor.

5.108 FASB ASC 940-20-25-3 explains that at the date of the statement of financial condition, the broker-dealer should analyze both the commission income generated from soft-dollar customers and the research provided to the soft-dollar customers to determine whether a liability should be accrued for research due to customers based on the commission income generated or whether any soft-dollar expenses have been prepaid and need to be deferred.

5.109 The realizability of any prepaid expenses should be evaluated as of the financial statement date.

Mandatorily Redeemable Instruments[18]

5.110 A *mandatorily redeemable instrument* is a financial instrument issued in the form of shares[19] that embody an unconditional obligation requiring the issuer[20] to redeem the instrument by transferring its assets at specified or determinable date(s) or upon an event that is certain to occur. FASB ASC 480, *Distinguishing Liabilities from Equity*, establishes standards for how an issuer classifies and measures in its statement of financial position certain financial instruments with characteristics of both liabilities and equity. FASB ASC 480-10-25 requires that an issuer classify a financial instrument within its scope as a liability (or an asset in some circumstances) because that financial instrument embodies an obligation of the issuer.

5.111 Such obligation as mentioned in the previous paragraph may arise from the terms of an operating, a partnership, or an incorporation agreement or the operation of state law.

5.112 Under FASB ASC 480-10, broker-dealers that have issued shares that must be sold back to the company upon the holder's death or termination of employment should record those shares as liabilities, rather than equity because the shares are mandatorily redeemable upon an event certain to occur. As a result, some broker-dealers may report minimal or no equity in their GAAP financial statements. From a regulatory standpoint, application of FASB ASC 480 can cause a broker-dealer to fall below its minimum net capital requirements under SEC Rule 15c3-l(a) or cause its subordinated debt to debt-equity total to increase above the 70 percent limit set forth in Rule 15c3-l(d). Broker-dealers may have amended, partnership, operating (such as limited liability

---

[18] The effective date for the classification, measurement, and disclosure provisions of FASB ASC 480, *Distinguishing Liabilities from Equity*, is deferred indefinitely for certain mandatorily redeemable financial instruments of certain nonpublic entities and certain mandatorily redeemable noncontrolling interests, as discussed in FASB ASC 480-10-65-1. Mandatorily redeemable financial instruments issued by SEC registrants are not eligible for the effective date deferral. Because registered broker-dealers are required to submit financial statements to the SEC, they are within the scope of SEC registrant in this guidance and, therefore, are subject to the guidance in FASB ASC 480-10.

[19] For the purpose of this guidance, shares include various forms of ownership that may or may not take the legal form of securities (for example, partnership interests).

[20] An *issuer*, for the purpose of this guidance, is the entity that issued the financial instrument.

company), shareholder, or other agreements to avoid the potential adverse impacts of FASB ASC 480 on net capital.

Statement of Income or Loss Considerations

> **© Update 5-6 *Accounting and Reporting*: Revenue from Contracts with Customers**[21]
>
> The "Pending Content" that links to FASB ASC 606-10-65-1, is effective for annual reporting periods beginning after December 15, 2017, including interim reporting periods within that reporting period, for a public business entity, a not-for-profit entity that has issued, or is a conduit bond obligor for, securities that are traded, listed, or quoted on an exchange or an over-the-counter market, and an employee benefit plan that files or furnishes financial statements with or to the SEC. Earlier application is permitted only as of annual reporting periods beginning after December 15, 2016, including interim reporting periods within that reporting period.
>
> For other entities, FASB ASC 606 is effective for annual reporting periods beginning after December 15, 2018, and interim periods within annual periods beginning after December 15, 2019. Other entities may elect to adopt the standard earlier, however, only as of either
>
> - an annual reporting period beginning after December 15, 2016, including interim periods within that reporting period, or
> - an annual reporting period beginning after December 15, 2016, and interim periods within annual periods beginning one year after the annual reporting period in which an entity first applies the "Pending Content" that links to FASB ASC 606-10-65-1.
>
> FASB ASC 606 provides a framework for revenue recognition and supersedes or amends several of the revenue recognition requirements in FASB ASC 605, as well as guidance within the 900 series of industry-specific topics. The standard applies to any entity that either enters into contracts with customers to transfer goods or services or enters into contracts for the transfer of nonfinancial assets unless those contracts are within the scope of other standards (for example, insurance or lease contracts).
>
> Readers are encouraged to consult the full text of FASB ASC 606 on FASB's website at www.fasb.org.
>
> For more information, see appendix E of this guide.

Underwriting Revenues and Expenses

5.113   As noted in FASB ASC 940-20-05-10, there are several different ways in which a broker-dealer may participate in the underwriting of a new issue of securities. The broker-dealer may be the managing or lead underwriter, a member of the syndicate, or a member of the selling group. Such participation may be on one of the following bases:

- Firm commitment

---

[21] See footnote 1.

- Standby
- Best efforts
- All or none

5.114 FASB ASC 940-340-05-1b notes that in connection with its participation in an underwriting of securities, a broker-dealer may receive various types of revenues, as well as incur various related expenses. Such revenues include management fees (in the case of the lead or comanaging underwriter), underwriting fees (in the case of the lead underwriter and other members of the syndicate), and selling concession fees (in the case of all selling group members). The related expenses include, but are not limited to, marketing and advertising fees, legal fees, stabilization costs, and the other costs associated with setting up the syndicate group. These expenses are accumulated by the lead underwriter and allocated to the other members of the syndicate on a pro rata basis.

5.115 As discussed in FASB ASC 940-605-25-2, the fee revenue relating to the underwriting commitment should be recorded when all significant items relating to the underwriting cycle have been completed and the amount of the underwriting revenue has been determined. This will generally be at the point at which all of the following have occurred (which may or may not be prior to the settlement date of the issue):

- The issuer's registration statement has become effective with the SEC, or other offering documents are finalized (as opposed to the closing or settlement date).
- The broker-dealer has made a firm commitment for the purchase of the shares or debt from the issuer.
- The broker-dealer has been informed of the exact number of shares or the principal amount of debt that it has been allotted (if it is not the lead underwriter of an undivided offering).

5.116 FASB ASC 940-340-25-3 and 940-340-35-3 state that when the related underwriting expenses described previously are incurred prior to the actual issuance of the securities, such expenses are deferred and recognized at the time the related revenues are recorded. In the event that the transaction is not completed and the securities are not issued, the entities that have agreed to participate in the costs associated with the underwriting write those costs off to expense.

5.117 According to FASB ASC 940-20-35-3, with respect to the underwriting of issues that trade prior to the settlement date, the broker-dealer should subsequently measure at fair value any shares that it is firmly committed to purchase but that have not yet been subscribed to by customers.

Mutual Fund Distribution Costs

5.118 FASB ASC 940-20-05-5 notes that broker-dealers may contract with one or more mutual funds to act as the registered distributor of the mutual fund's shares, assisting the fund in selling and distributing its shares. If a broker-dealer undertakes the responsibility for selling and distributing fund shares, it will incur different types of costs, the most common of which are commissions paid to those of its representatives who arrange fund sales. To compensate a broker-dealer for those selling efforts, mutual funds may establish some form of a fund-charge and shareholder-commission structure that provides fees to the broker-dealer either at the time of sale or over a specified period of time. Two common forms of compensation are the following:

- A front-end commission paid to the broker-dealer by the fund shareholder at the time of sale.

- A 12b-1 distribution fee that is paid by the fund over a period of time based on a percentage of the fund's daily net asset levels, together with a deferred sales charge that is a commission paid to the broker-dealer by the shareholder at the time the shareholder exits the fund. Deferred sales charges are often charged to the shareholder in decreasing amounts over time.

5.119 In accordance with FASB ASC 940-605-25-3, a front-end commission should be recorded in full by the broker-dealer at the time it is earned (the trade date). FASB ASC 940-605-25-4 further notes that with respect to 12b-1 fees and deferred sales charges, the broker-dealer generally defers its incremental direct costs associated with the selling of the fund shares (such as sales representatives' commissions and direct marketing costs) and amortizes these costs over the period in which the fees from the fund or fund shareholders are expected to be received. Indirect costs associated with selling the fund shares are expensed as incurred.

Half-Turn Convention

5.120 According to FASB ASC 940-605-30-1, commissions on certain contracts, such as commodity futures and options, may be billed to customers on a round-turn basis. The FASB ASC glossary defines *round turn* as a purchase and subsequent sale or a sale and subsequent purchase of a commodity futures contract. As explained in FASB ASC 940-605-30-2, even though the round-turn commissions may be reflected in the customer's account upon entering into the transaction or on the date of the round turn, this commission income should be recognized in the statement of income on a half-turn basis. Per the FASB ASC glossary, *half turn* is a transaction involving the purchase or sale as either an opening or a closing transaction of a commodity futures contract.

Interest, Dividends, and Rebates

5.121 The income statement classification of interest, dividends, and rebate income and expense varies, because certain transactions are entered into as financings and others are entered into as part of trading strategies.

5.122 FASB ASC 940-405-45-1 states that stock-loan and repo transactions may be entered into for the purpose of financing positions (such as in lieu of a bank loan). If such transactions are accounted for as financing transactions (see the "Secured Borrowings" section of this chapter), the rebate or interest expense should be reflected in the income statement as an expense separate and apart from any trading gains or losses.

5.123 However, FASB ASC 940-320-05-3 notes that broker-dealers frequently enter into matched-stock borrow and loan transactions as a finder or conduit, or enter into repo and reverse repo agreements as part of a matched-book trading strategy. Further, complex trading strategies often involve numerous long and short positions in different products so that those positions reflect a trading position that is different from its individual components (for example, box spreads, conversions, and reversals). FASB ASC 940-320-45-6 further states that for those activities, the resulting income and expense may be reflected net in the income statement, with disclosure of the gross components either on the face of the income statement or in the notes to the financial statements.

Costs Associated With Exit or Disposal Activities

5.124 FASB ASC 420, *Exit or Disposal Cost Obligations*, provides guidance on accounting and reporting for costs associated with exit or disposal activities, such as during a restructuring. Examples of costs include, but are not limited to, costs to consolidate or close facilities and relocate employees and costs to terminate a contract that is not a capital lease. Appropriate disclosure of any exit or disposal activity should be in the notes to the financial statements and the financial effects should be disclosed in the financial statements, as required by FASB ASC 420-10-50.

Chapter 6

Financial Statement Presentation and Classification

℗ Update 6-1 FASB *Accounting Standards Codification* (ASC) 606, *Revenue from Contracts with Customers*[1]

The "Pending Content" that links to FASB ASC 606-10-65-1, is effective for annual reporting periods beginning after December 15, 2017, including interim reporting periods within that reporting period, for a public business entity, a not-for-profit entity that has issued, or is a conduit bond obligor for, securities that are traded, listed, or quoted on an exchange or an over-the-counter market, and an employee benefit plan that files or furnishes financial statements with or to the SEC. Earlier application is permitted only as of annual reporting periods beginning after December 15, 2016, including interim reporting periods within that reporting period.

For other entities, FASB ASC 606 is effective for annual reporting periods beginning after December 15, 2018, and interim periods within annual periods beginning after December 15, 2019. Other entities may elect to adopt the standard earlier, however, only as of either

- an annual reporting period beginning after December 15, 2016, including interim periods within that reporting period, or

- an annual reporting period beginning after December 15, 2016, and interim periods within annual periods beginning one year after the annual reporting period in which an entity first applies the "Pending Content" that links to FASB ASC 606-10-65-1.

FASB ASC 606 provides a framework for revenue recognition and supersedes or amends several of the revenue recognition requirements in FASB ASC 605, *Revenue Recognition*, as well as guidance within the 900 series of industry-specific topics, including FASB ASC 940, *Financial Services—Brokers and Dealers*. The standard applies to any entity that either enters into contracts with customers to transfer goods or services or enters into contracts for the transfer of nonfinancial assets unless those contracts are within the scope of other standards (for example, insurance or lease contracts).

Readers are encouraged to consult the full text of FASB ASC 606 on FASB's website at www.fasb.org.

The AICPA has formed 16 industry task forces to assist in developing a new Accounting Guide on revenue recognition that will provide helpful hints and

---

[1] At the July 20, 2017 meeting of the Emerging Issues Task Force (EITF), the SEC staff announced that it would not object to elections by certain public business entities to use the nonpublic business entities effective dates for the sole purpose of adopting FASB *Accounting Standards Codification* (ASC) 606, *Revenue from Contracts with Customers*, and FASB ASC 842, *Leases*. The staff announcement makes clear that the ability to use the nonpublic business entities effective dates for adopting these new standards is limited to the subset of public business entities "that otherwise would not meet the definition of a public business entity except for a requirement to include or inclusion of its financial statements or financial information in another entity's filings with the SEC." Generally, this election would not be applicable to broker-dealers, however, readers should consult with their regulators and auditors if they believe it is.

illustrative examples for how to apply the new standard. Revenue recognition implementation issues identified by the Brokers and Dealers in Securities Revenue Recognition Task Force are available for informal comment, after review by the AICPA Financial Reporting Executive Committee, at www.aicpa.org/interestareas/frc/accountingfinancialreporting/revenuerecognition/pages/rrtf-brokerdealer.aspx.

Readers are encouraged to submit comments to revreccomments@aicpa.org.

As of the date of this publication, nine accounting implementation issues specific to the broker-dealer industry have been identified. Of the nine identified issues, three issues have been finalized and incorporated in the 2017 AICPA Audit and Accounting Guide *Revenue Recognition*. These finalized issues include:

- Considerations for broker-dealers in applying the guidance in FASB ASC 606 to trade-based commission income earned by providing trade facilitation, execution, clearance and settlement, custody, and trade administration services to its customers
- Whether the trade execution performance obligation is satisfied on the trade date or the settlement date
- Considerations for broker-dealers in applying the guidance in FASB ASC 606 when costs are incurred to obtain a contract to provide advisory services to a customer
- Clarification that the recognition of realized and unrealized gains and losses on proprietary transactions involving the purchase and sale of financial instruments and interest and dividend income on financial instrument contracts held by broker dealers are excluded from the scope of FASB ASC 606

For more information, see appendix E, "The New Revenue Recognition Standard: FASB ASC 606," of this guide.

© **Update 6-2 *Accounting and Reporting*: Recognition and Measurement of Financial Assets and Financial Liabilities**

FASB Accounting Standards Update (ASU) No. 2016-01, *Financial Instruments—Overall (Subtopic 825-10): Recognition and Measurement of Financial Assets and Financial Liabilities*, issued in January 2016, is effective for public entities for fiscal years beginning after December 15, 2017 and interim periods within those fiscal years. Early adoption is not permitted by public business entities; however, the ASU provides for early adoption of certain specified amendments upon issuance as of the beginning of the fiscal year of adoption.

For all other entities, including not-for-profit entities and employee benefit plans within the scope of FASB ASC 960, *Plan Accounting—Defined Benefit Pension Plans* through FASB ASC 965, *Plan Accounting—Health and Welfare Benefit Plans* topics for plan accounting, the amendments are effective for fiscal years beginning after December 15, 2018 and interim periods within fiscal years ending after December 15, 2019. Early adoption is permitted by entities other than public business entities as of the fiscal years beginning after December 15, 2017 and interim periods within those fiscal years.

FASB ASU No. 2016-01 amends guidance for recognition, measurement, presentation, and disclosure of financial instruments.

This edition of the guide has not been updated to reflect changes as a result of this ASU, however, this chapter will be updated in a future edition to reflect the amendments in this ASU, particularly an amendment that requires an entity to present separately in other comprehensive income the portion of the total change in the fair value of a liability that results from a change in the instrument-specific credit risk for financial liabilities that the entity has elected to measure at fair value in accordance with the fair value option.

Readers are encouraged to consult the full text of the ASU on FASB's website at www.fasb.org. For more information on FASB ASU No. 2016-01, see appendix G, "Accounting for Financial Instruments," of this guide.

© **Update 6-3 FASB ASU No. 2016-02, *Leases (Topic 842)*[2]**

FASB ASU No. 2016-02, issued in February 2016, is effective for fiscal years beginning after December 15, 2018, including interim periods within those fiscal years, for any of the following: (1) a public business entity; (2) a not-for-profit entity that has issued, or is a conduit bond obligor for, securities that are traded, listed, or quoted on an exchange or an over the-counter market; or (3) an employee benefit plan that files financial statements with the SEC.

For all other entities, the amendments in this update are effective for fiscal years beginning after December 15, 2019, and interim periods within fiscal years beginning after December 15, 2020.

Early application of the amendments in this update is permitted for all entities.

Readers are encouraged to consult the full text of this ASU on FASB's website at www.fasb.org.

This edition of the guide has not been updated to reflect changes as a result of this ASU, however, this chapter will be updated in a future edition. For more information on FASB ASU No. 2016-02, see appendix F, "The New Leases Standard: FASB ASU No. 2016-02," of this guide.

© **Update 6-4 FASB ASU No. 2016-13, *Financial Instruments—Credit Losses (Topic 326): Measurement of Credit Losses on Financial Instruments***

FASB ASU No. 2016-13 was issued in June 2016. For public business entities that are SEC filers, the amendments in this ASU are effective for fiscal years beginning after December 15, 2019, including interim periods within those fiscal years. For all other public business entities, the amendments in this update are effective for fiscal years beginning after December 15, 2020, including interim periods within those fiscal years.

For all other entities, including not-for-profit entities and employee benefit plans within the scope of FASB ASC 960 through FASB ASC 965 on plan accounting, the amendments in this ASU are effective for fiscal years beginning

---

[2] See footnote 1.

after December 15, 2020, and interim periods within fiscal years beginning after December 15, 2021.

All entities may adopt the amendments in this ASU earlier as of the fiscal years beginning after December 15, 2018, including interim periods within those fiscal years. See FASB ASU No. 2016-13 for additional information regarding the effective date of this ASU.

This edition of the guide has not been updated to reflect changes as a result of this ASU, however, this chapter will be updated in a future edition. Readers are encouraged to consult the full text of this ASU on FASB's website at www.fasb.org.

Ⓒ **Update 6-5 FASB ASU No. 2017-12,** *Derivatives and Hedging (Topic 815): Targeted Improvements to Accounting for Hedging Activities*

FASB ASU No. 2017-12 was issued in August 2017. For public business entities, the amendments in this ASU are effective for fiscal years beginning after December 15, 2018, and interim periods within those fiscal years. For all other entities, the amendments are effective for fiscal years beginning after December 15, 2019, and interim periods beginning after December 15, 2020.

Early application is permitted in any interim period after issuance of the ASU. All transition requirements and elections should be applied to hedging relationships existing (that is, hedging relationships in which the hedging instrument has not expired, been sold, terminated, or exercised or the entity has not removed the designation of the hedging relationship) on the date of adoption. The effect of adoption should be reflected as of the beginning of the fiscal year of adoption (that is, the initial application date).

This edition of the guide has not been updated to reflect changes as a result of this ASU, however, this chapter will be updated in a future edition. Readers are encouraged to consult the full text of this ASU on FASB's website at www.fasb.org.

Introduction

6.01 Broker-dealers are guided in their preparation of financial statements primarily by accounting principles generally accepted in the United States of America (GAAP). However, broker-dealers are further subject to SEC Rule 17a-5 and the Financial and Operational Combined Uniform Single (FOCUS) forms thereunder. SEC Rule 17a-5 requires, in addition to monthly and quarterly filings on the prescribed forms (Form X-17A-5—FOCUS Parts I, II, and IIA), annual audited financial statements that include a statement of financial condition, a statement of income or operations, a statement of cash flows, a statement of changes in ownership equity (stockholders' or members' equity or partners' or sole proprietor's capital), and a statement of changes in liabilities subordinated to claims of general creditors, and the applicable supplementary schedules (discussed in the "Supplementary Schedules" section of this chapter). Paragraph (d)(2) of SEC Rule 17a-5 requires that the annual audited financial statements are presented in a format consistent with Form X-17A-5 Part II or Form X-17a-5 Part IIA, as applicable.

6.02 In addition to annual audited financial statements, broker-dealers are required to distribute a mid-year statement of financial condition, including a footnote containing a statement of net capital and required net capital to requesting customers (as defined by paragraph (c)(4) of SEC Rule 17a-5). Paragraph (c)(3) of SEC Rule 17a-5 requires that these unaudited statements are dated six months from the date of the audited statements and are to be furnished within 65 days after the date of the unaudited statements. Certain financial information may be excluded from these statements if requirements prescribed in paragraph (c)(5) of SEC Rule 17a-5 are met.

6.03 SEC Rule 17a-5(d) requires disclosure of a reconciliation of the net capital and reserve requirement computations presented as supplementary schedules to the audited financial statements and those within the filed FOCUS report, should material differences exist.

6.04 In addition to the disclosures shown in exhibit 6-8, there may be certain other disclosures required under SEC Regulation S-X for those companies that are registered under Section 12(b) or 12(g) of the Securities Exchange Act of 1934 (the 1934 Act). Regulation S-X does not apply to the financial statements filed with the SEC under Rule 17a-5.

6.05 Broker-dealers commonly prepare their financial statements on a single-year basis, which complies with the requirements of SEC Rule 17a-5. Coexisting financial statements for other than regulatory filings (such as bank lending requirements or reports to shareholders) are also generally prepared on a single-year basis.

6.06 In accordance with paragraph (d)(5) of SEC Rule 17a-5 broker-dealers are required to file annual reports, including the annual audited financial statements (as discussed in paragraph 6.01), a compliance report or exemption report, and the accompanying opinion letters and reports from the independent accountant (see chapter 3, "Regulatory Considerations"), within 60 calendar days after the end of each fiscal year.

6.07 *Compliance report.*[3] In accordance with paragraph (d)(3) of SEC Rule 17a-5, a broker-dealer subject to the customer protection requirements of SEC Rule 15c3-3 (a "carrying broker-dealer") must file an annual "Compliance Report" containing five statements concerning their Internal Controls Over Compliance with the Financial Responsibility Rules, defined by paragraph (d)(3) of SEC Rule 17a-5 as those included in SEC Rules 15c3-1, 15c3-3, 17a-13, or any rule of the designated examining authority of the broker-dealer that requires account statements to be sent to the customers of the broker-dealer ("Account Statement Rule"). The following statements must be included within the compliance report:

- Whether the broker-dealer has established and maintained Internal Control Over Compliance, which is defined as internal controls that provide reasonable assurance that noncompliance will be prevented or detected on a timely basis;

- Whether the Internal Control Over Compliance of the broker-dealer was effective during the most recent fiscal year and, if applicable, a description of each identified *material weakness*, as defined in SEC Rule 17a-5;

---

[3] See appendix B, "Illustrative Example of Compliance Report Required by SEC Rule 17a-5," of this guide.

- Whether the Internal Control Over Compliance of the broker-dealer was effective as of the end of the most recent fiscal year and, if applicable, a description of each identified *material weakness*, as defined in SEC Rule 17a-5;

- Whether the broker-dealer was in compliance with SEC Rule 15c3-1 and paragraph (e) of SEC Rule 15c3-3 as of the end of the most recent fiscal year and, if applicable, a description of any instance(s) of noncompliance with those rules;

- The information the broker-dealer used to state whether it was in compliance with SEC Rule 15c3-1 and paragraph (e) of SEC Rule15c3-3 as of the end of the most recent fiscal year was derived from the books and records of the broker-dealer.

6.08 *Examination report.* With its compliance report, a broker-dealer must file an examination report prepared by its independent public accountant, which provides the accountant's assessment of certain statements made in the broker-dealer's compliance report.

6.09 *Exemption report.*[4] A noncarrying broker-dealer that claimed an exemption per the provisions in paragraph (k) of SEC Rule 15c3-3 throughout the most recent fiscal year must file an exemption report specifying the exemption on which it is relying. A broker-dealer must state in the report that it met the exemption provisions throughout the year without exceptions or with exceptions which must be described in the report to the broker-dealer's best knowledge and belief.

6.10 *Review report.* With its exemption report, a broker-dealer must file a review report prepared by its independent public accountant, which provides the accountant's assessment of the statements made in the broker-dealer's exemption report.

6.11 A broker-dealer that is a member of the Securities Investor Protection Corporation (SIPC) must file its annual reports with SIPC concurrently with their filing with the SEC. In addition, all broker-dealers are required to file an agreed-upon procedures report with SIPC over the SIPC filing.

6.12 *Access to audit documentation of clearing brokers.* Carrying and clearing broker-dealers are required to permit their independent public accountants to make available to the SEC and other regulators audit documentation associated with the annual audit reports required under SEC Rule 17a-5.

Financial Statements

Statement of Financial Condition

6.13 The statement of financial condition should be in a format and on a basis consistent with the totals reported on the statement of financial condition contained in Part II or IIA of the FOCUS report as filed by the broker-dealer. This presentation should be in accordance with GAAP. However, as discussed in FASB ASC 940-20-45-1, current and noncurrent classifications are ordinarily not presented in the statement of financial condition because such a distinction normally has little meaning for broker dealers.

---

[4] See appendix C, "Illustrative Example of Exemption Report Required by SEC Rule 17a-5," of this guide.

6.14 Consideration should be given to the materiality of each asset and liability account in determining the accounts warranting separate line items on the statement of financial condition.

6.15 In accordance with the "Pending Content" in FASB ASC 810-10-45-25, a reporting entity should present (a) assets of a consolidated variable interest entity (VIE) that can be used only to settle obligations of the consolidated VIE and (b) liabilities of a consolidated VIE for which creditors (or beneficial interest holders) do not have recourse to the general credit of the primary beneficiary separately on the face of the statement of financial condition. Additionally, information pertaining to a broker-dealer's consolidated VIEs under FASB ASC 810-10 should be disclosed. Refer to exhibit 6-3 for an illustration.

Statement of Income or Operations

6.16 The statement of income or operations should be in a format that is consistent with the statement contained in Part II or Part IIA of the FOCUS report, and it should disclose separately the sources of the broker-dealer's revenues (such as commissions, trading and investment gains or losses [principal transactions], underwriting profits or losses [investment banking], fee income, dividends, and interest).

6.17 Expenses should be reported by major types (such as employee compensation and benefits, technology and communications, occupancy and equipment, interest and dividends, floor brokerage, exchange and clearance fees).

6.18 Consideration should be given to the materiality of each revenue source and expense type in determining the accounts warranting separate line items on the statement of income or operations.

6.19 Generally, expenses incurred by a broker-dealer related to revenue-generating activities should be recorded on a gross basis. For cases in which the broker-dealer is acting in an "agent" capacity only, revenue may be recorded net of certain expenses meeting the criteria set forth in FASB ASC 605-45. For taxes collected from customers and remitted to governmental authorities, it is an accounting policy decision whether to present on a gross basis or net basis.

Statement of Cash Flows

> © **Update 6-6** *Accounting and Reporting*: **Statement of Cash Flows**
>
> FASB ASU No. 2016-15, *Statement of Cash Flows (Topic 230): Classification of Certain Cash Receipts and Cash Payments*, issued in August 2016, is effective for fiscal years, including interim periods within those fiscal years, of a public business entity beginning after December 15, 2017.
>
> For all other entities, FASB ASU No. 2016-15 is effective for fiscal years beginning after December 15, 2018, and interim periods within fiscal years beginning after December 15, 2019. Early adoption is permitted, including adoption in an interim period. If an entity early adopts the amendments in an interim period, any adjustments should be reflected as of the beginning of the fiscal year that includes that interim period. An entity that elects early adoption must adopt all of the amendments in the same period.
>
> FASB ASU No. 2016-15 addresses the following eight specific cash flow issues: debt prepayment or debt extinguishment costs; settlement of zero-coupon debt instruments or other debt instruments with coupon interest rates that

are insignificant in relation to the effective interest rate of the borrowing; contingent consideration payments made after a business combination; proceeds from the settlement of insurance claims; proceeds from the settlement of corporate-owned life insurance policies (including bank-owned life insurance policies; distributions received from equity method investees; beneficial interests in securitization transactions; and separately identifiable cash flows and application of the predominance principle.

This edition of the guide has not been updated to reflect changes as a result of this ASU, however, this section will be updated in a future edition. Readers are encouraged to consult the full text of this ASU on FASB's website at www.fasb.org.

☉ Update 6-7 *Accounting and Reporting*: Restricted Cash

FASB ASU No. 2016-18, *Statement of Cash Flows (Topic 230): Restricted Cash*, issued in November 2016, is effective for fiscal years, including interim periods within those fiscal years, of a public business entity beginning after December 15, 2017.

For all other entities, FASB ASU No. 2016-18 is effective for fiscal years beginning after December 15, 2018, and interim periods within those fiscal years beginning after December 15, 2019. Early adoption is permitted, including adoption in an interim period. If an entity early adopts the amendments in an interim period, any adjustments should be reflected as of the beginning of the fiscal year that includes that interim period.

FASB ASU No. 2016-18 requires that a statement of cash flows explain the change during the period in total of cash, cash equivalents, and amount generally described as restricted cash or restricted cash equivalents. Therefore, amounts generally described as restricted cash and restricted cash equivalents should be included with cash and cash equivalents when reconciling the beginning-of-period and end-of-period total amounts shown on the statement of cash flows.

This edition of the guide has not been updated to reflect changes as a result of this ASU, however, this section will be updated in a future edition. Readers are encouraged to consult the full text of this ASU on FASB's website at www.fasb.org.

6.20   As noted in FASB ASC 230-10-15-3, a business entity that provides a set of financial statements that presents both the statement of financial condition and statement of income or operations should also provide a statement of cash flows for each period for which a statement of income or operations is provided.

6.21   FASB ASC 940-320-45-7 states that broker-dealers should report their trading securities activities in the operating section of the statement of cash flows. This presentation is appropriate for the securities industry because, unlike other industries, a broker-dealer's business is to buy, sell, and finance securities and other financial instruments.

Statement of Changes in Ownership Equity

6.22   The statement of changes in ownership equity should be in a format that is consistent with the statement contained in Part II or Part IIA of the

FOCUS report. This statement is required regardless of whether the reporting broker-dealer is a corporation, limited liability company, partnership, or sole proprietorship. It should disclose the principal changes in the equity accounts of the broker-dealer during the periods for which a statement of income or operations is presented.

6.23 FASB ASC 480, *Distinguishing Liabilities from Equity*, provides guidance regarding certain instruments that should not be considered equity but, instead, should generally be considered a liability and classified as such (with changes reflected as a component of the income statement). Examples include certain mandatorily redeemable preferred and common stock, general partner buy-sell arrangements, and other similar arrangements. (See chapter 5, "Accounting Standards," of this guide for more information.) Separate classification on the face of the financial statements and disclosure in the footnotes should be made for any redeemable forms of equity. See paragraphs 1–2 of FASB ASC 480-10-45 and paragraphs 1–4 of FASB ASC 480-10-50 for additional guidance.

Statement of Changes in Subordinated Borrowings

6.24 The SEC requires a statement showing the changes in liabilities subordinated to claims of general creditors for each year being reported on. This statement is generally included even if no changes in subordinated liabilities occur during the year; however, generally a statement is not included if no subordinated liabilities existed at any time during the year. Broker-dealers dually registered with the Commodities Futures Trading Commission (CFTC) should note that CFTC Regulation 1.10, *Financial reports of futures commission merchants and introducing brokers*, section (d)(iii) requires this statement in all cases.

Consolidation of Subsidiaries

6.25 Annual audited financial statements of a company and its subsidiaries that are presented in conformity with GAAP are presented on a consolidated basis in accordance with FASB ASC 810, *Consolidation*; FASB ASC 860, *Transfers and Servicing*; and FASB ASC 805, *Business Combinations*. However, the financial statements filed as Part II or Part IIA on the FOCUS report may have different consolidation requirements than the audited financial statements prepared under GAAP. The SEC requires that such differences, if material, be disclosed in a note to the audited financial statements or included as supplementary information.

6.26 Net capital is computed on an unconsolidated basis. For subsidiaries consolidated under the flow-through capital benefits of Appendix C of SEC Rule 15c3-1, the effect of the consolidation on net capital and required net capital of the broker-dealer should be disclosed in the notes to the financial statements or in the net capital supplementary schedule as required by paragraph (c)(ii) of SEC Rule 17a-5.

6.27 FASB ASC 940-810-45-1 states that a majority-owned entity that is not in the scope of the "Variable Interest Entities" subsection of FASB ASC 810-10-15 and in which a parent has a controlling financial interest should not be consolidated if the parent is a broker-dealer within the scope of FASB ASC 940 and control is likely to be temporary.

Going Concern

6.28 As discussed in the "Pending Content" in FASB ASC 205-40,[5] in connection with preparing financial statements for each annual and interim reporting period, an entity's management should evaluate whether there are conditions or events, considered in the aggregate, that raise substantial doubt about the entity's ability to continue as a going concern within one year after the date that the financial statements are issued (or within one year after the date that the financial statements are available to be issued when applicable). Management's evaluation should be based on relevant conditions and events that are known and reasonably knowable at the date that the financial statements are issued (or at the date that the financial statements are available to be issued when applicable).

6.29 If conditions or events raise substantial doubt about an entity's ability to continue as a going concern, but the substantial doubt is alleviated as a result of consideration of management's plans, the entity should disclose information that enables users of the financial statements to understand all of the following (or refer to similar information disclosed elsewhere in the footnotes):

  a. Principal conditions or events that raised substantial doubt about the entity's ability to continue as a going concern (before consideration of management's plans)

  b. Management's evaluation of the significance of those conditions or events in relation to the entity's ability to meet its obligations

  c. Management's plans that alleviated substantial doubt about the entity's ability to continue as a going concern

6.30 If conditions or events raise substantial doubt about an entity's ability to continue as a going concern, and substantial doubt is not alleviated after consideration of management's plans, an entity should include a statement in the footnotes indicating that there is substantial doubt about the entity's ability to continue as a going concern within one year after the date that the financial statements are issued (or available to be issued). Additionally, the entity should disclose information that enables users of the financial statements to understand all of the following:

  a. Principal conditions or events that raise substantial doubt about the entity's ability to continue as a going concern

  b. Management's evaluation of the significance of those conditions or events in relation to the entity's ability to meet its obligations

  c. Management's plans that are intended to mitigate the conditions or events that raise substantial doubt about the entity's ability to continue as a going concern

---

[5] FASB Accounting Standards Update (ASU) No. 2014-15, *Presentation of Financial Statements—Going Concern (Subtopic 205-40): Disclosure of Uncertainties about an Entity's Ability to Continue as a Going Concern,* was issued in August 2014. The amendments in this ASU were effective for the annual period ending after December 15, 2016, and for annual periods and interim periods thereafter. Readers are encouraged to read the full text of the ASU, available at www.fasb.org. Readers should apply the appropriate guidance based on their facts and circumstances.

Supplementary Schedules

6.31 Certain supplementary schedules are required to be filed along with, and as of the same date as, the financial statements, when submitting the financial statements to certain regulators, such as the SEC. These supplementary schedules should be presented in the format that presents the relevant details required by applicable SEC and CFTC rules. The independent auditors' report is required to cover these schedules. See exhibit 6-9 for illustrative examples of these supplementary schedules.

6.32 For the following supplementary schedules, a reconciliation is required if material differences exist between the computations reported on by the independent auditor and the computations filed previously by the broker-dealer in the original unaudited FOCUS report. If no material differences exist, a statement to that effect should be made in the schedule(s). However, it should be noted that as permitted under the "SEC Letter to New York Stock Exchange (NYSE)" dated April 24, 1987, if a broker-dealer files an amended FOCUS report that contains the reconciliation and explanation of material differences between the amended report and original report, the auditor's report may be reconciled with the amended FOCUS report and would include a statement about whether any material differences exist between the amended FOCUS report and the audited financial statements. The date of the amended FOCUS filing must also be included.

Computation of Net Capital Pursuant to SEC Rule 15c3-1

6.33 This schedule shows the computation of the broker-dealer's net capital requirements and excess net capital as of the period end. A reconciliation is required if material differences exist between the computations reported on by the independent auditor and the computations filed previously by the broker-dealer in the unaudited FOCUS report (as discussed in paragraph 6.32). If no material differences exist, a statement to that effect should be made in the schedule(s).

Computations for Determination of Reserve Requirements Pursuant to SEC Rule 15c3-3

6.34 These schedules show the broker-dealer's computations of the required deposits in special reserve bank accounts for the exclusive benefit of customers and proprietary accounts of broker-dealers (PAB). SEC Rule 17a-5 requires both a supplementary schedule detailing the computation of the reserve requirement for customers and a separate supplementary schedule for the PAB computation.

6.35 A reconciliation is required if material differences exist between the computations reported on by the independent auditor and the computations filed previously by the broker-dealer in the unaudited FOCUS report (as discussed in paragraph 6.34). If no material differences exist, a statement to that effect should be made in the schedule(s).

Information Relating to Possession or Control Requirements Under SEC Rule 15c3-3

6.36 This schedule discloses the number of security positions and the related fair value of securities required to be in possession or control that had not been reduced to possession or control in the proper time frame because (*a*) properly issued segregation instructions were not acted upon, or (*b*) segregation instructions were not issued. In addition, for those items not in possession or control, the current status of the reduction of those items to possession or control should be included within the schedule, consistent with Note B within the "Information for Possession or Control Requirements Under Rule 15c3-3" section on the FOCUS report. A reconciliation is required if material differences exist between the schedule reported on by the independent auditor and the schedule filed previously by the broker-dealer in the unaudited FOCUS report (as discussed in paragraph 6.32). If no material differences exist, a statement to that effect should be made in the schedule(s).

6.37   SEC Rule 15c3-3(b)(5) also requires carrying broker-dealers to obtain and maintain possession or control of securities carried for PAB accounts unless the clearing broker-dealer has provided written notice to the PAB account holder that the securities may be used in the ordinary course of business, and has provided an opportunity for the account holder to object. Along with customer-related disclosures, possession or control information for those "objecting" PAB accounts must be included in the broker-dealer's "Information for Possession or Control Requirements Under Rule 15c3-3" section of the FOCUS report and the corresponding supplementary schedule.

Schedules of Segregation Requirements and Funds in Segregation for Customers' Trading Pursuant to the Commodity Exchange Act

6.38   The segregation schedule shows the computation of the amount of funds that should be segregated for customers trading on U.S. commodity exchanges and the total funds segregated by the broker-dealer to meet those requirements. In addition, a secured amount schedule showing the computation of funds required to be set aside in separate accounts for customers trading on non-U.S. commodity exchanges and the amount of funds in such separate accounts should be included in the filing. Lastly, a cleared swaps amount schedule that shows the computation of cleared swaps segregation requirements and funds in cleared swaps customer accounts must also be included in the schedule. A reconciliation is required if material differences exist between the computations reported on by the independent auditor and the computations filed previously by the broker-dealer in the original unaudited FOCUS report. See paragraph 6.32. If no material differences exist, a statement to that effect should be made in the schedule(s). See the illustrative example presented in schedule VI, "Statement of Cleared Swaps Customer Segregation Requirements and Funds in Cleared Swaps Customer Accounts Under 4D(f) of the Commodity Exchange Act" in this chapter.

Statement of Financial Condition Account Descriptions

6.39   Although, many statement of financial condition accounts within a broker-dealer's general ledger are self-explanatory, the accounts discussed in the following paragraphs require special comment because they contain certain characteristics or are related to certain transactions unique to broker-dealers.

Cash and Securities Segregated Under Federal and Other Regulations

6.40   Cash or securities in banks subject to withdrawal restrictions, restricted deposits held as compensating balances, and cash segregated in compliance with federal or other regulations (such as cash deposited in a special reserve bank account for the exclusive benefit of customers pursuant to SEC Rule 15c3-3) should be classified separately in the statement of financial condition as segregated or disclosed in the notes to the financial statements, as such. Additionally, because of the attributes of segregated cash and related assets under SEC and CFTC rules and regulations, many futures commission merchants and some broker-dealers disclose in the notes a summary of the funds in segregation.

Memberships in Exchanges

6.41 As discussed in FASB ASC 940-340-05-1, exchange memberships provide the broker-dealer with the right to do business on the exchanges of which the broker-dealer is a member. Some exchange memberships also represent an ownership interest in the exchange. Due to the demutualization of many exchanges, membership may not be aligned with ownership in the exchange as trading privileges are disaggregated from ownership. Many broker-dealers have memberships in several exchanges and more than one membership in any particular exchange.

6.42 To the extent that a broker-dealer holds the minimum exchange membership required in order to conduct business on the exchange, the asset is held at cost. Any exchange memberships held in excess of the minimum requirements would be considered an investment and would typically be held at fair value.

6.43 Memberships are usually registered in the names of individuals who are affiliated with the broker-dealer. FASB ASC 940-340-25-2 states that a membership held in the name of an individual is considered to be an asset of the broker-dealer if it is held by the broker-dealer under an agreement that would require the member to take specific action upon leaving the broker-dealer.

6.44 As noted in FASB ASC 940-340-25-1, the accounting for exchange memberships depends on the rights they convey and the reasons they are held as assets, as follows:

    a. *Intangible asset.* If an exchange membership represents only the right to conduct business on an exchange, the entity should account for the exchange membership as an intangible asset according to the guidance in FASB ASC 350-10, including the "Pending Content." Such memberships may have finite or indefinite lives based on the terms of the arrangement and the estimated life of the membership.

    b. *Ownership interest in the exchange.* An exchange membership should be accounted for as an ownership interest in the exchange, which should be measured initially at cost in accordance with FASB ASC 940-340-30-1, if either of the following conditions is met:

        i. The exchange membership represents both an ownership interest and the right to conduct business on the exchange, which are owned by a broker-dealer and held for operating purposes.

        ii. The exchange membership represents an ownership interest, which must be held by a broker-dealer to conduct business on the exchange.

    c. *Contributed interest.* A membership may be considered to be an asset of the broker-dealer if its use has been contributed to the broker-dealer under a formal or informal subordination agreement. An exchange membership contributed for the use of the broker-dealer and subordinated to claims of general creditors should be accounted for as a contributed interest, measured initially at fair value, and the equal and offsetting liability subordinated to claims of general creditors in accordance with FASB ASC 940-340-30-2.

6.45 Additional interests that are provided by the exchange that are above those that are required to trade on the exchange should be evaluated separately (for example, these interests are often additional financial instruments that are eligible for trading and should be carried as inventory.)

Securities Sold Under Agreements to Repurchase and Securities Purchased Under Agreements to Resell

6.46 A repurchase transaction (repo) is a sale of a security coupled with an agreement by the seller to repurchase the same or substantially the same security from the same counterparty at a fixed or determinable price (generally the original sales price plus accrued interest) within a fixed or variable time period. The meaning of *substantially the same* is discussed in FASB ASC 860-10-40-24a.

6.47 FASB ASC 860 provides specific criteria for determining whether repos should be accounted for as sales or secured borrowings. In accordance with FASB ASC 860-10-40-5, transfers of financial assets, including repos, should be accounted for as sales if and only if the transferred assets have been isolated from the transferor, the transferee has the right to pledge or exchange the asset of beneficial interest received, and transferor does not maintain effective control over the transferred asset. If any of these conditions are not met, the agreement should be accounted for as a secured borrowing. See the discussion in chapter 5 of this guide for more information related to transfers of financial assets.

6.48 A reverse repurchase agreement (reverse repo or resale) is the purchase of a security at a specified price with an agreement to sell the same or substantially the same security to the same counterparty at a fixed or determinable price at a future date.

6.49 Repos and reverse repos that are accounted for as collateralized borrowings should be recorded as both assets and liabilities on the statement of financial condition and may be netted if the conditions of FASB ASC 210-20-45-11 are met (see paragraph 6.52).

6.50 FASB ASC 210-20-05-1 states that it is a general principle of accounting that the offsetting of assets and liabilities in the balance sheet is improper except if a "right of setoff" exists, which is defined as a debtor's legal right, by contract or otherwise, to discharge all or a portion of the debt owed to another party by applying against the debt an amount that the other party owes to the debtor. FASB ASC 210-20-45-1 provides that a right of setoff exists when all of the following conditions are met:

    a. Each of two parties owes the other determinable amounts.

    b. The reporting party has the right to set off the amount owed with the amount owed by the other party.

    c. The reporting party intends to set off.

    d. The right of setoff is *enforceable at law* (as defined in FASB ASC 210-20-45-9).

6.51 The required disclosures when right of setoff exists are discussed in the "Balance Sheet Offsetting Disclosures" section of this chapter.

6.52 In accordance with FASB ASC 210-20-45-11, if the intent to set off condition in FASB ASC 210-20-45-1 is not met, a broker-dealer may, but is not required to, offset repo liabilities and reverse repo assets accounted for as collateralized borrowings if all of the following conditions are met:

    a. The repo and reverse repo agreements are executed with the same counterparty.

    b. The repo and reverse repo agreements have the same explicit settlement date specified at the inception of the agreement.

    c. The repo and reverse repo agreement are executed in accordance with a master netting agreement.

    d. The repo and reverse repo agreements will be settled on a securities transfer system that operates in the manner described in paragraphs 14–17 of FASB ASC 210-20-45, and the entity must have associated banking arrangements in place as described in those paragraphs. Cash settlements for securities transferred should be made under established banking arrangements that provide that the entity will need available cash on deposit only for any net amounts that are due at the end of the business day. It must be probable (likely to occur) that the associated banking arrangements will provide sufficient daylight overdraft or other intraday credit at the settlement date for each of the parties.

    e. The entity intends to use the same account at the clearing bank or other financial institution at the settlement date in transacting both the cash inflows resulting from the settlement of the reverse repo agreement and the cash outflows in settlement of the offsetting repo agreement.

Securities Borrowed and Securities Loaned

6.53 *Securities borrowed.* Broker-dealers borrow securities from other broker-dealers or institutions for the following purposes:

- To deliver securities to customers who have sold short (for example, sold a security not owned) or lack proper endorsements of securities preventing delivery to buyers

- To fulfill their own delivery obligations as a broker-dealer

- To obtain a security for the purpose of lending in connection with finder or conduit transactions

- To be used for other purposes permitted under Federal Reserve Regulation T (Regulation T) of the Board of Governors of the Federal Reserve System

- To obtain possession or control of a security in deficit, as required by SEC Rule 15c3-3

6.54 *Securities loaned.* Securities are loaned to other broker-dealers as a method of financing (for example, to utilize securities inventory in order to receive cash) or in finder or conduit transactions.

6.55 Broker-dealers may advance cash, pledge securities as allowed under Regulation T (permitted securities), or issue letters of credit as collateral for borrowed securities. Cash collateral posted by the broker-dealer borrowing the security is typically in excess of the fair value of the securities borrowed.

6.56 In certain transactions as described in FASB ASC 860-30, cash collateral should be derecognized by the payer and recognized by the recipient not as collateral but, rather, as proceeds of either a sale or borrowing. Accordingly, the amount recorded on the general ledger as Securities Borrowed represents the value of cash collateral posted, rather than the actual market value of the securities borrowed. For broker-dealers lending securities, the amount recorded on the general ledger as Securities Loaned represents the cash collateral received.

6.57 The amount of collateral required may increase or decrease based on changes in the value of the securities. If the value of the borrowed securities falls below a level, as pre-determined between the borrower and lender, the borrower of the security will request a return of excess cash collateral. This would result in a receipt of cash and decrease in the Securities Borrowed account for the borrowing broker-dealer, and a payment of cash and decrease in the Securities Loaned account for the lending broker-dealer. Conversely, if the value of a security increases, the lender of the security will generally request additional cash collateral to cover potential exposure to credit risk. This would result in a payment of cash to the lender and an increase in the Securities Borrowed account for the borrowing broker-dealer, and a receipt of cash and an increase to the Securities Loaned account for the lending broker-dealer.

6.58 The borrowing broker-dealer normally receives interest (rebate) on the cash it posted as collateral for the securities borrowed. Interest is accrued throughout the period based on the cash collateral amount outstanding. Therefore, the borrowing broker-dealer will typically record interest income on the transaction and the lending broker-dealer will record interest expense. Rebate rates in these transactions are agreed upon between the borrower and lender and are typically derived from standard interest rates (for example, Federal Funds Rate).

6.59 FASB ASC 940-405-55-1 states that securities lending transactions that do not have explicit settlement dates do not meet the requirement in FASB ASC 210-20-45-1 for a right of setoff. Therefore, balances arising from securities borrowed and loaned transactions that are accounted for as secured borrowings are presented gross on the statement of financial condition because they do not have explicit settlement dates.

6.60 FASB ASC 860 provides specific criteria for determining whether a securities lending transaction is to be accounted for as a sale or secured borrowing and provides an illustration of the latter. See chapter 5 of this guide for further discussion of secured borrowings.

Securities Received as Collateral and Obligation to Return Securities Received as Collateral

6.61 As previously described, securities lending transactions are typically collateralized with cash or cash equivalents. However, broker-dealers may engage in securities lending activities with customers or other broker-dealers in which collateral for securities loaned is provided in the form of other securities. These transactions are usually governed by specific securities lending agreements between the broker-dealer and the counterparty or customer, and will usually require that the securities are identical in type, nominal value, description, and amount.

6.62 To the extent that the reporting broker-dealer is the lender in this type of transaction, in accordance with FASB ASC 860-30-25-8 the broker-dealer must record the securities received on the statement of financial condition as an asset (Securities Received as Collateral) and an equal and offsetting liability (Obligation to Return Securities Received as Collateral), similar to how it would record cash received.

6.63 If the reporting broker-dealer engages in "borrow versus pledge" transactions as the borrowing party, usually designated by securities lending agreement terms and fee payment, there should be no recognition on the statement of financial condition.

Receivables From and Payables to Broker-Dealers, Clearing Organizations, and Others

6.64 Receivables from broker-dealers, clearing organizations, and others may include amounts receivable for securities failed to deliver; amounts receivable from clearing organizations relating to open transactions, margin deposits used as performance bonds for open trades, and good-faith funds on deposit regardless of activity; and commissions and floor-brokerage receivables. Payables to broker-dealers and clearing organizations include amounts payable for securities failed to receive, certain deposits received for securities loaned, amounts payable to clearing organizations on open transactions, and floor-brokerage payables. In addition, the net receivable or payable arising from unsettled trades would be reflected in either the receivable or payable line item on the statement of financial condition.

6.65 If a broker-dealer clears transactions on behalf of correspondents, or has its transactions cleared through other correspondents, there may be balances in the omnibus accounts with one or more of the correspondents. Balances included in this category may be shown separately on the statement of financial condition as due from or due to correspondent brokers.

6.66 If a broker-dealer provides a trading platform for mutual fund shares, any trades that are unsettled as of the date of the statement of financial condition should be reported as receivables and payables for redemptions and purchases, respectively. These balances may be listed as "Receivables from Mutual Funds" or "Payable to Mutual Funds" on the statement of financial condition or combined with another receivable line item, depending on the materiality of the balances.

6.67 A broker-dealer that provides derivatives clearing services to its customers collects *initial margin* (IM), typically in cash or security form, from its customers and remits such IM to the clearing house (CCP) or segregates it at a custodian bank. IM generally serves as collateral posted by the customer, through the broker-dealer clearing member, to establish a trading relationship with the CCP. The CCP sets a minimum IM requirement for each listed derivative position based upon the market risk of the derivative. The broker-dealer clearing member may be further required (for example, under CFTC Regulation 39.13) to collect IM from customers in an amount that is in excess of the CCP minimum requirements. The broker-dealer clearing member also may, in its discretion, impose additional IM requirements on a customer based on such customer's specific credit risk profile and current trading positions. This additional amount may be adjusted periodically to reflect changes in those risk attributes. IM is returned to the customer when trade positions are liquidated with the CCP or when the customer terminates its trading the relationship and closes its account.

6.68 The broker-dealer would assess various factors surrounding control and risk and rewards over the assets and liabilities to determine whether the broker-dealer clearing member may have to record on its balance sheet, the cash IM amount received from the customer as a *due to customer* (*payable*) and the cash IM amount remitted to the CCP or custodian bank as a due from *CCP/bank* (*receivable*). These factors may include, but are not limited to, whether (and to what degree) the broker-dealer clearing member

- retains control over the cash IM (for example, retaining transformation rights and making permitted investments with the cash under CFTC Regulation 1.25), or

- has a right to potential economic benefits earned from the customer's cash IM in excess of a market-based fee that is commensurate with the clearing services it provides, (for example, earns yield on permitted investments of the cash or does not pass through to customers the interest received from [or fees assessed by] the CCPs or custodian bank), or

- has an obligation for potential economic costs (for example, foreign exchange risk or payment of negative interest), or guarantees the CCP's or custodian bank's performance to the customer and whether the cash IM would be subject to customer protection and prioritization as customer property in the event of the broker-dealer clearing member's bankruptcy.

Each broker-dealer clearing member will need to consider their individual facts and circumstances and the factors considered to be relevant when evaluating whether cash IM should be recorded on its balance sheet.

6.69 *Fail-to-deliver.* According to FASB ASC 940-20-25-4, a broker-dealer that sells securities, either for its own account or a customer's account, but does not deliver the securities on the settlement date should record the fail-to-deliver as an asset in the receivable due from broker-dealers account. FASB ASC 940-20-30-1 states that a fail-to-deliver asset should be measured initially at the selling price of the security, including any accrued interest in the case of a fixed income security. Fail-to-deliver assets are collected upon delivery of the securities by the selling broker-dealer.

6.70 *Fail-to-receive.* FASB ASC 940-20-25-5 notes that a broker-dealer that purchases securities, either for its own account or a customer's account, but does not receive the securities on the settlement date should record the fail-to-receive as a liability to the selling broker-dealer. FASB ASC 940-20-30-2 states that a fail-to-receive liability should be measured initially at the purchase price of the security, including any accrued interest in the case of a fixed income security. Fail-to-receive liabilities are paid when the securities are received by the purchasing broker-dealer.

6.71 *Clearing organizations receivables and payables.* As described in chapter 1, "The Securities Industry," clearing organizations provide efficient and orderly trade clearance and settlement services for which clearing broker-dealers pay fees.

6.72 All continuous net settlement (CNS) transactions (see chapter 1 for a description of these transactions) are netted at each clearing organization to one cash settlement position due to or due from the broker-dealer. Therefore, if the contract amount of the securities to be received (purchased) is greater than that to be delivered (sold), the clearing broker-dealer records a payable to the clearing organization for the net movement. In practice, many broker-dealers pay or receive payment for their daily CNS balance at the end of each business day and therefore the outstanding CNS receivable or payable as of the financial reporting period would be zero, unless there were fails-to-deliver or fails-to-receive.

Receivables From and Payables to Customers

6.73 The term *customers* generally excludes other broker-dealers; persons who are principal officers, directors, and stockholders; and persons whose securities or funds are part of the regulatory net capital of the broker-dealer. Another broker-dealer's account may be classified as a customer if the account is carried as an omnibus account in compliance with Regulation T. The accounts of principal officers, directors, and stockholders may be combined in the customer captions if they are not material, and the combination is disclosed in the oath accompanying the annual audited financial statements.

6.74 Receivables from and payables to customers may include balances arising from customer securities and margin transactions. Upon receipt of a customer cash deposit, the clearing broker-dealer will record a payable to customer. Payables to customers may be reduced through customer trading activity, recorded on a settlement date basis. An account in a payable position typically represents excess cash in the customer account. To the extent that a broker-dealer extends credit to a customer, a receivable is recorded upon the margin loan initiation, which is typically the settlement date for the related trade. Interest is earned on these customer margin loans, which often comprises a significant portion of a broker-dealer's interest income. Interest expense may be incurred on customer payables; however, as the rates at which this interest accrues are generally much lower than that of margin loans, this interest expense is often not material for broker-dealers.

6.75 As the majority of clearing brokers directly debit fees from customer accounts on a monthly basis (for example, at the beginning of the month for services provided the prior month), receivables from customers due to accrued interest, trade commissions, and management fees generally represent one month's worth of various customer fee earnings.

6.76 In the event that a broker-dealer fails to deliver or fails to receive a security in conjunction with a customer transaction, a corresponding payable to or receivable from, respectively, would be recorded on the settlement date. Refer to the "Receivables From and Payables to Broker-Dealers, Clearing Organizations, and Others" section in this chapter for further information.

Deferred Dealer Concessions

6.77 When a broker-dealer is a mutual fund distributor, it may incur distribution costs and in turn receive 12b-1 fees, or fees paid to a broker-dealer for marketing or distributing mutual funds, from the fund as compensation for these costs. In some situations a broker-dealer also pays an upfront commission to a broker who sells the fund. If this upfront cost is combined with the right to receive 12b-1 fees and contingent deferred sales charges (CDSC) from the fund, the broker-dealer should capitalize the cost of the payment and amortize it over the period during which it will receive fees, and analyze the asset for impairment, on a regular basis, based on the future cash flows relating to the 12b-1 fees to be earned. A broker-dealer may also finance the cost of the upfront commission, and therefore should record the cash received and a liability. Additionally, if the broker-dealer sells the right to receive revenue, the broker-dealer should record revenue for the sale and expense the deferred dealer concession.

Securities Owned and Securities Sold, Not Yet Purchased

6.78 According to FASB ASC 940-320-45-2, proprietary securities transactions entered into by the broker-dealer for trading or investment purposes are included in "securities owned" and "securities sold, not yet purchased." As discussed in FASB ASC 940-320-25, all regular-way firm trades should be recorded in the broker-dealer's inventory on a trade-date basis. The corresponding account to this entry would be a receivable or payable to broker-dealer for unsettled regular-way trades. If the trade does not settle on the settlement date, a fail-to-deliver or fail-to-receive will be recorded.

6.79 Although proprietary trading is frequently thought of as purchasing securities for sale to others, trading securities for the broker-dealer's own account sometimes leads to a liability for the fair value of securities sold but not yet purchased (that is, sold short). The broker-dealer is then obligated to purchase the securities at a future date at the then-current market price.

6.80 FASB ASC 940-320-30-2 and FASB ASC 940-320-35-1 state that security positions resulting from proprietary trading are measured initially and subsequently at fair value. According to FASB ASC 940-320-35-2, any unrealized gains or losses resulting from subsequent measurement of these to fair value are included in profit or loss. As noted in FASB ASC 940-320-45-4, the fair value of fixed-income securities owned that were purchased at a discount or premium comprises accreted interest income, changes in the fair value of the securities, or both. Consideration should be given to reporting these components separately as interest income and trading gains and losses, respectively.

6.81 See chapter 5 for a discussion of fair value measurement under FASB ASC 820, *Fair Value Measurement*.

6.82 To the extent that a broker-dealer holds proprietary derivative positions, these should also be recorded on the balance sheet, and may be combined with securities in "Financial Instruments Owned" and "Financial Instruments Sold, Not Yet Purchased" or presented alone or combined with a different line item, as determined by the broker-dealer based on the materiality of the positions. FASB ASC 820 would apply to the measurement of the positions on the balance sheet.

6.83 Specific requirements regarding joint accounts with other broker-dealers are included in the instructions to the FOCUS report. For joint accounts carried by the broker-dealer, the applicable portion of the securities or other positions should be included in the appropriate securities owned or other classifications, and the other parties' interests in the ledger balance are included in receivables or payables. If the joint account is carried by another broker-dealer, the share of the broker-dealer being reported on should be determined and disclosed with a contra-liability to, or receivable from, the carrying broker-dealer.

6.84 FASB ASC 860-30-25 addresses the accounting for collateral and requires, in some cases, that a debtor reclassify an asset pledged as collateral to indicate it is encumbered. The standards for accounting for noncash collateral in FASB ASC 860-30-25-5 state that if the secured party has the right by contract or custom to sell or repledge the collateral, then the transferor should reclassify that asset and report it in the statement of financial position separately from other assets that are not encumbered. Therefore, a broker-dealer may separately report Security Pledged to Creditors as a line item on the statement of financial condition or within a parenthetical disclosure to securities owned.

6.85 Per FASB ASC 940-20-50, broker-dealers acting as principals in underwriting and when-issued contracts have contractual commitments. Disclosure should be made of such commitments (see the "Commitments and Guarantees" section of this chapter). The broker-dealer's share (assuming such share is not merely contingent) in underwriting or joint accounts with other broker-dealers for issued securities should be included with its trading accounts.

Other Borrowed Funds

6.86 The activities of broker-dealers are funded through various sources, including short and long term borrowings with banks and affiliates, issuing commercial paper, or the securities financing activities described previously. These loans may be secured or unsecured. Short-term secured loans with non-affiliate financial institutions are generally collateralized by marketable securities.

6.87 Generally, broker-dealers reflect these liabilities on the statement of financial condition at the face value amount outstanding as of the period end. However, the broker-dealer may elect to present the liabilities at fair value under FASB ASC 825-10-25. If these financial liabilities are not held at fair value, the broker-dealer is required to disclose the difference between the carrying value and the estimated fair value within the notes to the financial statements.

6.88 Broker-dealers should disclose in the notes to the financial statements the general attributes of the loans outstanding, including the collateral pledged. For long-term debt, per FASB ASC 470-10-50, the broker-dealer must disclose the aggregate amount of maturities and sinking fund requirements for each of the five years following the date of the statement of financial condition. In industry practice, broker-dealers typically disclose additional information regarding their loans outstanding, including interest rates and maturity dates.

Subordinated Borrowings

6.89 Broker-dealers often have loans with affiliated entities or persons of the broker-dealer (for example, a partner, parent entity, principal shareholder, officer, employee, or family relation of the foregoing). These loans may be cash loans or secured demand notes.

6.90 In a typical subordinated cash loan agreement, the lender lends cash to the broker-dealer and in return receives from the broker-dealer a written promise in the form of a note that sets forth the repayment terms, interest rate, and provisions under which the lender agrees to subordinate its claims to the claims of the general creditors of the broker-dealer. The broker-dealer records this liability on their general ledger.

6.91 A *secured demand note* is an interest-bearing promissory note executed by the lender and is payable upon demand of the broker-dealer to which it is contributed. These notes are generally collateralized by marketable securities, of which the lender retains ownership. Upon demand, the note becomes due and collectible. The right to demand payment may be conditioned upon the occurrence of certain events. The securities received as collateral and cash, if any, would be recorded in a secured demand note account similar to a customer account. (See paragraph 6.84, which discusses the financial reporting treatment of collateral.)

6.92 Subordinated borrowings should be subject to a satisfactory subordination agreement or secured demand note approved by the broker-dealer's designated examining authority or self-regulatory organization in order to qualify as capital for purposes of computing the broker-dealer's net capital in accordance with Appendix D of SEC Rule 15c3-1. Although treated similarly for net capital purposes, subordinated borrowings and ownership equity must be presented separately on the statement of financial condition.

6.93 Because of the unique characteristics of qualifying subordinated borrowings, disclosure of the amount of subordinated debt for which six months' notice has been given of intent to withdraw should be made in the notes to the financial statements.

Commitments and Guarantees

6.94 FASB ASC 440, *Commitments*, provides disclosure requirements for commitments such as unused letters of credit, long-term leases, cumulative preferred stock dividends in arrears, commitments for plant acquisitions, obligations to reduce debts, and obligations to restrict dividends.

6.95 FASB ASC 460, *Guarantees*, discusses several transactions that may be interpreted to be a guarantee, which may require specific recognition and measurement within the financial statements. Examples include a parent's guarantee of a subsidiary's debt, indemnifications to service providers or counterparties, certain written options, and certain credit default swaps. This topic elaborates on the disclosures to be made by a guarantor in its interim and annual financial statements about its obligations under certain guarantees it has issued. It also clarifies that a guarantor is required to recognize, at the inception of certain guarantees, a liability for the fair value of the obligation undertaken in issuing the guarantee. FASB ASC 460-10-25-1 lists the types of guarantees that are not subject to its initial recognition and measurement provisions, but are subject to its disclosure requirements.

Equity

6.96 FASB ASC 505-10-50 requires that broker-dealers disclose the individual components of ownership equity (for example, preferred stock, common stock, additional paid-in capital, and retained earnings) either on the face of the statement of financial condition or in the notes to the financial statements. Additionally, changes to these components throughout the financial statement period should also be disclosed. For single-member LLC broker-dealer entities wholly-owned by a parent, the detail of ownership equity components would not be required to be disclosed.

Statement of Income or Operations Account Descriptions

© **Update 6-8** *Accounting and Reporting*: **Revenue from Contracts with Customers**[6]

The "Pending Content" that links to FASB ASC 606-10-65-1, is effective for annual reporting periods beginning after December 15, 2017, including interim reporting periods within that reporting period, for a public business entity, a not-for-profit entity that has issued, or is a conduit bond obligor for, securities that are traded, listed, or quoted on an exchange or an over-the-counter market, and an employee benefit plan that files or furnishes financial statements with or to the SEC. Earlier application is permitted only as of annual reporting periods beginning after December 15, 2016, including interim reporting periods within that reporting period.

For other entities, FASB ASC 606 is effective for annual reporting periods beginning after December 15, 2018, and interim periods within annual periods beginning after December 15, 2019. Other entities may elect to adopt the standard earlier, however, only as of either

- an annual reporting period beginning after December 15, 2016, including interim periods within that reporting period, or
- an annual reporting period beginning after December 15, 2016, and interim periods within annual periods beginning one year after the annual reporting period in which an entity first applies the "Pending Content" that links to FASB ASC 606-10-65-1.

FASB ASC 606 provides a framework for revenue recognition and supersedes or amends several of the revenue recognition requirements in FASB ASC 605, as well as guidance within the 900 series of industry-specific topics. The standard applies to any entity that either enters into contracts with customers to transfer goods or services or enters into contracts for the transfer of nonfinancial assets unless those contracts are within the scope of other standards (for example, insurance or lease contracts).

Readers are encouraged to consult the full text of FASB ASC 606 on FASB's website at www.fasb.org.

For more information, see appendix E of this guide.

6.97 Many statement of income or operations accounts of broker-dealers are analogous to those of other entities. This guide discusses those income statement accounts that arise based on transactions that are unique to broker-dealers.

Commission Income and Related Expense

6.98 *Commission income.* Broker-dealers may earn trade-based commission income by providing trade facilitation, execution, clearance and settlement,

---

[6] See footnote 1.

custody, and trade administration services to its customers. Income earned on riskless principal transactions may also be classified as commission income.

6.99 As noted in FASB ASC 940-20-25-2, for securities purchased, the commission is recorded as a receivable from customers; for securities sold, it is recorded as reductions in the payable to customers. The commission income (and the related expenses) should be recorded on the trade date because substantially all the efforts in generating the commissions have been completed.

6.100 Broker-dealers may incur expenses directly related to earning commission revenue (for example, exchange fees incurred by a clearing broker when providing clearance and settlement services to its customers or clearing commissions paid by introducing brokers to clearing brokers). Broker-dealers should consider the terms of the contract to consider gross versus net presentation based on the criteria set forth in FASB ASC 605-45-05.

6.101 *Soft dollar income.* FASB ASC 940-20-05-4 explains that soft-dollar arrangements with customers (typically buy-side institutional investors or money managers) generate commission income for the broker-dealer. Many of these soft-dollar arrangements are agreed orally, and the value of the research to be provided is typically based on a percentage of commission income.

Interest Income and Interest Expense

6.102 Common significant sources of interest income earned by a broker-dealer include the following:

- Interest earned on reverse repurchase transactions.

- Interest charged on debit balances in customer margin accounts. A broker provides financing to its customers by allowing them to purchase on credit in return for which the broker-dealer charges interest.

- Interest income earned by the broker-dealer on its trading and investment portfolio, including the accretion of discounts and the amortization of premiums.

- Interest received on margin deposits.

- Interest earned on securities-borrowed transactions in which the broker-dealer has borrowed securities from another broker-dealer and in return has deposited cash with the other broker-dealer. The other broker-dealer pays interest (commonly known as a rebate) for the use of the cash.

6.103 Interest expense typically arises from the following:

- Interest on cash borrowings (for example, to finance payment for securities purchased)

- Interest paid to customers on credit balances

- Interest or rebates paid on cash collateral received for securities loaned to others

- Interest on cash collateral received in repurchase transactions

- Interest on borrowings to subordinated and other lenders

Dividend Income and Dividend Expense

6.104 Broker-dealers may earn dividend income from equity securities owned and may incur payments in lieu of dividends from equity securities sold, but not yet purchased. Dividend income and the related receivable and, conversely, dividend expense and the related payable, should be recorded on a gross basis as of the record date of the dividend.

Principal Transactions (Trading Gains and Losses)

6.105 As noted in FASB ASC 940-320-05-3, a broker-dealer may buy and sell securities for its own trading account. FASB ASC 940-320-35-3 states that the profit or loss for these firm transactions is measured by the difference between the acquisition cost and the fair value, which, like the underlying trading securities, is recorded on a trade-date basis. According to FASB ASC 940-320-45-5, trading gains and losses (also referred to as principal transactions in industry practice), which comprise both realized and unrealized gains and losses, are generally presented as one balance, of net gains and losses.

Investment Banking Fees and Expenses

6.106 *Underwriting income.* FASB ASC 940-605-25-1 describes how a broker-dealer may underwrite a security offering by contracting to buy the issue either at a fixed price or a price based on selling the offering on a best-effort basis. FASB ASC 940-605-25-2 provides guidance on the timing of recognition of such revenue. The difference between the price paid by the public and the contract price less certain direct related expenses represents the underwriting income or loss.

6.107 *Underwriting expenses.* FASB ASC 940-340-35-3 states that underwriting expenses deferred under the guidance in FASB ASC 940-340-25-3 should be recognized at the time the related revenues are recorded. In the event that the transaction is not completed and the securities are not issued, the entities that have agreed to participate in the costs associated with the underwriting will write those costs off to expense.

6.108 *Advisory fees.* Broker-dealers may offer certain advisory services to customers (for example, advisory services on particular transactions, such as a merger or acquisition) in exchange for a fee. In accordance with FASB ASC 605-10-25, these fees, typically specified in an agreement or mandate letter, should generally be recorded on an accrual basis throughout the course of the service engagement.

6.109 *Advisory expenses.* A broker-dealer may incur reimbursable expenses in performing advisory services on behalf of a client. As discussed in paragraph 6.19, expenses incurred by a broker-dealer related to revenue-generating activities should generally be recorded on a gross basis.

Asset Management and Investment Advisory Income

6.110 Many broker-dealers provide investment advice, research, and administrative services for customers. These services may only be in an advisory capacity where the broker-dealer provides asset recommendations, or the broker-dealer may also have the discretion to manage the assets on an ongoing basis without receiving explicit instruction from the client to buy and sell securities. For such services, the broker-dealer receives a fee that may be based on the net assets of the fund or account instead of a traditional trading commission on each security transaction. Therefore, such income may correlate with the size of the funds or accounts managed. In addition, depending on the materiality of this revenue stream, some broker-dealers may choose to combine the revenue earned from these services with another line item, such as commissions, for presentation on the statement of income or operations.

Mutual Fund Fees

6.111 Broker-dealers acting as mutual fund distributors may earn 12b-1 fees, paid by the fund to the broker-dealer to cover distribution expenses which encompass marketing and selling of fund shares (including expenses related to advertising the fund and printing and mailing the fund prospectuses), and are normally calculated based on a set rate multiplied by the fund balance. Similarly, a broker-dealer may also earn other mutual fund fees for providing a trading platform and other programs which enable a fund's shares to be traded. For both revenue streams, the broker-dealer often acts in an agent capacity and therefore pays out some or most of the revenue received from the fund to their correspondent brokers or advisers who perform related services for the fund, at agreed-upon rates between the two parties. In these situations, broker-dealers should apply the criteria in FASB ASC 605-45 for determining the gross versus net presentation of the funds received and the payout for both the 12b-1 fees and mutual fund fees.

Floor Brokerage, Exchange Fee, and Clearance Expenses

6.112 *Floor brokerage.* Broker-dealers often use other brokers to execute trades on their behalf. The trading broker-dealer becomes a customer of the executing broker-dealer and pays a floor brokerage fee. Such fees are paid periodically either directly to the executing broker-dealer or through a clearinghouse.

6.113 *Exchange fees.* Exchange fees are charged by securities exchanges and clearing houses for the privilege of trading securities listed on that exchange. Some fees vary with the related volume, whereas others are fixed. For transaction charges, each broker-dealer submits a monthly report of net commissions earned on transactions executed on the exchange. This report is used for the self-determination of the exchange fee. Floor brokerage and exchange fees generally vary proportionally with the volume of trades executed by the broker-dealer on the exchange.

6.114 *Clearance expenses.* Introducing broker-dealers may employ a securities clearing firm to clear and settle trades with other parties or with an external clearing corporation. The clearing firm will charge clearance expenses to the broker-dealer for performing these services.

Occupancy and Equipment Expenses

6.115 Occupancy and equipment expenses generally include rent, electricity, and depreciation on fixed assets. Rent can be a significant expense for broker-dealers with large retail networks and numerous branch offices. For this reason, retail broker-dealers tend to have higher occupancy costs than large institutional dealers, which tend to have more concentrated office sites.

Employee Compensation and Benefits Expenses

6.116 Employee compensation for a broker-dealer may include commissions paid to brokers or registered representatives based on the revenue they generate for the broker-dealer, as well as employee benefits, contractual salaries, and discretionary bonuses paid to their employees.

6.117 Employee salaries, bonuses, payroll taxes, and employee benefits expenses are not significantly different for broker-dealers than for other industries, except that at broker-dealers, bonuses usually represent a greater percentage of an individual's total compensation. Such compensation may be discretionary or nondiscretionary, and proper timing of recognition may involve judgment. In the event account executives or employees of a broker-dealer are compensated with equity of the broker-dealer or a related entity, FASB ASC 718, *Compensation—Stock Compensation*, should be referred to for guidance. Compensation cost should be recognized in the period in which it becomes probable that the performance target will be achieved and should represent the compensation cost attributable to the period(s) for which the requisite service has already been rendered.

6.118 In addition to employees of the broker-dealer, for those employees of an affiliate of the broker-dealer who provides services to the broker-dealer, compensation and benefits expense should be allocated on a reasonable basis (see the "Management and Allocated Corporate Overhead Expense" section of this chapter).

Technology and Communications Expense

6.119 Technology and communications expenses tend to be significant for broker-dealers because of their dependence on communication and information networks. Traders, account executives, and investment bankers constantly use the telephone to interact with customers, other broker-dealers, and branch locations; they use communication lines to receive quotation, ticker, and news services; and they use direct computer links to other broker-dealers, branches, clearing organizations, exchanges, analytical services, and major customers.

Management and Allocated Corporate Overhead Expense

6.120 Broker-dealers that are subsidiaries of a parent organization will generally have various corporate overhead expenses allocated to the broker-dealer entity. Per Financial Industry Regulatory Authority (FINRA) Notice to Members 03-63 these expenses should be allocated on a reasonable and consistent basis and recorded based on an appropriate "cost driver" (for example, usage), and such basis must be documented within a written expense sharing agreement. In many cases, revenue is not an appropriate allocation base for expenses. Therefore, broker-dealers should evaluate the facts and circumstances related to their use of resources in detail to determine the appropriate expense allocation bases.

Disclosures

Fair Value Disclosures

6.121 FASB ASC 820-10-50 discusses the disclosures required for assets and liabilities measured at fair value. As noted in FASB ASC 820-10-50-1, the reporting entity should disclose information that would help users of its financial statements understand and assess the following:

    a. For assets and liabilities that are measured at fair value on a recurring or nonrecurring basis in the statement of financial position after initial recognition, the valuation techniques and inputs used to develop those measurements; and

    b. For recurring fair value measurements using significant unobservable inputs (level 3), the effect of the measurements on earnings (or changes in net assets) or other comprehensive income for the period.

6.122 To meet the objectives noted in the preceding paragraph, FASB ASC 820-10-50-1A states that a reporting entity should consider all of the following:

    a. The level of detail necessary to satisfy the disclosure requirements

    b. How much emphasis to place on each of the various requirements

    c. How much aggregation or disaggregation to undertake

    d. Whether users of financial statements need additional information to evaluate the quantitative information disclosed

If the disclosures set forth in the guidance are insufficient to meet the objectives in the preceding paragraph, a reporting entity should disclose additional information necessary to meet those objectives.

6.123 The required disclosures related to fair value are extensive and detailed. FASB ASC 820-10-50 provides details of the information that should, at a minimum, be disclosed by the reporting entity. FASB ASC 820-10-50 also provides information on other required disclosures related to fair value. Paragraphs 99–107 of FASB ASC 820-10-55 provide illustrative disclosures about fair value measurements.

6.124 FASB ASC 940-820-50-1, which contains disclosure requirements specific to broker-dealers, states that notes to the financial statements should disclose all of the following if financial instruments' fair values are measured at lower than quoted prices (see the example in FASB ASC 820-10-55-52):

    a. Description of the financial instrument;

    b. The quoted price of the financial instrument;

    c. Fair value reported in the statement of financial condition; and

    d. Methods and significant assumptions used to value the instrument at lower than the quoted price.

Disclosures Related to Transfers of Financial Assets Accounted for as Sales

6.125 FASB ASC 860-20-50 discusses the disclosures required for transfers of financial assets accounted for as sales. To provide an understanding of the nature of the transactions, the transferor's continuing exposure to the transferred financial assets, and the presentation of the components of the transaction in the financial statements, FASB ASC 860-20-50-4D states that an entity should disclose the following for outstanding transactions at the reporting date that meet the scope guidance in paragraphs 4A–4B of FASB ASC 860-20-50 by type of transaction (for example, repurchase agreements, securities lending transactions, and other transactions economically similar to these), with the exception of those transactions excluded from the scope, as described in FASB ASC 860-20-50-4C:

    a. The carrying amount of assets derecognized as of the date of derecognition:

i. If the amounts that have been derecognized have changed significantly from the amounts that have been derecognized in prior periods or are not representative of the activity throughout the period, a discussion of the reasons for the change should be disclosed.

   b. The amount of gross cash proceeds received by the transferor for the assets derecognized as of the date of derecognition.

   c. Information about the transferor's ongoing exposure to the economic return on the transferred financial assets:

i. As of the reporting date, the fair value of assets derecognized by the transferor.

ii. Amounts reported in the statement of financial position arising from the transaction (for example, the carrying value or fair value of forward repurchase agreements or swap contracts). To the extent that those amounts are captured in the derivative disclosures presented in accordance with FASB ASC 815-10-50-4B, an entity should provide a cross-reference to the appropriate line item in that disclosure.

iii. A description of the arrangements that result in the transferor retaining substantially all of the exposure to the economic return on the transferred financial assets and the risks related to those arrangements.

6.126 FASB ASC 860-20-55-108 provides an illustration of one approach for satisfying the quantitative disclosure requirements discussed in the preceding paragraph.

Disclosures Related to Transfers of Financial Assets Accounted for as Secured Borrowings

6.127 To provide transparency about the types of collateral pledged and the associated risks of short-term collateralized liabilities, FASB ASC 860-30-50-7 requires the following disclosures for repurchase agreements, securities lending transactions, and repurchase-to-maturity transactions that are accounted for as secured borrowings:

   a. A disaggregation of the gross obligation by the class of collateral pledged, which should be determined by the reporting entity based on the nature, characteristics, and risks of the collateral pledged.

i. Total borrowings under those agreements should be reconciled to the amount of gross liability for repurchase agreements and securities lending transactions disclosed in accordance with FASB ASC 210-20-50-3a before any adjustments for offsetting. Any difference between these amounts should be presented as a reconciling item(s).

   b. The remaining contractual maturity of the agreements, which should be disclosed in maturity intervals determined by the reporting entity to convey an understanding of the overall maturity profile of the entity's financing agreements.

c. A discussion of the potential risks associated with the agreements and the related collateral pledged, including obligations arising from a decline in the fair value of the collateral pledged and how those risks are managed.

Disclosures of Certain Significant Risks and Uncertainties and Contingencies

6.128 FASB ASC 275, *Risks and Uncertainties*, requires entities to include in their financial statements disclosures about risks and uncertainties existing as of the date of the financial statements. Two of the areas of disclosure are (*a*) the nature of their operations and (*b*) the use of estimates in the preparation of their financial statements. Following are illustrations of the application of these disclosure requirements by a broker-dealer:

- *Nature of operations.* Standard broker-dealer operates seven branches in rural and suburban communities in Minnesota and Nebraska. The broker-dealer's primary source of revenue is providing brokerage services to customers who are predominately small and middle-market businesses and middle-income individuals.

- *Use of estimates in the preparation of financial statements.* The preparation of financial statements in conformity with GAAP requires management to make estimates and assumptions that affect the reported amounts of assets and liabilities and disclosure of contingent assets and liabilities at the date of the financial statements and the reported amounts of revenues and expenses during the reporting period. Actual results could differ from those estimates.

6.129 If specified disclosure criteria are met, FASB ASC 275 also requires entities to include in their financial statements disclosures about (*a*) certain significant estimates and (*b*) current vulnerability due to certain concentrations. The following paragraphs contain a discussion of the application of FASB ASC 275 by an entity to exemplify events and circumstances that meet the disclosure criteria.

6.130 *Certain significant estimates.* Paragraphs 7–8 of FASB ASC 275-10-50 require disclosure regarding estimates used in the determination of the carrying amounts of assets or liabilities or disclosure of gain or loss contingencies if known information available prior to issuance of the financial statements indicates that both of the following criteria are met:

a. It is at least reasonably possible that the estimate of the effect on the financial statements of a condition, situation, or set of circumstances that existed at the date of the financial statements will change in the near term due to one or more future confirming events.

b. The effect of the change would be material to the financial statements.

6.131 FASB ASC 275-10-50-9 states that the disclosure should indicate the nature of the uncertainty and include an indication that it is at least reasonably possible that a change in the estimate will occur in the near term.

6.132 If the estimate involves a loss contingency covered by FASB ASC 450-20, the disclosure should also include an estimate of the possible loss or range of loss, or state that such an estimate cannot be made. Paragraphs 3–4 of FASB ASC 450-20-50 state that disclosure of the contingency should be made if there is at least a reasonable possibility that a loss or an additional loss may have been incurred and either of the following conditions exists:

    a. An accrual is not made for a loss contingency because any of the conditions in FASB ASC 450-20-25-2 are not met.

    b. An exposure to loss exists in excess of the amount accrued pursuant to the provisions of FASB ASC 450-20-30-1.

Such disclosure should include the nature of the contingency and an estimate of the possible loss or range of loss or should state that such an estimate cannot be made.

6.133 Examples of uncertainties that may fall into one or more of these categories found at certain broker-dealers include the following:

- Significant trading inventory positions that were valued as of a specific time

- Estimates made regarding the value of securities in markets that are not active (such as valuations made in good faith by management)

6.134 FASB ASC 275-10-50-15 gives examples of assets and liabilities and related revenues and expenses and of disclosure of gain or loss contingencies included in financial statements that, based on facts and circumstances existing at the date of the financial statements, may be based on estimates that are particularly sensitive to change in the near term.

6.135 Besides valuations of securities made by management, examples of similar estimates often included in broker-dealers' financial statements include the following:

- Impairment of long-lived assets (for example, assets related to marginal branches)

- Estimates involving assumed prepayments (for example, mortgage-related derivatives)

- Lives of identifiable intangible assets

6.136 *Current vulnerability due to certain concentrations.* FASB ASC 275-10-50-16 requires entities to disclose the concentrations described in FASB ASC 275-10-50-18 if, based on information known to management prior to issuance of the financial statements, all of the following criteria are met:

    a. The concentration exists at the date of the financial statements.

    b. The concentration makes the entity vulnerable to the risk of a near-term severe impact.

    c. It is at least reasonably possible that the events that could cause the severe impact will occur in the near term.

6.137 FASB ASC 275-10-50-18 states that concentrations, including known group concentrations, described in the following list require disclosure if they meet the criteria of FASB ASC 275-10-50-16. (Group concentrations exist if a number of counterparties or items that have similar economic characteristics collectively expose the reporting entity to a particular kind of risk.) Some concentrations may fall into more than one of the following categories:

a. *Concentrations in the volume of business transacted with a particular customer, supplier, lender, grantor, or contributor.* The potential for the severe impact can result, for example, from total or partial loss of the business relationship. For purposes of this topic, it is always considered at least reasonably possible that any customer will be lost in the near term.

b. *Concentrations in revenue from particular products, services, or fund-raising events.* The potential for the severe impact can result, for example, from volume or price changes or the loss of patent protection for the particular source of revenue.

c. *Concentrations in the available sources of supply of materials, labor, or services or of licenses or other rights used in the entity's operations.* The potential for the severe impact can result, for example, from changes in the availability to the entity of a resource or right.

d. *Concentrations in the market or geographic area in which an entity conducts its operations.* The potential for the severe impact can result, for example, from the negative effects of the economic and political forces within the market or geographic area. For purposes of this topic, it is always considered at least reasonably possible that operations located outside an entity's home country will be disrupted in the near term.

6.138 Examples of concentrations found at a broker-dealer that could meet the criteria requiring disclosure described in FASB ASC 275-10-50-18 include a significant portion of revenue that is earned from bond underwritings to a particular municipality or from a limited number of customers.

Derivative Instruments Disclosures

6.139 Derivative instruments are subject to many disclosure requirements, and those requirements may be located in a number of different FASB ASC topics. FASB ASC 815, *Derivatives and Hedging*, provides guidance on disclosure requirements for derivative instruments. Additional disclosure requirements for derivative instruments may be found in FASB ASC 210, *Balance Sheet*, 460, 820, and 825, *Financial Instruments*. FASB ASC 825-10-50 addresses the incremental disclosure provisions about the fair value of financial instruments, concentrations of credit risk of all financial instruments, and the market risk of all financial instruments. See chapter 5 for information on FASB ASC 815 and for disclosures required under FASB ASC 820.

6.140 FASB ASC 815-10-50-1 states that an entity with derivative instruments should disclose information to enable users of the financial statements to understand all of the following:

• How and why the entity uses derivative instruments

• How derivative instruments and related hedged items are accounted for

• How derivative instruments and related hedged items affect the entity's financial position, financial performance, and cash flows

6.141 For every annual and interim reporting period for which a statement of financial position and statement of financial performance are presented, FASB ASC 815-10-50-1A states that the entity that holds or issues derivatives instruments should disclose the following:

- Its objectives for holding or issuing those instruments
- The context needed to understand those objectives
- Its strategies for achieving those objectives
- Information that would enable users of its financial statements to understand the volume of activity in those instruments

FASB ASC 815-10-50 provides more information about the detail that should be disclosed for a particular situation and the form the disclosure should take (tabular or nontabular format). Additional guidance regarding disclosures may also be found at the subtopic level of FASB ASC 815 (for example, FASB ASC 815-30-50 provides additional guidance regarding disclosures for cash flow hedges).

6.142 For derivative instruments that are not designated or do not qualify as hedging instruments under FASB ASC 815, FASB ASC 815-10-50-4F notes that if the entity's policy is to include those derivative instruments in its trading activities (for example, as part of its trading portfolio that includes both derivative and nonderivative or cash instruments), the entity can elect to not separately disclose gains and losses as required by FASB ASC 815-10-50-4Ce, provided that certain information is disclosed about its trading activities (including both derivative and nonderivative instruments).

Guarantee Disclosures

6.143 Under FASB ASC 460-10-50-4, guarantors are required to disclose the following for each guarantee, or group of similar guarantees, even if the likelihood of the guarantors having to make any payments under the guarantee is remote:

    a. The nature of the guarantee, including all of the following:

        i. The approximate term of the guarantee

        ii. How the guarantee arose

        iii. The events and circumstances that would require the guarantor to perform under the guarantee

        iv. The current status (that is, as of the date of the statement of financial position) of the payment/performance risk of the guarantee

        v. If the entity uses internal groupings for purposes of item iv, how those groupings are determined and used for managing risk

    b. The following information about the maximum potential amount of future payments under the guarantee, as appropriate:

        i. The maximum potential amount of future payments (undiscounted) that the guarantor could be required to make under the guarantee, not reduced by any recourse or collateralization provisions in the guarantee

    ii. If the terms of the guarantee provide for no limitation to the maximum potential future payments under the guarantee, that fact

    iii. If the guarantor is unable to develop an estimate of the maximum potential amount of future payments under its guarantee, the reasons why it cannot estimate the maximum potential amount

    c. The current carrying amount of the liability, if any, for the guarantor's obligations under the guarantee, regardless of whether the guarantee is freestanding or embedded in another contract

    d. The nature of any recourse provisions that would enable the guarantor to recover from third parties any amounts paid under the guarantee

    e. The nature of any assets held either as collateral or by third parties that, upon the occurrence of any triggering event or condition under the guarantee, the guarantor can obtain and liquidate to recover all or a portion of the amounts paid under the guarantee

    f. If estimable, the approximate extent to which the proceeds from liquidation of assets held either as collateral or by third parties would be expected to cover the maximum potential amount of future payments under the guarantee

6.144 Freestanding written put options and certain contracts that function as fair value guarantees on a financial asset that is owned by the guaranteed party, even when classified as derivatives under FASB ASC 815, are within the scope of the disclosure provisions of FASB ASC 460.

Related Party Disclosures

6.145 FASB ASC 850-10 provides guidance when related party transactions exist and should be disclosed. Examples of related parties are

    a. an entity and its affiliates;

    b. entities for which investments in their equity securities would be required, absent the election of the fair value option under FASB ASC 825-10-15, to be accounted for by the equity method by the investing entity;

    c. an entity and trusts for the benefit of employees, such as pension and profit-sharing trusts that are managed by or under the trusteeship of the entity's management;

    d. an entity and its principal owners or members of their immediate families;

    e. an entity and its management and members of their immediate families;

    f. other parties that can significantly influence the management or operating policies of the transacting parties or that have an ownership interest in one of the transacting parties and can significantly influence the other to an extent that one or more of the transacting parties might be prevented from fully pursuing its own separate interests; and

g. entities for which investments in their equity securities would be required, absent the election of the fair value option under FASB ASC 825-10-15, to be accounted for by the equity method by the investing entity.

h. executive officers (as defined by Schedule A of Form BD), such as broker's or dealer's chief executive officer, chief financial officer, chief operations officer, chief legal officer, chief compliance officer, director, and individuals with similar status or functions.

6.146 Transactions between related parties commonly occur in the normal course of business. Transactions between related parties are considered to be related party transactions even though they may not be given accounting recognition. For example, an entity may receive services from a related party without charge and would not record receipt of the services as an expense or payable. However, in accordance with paragraphs 4–5 of FASB ASC 850-10-05, disclosure of these transactions is required. Examples of common transactions with related parties are

a. sales, purchases, and transfers of real and personal property;

b. services received or furnished, such as accounting, management, engineering, and legal services;

c. use of property and equipment by lease or otherwise;

d. borrowings, lendings, and guarantees;

e. maintenance of compensating bank balances for the benefit of a related party;

f. intra-entity billings based on allocations of common costs; and

g. filings of consolidated tax returns.

6.147 In accordance with FASB ASC 850, *Related Party Disclosures*, the financial statements should include disclosures of material related party transactions, other than compensation arrangements, expense allowances, and other similar items in the ordinary course of business. In some cases, aggregation of similar transactions by type of related party may be appropriate. However, disclosure of transactions that are eliminated in the preparation of consolidated or combined financial statements is not required in those statements. The disclosures should include

a. the nature of the relationship(s) involved.

b. a description of the transactions, including transactions to which no amounts or nominal amounts were ascribed, for each of the periods for which income statements are presented, and such other information deemed necessary to an understanding of the effects of the transactions on the financial statements.

c. the dollar amounts of transactions for each of the periods for which income statements are presented and the effects of any change in the method of establishing the terms from that used in the preceding period.

d. amounts due from or to related parties as of the date of each balance sheet presented and, if not otherwise apparent, the terms and manner of settlement.

e. the information required by FASB ASC 740-10-50-17 for an entity that is a member of a group that files a consolidated tax return.

6.148 In addition, notes or receivables from officers, employees, or affiliated entities, should be shown separately and not included under a general heading such as notes receivable or accounts receivable.

6.149 It may be appropriate to aggregate similar transactions by type of related party, such as when the effect of the relationship between the parties may be so pervasive that disclosure of the relationship alone will be sufficient. The name of the related party should be disclosed if it is necessary to understanding the relationship between the party and the broker-dealer.

6.150 Paragraph 5 of FASB ASC 850-10-50 states that transactions involving related parties cannot be presumed to be carried out on an arm's-length basis, as the requisite conditions of competitive, free-market dealings may not exist. Representations about transactions with related parties, if made, should not imply that the related party transactions were consummated on terms equivalent to those that prevail in arm's-length transactions unless such representations can be substantiated. FASB ASC 850-10-50 also discusses additional considerations regarding related parties, including the arm's-length bases of transactions and control relationship.

Subsequent Events Disclosures

6.151 FASB ASC 855, *Subsequent Events*, provides guidance on subsequent events, including the time period through which subsequent events should be evaluated and the disclosures that are required.

6.152 The guidance in FASB ASC 855 notes that an entity should recognize in the financial statements the effects of all subsequent events that provide additional evidence about conditions that existed at the date of the statement of financial condition, including estimates inherent in the process of preparing the financial statements. See FASB ASC 855-10-55-1 for examples of recognized subsequent events.

6.153 FASB ASC 855-10-25-1A states that an SEC filer should evaluate subsequent events through the date the financial statements are issued. With respect to the guidance in FASB ASC 855, an *SEC filer* is defined as an entity that is required to file or furnish its financial statements with either the SEC or the appropriate agency under Section 12(i) of the 1934 Act. Nonissuer broker-dealers that are registered with the SEC fall under this definition.

Balance Sheet Offsetting Disclosures

6.154 FASB ASC 210-20-50 articulates disclosures about financial instruments and derivative instruments that are either offset in accordance with GAAP or are subject to an enforceable master netting arrangement or similar agreement. The objective of the disclosures is to improve comparability between those entities that prepare their financial statements on a GAAP basis and those entities that prepare their financial statements on an International Financial Reporting Standards basis.

6.155 FASB ASC 210-20-50-1 establishes the scope of the disclosure requirements found in paragraphs 2–5 of FASB ASC 210-20-50 by stating the disclosures are only applicable to the following recognized assets and liabilities:

a. Recognized derivative instruments accounted for in accordance with FASB ASC 815, including bifurcated embedded derivatives, repurchase agreements accounted for as collateralized borrowings (repos), and reverse repurchase agreements (reverse repos), and securities borrowing and securities lending transactions that are offset in accordance with either FASB ASC 210-20-45 or FASB ASC 815-10-45.

b. Recognized derivative instruments accounted for in accordance with FASB ASC 815, including bifurcated embedded derivatives, repos, and reverse repos, and securities borrowing and securities lending transactions that are subject to an enforceable master netting arrangement or similar agreement, irrespective of whether they are offset in accordance with either FASB ASC 210-20-45 or FASB ASC 815-10-45.

6.156 When applying this guidance, readers may need to consider the legal structure of master securities lending agreements and determine which parties have the legal right of offset. Legal counsel could be consulted when determining if a legal right of offset exists.

6.157 Pursuant to FASB ASC 210-20-50-3, reporting entities, including broker-dealers, will be required to disclose the following information for applicable financial instruments and derivative instruments:

a. The gross amounts of those recognized assets and those recognized liabilities

b. The amounts offset to determine the net amounts presented in the statement of financial position

c. The net amounts presented in the statement of financial position

d. The amounts subject to an enforceable master netting arrangement or similar agreement not otherwise included in item b

e. The net amount after deducting the amounts in item d from the amounts in item c

6.158 FASB ASC 210-20-50-4 explains that presentation of this information in tabular format, separately for assets and liabilities, is required unless another format is more appropriate. FASB ASC 210-20-50-5 also requires reporting entities to provide a description of the rights (including the nature of those rights) of setoff associated with an entity's recognized assets and recognized liabilities subject to an enforceable master netting arrangement or similar agreement. In addition, the standard requires disclosure of collateral received and posted in connection with master netting agreements or similar arrangements. When applying this disclosure guidance, readers may consider whether previously existing disclosures required by other FASB ASC topics for certain assets and liabilities may also address requirements set forth in FASB ASC 210-20-50-3. However, FASB ASC 210-20-50-6 explains that cross-referencing is required when the required disclosures exist in more than a single note to the financial statements.

6.159 FASB ASC 210-20-55 explains that the disclosures may be made by instrument or by counterparty. Additional implementation guidance is provided in paragraphs 1–18A of FASB ASC 210-20-55, and illustrative example disclosure tables are provided in paragraphs 19–22 of FASB ASC 210-20-55.

Financial Statements and Schedules

6.160 The financial statements required to be filed under SEC Rule 17a-5 are not required to be in comparative form, and therefore the following illustrative financial statement exhibits are prepared on a single year basis. However, if comparative financial statements are prepared, there is not a requirement to present the supplementary information on a comparative basis.

6.161 The following financial statement and schedule exhibits include the required facing page and the oath or affirmation form on Form X-17A-5. These exhibits are illustrative only and have been prepared to show how various items might be presented, assuming they are material in the particular circumstances. The financial statements of individual companies may vary from these illustrations depending on facts or circumstances present at the time of issuance.

6.162 The financial statements should contain a signed independent auditor's report delineating management's and the auditor's respective responsibilities with regard to the financial statements, as well as the auditor's opinion on the financial statements.

6.163 The illustrative financial statements and footnote disclosures included in this guide have been updated to reflect FASB ASC. However, in FASB's Notice to Constituents, it suggests the use of plain English to describe broad FASB ASC topic references. It suggests a reference similar to "as required by the Derivatives and Hedging Topic of the FASB *Accounting Standards Codification*." Entities might consider revising their financial statement references to reflect this plain English referencing rather than the use of specific FASB ASC references. We have provided these detailed references in this guide as a learning tool to familiarize constituents with the basis for the disclosures.

Exhibit 6-1[7]

UNITED STATES
SECURITIES AND EXCHANGE COMMISSION
WASHINGTON, D.C. 20549

ANNUAL AUDITED REPORT
FORM X-17A-5
PART III

FACING PAGE

Information Required of Brokers and Dealers	SEC FILE
Pursuant to Section 17 of the Securities	8-12345
Exchange Act of 1934 and Rule 17a-5 Thereunder	

REPORT FOR THE PERIOD BEGINNING	**01/01/X1**	AND ENDING	**12/31/X1**
	MM/DD/YY		MM/DD/YY

A. REGISTRANT IDENTIFICATION

NAME OF BROKER-DEALER:

OFFICIAL
USE ONLY

Standard Stockbrokerage Co., Inc.

ADDRESS OF PRINCIPAL PLACE OF BUSINESS: (Do not use P.O. Box No.)

1 Main Street

(No. and Street)

New York	**New York**	10004
(City)	(State)	(Zip Code)

NAME AND TELEPHONE NUMBER OF PERSON TO CONTACT IN REGARD
TO THIS REPORT

Joseph P. Brokestock   *(212) 555-1212*

(Area Code - Telephone No.)

B. ACCOUNTANT IDENTIFICATION

INDEPENDENT PUBLIC ACCOUNTANT (Whose opinion is contained in this
Report*)

Accounting Firm

(Name—*if individual, state last, first, middle name*)

2 Main Street	**New York**	**New York**	10004
(Address)	(City)	(State)	(Zip Code)

CHECK ONE:

x Certified Public Accountant
o Public Accountant
o Accountant not resident in United States or any of its possessions.

FOR OFFICIAL USE ONLY

---

* *Claims for exemption from the requirement that the annual report be covered by the opinion of an independent public accountant must be supported by a statement of facts and circumstances relied on at the bureau of the exemption. See Section 240.17a-5(e)(2).*

---

[7] The Financial and Operational Combined Uniform Single (FOCUS) Report forms are available on the SEC website at www.sec.gov/forms, readers should be aware that these forms may change and are encouraged to obtain the current forms from the SEC website.

Exhibit 6-2[8]

Oath or Affirmation

I,   JOSEPH P. BROKESTOCK   , swear (or affirm) that, to the best of my knowledge and belief, the accompanying financial statement and supporting schedules pertaining to the firm of STANDARD STOCKBROKERAGE CO., INC., as of   DECEMBER 31   , 20X1, are true and correct. I further swear (or affirm) that neither the Company nor any partner, proprietor, principal officer, or director has any proprietary interest in any account classified solely as that of a customer, except as follows:

SECURITY ACCOUNTS OF PRINCIPAL OFFICERS AND DIRECTORS THAT ARE CLASSIFIED AS CUSTOMER ACCOUNTS (DEBITS $316,513, CREDITS $273,412)

_____
Signature
VICE PRESIDENT — FINANCE
Title

Subscribed and sworn to
before me
this _____ day of _____ 20X2

_____
JOAN P. NOTARY
Notary Public

This report * contains (check all applicable boxes)

x (a) Facing page.

x (b) Statement of financial condition.

x (c) Statement of income (loss).

x (d) Statement of changes in financial condition.

x (e) Statement of changes in stockholders' equity or partners' or sole proprietor's capital.

x (f) Statement of changes in borrowings subordinated to claims of creditors.

x (g) Computation of net capital.

x (h) Computation for determination of reserve requirements pursuant to Rule 15c3-3.

x (i) Information relating to the possession or control requirements under Rule 15c3-3.

o (j) A reconciliation, including appropriate explanation, of the computation of net capital under Rule 15c3-1 and the computation for determination of the reserve requirements under exhibit A of Rule 15c3-3.

o (k) A reconciliation between the audited and unaudited statements of financial condition with respect to methods of consolidation.

x (l) An oath or affirmation.

x (m) A copy of the Securities Investor Protection Corporation (SIPC) supplemental report.[9]

o (n) A report describing any material weaknesses found to exist or found to have existed since the date of the previous audit.

_____

* *For conditions of confidential treatment of certain portions of this filing, see Section 240.17a–5(e)(3).*

Note: Various exchanges may require an additional letter of attestation.

_____

[8] See footnote 7.

[9] SEC Rule 17a-5(e)(4) states that the Securities Investor Protection Corporation supplemental report should be bound separately.

Exhibit 6-3

Standard Stockbrokerage Co., Inc. and Subsidiaries
Consolidated Statement of Financial Condition
December 31, 20X1
(*Dollars in Thousands, Except Share Data*)
Assets

Cash	$2,647
Cash and securities segregated under federal and other regulations (cash of $375 and securities with a fair value of $630)	1,005
Collateralized Agreements:	
Securities borrowed	2,500
Securities purchased under agreements to resell, at fair-value	3,782
Securities received as collateral	200
Deposits with clearing organizations and others (cash of $345 and securities with a fair value of $1,400)	1,745
Receivable from broker-dealers and clearing organizations	25,476
Receivable from customers[†]	40,360
Financial instruments owned, at fair value ($28,468 pledged as collateral)[*(a)]	35,679
Secured demand notes	5,215
Memberships in exchanges owned, at adjusted cost (fair value $2,500)	2,475
Furniture, equipment, and leasehold improvements, at cost, less accumulated depreciation and amortization of $2,425	4,744
Deferred dealer concessions	137
Other assets	523
	$126,488

Liabilities and Stockholders' Equity

Liabilities:

Other borrowed funds	$29,110
Collateralized Agreements:	
Securities loaned	1,800
Securities sold under agreements to repurchase, at fair value	3,790
Payable to broker-dealers and clearing organizations	19,164
Payable to customers	12,288
Financial instruments sold, not yet purchased, at fair value	1,862
Obligation to return securities received as collateral	200
Income taxes payable, including deferred taxes of $1,200	2,276
Accounts payable, accrued expenses, and other liabilities	2,449
Long-term notes payable	3,000
Beneficial interests issued by consolidated variable interest entities (VIEs)[a]	933
Subordinated borrowings	9,897
	86,769

Stockholders' equity:

Preferred stock, $5 cumulative, $100 par value, authorized 100,000 shares, outstanding 50,000 shares	5,000
Common stock, $1 par value, authorized 10,000,000 shares, issued 6,000,000 shares	6,000
Additional paid-in capital	2,200
Retained earnings	27,719
	40,919
Less 199,100 shares of common stock in treasury, at cost	(1,200)
Total stockholders' equity	39,719
	$126,488

---

[a] The following table presents information on assets and liabilities related to VIEs that are consolidated by the Company at December 31, 20X1. The difference between total VIE assets and liabilities represents the Company's interest, in those entities, which are eliminated in consolidation.

Assets:
    Securities owned, at fair value   974

Liabilities:
    Beneficial interests issued by consolidated VIEs   933

The accompanying notes are an integral part of these consolidated financial statements.

* To the extent that collateral has been pledged and the counterparty has the right by contract or custom to sell or repledge the collateral, separate captions or parenthetical disclosures in the statement of financial condition may be needed as illustrated in FASB ASC 860-30.

† Valuation allowances should be shown, if material, either parenthetically or in a note. or in a note.

Exhibit 6-4

Standard Stockbrokerage Co., Inc. and Subsidiaries

**Consolidated Statement of Income
for the Year Ended December 31, 20X1**

(Dollars in Thousands, Except Earnings Per Share)

Revenues

Commissions	$26,549
Principal transactions	6,707
Investment banking	5,689
Interest and dividends	4,253
Asset management fees	2,120
Mutual fund fees	570
Other income	130
	46,018

Expenses:

Employee compensation and benefits	12,815
Floor brokerage, exchange, and clearance fees	7,128
Technology and communications	5,723
Interest and dividends	3,896
Occupancy and equipment	1,625
Management fees and allocated corporate overhead	340
Other expenses	787
	32,314
Income before income taxes	13,704
Provision for income taxes	7,100
Net income	$6,604

The accompanying notes are an integral part of these consolidated financial statements.

Exhibit 6-5

Standard Stockbrokerage Co., Inc. and Subsidiaries
Consolidated Statement of Changes in Subordinated Borrowings
for the Year Ended December 31, 20X1

(Dollars in Thousands)

Subordinated borrowings at January 1, 20X1	$4,204
Increases:	
Secured demand note collateral agreements	3,325
Issuance of subordinated notes	3,675
Decreases:	
Payment of subordinated notes	(1,307)
Subordinated borrowings at December 31, 20X1	$9,897

The accompanying notes are an integral part of these
consolidated financial statements.

Exhibit 6-6

Standard Stockbrokerage Co., Inc. and Subsidiaries
Consolidated Statement of Changes in Stockholders' Equity
for the Year Ended December 31, 20X1

(Dollars in Thousands, Except Share Data)

	Capital Stock				Additional Paid-in Capital	Retained Earnings	Treasury Stock—Common		Total Stockholders' Equity
	Preferred		Common						
	Shares	Amount	Shares	Amount	Amount	Amount	Shares	Amount	Amount
Balances at January 1, 20X1	52,500	$5,250	6,000,000	$6,000	$2,212	$21,365	195,700	$(1,098)	$33,729
Net Income						6,604			6,604
Purchase and retirement of preferred shares	(2,500)	(250)			(12)				(262)
Dividends on preferred stock $5 a share						(250)			(250)
Net purchase of common shares for treasury							3,400	(102)	(102)
Balance at December 31, 20X1	50,000	$5,000	6,000,000	$6,000	$2,200	$27,719	199,100	$(1,200)	$39,719

The accompanying notes are an integral part of these consolidated financial statements.

Exhibit 6-7

⊘ Update 6-9 *Accounting and Reporting*: Statement of Cash Flows

FASB ASU No. 2016-15, issued in August 2016, is effective for fiscal years, including interim periods within those fiscal years, of a public business entity beginning after December 15, 2017.

For all other entities, FASB ASU No. 2016-15 is effective for fiscal years beginning after December 15, 2018, and interim periods within fiscal years beginning after December 15, 2019. Early adoption is permitted, including adoption in an interim period. If an entity early adopts the amendments in an interim period, any adjustments should be reflected as of the beginning of the fiscal year that includes that interim period. An entity that elects early adoption must adopt all of the amendments in the same period.

FASB ASU No. 2016-15 addresses the following eight specific cash flow issues: debt prepayment or debt extinguishment costs; settlement of zero-coupon debt instruments or other debt instruments with coupon interest rates that are insignificant in relation to the effective interest rate of the borrowing; contingent consideration payments made after a business combination; proceeds from the settlement of insurance claims; proceeds from the settlement of corporate-owned life insurance policies (including bank-owned life insurance policies; distributions received from equity method investees; beneficial interests in securitization transactions; and separately identifiable cash flows and application of the predominance principle.

This edition of the guide has not been updated to reflect changes as a result of this ASU, however, this section will be updated in a future edition. Readers are encouraged to consult the full text of this ASU on FASB's website at www.fasb.org.

⊘ Update 6-10 *Accounting and Reporting*: Restricted Cash

FASB ASU No. 2016-18, issued in November 2016, is effective for fiscal years, including interim periods within those fiscal years, of a public business entity beginning after December 15, 2017.

For all other entities, FASB ASU No. 2016-18 is effective for fiscal years beginning after December 15, 2018, and interim periods within those fiscal years beginning after December 15, 2019. Early adoption is permitted, including adoption in an interim period. If an entity early adopts the amendments in an interim period, any adjustments should be reflected as of the beginning of the fiscal year that includes that interim period.

FASB ASU No. 2016-18 requires that a statement of cash flows explain the change during the period in total of cash, cash equivalents, and amount generally described as restricted cash or restricted cash equivalents. Therefore, amounts generally described as restricted cash and restricted cash equivalents should be included with cash and cash equivalents when reconciling the beginning-of-period and end-of-period total amounts shown on the statement of cash flows.

This edition of the guide has not been updated to reflect changes as a result of this ASU, however, this section will be updated in a future edition.

> Readers are encouraged to consult the full text of this ASU on FASB's web-site at www.fasb.org.

Standard Stockbrokerage Co., Inc. and Subsidiaries

Consolidated Statement of Cash Flows
for the Year Ended December 31, 20X1

(Dollars in Thousands)

Cash flows from operating activities:		
Net income		$ 6,604
Adjustments to reconcile net income to net cash provided by operating activities:		
Depreciation and amortization	$582	
Deferred taxes	376	
(Increase) decrease in operating assets:		
Cash and securities segregated under federal and other regulations	500	
Deposits with clearing organizations and others	900	
Net receivable from broker-dealers and clearing organizations	4,785	
Net receivable from customers	(11,830)	
Securities borrowed, net of securities loaned	(50)	
Securities purchased under agreements to resell*	2,648	
Financial instruments owned, net	1,691	
Increase (decrease) in operating liabilities:		
Securities sold under agreements to repurchase*	587	
Other, net	(691)	
Total adjustments		(502)
Net cash provided by operating activities		6,102
Cash flows from investing activities:		
Proceeds from sale of long-term investments	110	
Purchase of long-term investments	(50)	
Purchase of furniture, equipment, and leasehold improvements	(75)	
Net cash used in investing activities		(15)

(continued)

Cash flows from financing activities:

Payment of short-term bank loans	(7,762)
Proceeds from issuance of derivatives with a financing element, net [†]	100
Proceeds from issuance of common stock from treasury	78
Purchase of common stock for treasury	(180)
Proceeds from issuance of subordinated notes	3,675
Payments of subordinated notes	(1,307)
Payments of long-term notes payable	(500)
Purchase and retirement of preferred stock	(262)
Dividend on preferred stock	(250)
Net cash used in financing activities	(6,408)
Decrease in cash	(321)
Cash at beginning of the year	2,968
Cash at end of the year	$2,647

Supplemental cash flows disclosures:

Income tax payments (paid to parent)	$6,700
Interest payments	$3,618
Noncash financing activity— borrowings under secured demand note collateral agreements	$3,325

The accompanying notes are an integral part of these consolidated financial statements.

---

[*] Depending on the nature of the activity, securities purchased under agreements to resell can be classified as operating or investing; likewise, securities sold under agreements to repurchase can be classified as operating or financing.

[†] Paragraphs 11–15 of FASB 815-10-45 require all cash flows associated with a derivative that contains an other-than-insignificant financing element at inception, other than a financing element inherently included in an at-the-market derivative instrument with no prepayments (that is, the forward points in an at-the-money forward contract), to be reported as cash flows from financing activities in the statement of cash flows as opposed to reporting only the cash flows related to a financing element of a derivative as a financing activity.

Exhibit 6-8

© **Update 6-11 *Accounting and Reporting*: Recognition and Measurement of Financial Assets and Financial Liabilities**

FASB ASU No. 2016-01, issued in January 2016, is effective for public entities for fiscal years beginning after December 15, 2017 and interim periods within those fiscal years. Early adoption is not permitted by public business entities; however, the ASU provides for early adoption of certain specified amendments upon issuance as of the beginning of the fiscal year of adoption.

For all other entities, including not-for-profit entities and employee benefit plans within the scope of FASB ASC 960 through FASB ASC 965 topics for plan accounting, the amendments are effective for fiscal years beginning after December 15, 2018 and interim periods within fiscal years ending after December 15, 2019. Early adoption is permitted by entities other than public business entities as of the fiscal years beginning after December 15, 2017 and interim periods within those fiscal years.

FASB ASU No. 2016-01 amends guidance for recognition, measurement, presentation, and disclosure of financial instruments.

This edition of the guide has not been updated to reflect changes as a result of this ASU, however, the following section will be updated in a future edition to reflect the amendments in this ASU, particularly an amendment that requires an entity to present separately in other comprehensive income the portion of the total change in the fair value of a liability that results from a change in the instrument-specific credit risk for financial liabilities that the entity has elected to measure at fair value in accordance with the fair value option.

Readers are encouraged to consult the full text of the ASU on FASB's website at www.fasb.org. For more information on ASU No. 2016-01, see appendix G of this guide.

Standard Stockbrokerage Co., Inc. and Subsidiaries

Notes to Consolidated Financial Statements[10]

December 31, 20X1

(Dollars in Thousands)

The following notes to financial statements are illustrative only. In some situations, the information in the notes may be better presented within the financial statements; in other situations, information not required by regulation may not be sufficiently material to warrant disclosure. In addition, these notes may not include all disclosures required by Regulation S-X.[11]

1. Organization and Nature of Business

Standard Stockbrokerage Co., Inc., (the Company) is a broker-dealer registered with the SEC and is a member of various exchanges and the Financial Industry

---

[10] These notes do not reflect all disclosures required under accounting principles generally accepted in the United States of America. The notes will continue to be updated in future editions of this guide to the extent applicable.

[11] A discussion of the disclosures related to significant risks and uncertainties is included in the "Disclosures of Certain Significant Risks and Uncertainties" section of this chapter.

Regulatory Authority (FINRA). The Company is a Delaware Corporation that is a majority-owned subsidiary of Standard Stockbrokerage Holding Company, Inc. (Parent). The U.S. dollar ($) is the functional currency of the Company.

2. Significant Accounting Policies

Basis of Presentation

The consolidated financial statements include the accounts of the Company and its wholly-owned subsidiaries. The Company is engaged in a single line of business as a securities broker-dealer, which comprises several classes of services, including principal transactions, agency transactions, investment banking, investment advisory, and venture capital businesses. All material intercompany balances and transactions are eliminated in consolidation.

Use of Estimates

The preparation of financial statements in conformity with U.S. GAAP requires management to make estimates and assumptions that affect the reported amounts of assets and liabilities and disclosure of contingent assets and liabilities at the date of the financial statements and the reported amounts of revenues and expenses during the reporting period. Actual results could differ from those estimates.

Financial Instruments Owned

Proprietary securities transactions in regular-way trades are recorded on the trade date, as if they had settled. Profit and loss arising from all securities and commodities transactions entered into for the account and risk of the Company are recorded on a trade date basis. Customers' securities and commodities transactions are reported on a settlement date basis with related commission income and expenses reported on a trade date basis.[12]

Amounts receivable and payable for securities transactions that have not reached their contractual settlement date are recorded net on the consolidated statement of financial condition.

Securities and derivative positions are recorded at fair value in accordance with FASB ASC 820, *Fair Value Measurement*.

Offsetting of Amounts Related to Certain Contracts

When the requirements of FASB ASC 815-10-45-5 are met, the Company offsets certain fair value amounts recognized for cash collateral receivables or payables against fair value amounts recognized for net derivative positions executed with the same counterparty under the same master netting arrangement. (See note 14 for more information related to offsetting securities financing transactions and note 13 related to derivative transactions.)

Investment Banking

Investment banking revenues include gains, losses, and fees, net of syndicate expenses, arising from securities offerings in which the Company acts as an underwriter or agent. Investment banking revenues also include fees earned from providing merger-and-acquisition and financial restructuring advisory services. Investment banking management fees are recorded on offering date, sales concessions on settlement date, and underwriting fees at the time the underwriting is completed and the income is reasonably determinable. Underwriting expenses that are deferred under the guidance in FASB ASC 940-340-25-3

---

[12] See chapter 5, "Accounting Standards," of this guide regarding settlement-date-basis versus trade-date-basis accounting.

are recognized at the time the related revenues are recorded, in the event that transactions are not completed and the securities are not issued, the Company expenses those costs.

Commissions

Commissions and related clearing expenses are recorded on a trade-date basis as securities transactions occur.

Investment Advisory Income

Investment advisory fees are received quarterly but are recognized as earned on a pro rata basis over the term of the contract.

Translation of Foreign Currencies

Assets and liabilities denominated in foreign currencies are translated at year-end rates of exchange, whereas the income statement accounts are translated at average rates of exchange for the year. Gains or losses resulting from foreign currency transactions are included in net income.

Income Taxes

The Company and its subsidiaries are included in the consolidated federal income tax return filed by the Parent. Federal income taxes are calculated as if the companies filed on a separate return basis, and the amount of current tax or benefit calculated is either remitted to or received from the Parent. The amount of current and deferred taxes payable or refundable is recognized as of the date of the financial statements, utilizing currently enacted tax laws and rates. Deferred tax expenses or benefits are recognized in the financial statements for the changes in deferred tax liabilities or assets between years.

The Company recognizes and measures its unrecognized tax benefits in accordance with FASB ASC 740, *Income Taxes*. Under that guidance the Company assesses the likelihood, based on their technical merit, that tax positions will be sustained upon examination based on the facts, circumstances and information available at the end of each period. The measurement of unrecognized tax benefits is adjusted when new information is available, or when an event occurs that requires a change.

Depreciation

Depreciation is provided on a straight-line basis using estimated useful lives of five to ten years. Leasehold improvements are amortized over the lesser of the economic useful life of the improvement or the term of the lease.

Drafts Payable

Drafts payable represent amounts drawn by the Company against a bank and sight overdrafts under a sweep agreement with a bank.

Exchange Memberships

The Company's exchange memberships, which represent ownership interests in the exchanges and provide the Company with the right to conduct business on the exchanges, are recorded at cost or, if an other than temporary impairment in value has occurred, at a value that reflects management's estimate of the impairment. Management believes that such impairment in value occurred in 20W7, at which time the Company wrote down the cost of its exchange memberships. There were no exchange membership impairments in 20X1. At December 31, 20X1, the fair value of exchange memberships was $2,500.

Statement of Cash Flows

For purposes of the Consolidated Statement of Cash Flows, the Company has defined cash equivalents as highly liquid investments, with original maturities of less than three months, that are not held for sale in the ordinary course of business.

3. Fair Value

Fair Value Hierarchy

FASB ASC 820 defines fair value, establishes a framework for measuring fair value, and establishes a hierarchy of fair value inputs. Fair value is the price that would be received to sell an asset or paid to transfer a liability in an orderly transaction between market participants at the measurement date. A fair value measurement assumes that the transaction to sell the asset or transfer the liability occurs in the principal market for the asset or liability or, in the absence of a principal market, the most advantageous market. Valuation techniques that are consistent with the market, income or cost approach, as specified by FASB ASC 820, are used to measure fair value.

The fair value hierarchy prioritizes the inputs to valuation techniques used to measure fair value into three broad levels:

- *Level 1.* Quoted prices (unadjusted) in active markets for identical assets or liabilities that the Company can access at the measurement date.

- *Level 2.* Inputs other than quoted prices included within level 1 that are observable for the asset or liability either directly or indirectly.

- *Level 3.* Unobservable inputs for the asset or liability.

The availability of observable inputs can vary from security to security and is affected by a wide variety of factors, including, for example, the type of security, the liquidity of markets, and other characteristics particular to the security. To the extent that valuation is based on models or inputs that are less observable or unobservable in the market, the determination of fair value requires more judgment. Accordingly, the degree of judgment exercised in determining fair value is greatest for instruments categorized in level 3.

The inputs used to measure fair value may fall into different levels of the fair value hierarchy. In such cases, for disclosure purposes, the level in the fair value hierarchy within which the fair value measurement falls in its entirety is determined based on the lowest level input that is significant to the fair value measurement in its entirety.

Processes and Structure

The Fair Valuation Committee (FVC), established by the Parent, is responsible for the Company's fair value valuation policies, processes, and procedures. FVC is independent of the business units and reports to the CFO of the Parent, who has final authority over the valuation of the Company's financial instruments. FVC implements valuation control processes to validate the fair value of the Company's financial instruments measured at fair value, including those derived from pricing models. These control processes are designed to assure that the values used for financial reporting are based on observable inputs wherever possible. In the event that observable inputs are not available, the control processes are designed to assure that the valuation approach utilized is appropriate and consistently applied and that the assumptions are reasonable.

The Company's control processes for financial instruments categorized in level 3 of the fair value hierarchy include the following:

Model Review. FVC, in conjunction with the Risk Department (RD), which reports to the chief risk officer (CRO) of the Parent, independently reviews valuation models' theoretical soundness, the appropriateness of the valuation methodology, and calibration techniques developed by the business units using observable inputs. When inputs are not observable, FVC reviews the appropriateness of the proposed valuation methodology to ensure it is consistent with how a market participant would arrive at the unobservable input. The valuation methodologies utilized in the absence of observable inputs may include extrapolation techniques and the use of comparable observable inputs. As part of the review, FVC develops a methodology to independently verify the fair value generated by the business unit's valuation models. Before trades are executed using new valuation models, those models are required to be independently reviewed. All of the Company's valuation models are subject to an independent annual FVC review.

Independent Price Verification. The business units are responsible for determining the fair value of financial instruments using approved valuation models and valuation methodologies. Generally, on a monthly basis, FVC independently validates the fair values of financial instruments determined using valuation models by determining the appropriateness of the inputs used by the business units and by testing compliance with the documented valuation methodologies approved in the model review process described previously.

FVC uses recently executed transactions and other observable market data such as exchange data, broker-dealer quotes, third-party pricing vendors, and aggregation services for validating the fair values of financial instruments generated using valuation models. FVC assesses the external sources and their valuation methodologies to determine if the external providers meet the minimum standards expected of a third-party pricing source. Pricing data provided by approved external sources are evaluated using a number of approaches; for example, by corroborating the external sources' prices to executed trades, by analyzing the methodology and assumptions used by the external source to generate a price and/or by evaluating how active the third-party pricing source (or originating sources used by the third-party pricing source) is in the market. Based on this analysis, FVC generates a ranking of the observable market data to ensure that the highest ranked market data source is used to validate the business unit's fair value of financial instruments.

The results of this independent price verification and any adjustments made by FVC to the fair value generated by the business units are presented to management, the CFO and the CRO on a regular basis.

Review of New Level 3 Transactions. FVC reviews the models and valuation methodology used to price all new material level 3 transactions and RD management must approve the fair value of the trade that is initially recognized.

Fair Value Measurements

Many cash instruments and OTC derivative contracts have bid and ask prices that can be observed in the marketplace. *Bid prices* reflect the highest price that a party is willing to pay for an asset. *Ask prices* represent the lowest price that a party is willing to accept for an asset. For financial instruments whose inputs are based on bid-ask prices, the Company does not require that the fair value estimate always be a predetermined point in the bid-ask range. The Company's policy is to allow for midmarket pricing and to adjust to the point within the bid-ask range that meets the Company's best estimate of fair value. For offsetting positions in the same financial instrument, the same price within the bid-ask spread is used to measure both the long and short positions.

Fair value for many cash instruments and OTC derivative contracts is derived using pricing models. Pricing models take into account the contract terms (including maturity) as well as multiple inputs, including, when applicable, commodity prices, equity prices, interest rate yield curves, credit curves, correlation, creditworthiness of the counterparty, creditworthiness of the Company, option volatility, and currency rates. When appropriate, valuation adjustments are made to account for various factors such as liquidity risk (bid-ask adjustments), credit quality, model uncertainty, and concentration risk. Adjustments for liquidity risk adjust model-derived midmarket levels of level 2 and level 3 financial instruments for the bid-mid or mid-ask spread required to properly reflect the exit price of a risk position. Bid-mid and mid-ask spreads are marked to levels observed in trade activity, broker quotes, or other external third-party data. When these spreads are unobservable for the particular position in question, spreads are derived from observable levels of similar positions. The Company applies credit-related valuation adjustments to its OTC derivatives. For OTC derivatives, the effect of changes in both the Company's and the counterparty's credit standing is considered when measuring fair value. In determining the expected exposure, the Company simulates the distribution of the future exposure to a counterparty, then applies market-based default probabilities to the future exposure, leveraging external third-party credit default swap (CDS) spread data. When CDS spread data are unavailable for a specific counterparty, bond market spreads, CDS spread data based on the counterparty's credit rating or CDS spread data that reference a comparable counterparty may be utilized. The Company also considers collateral held and legally enforceable master netting agreements that mitigate the Company's exposure to each counterparty. Adjustments for model uncertainty are taken for positions whose underlying models rely on significant inputs that are neither directly nor indirectly observable, hence requiring reliance on established theoretical concepts in their derivation. These adjustments are derived by making assessments of the possible degree of variability using statistical approaches and market-based information where possible. The Company generally subjects all valuations and models to a review process initially and on a periodic basis thereafter.

Fair value is a market-based measure considered from the perspective of a market participant rather than an entity-specific measure. Therefore, even when market assumptions are not readily available, the Company's own assumptions are set to reflect those that the Company believes market participants would use in pricing the asset or liability at the measurement date.

A description of the valuation techniques applied to the company's major categories of assets and liabilities measured at fair value on a recurring basis follows.

U.S. Government Securities. U.S. government securities are valued using quoted market prices. Valuation adjustments are not applied. Accordingly, U.S. government securities are generally categorized in level 1 of the fair value hierarchy.

U.S. Agency Securities. U.S. agency securities are composed of three main categories consisting of agency-issued debt, agency mortgage pass-through pool securities, and collateralized mortgage obligations. Noncallable agency issued debt securities are generally valued using quoted market prices. Callable agency-issued debt securities are valued by benchmarking model-derived prices to quoted market prices and trade data for identical or comparable securities. The fair value of agency mortgage pass-through pool securities is model-driven based on spreads of the comparable to-be-announced (TBA) security. Collateralized mortgage obligations are valued using quoted market prices and trade data adjusted by subsequent changes in related indices for identical or comparable securities. Actively traded noncallable agency issued debt securities are generally categorized in level 1 of the fair value hierarchy. Callable agency issued debt securities, agency mortgage pass-through pool securities, and collateralized mortgage obligations are generally categorized in level 2 of the fair value hierarchy.

Corporate Bonds. The fair value of corporate bonds is determined using recently executed transactions, market price quotations (when observable), bond spreads or credit default swap spreads obtained from independent external parties, such as vendors and brokers, adjusted for any basis difference between cash and derivative instruments. The spread data used are for the same maturity as the bond. If the spread data do not reference the issuer, then data that reference a comparable issuer are used. When position-specific external price data are not observable, fair value is determined based on either benchmarking to similar instruments or cash flow models with yield curves, bond, or single-name credit default swap spreads and recovery rates as significant inputs. Corporate bonds are generally categorized in level 2 of the fair value hierarchy; in instances when prices, spreads, or any of the other aforementioned key inputs are unobservable, they are categorized in level 3 of the fair value hierarchy.

Residential Mortgage-Backed Securities (RMBS) and Asset-Backed Securities (ABS). RMBS and ABS may be valued based on price or spread data obtained from observed transactions or independent external parties such as vendors or brokers. When position-specific external price data are not observable, the fair value determination may require benchmarking to similar instruments and/or analyzing expected credit losses, default, and recovery rates. In evaluating the fair value of each security, the Company considers security collateral-specific attributes including payment priority, credit enhancement levels, type of collateral, delinquency rates, and loss severity. In addition, for RMBS borrowers, Fair Isaac Corporation scores and the level of documentation for the loan are also considered. Market standard models, such as Intex, Trepp, or others, may be deployed to model the specific collateral composition and cash flow structure of each transaction. Key inputs to these models are market spreads, forecasted credit losses, default and prepayment rates for each asset category. Valuation levels of RMBS indexes are also used as an additional data point for benchmarking purposes or to price outright index positions.

RMBS and ABS are generally categorized in level 2 of the fair value hierarchy. If external prices or significant spread inputs are unobservable or if the comparability assessment involves significant subjectivity related to property type differences, cash flows, performance, and other inputs, then RMBS and ABS are categorized in level 3 of the fair value hierarchy.

Exchange-Traded Equity Securities. Exchange-traded equity securities are generally valued based on quoted prices from the exchange. To the extent these securities are actively traded, valuation adjustments are not applied, and they are categorized in level 1 of the fair value hierarchy; otherwise, they are categorized in level 2 or level 3 of the fair value hierarchy.

Listed Derivative Contracts. Listed derivatives that are actively traded are valued based on quoted prices from the exchange and are categorized in level 1 of the fair value hierarchy. Listed derivatives that are not actively traded are valued using the same approaches as those applied to OTC derivatives; they are generally categorized in level 2 of the fair value hierarchy.

OTC Derivative Contracts. OTC derivative contracts include forward, swap, and option contracts related to interest rates, foreign currencies, credit standing of reference entities, equity prices, or commodity prices.

Depending on the product and the terms of the transaction, the fair value of OTC derivative products can be either observed or modeled using a series of techniques and model inputs from comparable benchmarks, including closed-form analytic formulas, such as the Black-Scholes option-pricing model, and simulation models or a combination thereof. Many pricing models do not entail material subjectivity because the methodologies employed do not necessitate significant judgment, and the pricing inputs are observed from actively quoted markets, as is the case for generic interest rate swaps, certain option contracts and certain credit default swaps. In the case of more established derivative products, the pricing models used by the Company are widely accepted by the financial services industry. A substantial majority of OTC derivative products valued by the Company using pricing models fall into this category and are categorized in level 2 of the fair value hierarchy; otherwise, they are categorized in level 3 of the fair value hierarchy.

For further information on derivative instruments, see note 13.

Reverse Repurchase Agreements and Repurchase Agreements. The fair value of a reverse repurchase agreement or repurchase agreement is computed using a standard cash flow discounting methodology. The inputs to the valuation include contractual cash flows and collateral funding spreads, which are estimated using various benchmarks, interest rate yield curves, and option volatilities. In instances where the unobservable inputs are deemed significant, reverse repurchase agreements and repurchase agreements are categorized in level 3 of the fair value hierarchy; otherwise, they are categorized in level 2 of the fair value hierarchy.

The following table presents the Company's fair value hierarchy for those assets and liabilities measured at fair value on a recurring basis as of December 31, 20X1.

Fair Value Measurements on a Recurring Basis
As of December 31, 20X1
(Dollars in Thousands)

	Level 1	Level 2	Level 3	Netting and Collateral	Total
ASSETS					
Cash and securities segregated under federal and other regulations	$630	$—	$—	$—	$630
Securities purchased under agreements to resell	—	3,782	—	—	3,782
Deposits with Clearing Organizations	1,400	—	—	—	1,400
Securities owned:					
U.S. government and agency	6,321	5,859	—	—	12,180
Corporate bonds	1,074	4,468	4,698	—	10,240
Residential mortgage and other asset backed securities	—	4,482	1,897	—	6,379
Equities	4,555	—	—	—	4,555
Derivatives	50	709	466	(300)	925
Securities received as collateral	200	—	—	—	200
TOTALS	$14,230	$19,300	$7,061	$(300)	$40,291
LIABILITIES					
Securities sold under agreements to repurchase	$—	$3,790	$—	$—	$3,790
Securities sold, not yet purchased:					
U.S. government and agency	430	150	—	—	580
Corporate and other debt	—	10	—	—	10
Equities	622	—	—	—	622
Derivatives	—	500	200	(50)	650
Obligation to return securities received as collateral	200	—	—	—	200
TOTALS	$1,252	$4,450	$200	$(50)	$5,852

There were no transfers between level 1 and level 2 during the year.

The following is a reconciliation of the beginning and ending balances for assets and liabilities measured at fair value on a recurring basis using significant unobservable inputs (level 3) during the year ended December 31, 20X1:

Level 3 Financial Assets and Liabilities
Year ended December 31, 20X1
(Dollars in Thousands)

| | Beginning Balance | Total Gains/Losses Included in Income — Principal Transactions | | Total Gains/Losses Included in Income — Investment Banking | Purchases, Issuances, and Settlements | Transfers In (Out) | Ending Balance |
		Unrealized Gains and (Losses) Related to Assets Held at Year End	Realized Gains and (Losses) Related to Assets No Longer Held	Realized Gains and (Losses) No Positions Held at Year End			
ASSETS							
Corporate bonds	$4,258	$28	$182	$(75)	$(80)	$385	$4,698
Residential mortgages and other asset-backed securities	1,828	(33)	88	70	(81)	25	1,897
Derivatives	175	45	(10)	(70)	186	140	466
Total	$5,761	$40	$260	$(75)	$25	$550	$7,061
LIABILITIES							
Derivatives	$75	$60	$(5)	$(40)	$110	—	$200

Quantitative Information About and Sensitivity of Significant Unobservable Inputs Used in Recurring Level 3 Fair Value Measurements at December 31, 20X1[13]

The following disclosures provide information on the valuation techniques, significant unobservable inputs, and their ranges for each major category of assets and liabilities measured at fair value on a recurring basis with a significant level 3 balance. The level of aggregation and breadth of products cause the range of inputs to be wide and not evenly distributed across the inventory. Further, the range of unobservable inputs may differ across firms in the financial services industry because of diversity in the types of products included in each firm's inventory. The following disclosures also include qualitative information on the sensitivity of the fair value measurements to changes in the significant unobservable inputs.

	Balance at December 31, 20X1	Valuation Technique(s)	Significant Unobservable Input(s): Sensitivity of the Fair Value to Changes in the Unobservable Inputs	Range
ASSETS				
Corporate bonds	$4,698	Discounted cash flow	Discount rate: Significant increase (decrease) in the unobservable input in isolation would result in a significantly lower (higher) fair value measurement.	12% to 13%
Residential mortgages and other asset-backed securities	1,897	Comparable pricing	Comparable bond price: Significant increase (decrease) in the unobservable input in isolation would result in a significantly higher (lower) fair value measurement.	72–93 points
Derivatives	466	Option model	Interest rate volatility skew: Significant increase (decrease) in the unobservable input in isolation would result in a significantly higher (lower) fair value measurement.	10% to 90%
LIABILITIES				
Derivatives	$200	Option	At the money volatility: Significant increase (decrease) in the unobservable input in isolation would result in a significantly higher (lower) fair value measurement. There are no predictable relationships between the significant unobservable inputs.	20% to 45%

---

[13] Although not required for nonissuers, for level 3 measurements, issuers are required to provide a narrative description of the sensitivity of the fair value measurement to changes in unobservable inputs if a change in those inputs to a different amount might result in a significantly higher or lower fair value measurement. If there are interrelationships between those inputs and other unobservable inputs are used in the fair value measurement, an issuer should also provide a description of those interrelationships and how they might magnify or mitigate the effect of changes in the unobservable inputs on the fair value measurement.

Additional Disclosures About the Fair Value of Financial Instruments (Including Financial Instruments Not Carried at Fair Value)

GAAP requires disclosure of the estimated fair value of certain financial instruments, and the methods and significant assumptions used to estimate their fair values. Financial instruments within the scope of these disclosure requirements are included in the following table. Certain financial instruments that are not carried at fair value on the Consolidated Statement of Financial Condition are carried at amounts that approximate fair value due to their short-term nature and generally negligible credit risk. These instruments include cash, securities purchased under resale agreements with short-dated maturities, securities borrowed with short-dated maturities, short-term receivables and accrued interest receivable, commercial paper, securities sold under repurchase agreements with short-dated maturities, securities loaned with short-dated maturities, borrowings, accounts payable, and other liabilities.

The following table presents the carrying values and estimated fair values at December 31, 20X1, of financial assets and liabilities, excluding financial instruments that are carried at fair value on a recurring basis, and information is provided on their classification within the fair value hierarchy.

	Carrying Value	Level 1	Level 2	Level 3	Total Estimated Fair Value
ASSETS					
Cash	$2,647	$2,647	$—	$—	$2,647
Cash and securities segregated under federal and other regulations	375	375	—	—	375
Deposits with clearing organizations	345	345	—	—	345
Receivable from customers	40,360	—	40,360	—	40,360
Securities borrowed	2,500	—	2,500	—	2,500
Receivable from broker-dealers and clearing organizations	25,476	—	25,476	—	25,476
Secured demand notes	5,215	—	5,215	—	5,215
Memberships in exchanges owned	2,475	—	2,475	—	2,500
TOTALS	$79,393	$3,367	$76,026	$—	$79,418
LIABILITIES					
Other borrowed funds	$29,110	$—	$29,110	$—	$29,110
Payable to broker-dealers and clearing organizations	19,164	—	19,164	—	19,164
Payable to customers	12,288	—	12,288	—	12,288
Accounts payable, accrued expenses, and other liabilities	2,449	—	2,449	—	2,449
Securities loan	1,800	—	1,800	—	1,800
Long-term notes payable	3,000	—	3,000	—	3,000
Subordinated borrowings	9,897	—	9,897	—	9,897
TOTALS	$77,708	$—	$77,708	$—	$77,708

Fair Value Option[14]

FASB ASC 825, *Financial Instruments*, provides a fair value option election that allows entities to irrevocably elect fair value as the initial and subsequent measurement attribute for certain financial assets and liabilities. Changes in fair value are recognized in earnings as they occur for those assets and liabilities for which the election is made. The election is made on an instrument by instrument basis at initial recognition of an asset or liability or upon an event that gives rise to a new basis of accounting for that instrument. The fair value option has been elected for certain financial instruments that are not accounted for at fair value under other applicable accounting guidance.

At January 1, 20X1, the Company elected the fair value option on a prospective basis for securities purchased under agreements to resell and securities sold under agreements to repurchase.

The following table presents a summary of financial assets and liabilities for which the fair value option has been elected:

	Changes in Fair Value for the Year Ended December 31, 20X1 for Items Measured at Fair Value Pursuant to the Fair Value Option		
	Gains / Losses Principal Transactions	Gains Other Income	Total Changes in Fair Value
ASSETS			
Securities purchased under agreement to resell	$60	$5	$65
LIABILITIES			
Securities sold under agreement to repurchase	$(42)	$(17)	$(59)

4. Variable Interest Entities

The Company is involved with various special purpose entities (SPEs) in the normal course of business. In most cases, these entities are deemed to be variable interest entities (VIEs).

VIEs are defined as entities that either lack sufficient equity to permit the entity to finance its activities without additional subordinated financial support from other parties or have equity investors that do not have the ability to make significant decisions relating to the entity's operations through voting rights or do not have the right to receive residuals returns on equity nor the obligation to absorb expected losses. The Company applies accounting guidance for consolidation of VIEs to entities which fit the aforementioned VIE description

---

[14] FASB ASC 825, *Financial Instruments*, states that in annual periods only, an entity should disclose the methods and significant assumptions used to estimate the fair value of items for which the fair value option has been elected. In addition, as of each date for which a statement of financial position is presented, an entity should disclose certain other information that relates the information in the note to the financial statements numbers, and disclosure should be made of certain information regarding any partial elections within a group of similar eligible items. Also, FASB ASC 825 requires disclosures that relate to particular types of assets or liabilities for which the fair value option may be elected. This note is for illustrative purposes only and is not intended include all disclosures required under the topic. See FASB ASC 825-10-50 for more information on the disclosures required.

and whose primary beneficiary is the Company. The primary beneficiary of a VIE is the party that both (1) has the power to direct the activities of a VIE that most significantly affect the VIE's economic performance and (2) has an obligation to absorb losses or the right to receive benefits that in either case could potentially be significant to the VIE.

The Company determines whether it is the primary beneficiary of a VIE upon its initial involvement with the VIE and reassesses whether it is the primary beneficiary on an ongoing basis as long as it has any continuing involvement with the VIE. This determination is based upon an analysis of the design of the VIE, including the VIE's structure and activities, the power to make significant economic decisions held by the Company and by other parties, and the variable interests owned by the Company and other parties.

The Company's variable interests in VIEs include debt and equity interests. The Company's involvement with VIEs arises primarily from interests purchased in connection with secondary market-making activities including securitization. Primarily as a result of its client facilitation activities, the Company owned securities issued by securitization SPEs.[15] These securities totaled $974 at December 31, 20X1. The Company's primary risk exposure is to the securities issued by the SPE owned by the Company, with the risk highest on the most subordinate class of beneficial interests. These securities generally are included in Securities Owned and are measured at fair value. The Company does not provide additional support in these transactions through contractual facilities, such as liquidity facilities, guarantees or similar derivatives. The Company's maximum exposure to loss generally equals the fair value of the securities owned.

The Company's maximum exposure to loss does not include the offsetting benefit of any financial instruments that the Company may utilize to hedge these risks associated with the Company's variable interests. In addition, the Company's maximum exposure to loss is not reduced by the amount of collateral held as part of a transaction with the VIE or any party to the VIE directly against a specific exposure to loss.

5. Cash and Securities Segregated Under Federal and Other Regulations

Cash of $275 and U.S. government securities with a fair value of $630 are segregated under the Commodity Exchange Act and represent funds deposited by customers and funds accruing to customers as a result of trades or contracts.

Cash of $100 has been segregated in a special reserve bank account for the benefit of customers under Rule 15c3-3 of the SEC or agreements for proprietary accounts of brokers-dealers.[16]

---

[15] If the Company was involved in selling assets to a securitization vehicle, it should provide the disclosures required by FASB ASC 860, *Transfers and Servicing*.

[16] This is possible wording for those situations in which a deposit is required based on SEC Rule 15c3-3 or proprietary accounts of introducing brokers' computations, or both.

6. Receivable From and Payable to Broker-Dealers and Clearing Organizations

Amounts receivable from and payable to broker-dealers and clearing organizations at December 31, 20X1, consist of the following:

	Receivable	Payable
Deposits for securities borrowed/loaned	$7,756	$7,395
Securities failed-to-deliver/receive	13,646	1,014
Payable to clearing broker	—	9,350
Receivable from clearing organizations	2,173	—
Fees and commissions receivable/payable	1,312	1,196
Other	589	209
	$25,476	$19,164

The Company clears certain of its proprietary and customer transactions through another broker-dealer on a fully disclosed basis. The amount payable to the clearing broker relates to the aforementioned transactions and is collateralized by securities owned by the Company.

7. Receivable From and Payable to Customers

Accounts receivable from and payable to customers include amounts due on cash and margin transactions. Securities owned by customers are held as collateral for receivables.

	Receivable	Payable
Market value of customer accounts	$473	$8,438
Securities failed-to-deliver/receive	8,977	3,508
Commissions receivable	8,444	—
Margin loans	21,724	—
Other	742	342
	$40,360	$12,288

8. Other Borrowed Funds

Firm loans of $26,900 are collateralized by $31,800 of securities owned by the Company and $5,000 of securities held pursuant to secured demand note collateral agreements.

Short-term bank loans	$26,900
Drafts payable	2,210
	$29,110

9. Long-Term Notes Payable

The long-term notes payable of $3,000 bear interest at 6.5 percent and are payable in semiannual installments of $250 through July 1, 20X6. Furniture and equipment with a net carrying value of $2,500 has been pledged as sole recourse to secure the notes.

10. Related Parties

The Company is involved in significant financing and other transactions, and has significant related party balances with affiliates.

The following table sets forth the Company's related party assets and liabilities as of December 31, 20X1:

	December 31, 20X1
ASSETS	
Securities borrowed	$700
Securities purchased under agreements to resell, at fair value	880
Receivable from broker-dealers and clearing organizations	4,280
Receivable from customers	7,240
Securities owned, at fair value	529
Loans receivable from parent and affiliates (included in other assets)	125
Total assets	$13,754
LIABILITIES	
Securities loaned	$1,101
Securities sold under agreements to repurchase, at fair value	1,535
Payable to broker-dealers and clearing organizations	8,490
Payable to customers	2,424
Income taxes payable	2,276
Accounts payable, accrued expenses, and other liabilities	1,526
Subordinated borrowings	9,897
Total liabilities	$27,249

Included in the consolidated statement of income are revenues and expenses resulting from various securities trading and financing activities with certain affiliates, as well as fees for administrative services performed by the Company under the terms of various agreements.

The following table sets forth the Company's related party revenues and expenses for the year ended December 31, 20X1:

	20X1
Commissions	$724
Principal transactions	529
Investment banking	1,026
Interest Income	951
Other income	319
Total revenues	$3,549
Interest Expense	$226
Floor brokerage, clearance, and other operating expenses	$4,280
Total expenses	$4,506

11. Subordinated Borrowings[17]

The borrowings under subordination agreements at December 31, 20X1, are listed in the following:

Subordinated notes, 10 percent, due December 31, 20X2	$4,307
Secured demand note collateral agreements, 6 percent, due $1,000 in March 20X2, $1,200 in March 20X3, and $3,015 in December 20X3	5,215
Exchange memberships contributed for the use of the Company	375
	$9,897

The subordinated borrowings are with related parties and are available in computing net capital under the SEC's uniform net capital rule. To the extent that such borrowings are required for the Company's continued compliance with minimum net capital requirements, they may not be repaid. It is the Company's intention not to renew the secured demand note collateralizing agreements due on March 20X2.[18]

The fair value of subordinated borrowings is $10,800.

12. Preferred Stock

The preferred stock is redeemable at the option of the Company at $105 a share. There are no calls or puts on the preferred stock.

13. Financial Instruments[19]

Derivative financial instruments used for trading purposes, including economic hedges of trading instruments, are carried at fair value. Fair values for

---

[17] Significant restrictive covenants of debt agreements should be disclosed.

[18] Because of the unique characteristics of subordinated borrowings, additional disclosure of the amount for which six months' notice has been given of intent to withdraw is necessary.

[19] Readers should consider all the disclosure requirements of FASB ASC 815, *Derivatives and Hedging*, which may not be necessarily reflected in these financial statements and notes to the financial statements.

exchange-traded derivatives, principally futures and certain options, are based on quoted market prices. Fair values for over-the-counter derivative financial instruments, principally forwards, options, and swaps, are based on internal pricing models as no quoted market prices exist for such instruments. Factors taken into consideration in estimating the fair value of OTC derivatives include credit spreads, market liquidity, concentrations, and funding and administrative costs incurred over the life of the instruments.

Derivatives used for economic hedging purposes include swaps, forwards, futures, and purchased options. Unrealized gains or losses on these derivative contracts are recognized currently in the statement of income as principal transactions. The Company does not apply hedge accounting as defined in FASB ASC 815 because all financial instruments are recorded at fair value with changes in fair values reflected in earnings. Therefore, certain of the disclosures required under FASB ASC 815 are generally not applicable with respect to these financial instruments.

Fair values of forwards, swaps, and options contracts are recorded in securities owned or securities sold, not yet purchased, as appropriate. Open equity in futures transactions is recorded as receivables from and payables to broker-dealers and clearing organizations, as applicable.

Premiums and unrealized gains and losses for written and purchased option contracts, as well as unrealized gains and losses on interest rate swaps, are recognized gross in the consolidated statement of financial condition. The unrealized gains for delayed-delivery, TBA, and when-issued securities generally are recorded in the consolidated statement of financial condition net of unrealized losses by counterparty where master netting agreements are in place.

Principal Transactions[20]

The Company's principal transactions by reporting categories, including derivatives, at December 31, 20X1, are the following:

Fixed income	$2,607
Equity	3,500
Foreign exchange and other derivative financial instruments	600
	$6,707

---

[20] FASB ASC 815-10-50-4F provides an alternative disclosure option for derivative instruments that are not designated or qualifying as hedging instruments under FASB ASC 815-20. If an entity's policy is to include those derivative instruments in its trading activities, the entity may elect to not separately disclose gains and losses as required by FASB ASC 815-10-50-4Ce provided that the entity discloses all of the following:

    a. The gains and losses on its trading activities (including both derivative and nonderivative instruments) recognized in the statement of financial performance, separately by major types of items (such as fixed income or interest rates, foreign exchange, equity, commodity, and credit).

    b. The line items in the statement of financial condition in which trading activities gains and losses are included.

    c. A description of the nature of its trading activities and related risks, and how the entity manages those risks.

If this alternative disclosure option is elected, the entity should include a footnote in the required tables referencing the use of alternative disclosures for trading activities.

Fair Value of Financial Instruments[21]

The financial instruments of the Company are reported in the consolidated statement of financial condition at fair values, or at carrying amounts that approximate fair values because of the short maturity of the instruments, except long-term notes payable, and subordinated borrowings. The fair values of these financial instruments at December 31, 20X1, are as follows:[22]

	Assets (Liabilities)	
	Carrying Amount	Fair Value
Long-term notes payable	$(3,000)	$(3,300)
Subordinated borrowings	$(9,897)	$(10,800)

The fair value of the Company's long-term notes payable and subordinated borrowings are based on current rates offered to the Company for debt with substantially the same characteristics and maturities.

Financial Instruments With Off-Balance-Sheet Risk

The Company enters into various transactions involving derivatives and other off-balance sheet financial instruments. These financial instruments include futures, forward and foreign exchange contracts, exchange-traded and over-the-counter options, delayed deliveries, mortgage-backed TBAs, securities purchased and sold on a when-issued basis (when-issued securities), and interest rate swaps. These derivative financial instruments are used to meet the needs of customers, conduct trading activities, and manage market risks and are, therefore, subject to varying degrees of market and credit risk. Derivative transactions are entered into for trading purposes or to economically hedge other positions or transactions.

Futures and forward contracts and TBAs and when-issued securities provide for the delayed delivery of the underlying instrument. As a writer of options, the Company receives a premium in exchange for giving the counterparty the right to buy or sell the security at a future date at a contracted price. Interest rate swaps involve the exchange of payments based on fixed or floating rates applied to notional amounts. The contractual or notional amounts related to these financial instruments reflect the volume and activity and generally do not reflect the amounts at risk. Futures contracts are executed on an exchange, and cash settlement is made on a daily basis for market movements. Accordingly, futures contracts generally do not have credit risk. The credit risk for

---

[21] A nonpublic entity is not required to provide the disclosure in FASB ASC 825-10-50-10d for items disclosed at fair value but not measured at fair value in the statement of financial position. Except as noted in FASB ASC 825-10-50-3A, for annual reporting periods, FASB ASC 825-10-50-3 makes the disclosures about fair value of financial instruments optional for entities that meet all of the following criteria:

    a. The entity is a nonpublic entity.

    b. The entity's total assets are less than $100 million on the date of the financial statements.

    c. The entity has no instrument that, in whole or in part, is accounted for as a derivative instrument under FASB ASC 815, other than commitments related to the origination of mortgage loans to be held for sale, during the reporting period.

[22] When carrying amounts and fair values are the same, the table may be omitted if that is stated.

forward contracts, TBAs, options, swaps, and when-issued securities is limited to the unrealized fair valuation gains recorded in the statement of financial condition. Market risk is substantially dependent upon the value of the underlying financial instruments and is affected by market forces such as volatility and changes in interest and foreign exchange rates.

The Company had certain other transactions which, in accordance with industry practice, were not recorded on the statement of financial condition. At December 31, 20X1, the Company had commitments to enter into future resale and repurchase agreements. At December 31, 20X1, the Company had also borrowed securities and pledged securities against those borrowed securities.

In addition, the Company has sold securities that it does not currently own and will therefore be obligated to purchase such securities at a future date. The Company has recorded these obligations in the financial statements at December 31, 20X1, at fair values of the related securities and will incur a loss if the fair value of the securities increases subsequent to December 31, 20X1.

In the normal course of business, the Company's customer activities involve the execution, settlement, and financing of various customer securities transactions. These activities may expose the Company to off-balance-sheet risk in the event the customer or other broker is unable to fulfill its contracted obligations and the Company has to purchase or sell the financial instrument underlying the contract at a loss.

The Company's customer securities activities are transacted on either a cash or margin basis. In margin transactions, the Company extends credit to its customers, subject to various regulatory and internal margin requirements, collateralized by cash and securities in the customers' accounts. In connection with these activities, the Company executes and clears customer transactions involving the sale of securities not yet purchased, substantially all of which are transacted on a margin basis subject to individual exchange regulations. Such transactions may expose the Company to significant off-balance-sheet risk in the event margin requirements are not sufficient to fully cover losses that customers may incur. In the event the customer fails to satisfy its obligations, the Company may be required to purchase or sell financial instruments at prevailing market prices to fulfill the customer's obligations. The Company seeks to control the risks associated with its customer activities by requiring customers to maintain margin collateral in compliance with various regulatory and internal guidelines. The Company monitors required margin levels daily and, pursuant to such guidelines, requires the customer to deposit additional collateral or to reduce positions when necessary.

The Company's customer financing and securities settlement activities require the Company to pledge customer securities as collateral in support of various secured financing sources such as bank loans and securities loaned. In the event the counterparty is unable to meet its contractual obligation to return customer securities pledged as collateral, the Company may be exposed to the risk of acquiring the securities at prevailing market prices in order to satisfy its customer obligations. The Company controls this risk by monitoring the fair value of securities pledged on a daily basis and by requiring adjustments of collateral levels in the event of excess market exposure. In addition, the Company establishes credit limits for such activities and monitors compliance on a daily basis.

Quantitative Disclosures for Derivative Financial Instruments Used for Trading Purposes

As of December 31, 20X1, the gross contractual or notional amounts of derivative financial instruments are as follows:

	Notional or Contract Amount
Interest Rate:	
Swap agreements, including options, swaptions, caps, collars, and floors	$50
Futures contracts	5
Options held	2
Foreign Exchange:	
Futures contracts	5
Forward contracts	23
Options held	1
Options written	2
Mortgage-Backed Securities:	
Forward contracts	10
Equity:	
Swap agreements	22
Futures contracts	5
Options held	1
Options written	1
Total	$127

The majority of the Company's transactions with off-balance-sheet risk are short-term in duration with a weighted average maturity of approximately 1.65 years at December 31, 20X1. The remaining maturities for notional or contract amounts outstanding for derivative financial instruments are as follows:[23]

---

[23] The disclosure of the remaining maturities for notional or contract amounts for derivative financial instruments is encouraged but not required.

	Less Than 1 Year	1–3 Years	3–5 Years	Greater Than 5 Years	Total
Swap agreements	$20	$25	$16	$11	$72
Futures contracts	9	5	1	—	15
Forward contracts	33	—	—	—	33
Options held	4	—	—	—	4
Options written	3	—	—	—	3
Total	$69	$30	$17	$11	$127
Percent of total	54%	24%	13%	9%	100%

The fair values of derivative financial instruments included in securities owned and securities sold, not yet purchased as of December 31, 20X1, and the average monthly fair value of the instruments for the year ended December 31, 20X1, are as follows:

	Fair Value at Year-End		Average Fair Values	
	Assets	Liabilities	Assets	Liabilities
Swap agreements	$688	$348	$499	$226
Futures contracts	40	—	30	—
Forward contracts	169	61	31	15
Options held	328	—	203	—
Options written	—	291	—	123
Total derivatives	$1,225	$700	$763	$364
Cash collateral	(200)	(40)		
Netting	(100)	(10)		
Total carrying value	$925	$650		

In accordance with FASB ASC 210-20-50, the following tables present, as of December 31, 20X1, the gross and net derivatives receivables and payables by contract and settlement type under GAAP.[24] Derivatives receivables and payables have been netted on the Consolidated Statement of Financial Condition against derivative payables and receivables, respectively, to the same counterparty with respect to derivative contracts for which the Company has obtained an appropriate legal opinion with respect to the master netting agreement; where such a legal opinion has not been either sought or obtained, the receivables and payables are not eligible under GAAP for netting against related derivative payables on the Consolidated Statement of Financial

---

[24] In accordance with FASB ASC 210-20-50, an entity is allowed to present the gross and net derivative receivables and payables by either contract and settlement type or by counterparty.

Condition, and are shown separately in the following tables ("Derivative receivables not nettable under GAAP").

	Gross Derivative Receivables	Amounts Netted on the Consolidated Statement of Financial Condition	Net Derivative Receivables
GAAP nettable derivative receivables			
Interest rate contracts:			
Over-the-counter	$1,924	$(1,887)	$37
OTC-cleared	148	(92)	56
Exchange traded	977	(805)	172
Total interest rate contracts	3,049	(2,784)	265
Credit contracts:			
Over-the-counter	250	(250)	—
OTC-cleared	751	(672)	79
Total credit contracts	1,001	(922)	79
Foreign exchange contracts:			
Over-the-counter	98	—	98
Total foreign exchange contracts	98	—	98
Equity contracts:			
Over-the-counter	2,788	(2,363)	425
Exchange traded	739	(739)	—
Total equity contracts	3,527	(3,102)	425
Derivative receivables with an appropriate legal opinion	7,675	(6,808)	867
Derivative receivables where an appropriate legal opinion has not been either sought or obtained	58	—	58
Total derivative receivables recognized on the Consolidated Statement of Financial Condition	$7,733	$(6,808)	$925

	Gross Derivative Payables	Amounts Netted on the Consolidated Statement of Financial Condition	Net Derivative Payables
U.S. GAAP nettable derivative payables			
Interest rate contracts:			
Over-the-counter	$1,561	$(1,531)	$30
OTC-cleared	219	(186)	33
Exchange traded	985	(829)	156
Total interest rate contracts	2,765	(2,546)	219
Credit contracts:			
Over-the-counter	48	(48)	—
OTC-cleared	197	(129)	68
Total credit contracts	245	(177)	68
Foreign exchange contracts:			
Over-the-counter	124	—	124
Total foreign exchange contracts	124	—	124
Equity contracts:			
Over-the-counter	1,274	(1,122)	152
Exchange traded	987	(987)	—
Total equity contracts	2,261	(2,109)	152
Derivative payables with an appropriate legal opinion	5,395	(4,832)	563
Derivative payables where an appropriate legal opinion has not been either sought or obtained	87	—	87
Total derivative payables recognized on the Consolidated Statement of Financial Condition	$5,482	$(4,832)	$650

In addition to the cash collateral received and transferred that is presented on a net basis with net derivative receivables and payables, the Company receives and transfers additional collateral (financial instruments and cash). These amounts mitigate counterparty credit risk associated with the Company's derivative instruments but are not eligible for net presentation, because (a) the collateral is non-cash financial instruments (generally U.S. government and agency securities and other government bonds), (b) the amount of collateral held or transferred exceeds the fair value exposure, at the individual counterparty level, as of the date presented, or (c) the collateral relates to derivative receivables or payables where an appropriate legal opinion has not been either sought or obtained.

The following table presents information regarding certain financial instrument collateral received and transferred as of December 31, 20X1, that is not eligible for net presentation under GAAP. The collateral included in these tables relates only to the nettable derivative instruments with the appropriate legal opinions and excludes additional collateral that exceeds the fair value exposure and excludes all collateral related to derivative instruments.

Derivatives Receivable Collateral	Net Derivatives Receivables	Collateral Not Nettable on the Consolidated Statement of Financial Condition	Net Exposure
Derivative receivables with appropriate legal opinions	925	—	925

Derivatives Payable Collateral	Net Derivatives Payables	Collateral Not Nettable on the Consolidated Statement of Financial Condition	Net Exposure
Derivative payables with appropriate legal opinions	650	—	650

The following table summarizes the credit quality of the Company's over-the-counter derivatives by showing internal counterparty credit ratings for the net exposure (net of collateral of $200) of contracts in an asset position at December 31, 20X1.[25]

Rating*	Net Exposure
AAA	$525
AA	220
A	130
BBB and lower	100
Other†	50
Total	$1,025

* Rating Agency Equivalent

† *Other* indicates counterparties for which no credit was available from an independent third-party source. It does not necessarily indicate the counterparties' credit is below investment grade.

---

[25] Qualitative disclosure for derivative financial instruments, such as this table, is encouraged but not required.

Credit-Risk-Related Contingent Features in Derivatives

Certain of the Company's derivative instruments contain provisions that require the Company's debt to maintain an investment grade credit rating from each of the major credit rating agencies. If the Company's debt rating were to fall below investment grade, it would be in violation of these provisions, and the counterparties to the derivative instruments could request immediate payment or demand immediate and ongoing full overnight collateralization on derivative instruments in net liability positions. The aggregate fair value of all derivative instruments with such provisions that are in a liability position on December 31, 20X1, is $100 for which the Company has posted collateral of $40 in the normal course of business. If the credit-risk-related contingent features underlying these agreements were triggered on December 31, 20X1, the Company would be required to post an additional $15 of collateral to its counterparties.

Derivative Financial Instruments Used for Purposes Other Than Trading

The Company enters into derivative contracts to economically hedge exposures or to modify the characteristics of financial instruments or transactions.

Open derivative contracts, which are linked to assets or liabilities that are sold or otherwise disposed of, are terminated at the time of disposition. Unrealized gains or losses on such derivative contracts are recognized in the statement of income currently as revenue from principal transactions.

At December 31, 20X1, the Company had outstanding interest rate and currency swap agreements with a notional principal amount of $72. The swaps are recorded at fair value, and changes in fair value are included in income currently.

Concentrations of Credit Risk

The Company and its subsidiaries are engaged in various trading and brokerage activities in which counterparties primarily include broker-dealers, banks, and other financial institutions. In the event counterparties do not fulfill their obligations, the Company may be exposed to risk. The risk of default depends on the creditworthiness of the counterparty or issuer of the instrument. It is the Company's policy to review, as necessary, the credit standing of each counterparty.

14. Securities Financing

Transactions involving securities purchased under agreements to resell (reverse repurchase agreements or reverse repos) or securities sold under agreements to repurchase (repurchase agreements or repos) are accounted for as collateralized agreements or financings except where the Company does not have an agreement to sell (or purchase) the same or substantially the same securities before maturity at a fixed or determinable price. It is the policy of the Company and subsidiaries to obtain possession of collateral with a fair value equal to or in excess of the principal amount loaned under resale agreements. Collateral is valued daily, and the Company may require counterparties to deposit additional collateral or return collateral pledged when appropriate. Reverse repos and repos are carried at fair value. Interest on such contract amounts is accrued and is included in the consolidated statement of financial condition in receivables from and payables to broker-dealers and clearing organizations.[26] In accordance with FASB ASC 860-10-40, repurchase-to-maturity transactions should be accounted for as secured borrowings.

Securities borrowed and securities loaned transactions are generally reported as collateralized financings except where letters of credit or other securities are used as collateral. Securities borrowed transactions require the Company to deposit cash, letters of credit, or other collateral with the lender. With respect to securities loaned, the Company receives collateral in the form of cash or other collateral in an amount generally in excess of the fair value of securities loaned. The Company monitors the fair value of securities borrowed and loaned on a daily basis, with additional collateral obtained or refunded as necessary. Securities borrowed and securities loaned transactions are recorded at the amount of cash collateral advanced or received, adjusted for additional collateral obtained or received. Interest on such transactions is accrued and is included in the consolidated statement of financial condition in receivables from and payables to broker-dealers and clearing organizations.

In accordance with FASB ASC 210-20-50-3, the following table presents as of December 31, 20X1 the gross and net securities purchased under resale agreements and securities borrowed, and the gross and net securities sold under repurchase agreements and securities loaned.[27]

	Gross Amounts Recognized as Assets	Gross Amounts Offset in the Statement of Financial Condition	Net Amounts of Assets Presented in the Statement of Financial Condition
Securities purchased under resale agreements	4,704	(922)	3,782
Securities borrowed	2,500	—	2,500

	Gross Amounts Recognized as Liabilities	Gross Amounts Offset in the Statement of Financial Condition	Net Amounts of Liabilities Presented in the Statement of Financial Condition
Securities sold under resale agreements	4,797	(1,007)	3,790
Securities loaned	1,800	—	1,800

The following table presents, for those transactions accounted for as a sale and accompanied by an agreement that results in the Company retaining substantially all of the exposure to the economic returns of the transferred asset during the transaction's term, the carrying amount of assets derecognized and the gross amount of proceeds received at the transfer date and the related amounts reported as of December 31, 20X1:

[26] Alternatively, accrued interest could be reported either on its own line (for example,"accrued interest receivable") or as part of the "repurchase agreements" or "reverse repurchase agreements" lines.

[27] If the Company has amounts subject to enforceable netting arrangements but are not offset, those amounts should be disclosed in accordance with FASB ASC 210-20-50-3d.

	At the Date of Derecognition for Transactions Outstanding		As of December 31, 20X1		
	Carrying Amount Derecognized	Gross Cash Proceeds Received for Assets Derecognized	Fair Value of Transferred Assets	Gross Derivative Assets Recorded[a][b]	Gross Derivative Liabilities Recorded[a][b]
Securities sold under resale agreements	$45	$42	$48	$3	$
Sales and a total return swap	4	4	4	—	—
Securities loaned	176	178	170	—	6
Total	$225	$224	$222	$3	$6

[a] Balances are presented on a gross basis, before the application of counterparty and cash collateral netting.

[b] $3 of gross derivative assets and $6 of gross derivative liabilities are included as equity contracts in footnote 13 on derivative disclosures.

In accordance with FASB ASC 860-30-50-7 the following tables present, as of December 31, 20X1, the gross liability for securities sold under repurchase agreements and securities loaned disaggregated by class of collateral pledged and by remaining contractual maturity of the agreements.

	Securities Sold Under Resale Agreements	Securities Loaned	Total
U.S. Treasury and federal agency	4,413	342	4,755
State and municipal	48	18	66
Equity securities	336	1,440	1,776
Total	4,797	1,800	6,597

	Overnight and Open	Up to 30 days	30–90 days	Greater than 90 days	Total
Securities sold under resale agreements	4,317	192	48	240	4,797
Securities loaned	1333	467	—	—	1,800
Total	5,560	659	48	240	6,597

Note that the collateral pledged as part of repurchase agreements and securities loaned is subject to changes in market price and thus may decline in value during the time of the agreement. In this case, the Company may be required to post additional collateral to the counterparty to appropriately collateralize the contract (and similarly may receive a portion of the collateral posted back when the collateral posted experiences a market value increase). The market risk of the collateral posted is reviewed by the Company's risk function, and these risks are managed using a variety of mechanisms including review of the type and grade of securities posted as collateral and the Company entering into offsetting agreements to hedge a decline in the market value of collateral posted.

15. Commitments and Contingent Liabilities[28]

The Company is contingently liable as of December 31, 20X1, in the amount of $4,375 under bank guarantees and has outstanding letter-of-credit agreements aggregating $3,000 used in lieu of margin deposits. The Company has determined that these commitments do not meet the definition of a derivative, as defined by FASB ASC 815. These agreements are generally made for periods of six months to one year and bear interest at rates from 0.5 percent to 1 percent.

---

[28] If the Company is subject to any litigation, it should follow the guidance and provide disclosure in accordance with FASB ASC 450, *Contingencies*.

The Company and its subsidiaries have obligations under operating leases with initial noncancelable terms in excess of one year. Aggregate annual rentals for office space and equipment at December 31, 20X1, are approximately as listed as follows:

20X2	$1,492
20X3	1,440
20X4	1,006
20X5	982
20X6	901
Later years	1,164
	$6,985

Certain leases contain renewal options and escalation clauses. Rent expense for 20X1 aggregated to $1,519 and is included in the *Occupancy and equipment* expense line item on the Consolidated Statement of Income.

The Company and a subsidiary—together with various other broker-dealers, corporations, and individuals—have been named as defendants in several class action lawsuits that allege violations of federal and state securities laws and claim substantial damages. The Company is also a defendant in other lawsuits incidental to its securities and commodities business. Management of the Company, after consultation with outside legal counsel, believes that the resolution of these various lawsuits will not result in any material adverse effect on the Company's consolidated financial position.

In the normal course of business, the Company enters into underwriting commitments. Transactions relating to such underwriting commitments that were open at December 31, 20X1, and were subsequently settled had no material effect on the financial statements as of that date.

16. Guarantees

FASB ASC 460, *Guarantees*, requires the Company to disclose information about its obligations under certain guarantee arrangements. FASB ASC 460 defines guarantees as contracts and indemnification agreements that contingently require a guarantor to make payments to the guaranteed party based on changes in an underlying (such as an interest or foreign exchange rate, security or commodity price, an index or the occurrence or nonoccurrence of a specified event) related to an asset, liability or equity security of a guaranteed party. This guidance also defines guarantees as contracts that contingently require the guarantor to make payments to the guaranteed party based on another entity's failure to perform under an agreement as well as indirect guarantees of the indebtedness of others.

Derivative Contracts

Certain derivative contracts that the Company has entered into meet the accounting definition of a guarantee under FASB ASC 460. Derivatives that meet the FASB ASC 460 definition of guarantees include certain written options and credit default swaps. Because the Company does not track the counterparties' purpose for entering into a derivative contract, it has disclosed derivative contracts that are likely to be used to protect against a change in an underlying financial instrument, regardless of their actual use.

The maximum potential payout for certain derivative contracts, such as written interest rate caps and written foreign currency options, cannot be estimated as increases in interest or foreign exchange rates in the future could possibly be unlimited. Therefore, in order to provide information regarding the maximum potential amount of future payments that the Company could be required to make under certain derivative contracts, the notional amount of the contracts has been disclosed.

The Company records all derivative contracts at fair value. The Company does not monitor its risk exposure to derivative contracts based on derivative notional amounts but rather on a fair value basis. Aggregate market risk limits have been established, and market risk measures are routinely monitored against these limits. The Company also manages its exposure to these derivative contracts through a variety of risk mitigation strategies, including, but not limited to, entering into offsetting economic hedge positions, collateral, and setoff rights. The Company believes that the notional amounts of the derivative contracts generally overstate its exposure.

Indemnifications

In the normal course of its business, the Company indemnifies and guarantees certain service providers, such as clearing and custody agents, trustees and administrators, against specified potential losses in connection with their acting as an agent of, or providing services to, the Company or its affiliates. The Company also indemnifies some clients against potential losses incurred in the event specified third-party service providers, including subcustodians and third-party brokers, improperly executed transactions. The maximum potential amount of future payments that the Company could be required to make under these indemnifications cannot be estimated. However, the Company believes that it is unlikely it will have to make material payments under these arrangements and has not recorded any contingent liability in the consolidated financial statements for these indemnifications.

The Company provides representations and warranties to counterparties in connection with a variety of commercial transactions and occasionally indemnifies them against potential losses caused by the breach of those representations and warranties. The Company may also provide standard indemnifications to some counterparties to protect them in the event additional taxes are owed or payments are withheld, due either to a change in or adverse application of certain tax laws. These indemnifications generally are standard contractual terms and are entered into in the normal course of business. The maximum potential amount of future payments that the Company could be required to make under these indemnifications cannot be estimated. However, the Company believes that it is unlikely it will have to make material payments under these arrangements and has not recorded any contingent liability in the consolidated financial statements for these indemnifications.

Exchange Member Guarantees

The Company is a member of various exchanges that trade and clear securities or futures contracts or both. Associated with its membership, the Company may be required to pay a proportionate share of the financial obligations of another member who may default on its obligations to the exchange. Although the rules governing different exchange memberships vary, in general the Company's guarantee obligations would arise only if the exchange had previously exhausted its resources. In addition, any such guarantee obligation would be apportioned among the other nondefaulting members of the exchange. Any potential contingent liability under these membership agreements cannot be estimated. The Company has not recorded any contingent liability in the consolidated financial statements for these agreements and believes that any potential requirement to make payments under these agreements is remote.

Other Guarantees

The Company, in its capacity as an agency lender, occasionally indemnifies securities lending customers against losses incurred in the event that borrowers do not return securities and the collateral held is insufficient to cover the fair value of the securities borrowed. In addition, the Company provides letters of credit and other guarantees, on a limited basis, to enable clients to enhance their credit standing and complete transactions.

The following table sets forth the maximum payout/notional amounts associated with the Company's guarantees as of December 31, 20X1:

Maximum Potential Payout/Notional

Years to Maturity

Type of Guarantee	Less than 1	1–3	3–5	Over 5	Total	Carrying Amount	Collateral / Recourse
Derivative contracts	$1,267	$936	$397	$418	$3,018	$2,755	$2,113
Securities lending indemnifications	377	458	255	—	1,090	277	709
Letters of credit and other guarantees	38	77	69	8	192	192	137

17. Net Capital Requirements

The Company is subject to the SEC Uniform Net Capital Rule (SEC Rule 15c3-1), which requires the maintenance of minimum net capital and requires that the ratio of aggregate indebtedness to net capital, both as defined, should not exceed 15 to 1 (and the rule of the "applicable" exchange also provides that equity capital may not be withdrawn or cash dividends paid if the resulting net capital ratio would exceed 10 to 1).[29] The Company is also subject to the net capital requirements of the CFTC Regulation 1.17 and requirements of the National Futures Association, and is required to maintain "adjusted net capital", equivalent to the greater of $1,000,000 or 8 percent of customer and noncustomer risk maintenance margin requirements on all positions, as these terms are defined.[30] At December 31, 20X1, the Company had net capital of $33,584, which was $29,381 in excess of its required net capital of $4,203. The Company's net capital ratio was 1.7 to 1.[31]

18. Income Taxes

The Company is included in the consolidated federal income tax return filed by its Parent. Federal income taxes are calculated as if the Company filed a

---

[29] Various regulatory agencies and exchanges may impose additional capital requirements, which may be necessary to disclose.

[30] Only applicable if the broker-dealer is a futures commission merchant subject to Regulation 1.17 of the Commodity Futures Trading Commission.

[31] See illustrative schedule I in exhibit 6-9.

separate federal income tax return. The Company and its subsidiaries file their own state and local tax returns. The current and deferred portions of the income tax expense (benefit) included in the statement of operations as determined in accordance with FASB ASC 740 are as follows:

	Current	Deferred	Total
Federal	$5,204	$(304)	$4,900
State and local	1,280	680	1,960
Foreign	240	—	240
	$6,724	$376	$7,100

A reconciliation of the difference between the expected income tax expense or benefit computed at the U.S. statutory income tax rate and the Company's income tax expense is shown in the following table:[32]

Expected income tax expense at U.S. statutory tax rate	$4,659
The effect of:	
Nondeductible expenses	1,309
Increase due to state and local taxes, net of U.S. federal income tax effects	1,293
Tax-exempt income, net of related nondeductible interest expense	(427)
Other, net	266
Income tax expense[33]	$7,100

The Company recognizes the accrual of any interest and penalties related to unrecognized tax benefits in income tax expense. No interest or penalties were recognized in 20X1. The following is a reconciliation of the beginning and ending amounts of unrecognized tax benefits:

Balance at January 1, 20X1	$533
Additions based on tax positions related to the current year	72
Additions for tax positions of prior years	—
Reductions for tax positions of prior years	(17)
Settlements	(5)
Expiration of Statute of Limitations	—
Balance at December 31, 20X1	$583

---

[32] This is an optional disclosure for firms not subject to SEC Regulation S-X. An explanation of a disproportionate tax provision, however, is required under accounting principles generally accepted in the United States of America.

[33] See FASB ASC 740-10-50 for additional disclosures required, if material.

Of the balance at December 31, 20X1, approximately $63 represents the amount of unrecognized tax benefits that, if recognized, would favorably affect the effective tax rate in future years. The Company does not have any tax positions at the end of the year for which it is reasonably possible that the total amounts of unrecognized tax benefits will significantly increase or decrease within 12 months of the reporting date.

The following represents the approximate tax effect of each significant type of temporary difference giving rise to the deferred income tax liability.

Deferred tax asset:	
Employee benefits	$25
Other	11
Total	$36
Deferred tax liability:	
Property, plant, and equipment	42
Other	7
Total	$49
Deferred tax liability, net	$13

The Parent and the Company are no longer subject to federal, state, or local tax examinations by taxing authorities for years before 20W4. The IRS commenced an examination of the Parent's federal income tax returns for the years 20W6 and 20W7 in the last quarter of 20W9 that is anticipated to be completed by the end of 20X2. As of December 31, 20X1, the IRS has not proposed any adjustment to the Company's tax position.

19. Consolidated Subsidiaries[34,35]

The following is a summary of certain financial information of the Company's consolidated subsidiaries:

	Broker-Dealer Jr.	Investment Advisory	Venture Capital	Total
Total assets	$12,700	$1,700	$5,100	$19,500
Stockholders' equity	2,800	400	1,800	5,000

The $2,800 of stockholders' equity and $1,500 of the subordinated liabilities of the broker-dealer subsidiary are included as capital in a consolidated computation of the Company's net capital, because the assets of the subsidiary are readily available for the protection of the Company's customers, broker-dealers,

---

[34] Information in this note is presented to comply with FOCUS requirements (total assets and stockholders' equity of consolidated subsidiaries and treatment of the flow-through capital of the broker-dealer subsidiary). Readers should also consider FASB ASC 280, *Segment Reporting*, which requires that public business enterprises report financial and descriptive information about their reportable operating segments.

[35] See FASB ASC 810-10-50 for information on required disclosures related to consolidation. Note that the "Pending Content" in FASB ASC 810-10-15-10 states that a majority-owned subsidiary that is not within the scope of the "Variable Interest Entity" subsections and in which a parent has a controlling financial interest should not be consolidated if the parent is a broker-dealer within the scope of FASB ASC 940, *Financial Services—Brokers and Dealers*, and the control is likely to be temporary.

and other creditors, as permitted by Rule 15c3-1, which resulted in an increase in net capital and required net capital (after nonallowable assets and charges) of $1,838 and $500, respectively. The accounts of the other subsidiaries are not included in the computation.

20. Pledged Assets and Collateral

The Company pledges its financial instruments owned to collateralize repurchase agreements and other securities financings. Pledged securities that can be sold or repledged by the secured party are identified in the consolidated statement of financial condition. The carrying value and classification of securities owned by the Company that have been loaned or pledged to counterparties where those counterparties do not have the right to sell or repledge the collateral were as follows:

	At December 31, 20X1
Financial instruments owned:	
U.S. government and agency securities	$1,000
Corporate and other debt	500
Residential mortgages and other asset backed securities	600
Corporate equities	900
Total	$3,000

Under the Company's collateralized financing agreements, the Company either receives or provides collateral. In many cases, the Company is permitted to sell or repledge these securities held as collateral. At December 31, 20X1, the fair value of securities received as collateral where the Company is permitted to sell or repledge the securities was $2,570 and the fair value of the portion that had been sold or repledged was $2,387.

The Company additionally receives securities as collateral in connection with certain securities for securities transactions in which the Company is the lender. In instances where the Company is permitted to sell or repledge these securities, the Company reports the fair value of the collateral received and the related obligation to return the collateral in the consolidated statement of financial condition. At December 31, 20X1, $200, was reported as *Securities received as collateral* and an *Obligation to return securities received as collateral* in the consolidated statement of financial condition. Collateral received in connection with these transactions that was subsequently repledged was approximately $194 at December 31, 20X1.[36,37]

21. Subsequent Events

The Company has performed an evaluation of events that have occurred subsequent to December 31, 20X1, and through February XX, 20X2,[38] the date of the filing of this report. There have been no material subsequent events that occurred during such period that would require disclosure in this report or would be required to be recognized in the consolidated financial statements as of December 31, 20X1.

---

[36] FASB ASC 860-30-50 requires disclosure of information about the sources and uses of that collateral.

[37] See footnote 34.

[38] This date should correspond with the date of the filing of the report.

Exhibit 6-9

Supplementary Information
Pursuant to Rule 17a-5 of the
Securities Exchange Act of 1934

As of December 31, 20X1

The accompanying schedules are prepared in accordance with the requirements and general format of FOCUS Form X-17A-5. If desired, the preprinted FOCUS forms may be used for presenting the required supplementary information. The auditor should be aware of certain exemptive provisions under SEC Rule 15c3-3 regarding the determination of net capital requirements in the computation of net capital (Schedule I) and the computation for the determination of reserve requirements (Schedule II). If the exemptive provisions apply, a note should be added by the broker-dealer to the schedules, stating the basis under which the broker-dealer claims exemption.

Schedule I
Standard Stockbrokerage Co., Inc.
Computation of Net Capital Under Rule 15c3-1 of the Securities and Exchange Commission[*]
(Dollars in Thousands)
As of December 31, 20X1

Net Capital

Total consolidated stockholders' equity		$39,719
Deduct stockholders' equity not allowable for net capital[†]		2,200
Total stockholders' equity qualified for net capital		37,519
Add:		
Subordinated borrowings allowable in computation of net capital		9,897
Other (deductions) or allowable credits-deferred income taxes payable		1,200
Total capital and allowable subordinated borrowings		48,616
Deductions/charges:		
Nonallowable assets:		
Securities not readily marketable	$1,730	
Exchange memberships	2,475	
Furniture, equipment, and leasehold improvements, net[‡]	2,381	
Other assets[‖]	98	
	6,684	
Additional charges for customers' and noncustomers' security accounts	825	
Additional charges for customers' and noncustomers' commodity accounts	78	
Aged fails-to-deliver	42	
Aged short security differences	44	
Secured demand note deficiency	525	
Commodity futures contracts and spot commodities/ proprietary capital charges	163	
Other deductions/charges	514	8,875
Net capital before haircuts on securities positions (tentative net capital)		39,741
Haircuts on securities		
Contractual securities commitments	2,520	
Trading and investment securities		
Bankers' acceptances, certificates of deposit, and commercial paper	34	

(continued)

U.S. government agency and Canadian government obligations	1,155	
State and municipal government obligations	14	
Corporate obligations	1,242	
Stocks and warrants	893	
Options	212	
Undue concentrations	87	6,157
Net capital		$33,584

Aggregate indebtedness

Items included in consolidated statement of financial condition:#

Short-term bank loans (secured by customer's securities)	$18,400
Drafts payable	2,210
Payable to brokers and dealers	8,110
Payable to clearing broker	9,350
Payable to customers	11,716
Other accounts payable and accrued expenses	3,150

Items not included in consolidated statement of financial condition:

Fair value of securities borrowed for which no equivalent value is paid or credited	2,532
Other unrecorded amounts	1,158
Total aggregate indebtedness	$56,626

Computation of basic net capital requirement

Minimum net capital required:

Company	$ 3,775
Broker-dealer subsidiary	428
Total	$4,203
Excess net capital at 1,500 percent	$29,381
Excess net capital at 1,000 percent	$27,493
Ratio: Aggregate indebtedness to net capital	1.69 to 1

Reconciliation with Company's computation** (included in Part II of Form X-17A-5 as of December 31, 20X1)

Net capital, as reported in Company's Part II (unaudited) FOCUS report	$35,154

Allowable assets erroneously reported as nonallowable:

Deposits	582
Accrued interest receivable	378
Difference due to offsetting various asset accounts against related liabilities	(2,518)
Audit adjustments to record additional compensation	(600)

Other audit adjustments (net)	373
Other items (net)	215
Net capital per the preceding	$33,584

Computation of alternative net capital requirement[††]

2% of aggregate debit items (or $250,000, if greater) as shown in formula for reserve requirements pursuant to Rule 15c3-3 prepared as of date of net capital computation—Company	$1,077
Capital requirement of consolidated broker-dealer subsidiary electing alternative method	250
Total net capital requirement	$1,327
Excess net capital[‡‡]	$32,257

Net capital in excess of

4 percent of aggregate debit items	$31,106
5 percent of aggregate debit items	$30,236

---

* Broker-dealers should consider the impact of recently issued accounting and regulatory pronouncements when preparing this supplementary schedule.

† Excludes stockholders' equity of investment advisory and venture capital subsidiaries. See note 19.

‡ Excludes $2.5 million because of sole recourse of the related indebtedness.

|| Excludes $222 of good-faith deposits for underwritings.

\# Excludes balances of consolidated subsidiaries other than wholly-owned broker-dealer subsidiaries included in consolidated computation of net capital.

** If there is no material difference from the Company's computation and a reconciliation is not included, a statement to that effect is required. The following statement can be used to satisfy this requirement:

Note: There are no material differences between the preceding computation and the Company's corresponding unaudited Part II of Form X-17A-5 as of December 31, 20X1.

This note can be placed at the end of this schedule or on every page of the schedule.

†† To be included if the Company has elected to use the alternative method of computing net capital pursuant to Appendix C of Rule 15c3-1. In this case, aggregate indebtedness and the computation of basic net capital may be excluded.

‡‡ Net capital under the alternative method is computed on a basis similar to the basic net capital computation; the broker-dealer would incur a 1 percent charge on fails-to-deliver (offset by fails-to-receive).

Schedule II
Standard Stockbrokerage Co., Inc.
Computation for Determination of Customer Account Reserve of Brokers and Dealers
Under Rule 15c3-3 of the Securities and Exchange Commission[*]
(Standard Stockbrokerage Co., Inc. only)
(*Dollars in Thousands*)
As of December 31, 20X1

Credit balances

Free credit balances and other credit balances in customers' security accounts (including nonregulated commodity accounts, net of related margin deposits of $322,300)	$10,716
Monies borrowed, collateralized by securities carried for the accounts of customers	18,400
Monies payable against customers' securities loaned	1,825
Customers' securities failed to receive (including credit balances in continuous net settlement accounts)	6,276
Credit balances in firm accounts that are attributable to principal sales to customers	1,238
Fair value of stock dividends, stock splits, and similar distributions receivable outstanding over 30 calendar days	327
Fair value of short security count differences over 30 calendar days old[†]	5
Fair value of short securities and credits (not to be offset by "longs" or by debits) in all suspense accounts over 30 calendar days[†]	78
Fair value of securities that are in transfer in excess of forty calendar days and have not been confirmed to be in transfer by the transfer agent or the issuer	38
Total credit items	38,903

Debit balances

Debit balances in customers' cash and margin accounts
excluding unsecured accounts and accounts doubtful of
collection net of deductions pursuant to Rule 15c3-3[‡] ... 38,988

Securities borrowed to effectuate short sales by
customers and securities borrowed to make delivery
on customers' securities failed to deliver ... 1,318

Failed to deliver of customers' securities not older than
30 calendar days (including debit balances in
continuous net settlement accounts) ... 14,782

Other[ǁ] ... 438

Gross debits ... 55,526

Less 3 percent charge ... 1,666

Total debit items[‡] ... 53,860

Reserve computation[‡]

Excess of total debits over total credits ... $14,957

Required deposit ... None

Reconciliation with Company's computation[#]
(included in Part II of Form X-17A-5 as of
December 31, 20X1)

Excess debits as reported in Company's Part II FOCUS
report ... $15,496

Nonregulated commodity margin deposits erroneously
excluded from the Company's computation ... $322

Other items, net ... 217 ... (539)

Excess debits per the preceding computation ... $14,957

---

[*] Broker-dealers should consider the impact of recently issued accounting and regulatory pronouncements when preparing this supplementary schedule.

[†] Would be seven calendar days if the broker or dealer had elected the alternative net capital requirement under Rule 15c3-1(f).

[‡] Those firms calculating net capital under the basic method must reduce debit balances in customer accounts by 1 percent, whereas those calculating net capital under the alternative method are required to reduce total debits by 3 percent.

[ǁ] This caption may only include those interpretive items that do not belong in the captions specified by the rule.

[#] If there are no material differences from the Company's computation and a reconciliation is not included, a statement to that effect is required. The following statement can be used to satisfy this requirement:

Note: There are no material differences between the preceding computation and the Company's corresponding unaudited Part II of Form X-17A-5 as of December 31, 20X1.

This note can be placed at the end of this schedule or on every page of the schedule.

Schedule III
Standard Stockbrokerage Co., Inc.
Computation for Determination of PAB Account Reserve of Brokers and Dealers
Under Rule 15c3-3 of the Securities and Exchange Commission*
(Standard Stockbrokerage Co., Inc. only)
(*Dollars in Thousands*)
As of December 31, 20X1

Credit balances

Free credit balances and other credit balances in PAB security accounts	$492
Monies borrowed, collateralized by securities carried for the accounts of PAB	1,083
Monies payable against PAB securities loaned	366
PAB securities failed to receive	—
Credit balances in firm accounts that are attributable to principal sales to PAB	887
Fair value of stock dividends, stock splits, and similar distributions receivable outstanding over 30 calendar days	3
Fair value of short security count differences over 30 calendar days old †	—
Fair value of short securities and credits (not to be offset by "longs" or by debits) in all suspense accounts over 30 calendar days†	5
Fair value of securities that are in transfer in excess of 40 calendar days and have not been confirmed to be in transfer by the transfer agent or the issuer	—
Total PAB credit items	2,836

Debit balances

Debit balances in PAB cash and margin accounts excluding unsecured accounts and accounts doubtful of collection net of deductions pursuant to Rule 15c3-3‡	663
Securities borrowed to effectuate short sales by PAB and securities borrowed to make delivery on PAB securities failed to deliver	1,439
Failed to deliver of PAB securities not older than 30 calendar days (including debit balances in continuous net settlement accounts)	908

Margin required and on deposit with the Options Clearing Corporation for all option contracts written or purchased in PAB accounts	—
Margin required and on deposit with a registered clearing agency or a registered derivatives clearing organization related to the following types of positions written, purchased or sold in customer accounts: (1) security futures products and (2) futures contracts (and options thereon) carried in a securities account pursuant to an SRO portfolio margining rule	—
Other[ll]	14
Total PAB debit items[‡]	3,024

Reserve computation[‡]

Excess of total PAB debits over total PAB credits	$188
Required deposit	None

Reconciliation with Company's computation[#] (included in Part II of Form X-17A-5 as of December 31, 20X1)

Excess debits as reported in Company's Part II FOCUS report	$188

---

[*] Broker-dealers should consider the impact of recently issued accounting and regulatory pronouncements when preparing this supplementary schedule.

[†] Would be seven calendar days if the broker or dealer had elected the alternative net capital requirement under SEC Rule 15c3-1(f).

[‡] Those firms calculating net capital under the basic method must reduce debit balances in customer accounts by 1 percent, whereas those calculating net capital under the alternative method are required to reduce total debits by 3 percent.

[ll] This caption may only include those interpretive items that do not belong in the captions specified by the rule.

[#] If there are no material differences from the Company's computation and a reconciliation is not included, a statement to that effect is required. The following statement can be used to satisfy this requirement:

Note: There are no material differences between the preceding computation and the Company's corresponding unaudited Part II of Form X-17A-5 as of December 31, 20X1.

This note can be placed at the end of this schedule or on every page of the schedule.

Schedule IV

Standard Stockbrokerage Co., Inc.

**Information for Possession or Control Requirements
Under Rule 15c3-3 of the Securities and Exchange Commission**[*]

(Standard Stockbrokerage Co., Inc. only)

(Dollars in Thousands)

As of December 31, 20X1

1. Customers' fully paid and excess margin securities not in the respondent's possession or control as of the report date (for which instructions to reduce to possession or control had been issued as of the report date but for which the required action was not taken by respondent within the time frames specified under Rule 15c3-3):[†] $18

   A. Number of items   2

2. Customers' fully paid securities and excess margin securities for which instructions to reduce to possession or control had not been issued as of the report date, excluding items arising from "temporary lags which result from normal business operations" as permitted under Rule 15c3-3.[‡] $39

   A. Number of items   5

---

[*]   Broker-dealers should consider the impact of recently issued accounting and regulatory pronouncements when preparing this supplementary schedule.

[†]   If the customers' fully paid securities are subsequently reduced to possession or control, a statement to that effect should be included.

[‡]   In some instances, it may be impractical to determine the number of items in response to item 2. It may also be impractical to determine whether the Company has subsequently issued instructions to reduce those items to possession or control or to determine that such instructions were acted on.

Schedule V
Standard Stockbrokerage Co., Inc.
Schedule of Segregation Requirements and Funds in Segregation for Customers' Trading on U.S. Commodity Exchanges*
(Dollars in Thousands)
As of December 31, 20X1

Segregation requirements	
Net ledger balance:	
Cash	$976
Securities (at market)	784
Net unrealized profit (loss) in open futures contracts	(367)
Exchange traded options	
Add: fair value of open option contracts purchased on a contract market	143
Deduct: fair value of open option contracts granted (sold) on a contract market	(129)
Net equity (deficit)	1,407
Add: accounts liquidating to a deficit and accounts with debit balances with no open trades	138
Deduct: amount offset by customer owned securities	(60)
Amount required to be segregated	1,485
Funds on deposit in segregation	
Deposited in segregated funds bank accounts:	
Cash	105
Securities representing investments of customers' funds (at market)	141
Securities held for customers in lieu of cash margins (at market)	784
Margins on deposit with clearing organizations of contract markets:	
Cash	170
Securities representing investments of customers' funds (at market)	489
Settlement due from (to) contract market clearing organization	(28)
Exchange traded options:	
Add: unrealized receivables for option contracts purchased on contract markets	143
Deduct: unrealized obligations for option contracts granted (sold) on contract markets	(129)
Net equities with other FCMs	37
Segregated funds on hand†	50
Total amount in segregation	1,762
Excess funds (insufficiency) in segregation	$ 277
Management targeted amount for excess funds in segregation	$XX
Excess funds (insufficiency) segregation over (under) management target excess	$XX

---

* Broker-dealers should consider the impact of recently issued accounting and regulatory pronouncements when preparing this supplementary schedule.

† This is only applicable for those broker-dealers that are dually registered as futures commission merchants.

Schedule VI

Standard Stockbrokerage Co., Inc.

Statement of Cleared Swaps Customer Segregation Requirements and Funds in Cleared Swaps Customer Accounts Under 4D(f) of the Commodity Exchange Act[*][†]

(Dollars in Thousands)

As of December 31, 20X1

Cleared swaps customer requirements	
Net ledger balance:	
Cash	$144
Securities (at market)	—
Net unrealized profit (loss) in open cleared swaps	9
Cleared swaps options	
Fair value of open cleared swaps option contracts purchased	—
Fair value of open cleared swaps option contracts granted (sold)	—
Net equity (deficit)	153
Accounts liquidating to a deficit and accounts with debit balances	3
Deduct: amount offset by customer owned securities	—
Amount required to be segregated for cleared swaps customers	156
Funds in cleared swaps customer segregated accounts	
Deposited in cleared swaps customer segregated accounts at banks	
Cash	32
Securities held for customers in lieu of cash margins (at market)	—
Margins on deposit with derivatives clearing organizations in cleared swaps customer segregated accounts markets:	
Cash	148
Securities representing investments of customers' funds (at market)	5
Settlement due from (to) contract market clearing organization	(4)
Cleared swaps options	
Value of open cleared swaps long option contracts	—
Value of open cleared swaps short option contracts	—
Total amount in cleared swaps customer segregation	181

Excess funds (insufficiency) in cleared swaps customer segregation	$25
Management targeted amount for excess funds in cleared swaps customer segregation	$XX
Excess funds (insufficiency) in cleared swaps customer segregation over (under) management target excess	$XX

---

* Broker-dealers should consider the impact of recently issued accounting and regulatory pronouncements when preparing this supplementary schedule.

† This schedule is only applicable for those broker-dealers that are dually registered as futures commission merchants.

Appendix A

Information Sources

This appendix is nonauthoritative and is included for informational purposes only.

For further information on matters addressed in this guide, including the full text of standards and regulations, readers are encouraged to contact the various organizations listed in the table that follows. Many nongovernment and some government publications and services involve a charge or membership requirement.

Information Sources

Organization	General Information	Fax	Website Address/ Electronic Bulletin Board
American Institute of Certified Public Accountants	*Member Service Center* 220 Leigh Farm Rd. Durham, NC 27707-8110 888.777.7077 If outside of the U.S., call 919.402.4500	800.362.5066	www.aicpa.org
CME Group	20 South Wacker Drive Chicago, IL 60606 866.716.7274		www.cmegroup .com
Commodity Futures Trading Commission	Three Lafayette Center 1155 21st Street, NW Washington, DC 20581 202.418.5000	202.418.5521	www.cftc.gov
Financial Accounting Standards Board	401 Merritt 7 P.O. Box 5116 Norwalk, CT 06856-5116 203.847.0700	203.849.9714	www.fasb.org
Financial Industry Regulatory Authority (FINRA)	1735 K Street Washington, DC 20006 301.590.6500		www.finra.org
Futures Industry Association	2001 Pennsylvania Avenue, NW Suite 600 Washington, DC 20006 202.466.5460		www.futures industry.org

(continued)

Information Sources—*continued*

Organization	General Information	Fax	Website Address/ Electronic Bulletin Board
National Futures Association	300 S. Riverside Plaza #1800 Chicago, IL 60606-6615 *Main Number* 312.781.1300 *Information Center* 800.621.3570	312.781.1467	www.nfa.futures .org
NYSE Euronext	11 Wall Street New York, NY 10005 212.656.3000		www.nyse.com
Public Company Accounting Oversight Board	1666 K Street, NW Washington, DC 20006-2803 202.207.9100	202.862.8430	http://pcaobus .org
Securities Industry and Financial Markets Association (SIFMA)	120 Broadway, 35th FL New York, NY 10271 212.313.1200		www.sifma.org
Securities Investor Protection Corporation	1667 K St. NW Suite 1000 Washington, DC 20006-1620 202.371.8300	202.223.1679	www.sipc.org
U.S. Securities and Exchange Commission	100 F Street, NE Washington, DC 20549 202.942.8088	202.772.9295	www.sec.gov

Appendix B

Illustrative Example of Compliance Report Required by SEC Rule 17a-5

This appendix is nonauthoritative and is included for informational purposes only.

This sample compliance report, as jointly prepared by the AICPA and SIFMA's Financial Management Society, is for information purposes only. The compliance report required by SEC Rule 17a-5 is the responsibility of the firm making such report, it is recommended that firms seek the advice of their own legal and/or other advisers with respect to their compliance reports.

[Company]'s Compliance Report

[Name of Company] (the "Company") is a registered broker-dealer subject to Rule 17a-5 promulgated by the Securities and Exchange Commission (17 C.F.R. §240.17a-5, "Reports to be made by certain brokers and dealers"). As required by 17 C.F.R. §240.17a-5(d)(1) and (3), the Company states as follows:

(1)   The Company [has][has not] established and maintained Internal Control Over Compliance, as that term is defined in paragraph (d)(3)(ii) of Rule 17a-5.

(2)   The Company's Internal Control Over Compliance [was][was not] effective during the most recent fiscal year ended [date];

(3)   The Company's Internal Control Over Compliance [was][was not] effective as of the end of the most recent fiscal year ended [date];

(4)   The Company [was][was not] in compliance with 17 C.F.R. §240.15c3-1 and 17 C.F.R. §240.15c3-3(e) as of the end of the most recent fiscal year ended [date]; and

(5)   The information the Company used to state that the Company was in compliance with 17 C.F.R. §240.15c3-1 and 17 C.F.R. §240.15c3-3(e) [was][was not] derived from the books and records of the Company.

[If applicable, include a description of each material weakness in the Company's Internal Control Over Compliance during the most recent fiscal year ended [date].]

[If applicable, include a description of any instance of non-compliance with 17 C.F.R. §240.15c3-1 and 17 C.F.R. §240.15c3-3(e) as of the end of the most recent fiscal year ended [date].]

_____

[Name of Company]

I, _____, swear (or affirm) that, to my best knowledge and belief, this compliance report is true and correct.

By: [Signature]

Title:

[Date of report]

_____

Appendix C

Illustrative Example of Exemption Report Required by SEC Rule 17a-5

This appendix is nonauthoritative and is included for informational purposes only.

This sample exemption report, as jointly prepared by the AICPA and SIFMA's Financial Management Society, is for information purposes only. The exemption report required by SEC Rule 17a-5 is the responsibility of the firm making such report. It is recommended that firms seek the advice of their own legal and/or other advisers with respect to their exemption reports.

[Company]'s Exemption Report

[Name of Company] (the "Company") is a registered broker-dealer subject to Rule 17a-5 promulgated by the Securities and Exchange Commission (17 C.F.R. §240.17a-5, "Reports to be made by certain brokers and dealers"). This Exemption Report was prepared as required by 17 C.F.R. §240.17a-5(d)(1) and (4). To the best of its knowledge and belief, the Company states the following:

(1)   The Company claimed an exemption from 17 C.F.R. §240.15c3-3 under the following provisions of 17 C.F.R. §240.15c3-3 (k): [ ]

or

(1)   The Company may file an exemption report because the Company had no obligations under 17 C.F.R. §240.15c3-3.

(2)   The Company met the identified exemption provisions in 17 C.F.R. §240.15c3-3(k) throughout the most recent fiscal year without exception.

or

(2)   The Company had no obligations under 17 C.F.R. §240.15c3-3 throughout the most recent fiscal year without exception.

or

(2)   The Company met the identified exemption provisions in 17 C.F.R. §240.15c3-3(k) throughout the most recent fiscal year except as described below.

or

(2)   The Company had no obligations under 17 C.F.R. §240.15c3-3 throughout the most recent fiscal year except as described below.

[If applicable, identify each exception during the most recent fiscal year and briefly describe the nature of each exception and the approximate date(s) on which the exception existed.]

_____

[Name of Company]

I, _____, swear (or affirm) that, to my best knowledge and belief, this exemption report is true and correct.

By: [Signature line]

Title:

[Date of report]

_____

Appendix D

Overview of Statements on Quality Control Standards

This appendix is nonauthoritative and is included for informational purposes only.

This appendix is a partial reproduction of chapter 1 of the AICPA practice aid *Establishing and Maintaining a System of Quality Control for a CPA Firm's Accounting and Auditing Practice,* available at www.aicpa.org/interestareas/ frc/pages/enhancingauditqualitypracticeaid.aspx.

This appendix highlights certain aspects of the quality control standards issued by the AICPA. If appropriate, readers should also refer to the quality control standards issued by the PCAOB, available at www.pcaobus.org/standards/ qc/pages/default.aspx.

1.01 The objectives of a system of quality control are to provide a CPA firm with reasonable assurance[1] that the firm and its personnel comply with professional standards and applicable regulatory and legal requirements, and that the firm or engagement partners issue reports that are appropriate in the circumstances. QC section 10, *A Firm's System of Quality Control* (AICPA, *Professional Standards*), addresses a CPA firm's responsibilities for its system of quality control for its accounting and auditing practice. That section is to be read in conjunction with the AICPA Code of Professional Conduct and other relevant ethical requirements.

1.02 A system of quality control consists of policies designed to achieve the objectives of the system and the procedures necessary to implement and monitor compliance with those policies. The nature, extent, and formality of a firm's quality control policies and procedures will depend on various factors such as the firm's size; the number and operating characteristics of its offices; the degree of authority allowed to, and the knowledge and experience possessed by, firm personnel; and the nature and complexity of the firm's practice.

Communication of Quality Control Policies and Procedures

1.03 The firm should communicate its quality control policies and procedures to its personnel. Most firms will find it appropriate to communicate their policies and procedures in writing and distribute them, or make them available electronically, to all professional personnel. Effective communication includes the following:

- A description of quality control policies and procedures and the objectives they are designed to achieve
- The message that each individual has a personal responsibility for quality
- A requirement for each individual to be familiar with and to comply with these policies and procedures

---

[1] The term *reasonable assurance*, which is defined as a high, but not absolute, level of assurance, is used because absolute assurance cannot be attained. Paragraph .53 of QC section 10, *A Firm's System of Quality Control* (AICPA, *Professional Standards*), states, "Any system of quality control has inherent limitations that can reduce its effectiveness."

Effective communication also includes procedures for personnel to communicate their views or concerns on quality control matters to the firm's management.

Elements of a System of Quality Control

1.04 A firm must establish and maintain a system of quality control. The firm's system of quality control should include policies and procedures that address each of the following elements of quality control identified in paragraph .17 of QC section 10:

- Leadership responsibilities for quality within the firm (the "tone at the top")
- Relevant ethical requirements
- Acceptance and continuance of client relationships and specific engagements
- Human resources
- Engagement performance
- Monitoring

1.05 The elements of quality control are interrelated. For example, a firm continually assesses client relationships to comply with relevant ethical requirements, including independence, integrity, and objectivity, and policies and procedures related to the acceptance and continuance of client relationships and specific engagements. Similarly, the human resources element of quality control encompasses criteria related to professional development, hiring, advancement, and assignment of firm personnel to engagements, all of which affect policies and procedures related to engagement performance. In addition, policies and procedures related to the monitoring element of quality control enable a firm to evaluate whether its policies and procedures for each of the other five elements of quality control are suitably designed and effectively applied.

1.06 Policies and procedures established by the firm related to each element are designed to achieve reasonable assurance with respect to the purpose of that element. Deficiencies in policies and procedures for an element may result in not achieving reasonable assurance with respect to the purpose of that element; however, the system of quality control, as a whole, may still be effective in providing the firm with reasonable assurance that the firm and its personnel comply with professional standards and applicable regulatory and legal requirements and that the firm or engagement partners issue reports that are appropriate in the circumstances.

1.07 If a firm merges, acquires, sells, or otherwise changes a portion of its practice, the surviving firm evaluates and, as necessary, revises, implements, and maintains firm-wide quality control policies and procedures that are appropriate for the changed circumstances.

Leadership Responsibilities for Quality Within the Firm (the "Tone at the Top")

1.08 The purpose of the leadership responsibilities element of a system of quality control is to promote an internal culture based on the recognition that quality is essential in performing engagements. The firm should establish and maintain the following policies and procedures to achieve this purpose:

- Require the firm's leadership (managing partner, board of managing partners, CEO, or equivalent) to assume ultimate responsibility for the firm's system of quality control.

- Provide the firm with reasonable assurance that personnel assigned operational responsibility for the firm's quality control system have sufficient and appropriate experience and ability to identify and understand quality control issues and develop appropriate policies and procedures, as well as the necessary authority to implement those policies and procedures.

1.09 Establishing and maintaining the following policies and procedures assists firms in recognizing that the firm's business strategy is subject to the overarching requirement for the firm to achieve the objectives of the system of quality control in all the engagements that the firm performs:

- Assign management responsibilities so that commercial considerations do not override the quality of the work performed.

- Design policies and procedures addressing performance evaluation, compensation, and advancement (including incentive systems) with regard to personnel to demonstrate the firm's overarching commitment to the objectives of the system of quality control.

- Devote sufficient and appropriate resources for the development, communication, and support of its quality control policies and procedures.

Relevant Ethical Requirements

1.10 The purpose of the relevant ethical requirements element of a system of quality control is to provide the firm with reasonable assurance that the firm and its personnel comply with relevant ethical requirements when discharging professional responsibilities. Relevant ethical requirements include independence, integrity, and objectivity. Establishing and maintaining policies such as the following assist the firm in obtaining this assurance:

- Require that personnel adhere to relevant ethical requirements such as those in regulations, interpretations, and rules of the AICPA, state CPA societies, state boards of accountancy, state statutes, the U.S. Government Accountability Office, and any other applicable regulators.

- Establish procedures to communicate independence requirements to firm personnel and, where applicable, others subject to them.

- Establish procedures to identify and evaluate possible threats to independence and objectivity, including the familiarity threat that may be created by using the same senior personnel on an audit or attest engagement over a long period of time, and to take appropriate action to eliminate those threats or reduce them to an acceptable level by applying safeguards.

- Require that the firm withdraw from the engagement if effective safeguards to reduce threats to independence to an acceptable level cannot be applied.

- Require written confirmation, at least annually, of compliance with the firm's policies and procedures on independence from all firm personnel required to be independent by relevant requirements.

- Establish procedures for confirming the independence of another firm or firm personnel in associated member firms who perform part of the engagement. This would apply to national firm personnel, foreign firm personnel, and foreign-associated firms.[2]

- Require the rotation of personnel for audit or attest engagements where regulatory or other authorities require such rotation after a specified period.

Acceptance and Continuance of Client Relationships and Specific Engagements

1.11 The purpose of the quality control element that addresses acceptance and continuance of client relationships and specific engagements is to establish criteria for deciding whether to accept or continue a client relationship and whether to perform a specific engagement for a client. A firm's client acceptance and continuance policies represent a key element in mitigating litigation and business risk. Accordingly, it is important that a firm be aware that the integrity and reputation of a client's management could reflect the reliability of the client's accounting records and financial representations and, therefore, affect the firm's reputation or involvement in litigation. A firm's policies and procedures related to the acceptance and continuance of client relationships and specific engagements should provide the firm with reasonable assurance that it will undertake or continue relationships and engagements only where it

- is competent to perform the engagement and has the capabilities, including the time and resources, to do so;

- can comply with legal and relevant ethical requirements;

- has considered the client's integrity and does not have information that would lead it to conclude that the client lacks integrity; and

- has reached an understanding with the client regarding the services to be performed.

1.12 This assurance should be obtained before accepting an engagement with a new client, when deciding whether to continue an existing engagement, and when considering acceptance of a new engagement with an existing client. Establishing and maintaining policies such as the following assist the firm in obtaining this assurance:

---

[2] A *foreign-associated firm* is a firm domiciled outside of the United States and its territories that is a member of, correspondent with, or similarly associated with an international firm or international association of firms.

- Evaluate factors that have a bearing on management's integrity and consider the risk associated with providing professional services in particular circumstances.[3]

- Evaluate whether the engagement can be completed with professional competence; undertake only those engagements for which the firm has the capabilities, resources, and professional competence to complete; and evaluate, at the end of specific periods or upon occurrence of certain events, whether the relationship should be continued.

- Obtain an understanding, preferably in writing, with the client regarding the services to be performed.

- Establish procedures on continuing an engagement and the client relationship, including procedures for dealing with information that would have caused the firm to decline an engagement if the information had been available earlier.

- Require documentation of how issues relating to acceptance or continuance of client relationships and specific engagements were resolved.

Human Resources

1.13 The purpose of the human resources element of a system of quality control is to provide the firm with reasonable assurance that it has sufficient personnel with the capabilities, competence, and commitment to ethical principles necessary (a) to perform its engagements in accordance with professional standards and regulatory and legal requirements, and (b) to enable the firm to issue reports that are appropriate in the circumstances. Establishing and maintaining policies such as the following assist the firm in obtaining this assurance:

- Recruit and hire personnel of integrity who possess the characteristics that enable them to perform competently.

- Determine capabilities and competencies required for an engagement, especially for the engagement partner, based on the characteristics of the particular client, industry, and kind of service being performed. Specific competencies necessary for an engagement partner are discussed in paragraph .A27 of QC section 10.

- Determine the capabilities and competencies possessed by personnel.

- Assign the responsibility for each engagement to an engagement partner.

---

[3] Such considerations would include the risk of providing professional services to significant clients or to other clients for which the practitioner's objectivity or the appearance of independence may be impaired. In broad terms, the significance of a client to a member or a firm refers to relationships that could diminish a practitioner's objectivity and independence in performing attest services. Examples of factors to consider in determining the significance of a client to an engagement partner, office, or practice unit include (a) the amount of time the partner, office, or practice unit devotes to the engagement, (b) the effect on the partner's stature within the firm as a result of his or her service to the client, (c) the manner in which the partner, office, or practice unit is compensated, or (d) the effect that losing the client would have on the partner, office, or practice unit.

- Assign personnel based on the knowledge, skills, and abilities required in the circumstances and the nature and extent of supervision needed.
- Have personnel participate in general and industry-specific continuing professional education and professional development activities that enable them to accomplish assigned responsibilities and satisfy applicable continuing professional education requirements of the AICPA, state boards of accountancy, and other regulators.
- Select for advancement only those individuals who have the qualifications necessary to fulfill the responsibilities they will be called on to assume.

Engagement Performance

1.14 The purpose of the engagement performance element of quality control is to provide the firm with reasonable assurance (*a*) that engagements are consistently performed in accordance with applicable professional standards and regulatory and legal requirements, and (*b*) that the firm or the engagement partner issues reports that are appropriate in the circumstances. Policies and procedures for engagement performance should address all phases of the design and execution of the engagement, including engagement performance, supervision responsibilities, and review responsibilities. Policies and procedures also should require that consultation takes place when appropriate. In addition, a policy should establish criteria against which all engagements are to be evaluated to determine whether an engagement quality control review should be performed.

1.15 Establishing and maintaining policies such as the following assist the firm in obtaining the assurance required relating to the engagement performance element of quality control:

- Plan all engagements to meet professional, regulatory, and the firm's requirements.
- Perform work and issue reports and other communications that meet professional, regulatory, and the firm's requirements.
- Require that work performed by other team members be reviewed by qualified engagement team members, which may include the engagement partner, on a timely basis.
- Require the engagement team to complete the assembly of final engagement files on a timely basis.
- Establish procedures to maintain the confidentiality, safe custody, integrity, accessibility, and retrievability of engagement documentation.
- Require the retention of engagement documentation for a period of time sufficient to meet the needs of the firm, professional standards, laws, and regulations.
- Require that
  - consultation take place when appropriate (for example, when dealing with complex, unusual, unfamiliar, difficult, or contentious issues);

— sufficient and appropriate resources be available to enable appropriate consultation to take place;

— all the relevant facts known to the engagement team be provided to those consulted;

— the nature, scope, and conclusions of such consultations be documented; and

— the conclusions resulting from such consultations be implemented.

- Require that

— differences of opinion be dealt with and resolved;

— conclusions reached are documented and implemented; and

— the report not be released until the matter is resolved.

- Require that

— all engagements be evaluated against the criteria for determining whether an engagement quality control review should be performed;

— an engagement quality control review be performed for all engagements that meet the criteria; and

— the review be completed before the report is released.

- Establish procedures addressing the nature, timing, extent, and documentation of the engagement quality control review.

- Establish criteria for the eligibility of engagement quality control reviewers.

Monitoring

1.16 The purpose of the monitoring element of a system of quality control is to provide the firm and its engagement partners with reasonable assurance that the policies and procedures related to the system of quality control are relevant, adequate, operating effectively, and complied with in practice. Monitoring involves an ongoing consideration and evaluation of the appropriateness of the design, the effectiveness of the operation of a firm's quality control system, and a firm's compliance with its quality control policies and procedures. The purpose of monitoring compliance with quality control policies and procedures is to provide an evaluation of the following:

- Adherence to professional standards and regulatory and legal requirements

- Whether the quality control system has been appropriately designed and effectively implemented

- Whether the firm's quality control policies and procedures have been operating effectively so that reports issued by the firm are appropriate in the circumstances

1.17 Establishing and maintaining policies such as the following assist the firm in obtaining the assurance required relating to the monitoring element of quality control:

- Assign responsibility for the monitoring process to a partner or partners or other persons with sufficient and appropriate experience and authority in the firm to assume that responsibility.

- Assign performance of the monitoring process to competent individuals.

- Require the performance of monitoring procedures that are sufficiently comprehensive to enable the firm to assess compliance with all applicable professional standards and the firm's quality control policies and procedures. Monitoring procedures consist of the following:

  — Review of selected administrative and personnel records pertaining to the quality control elements.

  — Review of engagement documentation, reports, and clients' financial statements.

  — Summarization of the findings from the monitoring procedures, at least annually, and consideration of the systemic causes of findings that indicate that improvements are needed.

  — Determination of any corrective actions to be taken or improvements to be made with respect to the specific engagements reviewed or the firm's quality control policies and procedures.

  — Communication of the identified findings to appropriate firm management personnel.

  — Consideration of findings by appropriate firm management personnel who should also determine that any actions necessary, including necessary modifications to the quality control system, are taken on a timely basis.

  — Assessment of

    - the appropriateness of the firm's guidance materials and any practice aids;

    - new developments in professional standards and regulatory and legal requirements and how they are reflected in the firm's policies and procedures where appropriate;

    - compliance with policies and procedures on independence;

    - the effectiveness of continuing professional development, including training;

    - decisions related to acceptance and continuance of client relationships and specific engagements; and

    - firm personnel's understanding of the firm's quality control policies and procedures and implementation thereof.

- Communicate at least annually, to relevant engagement partners and other appropriate personnel, deficiencies noted as a result of the monitoring process and recommendations for appropriate remedial action.

- Communicate the results of the monitoring of its quality control system process to relevant firm personnel at least annually.
- Establish procedures designed to provide the firm with reasonable assurance that it deals appropriately with the following:
  - Complaints and allegations that the work performed by the firm fails to comply with professional standards and regulatory and legal requirements.
  - Allegations of noncompliance with the firm's system of quality control.
  - Deficiencies in the design or operation of the firm's quality control policies and procedures, or noncompliance with the firm's system of quality control by an individual or individuals, as identified during the investigations into complaints and allegations.

  This includes establishing clearly defined channels for firm personnel to raise any concerns in a manner that enables them to come forward without fear of reprisal and documenting complaints and allegations and the responses to them.

- Require appropriate documentation to provide evidence of the operation of each element of its system of quality control. The form and content of documentation evidencing the operation of each of the elements of the system of quality control is a matter of judgment and depends on a number of factors, including the following, for example:
  - The size of the firm and the number of offices.
  - The nature and complexity of the firm's practice and organization.

- Require retention of documentation providing evidence of the operation of the system of quality control for a period of time sufficient to permit those performing monitoring procedures and peer review to evaluate the firm's compliance with its system of quality control, or for a longer period if required by law or regulation.

1.18 Some of the monitoring procedures discussed in the previous list may be accomplished through the performance of the following:

- Engagement quality control review
- Review of engagement documentation, reports, and clients' financial statements for selected engagements after the report release date
- Inspection[4] procedures

---

[4] *Inspection* is a retrospective evaluation of the adequacy of the firm's quality control policies and procedures, its personnel's understanding of those policies and procedures, and the extent of the firm's compliance with them. Although monitoring procedures are meant to be ongoing, they may include inspection procedures performed at a fixed point in time. Monitoring is a broad concept; inspection is one specific type of monitoring procedure.

Documentation of Quality Control Policies and Procedures

1.19 The firm should document each element of its system of quality control. The extent of the documentation will depend on the size, structure, and nature of the firm's practice. Documentation may be as simple as a checklist of the firm's policies and procedures or as extensive as practice manuals.

Appendix E

The New Revenue Recognition Standard: FASB ASC 606

This appendix is nonauthoritative and is included for informational purposes only.

Overview

On May 28, 2014, the International Accounting Standards Board (IASB) and FASB issued a joint accounting standard on revenue recognition to address a number of concerns regarding the complexity and lack of consistency surrounding the accounting for revenue transactions. Consistent with each board's policy, FASB issued Accounting Standards Update (ASU) No. 2014-09, *Revenue from Contracts with Customers (Topic 606)*, and the IASB issued International Financial Reporting Standard (IFRS) 15, *Revenue from Contracts with Customers*. FASB ASU No. 2014-09 will amend the FASB *Accounting Standards Codification®* (ASC) by creating a new Topic 606, *Revenue from Contracts with Customers*, and a new Subtopic 340-40, *Other Assets and Deferred Costs—Contracts with Customers*. The guidance in ASU No. 2014-09 provides what FASB describes as a framework for revenue recognition and supersedes or amends several of the revenue recognition requirements in FASB ASC 605, *Revenue Recognition*, as well as guidance within the 900 series of industry-specific topics.

As part of the boards' efforts to converge U.S. generally accepted accounting principles (GAAP) and IFRSs, the standard eliminates the transaction- and industry-specific revenue recognition guidance under current GAAP and replaces it with a principles-based approach for revenue recognition. The intent is to avoid inconsistencies of accounting treatment across different geographies and industries. In addition to improving comparability of revenue recognition practices, the new guidance provides more useful information to financial statement users through enhanced disclosure requirements. FASB and the IASB have essentially achieved convergence with these standards, with some minor differences related to the collectibility threshold, interim disclosure requirements, early application and effective date, impairment loss reversal, and nonpublic entity requirements.

The standard applies to any entity that either enters into contracts with customers to transfer goods or services or enters into contracts for the transfer of nonfinancial assets, unless those contracts are within the scope of other standards (for example, insurance or lease contracts).

Effective or Applicability Date

The guidance in ASU No. 2014-09 was originally effective for annual reporting periods of public entities beginning after December 15, 2016, including interim periods within that reporting period. Early application was not permitted for public entities, including not-for-profit entities (NFPs) that have issued, or are conduit bond obligors for, securities that are traded, listed, or quoted on an exchange or an over-the-counter market and for employee benefit plans that file or furnish financial statements to the SEC.

For nonpublic entities, the amendments in the new guidance were originally effective for annual reporting periods beginning after December 15, 2017, and interim periods within annual periods beginning after December 15, 2018.

On August 12, 2015, FASB issued ASU No. 2015-14, *Revenue from Contracts with Customers (Topic 606): Deferral of the Effective Date*, to allow entities additional time to implement systems, gather data, and resolve implementation questions. This update allows for public business entities, certain NFPs, and certain employee benefit plans to apply the new requirements to annual reporting periods beginning after December 15, 2017, including interim reporting periods within that reporting period. Earlier application is permitted only as of annual reporting periods beginning after December 15, 2016, including interim reporting periods within that reporting period.

All other entities will now apply the guidance in ASU No. 2014-09 to annual reporting periods beginning after December 15, 2018, and interim reporting periods within annual reporting periods beginning after December 15, 2019. Application is permitted earlier only as of an annual reporting period beginning after December 15, 2016, including interim reporting periods within that reporting period, or an annual reporting period beginning after December 15, 2016, and interim reporting periods within annual reporting periods beginning one year after the annual reporting period in which an entity first applies the guidance in ASU No. 2014-09.

Overview of the New Guidance

The core principle of the revised revenue recognition standard is that an entity should recognize revenue to depict the transfer of goods or services to customers in an amount that reflects the consideration to which the entity expects to be entitled in exchange for those good or services.

To apply the proposed revenue recognition standard, ASU No. 2014-09 states that an entity should follow these five steps:

1. Identify the contract(s) with a customer.
2. Identify the performance obligations in the contract.
3. Determine the transaction price.
4. Allocate the transaction price to the performance obligations in the contract.
5. Recognize revenue when (or as) the entity satisfies a performance obligation.

Under the new standard, revenue is recognized when a company satisfies a performance obligation by transferring a promised good or service to a customer (which is when the customer obtains control of that good or service). See the following discussion of the five steps involved when recognizing revenue under the new guidance.

Understanding the Five-Step Process

Step 1: Identify the Contract(s) With a Customer

ASU No. 2014-09 defines a contract as "an agreement between two or more parties that creates enforceable rights and obligations." The new standard affects contracts with a customer that meet the following criteria:

- Approval (in writing, orally, or in accordance with other customary business practices) and commitment of the parties
- Identification of the rights of the parties
- Identification of the payment terms
- Contract has commercial substance
- Probable that the entity will collect substantially all the consideration to which it will be entitled in exchange for the goods or services that will be transferred to the customer

A contract does not exist if each party to the contract has the unilateral enforceable right to terminate a wholly unperformed contract without compensating the other party (parties).

Step 2: Identify the Performance Obligations in the Contract

A *performance obligation* is a promise in a contract with a customer to transfer a good or service to the customer.

At contract inception, an entity should assess the goods or services promised in a contract with a customer and identify as a performance obligation (possibly multiple performance obligations) each promise to transfer to the customer either

- a good or service (or bundle of goods or services) that is distinct, or
- a series of distinct goods or services that are substantially the same and that have the same pattern of transfer to the customer.

A good or service that is not distinct should be combined with other promised goods or services until the entity identifies a bundle of goods or services that is distinct. In some cases, that would result in the entity accounting for all the goods or services promised in a contract as a single performance obligation.

Step 3: Determine the Transaction Price

The transaction price is the amount of consideration (fixed or variable) the entity expects to receive in exchange for transferring promised goods or services to a customer, excluding amounts collected on behalf of third parties. To determine the transaction price, an entity should consider the effects of

- variable consideration,
- constraining estimates of variable consideration,
- the existence of a significant financing component,
- noncash considerations, and
- consideration payable to the customer.

If the consideration promised in a contract includes a variable amount, then an entity should estimate the amount of consideration to which the entity will be entitled in exchange for transferring the promised goods or services to a customer. An entity would then include in the transaction price some or all of an amount of variable consideration only to the extent that it is probable that a significant reversal in the amount of cumulative revenue recognized will not occur when the uncertainty associated with the variable consideration is subsequently resolved.

An entity should consider the terms of the contract and its customary business practices to determine the transaction price.

Step 4: Allocate the Transaction Price to the Performance Obligations in the Contract

The transaction price is allocated to separate performance obligations in proportion to the standalone selling price of the promised goods or services. If a standalone selling price is not directly observable, then an entity should estimate it. Reallocation of the transaction price for changes in the standalone selling price is not permitted. When estimating the standalone selling price, entities can use various methods, including the adjusted market assessment approach, expected cost plus a margin approach, and residual approach (only if the selling price is highly variable and uncertain).

Sometimes, the transaction price includes a discount or a variable amount of consideration that relates entirely to one of the performance obligations in a contract. Guidance under the new standard specifies when an entity should allocate the discount or variable consideration to one (or some) performance obligation(s), rather than to all the performance obligations in the contract.

Step 5: Recognize Revenue When (or as) the Entity Satisfies a Performance Obligation

The amount of revenue recognized when transferring the promised good or service to a customer is equal to the amount allocated to the satisfied performance obligation, which may be satisfied at a point in time or over time. Control of an asset refers to the ability to direct the use of, and obtain substantially all the remaining benefits from, the asset. Control also includes the ability to prevent *other entities* from directing the use of, and obtaining the benefits from, an asset.

When performance obligations are satisfied over time, the entity should select an appropriate method for measuring its progress toward complete satisfaction of that performance obligation. The standard discusses methods of measuring progress, including input and output methods, and how to determine which method is appropriate.

Additional Guidance Under the New Standard

In addition to the five-step process for recognizing revenue, ASU No. 2014-09 also addresses the following areas:

- Accounting for incremental costs of obtaining a contract, as well as costs incurred to fulfill a contract

- Licenses
- Warranties

Lastly, the new guidance enhances disclosure requirements to include more information about specific revenue contracts entered into by the entity, including performance obligations and the transaction price.

Transition Resource Group

Due to the potential for significant changes that may result from the issuance of the new standard, FASB and the IASB have received an abundance of implementation questions from interested parties. To address these questions, the boards have formed a joint Transition Resource Group (TRG) for revenue recognition to promote effective implementation and transition to the converged standard.

Since the issuance of the standard, the TRG has met several times to discuss implementation issues raised by concerned parties and actions to take to address these issues. Refer to FASB's TRG website for more information on this group and the status of their efforts, including meeting materials and meeting summaries.

Latest Developments

Based on discussions held thus far on individual areas affected by the new standard, the TRG informed the boards that technical corrections are needed to further articulate the guidance in the standard. As a result, FASB has issued updates to clarify guidance on performance obligations, licensing, principal versus agent considerations, and other narrow-scope improvements and practical expedients.

ASU No. 2016-08, *Revenue from Contracts with Customers (Topic 606): Principle versus Agent Considerations (Reporting Revenue Gross versus Net)*, was issued in March 2016 to clarify the guidance in FASB ASC 606 with respect to principal versus agent. There is little disagreement that an entity who is a principal recognizes revenue in the gross amount of consideration when a performance obligation is satisfied. An entity who is an agent (collecting revenue on behalf of the principal) recognizes revenue only to the extent of the commission or fee that the agent collects. This ASU hopes to eliminate the potential diversity in practice when determining whether an entity is a principal or an agent by clarifying the following:

- An entity determines whether it is a principal or an agent for each distinct good or service.
- An entity determines the nature of each specified good or service (including whether it is a right to a good or service)
- When an entity is a principal, it obtains control of
  - a good or another asset from the other party that it then transfers to the customer;
  - a right to a service that will be performed by another party, which gives the entity the ability to direct that party to provide the service to the customer on the entity's behalf; or

> — a good or service from the other party that it combines with other goods or services to provide the specified good or service to the customer.

- Indicators in the assessment of control may be more or less relevant or persuasive, or both, to the control assessment, depending on the facts and circumstances.

Additional illustrative examples are also provided in ASU No. 2016-08 to further assist practitioners in applying this guidance. The effective date of this update is in line with the guidance in ASU No. 2014-09, as amended by ASU No. 2015-14.

ASU No. 2016-10, *Revenue from Contracts with Customers (Topic 606): Identifying Performance Obligations and Licensing,* was issued in April 2016 to reduce potential for diversity in practice at initial application of FASB ASC 606, as well as the cost and complexity of applying FASB ASC 606 at transition and on an ongoing basis. When identifying promised goods and services in a contract, this ASU states that entities

- are not required to assess whether promised goods or services are performance obligations if they are immaterial to the contract.
- can elect to account for shipping and handling activities as an activity to fulfill promises within the contract, rather than as an additional promised service.

When assessing whether promised goods or services are distinct, this ASU emphasizes the need to determine whether the nature of the promise is to transfer

- each of the goods or services, or
- a combined item (or items) to which the promised goods or services are inputs.

With regards to licensing, ASU No. 2016-10 clarifies whether revenue should be recognized at a point in time or over time, based on whether the license provides a right to use an entity's intellectual property or a right to access the entity's intellectual property. Specifically,

- if the intellectual property has significant standalone functionality, the license does not include supporting or maintaining that intellectual property during the license period. Therefore, the performance obligation would be considered satisfied at a point in time. Examples of this type of intellectual property include software, biological compounds or drug formulas, and media.
- licenses for symbolic intellectual property include supporting or maintaining that intellectual property during the license period and, therefore, are considered to be satisfied over time. Examples of symbolic intellectual property include brands, team or trade names, logos, and franchise rights.

Lastly, ASU No. 2016-10 provides clarification on implementation guidance on recognizing revenue for sales-based or usage-based royalty promised in exchange for a license of intellectual property. The effective date of this ASU is in line with the guidance in ASU No. 2014-09, as amended by ASU No. 2015-14.

In addition to ASU Nos. 2016-08 and 2016-10, ASU No. 2016-12, *Revenue from Contracts with Customers (Topic 606): Narrow-Scope Improvements and Practical Expedients*, was issued in May 2016. Topics covered in this ASU include

- clarification on contract modifications. This amendment permits an entity to determine and allocate the transaction price on the basis of all satisfied and unsatisfied performance obligations in a modified contract as of the beginning of the earliest period presented in accordance with the guidance in FASB ASC 606. An entity would not be required to separately evaluate the effects of each contract modification. An entity that chooses to apply this practical expedient would apply the expedient consistently to similar types of contracts.

- how to assess the collectibility criterion. The amendment introduces new criteria to meet the collectibility requirement. An entity should assess the collectibility of the consideration promised in a contract for the goods or services that will be transferred to the customer, rather than assessing the collectibility of the consideration promised in the contract for all the promised goods or services.

- how to report sales taxes and similar taxes. This amendment states that an entity may make an accounting policy election to exclude from the measurement of the transaction price all taxes assessed by a governmental authority that are both imposed on and concurrent with a specific revenue-producing transaction and collected by the entity from a customer (for example, sales, use, value added, and some excise taxes). Taxes assessed on an entity's total gross receipts or imposed during the inventory procurement process should be excluded from the scope of the election. An entity that makes this election should exclude from the transaction price all taxes in the scope of the election and should comply with the applicable accounting policy guidance, including disclosure requirements.

- when to measure noncash consideration. This amendment clarifies that the measurement date for noncash consideration is contract inception. If the fair value of the noncash consideration varies because of the form of the consideration and for reasons other than the form of the consideration, an entity should apply the guidance on variable consideration only to the variability resulting from reasons other than the form of the consideration.

- how to apply transition guidance. This amendment clarifies that a completed contract for purposes of transition is a contract for which all (or substantially all) the revenue was recognized under legacy GAAP before the date of initial application. Accounting for elements of a contract that do not affect revenue under legacy GAAP are irrelevant to the assessment of whether a contract is complete. In addition, the amendment permits an entity to apply the modified retrospective transition method either to all contracts or only to contracts that are not completed contracts.

The effective date of this ASU is in line with the guidance in ASU No. 2014-09, as amended by ASU No. 2015-14.

FASB also issued ASU No. 2016-20, *Technical Corrections and Improvements to Topic 606, Revenue from Contracts with Customers*, in December 2016. These amendments affect narrow aspects of guidance issued in ASU No. 2014-09, including but not limited to, guidance on

- impairment testing. When performing impairment testing, an entity should consider expected contract renewals and extensions. In addition, the assessment should include both the amount of consideration it already has received but has not yet recognized as revenue, and the amount it expects to receive in the future.

- additional scope exceptions. The term "insurance" is removed from the scope exceptions of FASB ASC 606 to clarify that all contracts within the scope of FASB ASC 944, *Financial Services—Insurance*, are excluded.

- provisions for losses on construction-type and production-type contracts. Such provisions should be determined at least at the contract level; however, an entity can make an accounting policy election to determine the provision for losses at the performance obligation level.

- disclosure of remaining performance obligations. Optional exemptions from the disclosure requirement are provided for remaining performance obligations when an entity is not required to estimate variable consideration to recognize revenue.

Consistent with the other ASUs, the effective date of ASU No. 2016-20 is in line with the guidance in ASU No. 2014-09, as amended by ASU No. 2015-14.

In February 2017, the FASB issued ASU No. 2017-05, *Other Income—Gains and Losses from the Derecognition of Nonfinancial Assets (Subtopic 610-20): Clarifying the Scope of Asset Derecognition Guidance and Accounting for Partial Sales of Nonfinancial Assets*. The amendments in this ASU include, but are not limited to

- a definition of the term in substance nonfinancial asset, to clarify the scope of FASB ASC 610-20. An in substance nonfinancial asset is, in part, a financial asset promised to a counterparty in a contract if substantially all of the fair value of the assets (recognized and unrecognized) that are promised to the counterparty in the contract is concentrated in nonfinancial assets. An in substance nonfinancial asset also includes a financial asset that is held in an individual consolidated subsidiary within a contract if substantially all the fair value of the assets (recognized and unrecognized) that are promised to the counterparty in that subsidiary is concentrated in nonfinancial assets.

- a clarification that nonfinancial assets within the scope of FASB ASC 610-20 may include nonfinancial assets transferred within a legal entity to a counterparty. For example, a parent may transfer control of nonfinancial assets by transferring ownership interests in a consolidated subsidiary. A contract that includes the transfer of ownership interests in one or more consolidated subsidiaries is within the scope of Subtopic 610-20 if substantially all of the fair value of the assets that are promised to the counterparty in a contract is concentrated in nonfinancial assets.

- removal of the scope exception for transfers of equity method investment that were considered in substance nonfinancial assets. All transfers of equity method investments will be accounted for in accordance with FASB ASC 860, *Transfers and Servicing*.

- derecognition of each distinct nonfinancial asset or in substance nonfinancial asset promised to a counterparty. Each asset will be derecognized when a counterparty obtains control of it. The amendments also clarify that an entity should allocate consideration to each distinct asset by applying the guidance in FASB ASC 606 on allocating the transaction price to performance obligations.

- partial sales transactions. An entity will derecognize a distinct nonfinancial asset or distinct in substance nonfinancial asset in a partial sale transaction when it (1) does not have (or ceases to have) a controlling financial interest in the legal entity that holds the asset in accordance with FASB ASC 810, *Consolidation*, and (2) transfers control of the asset in accordance with FASB ASC 606. Once an entity transfers control of a distinct nonfinancial asset or distinct in substance nonfinancial asset, it is required to measure any noncontrolling interest it receives (or retains) at fair value. If an entity transfers ownership interests in a consolidated subsidiary and continues to have a controlling financial interest in that subsidiary, it does not derecognize the assets and liabilities of the subsidiary and accounts for the transaction as an equity transaction. Therefore, no gain or loss is recognized.

- contributions of nonfinancial assets to a joint venture or other non-controlled investee. These contributions will be within the scope of FASB ASC 610-20, and an entity will recognize a full gain or loss on transfers of nonfinancial assets to equity method investees.

Consistent with the other ASUs, the effective date of ASU No. 2017-05 is in line with the guidance in ASU No. 2014-09, as amended by ASU No. 2015-14.

Conclusion

Upon implementation of the new standard, consistency of revenue recognition principles across geography and industry will be enhanced and financial statement users will be provided better insight through improved disclosure requirements. To provide CPAs with guidance during this time of transition, the AICPA's Financial Reporting Center (FRC) offers invaluable resources on the topic, including a roadmap to ensure that companies take the necessary steps to prepare themselves for the new standard. In addition, the FRC includes a list of conferences, webcasts, and other products to keep you informed on upcoming changes in revenue recognition. Refer to www.aicpa.org/interestareas/frc/accountingfinancialreporting/revenuerecognition/pages/revenuerecognition.aspx to stay updated on the latest information available on revenue recognition.

_____

Appendix F

The New Leases Standard: FASB ASU No. 2016-02

This appendix is nonauthoritative and is included for informational purposes only.

Overview

Issuance and Objective

On February 25, 2016, FASB issued Accounting Standards Update (ASU) No. 2016-02, *Leases (Topic 842)*. The objective of the ASU is to increase transparency and comparability in financial reporting by requiring balance sheet recognition of leases and note disclosure of certain information about lease arrangements. This ASU codifies the new FASB ASC topic 842, *Leases*, and makes conforming amendments to other FASB ASC topics.

The new FASB ASC topic on leases consists of these subtopics:

- *a.* Overall
- *b.* Lessee
- *c.* Lessor
- *d.* Sale and leaseback transactions
- *e.* Leveraged lease arrangements

Applicability and Effective Date

ASU No. 2016-02 is applicable to any entity that enters into a lease and is effective as follows:

	Fiscal Years Beginning After	Interim Periods Within Fiscal Years Beginning After
Public business entities, certain not-for-profit entities with conduit financing arrangements, and employee benefit plans	December 15, 2018	December 15, 2018
All other entities	December 15, 2019	December 15, 2020

FASB ASC 842 applies to all leases and subleases of property, plant, and equipment; it specifically does not apply to the following nondepreciable assets accounted for under other FASB ASC topics:

- *a.* Leases of intangible assets
- *b.* Leases to explore for or use nonregenerative resources such as minerals, oil, and natural gas
- *c.* Leases of biological assets, such as timber

    d. Leases of inventory

    e. Leases of assets under construction

Main Provisions

Overall

Identifying a Lease

Key changes in the guidance are illustrated by comparing the definition of a lease in FASB ASC 840 (extant GAAP) and FASB ASC 842.

FASB ASC 840	*FASB ASC 842*
An agreement conveying the right to use property, plant, or equipment (land and/or depreciable assets) usually for a stated period of time.	A contract, or part of a contract, that conveys the right to control the use of identified property, plant, or equipment (an identified asset) for a period of time in exchange for consideration.

The identification of a lease under FASB ASC 842 should be based on the presence of key elements in the definition.

Separating Components of a Lease Contract

Under FASB ASC 842, a contract that contains a lease should be separated into lease and nonlease components. Separation should be based on the right to use; each underlying asset should be considered to be separate from other lease components when both of the following criteria are met:

    a. The lessee can benefit from the right-of-use of the asset (either alone or with other readily available resources)

    b. The right-of-use is neither highly dependent on or highly interrelated with other underlying assets in the contract

The consideration in the contract should be allocated to the separate lease and nonlease components in accordance with provisions of FASB ASC 842.

Lessees can make an accounting policy election to treat both lease and nonlease elements as a single lease component.

Lease Classification

When a lease meets any of the following specified criteria at commencement, the lease should be classified by the lessee and lessor as a finance lease and a sales-type lease, respectively. These criteria can be summarized as follows:

    a. Transfers ownership to lessee

    b. Purchase option reasonably certain to be exercised

    c. Lease term for major portion of asset's remaining economic life

    d. Present value of lease payments and residual value exceeds substantially all of the fair value of the underlying asset

    e. Specialized nature of underlying asset results in no expectation of alternative use after the lease term

If none of the above criteria are met, the lease should be classified as follows:

Lessee—classify as an operating lease

Lessor—classify as an operating lease unless (1) the present value of the lease payments and any residual value guarantee that equals or exceeds substantially all of the fair value of the underlying asset and (2) it is probable that the lessor will collect the lease payments plus any residual value guarantee. If both of these summarized criteria from FASB ASC 842-10-25-3 are met, the lessor should classify the lease as a direct financing lease.

Lease Term and Measurement

The lease term is the noncancellable period of the lease together with all of the following:

a. Period covered by the option for the lessee to extend the lease if the option is reasonably certain to be exercised

b. Period covered by option for lessee to terminate the lease if reasonably certain not to be exercised

c. Period covered by option for lessor to extend or not terminate the lease if option is controlled by lessor.

Lease Payments

Lease payments relating to use of the underlying asset during the lease term include the following at the commencement date:

a. Fixed payments less incentives payable to lessee

b. Variable lease payments based on an index or other rate

c. Exercise price of an option to purchase the underlying asset if it is reasonably certain to be exercised

d. Payments for penalties for terminating a lease if the lease term reflects exercise of lessee option

e. Fees paid by the lessee to the owners of a special purpose entity for structuring the lease

f. For lessee only, amounts probable of being owed under residual value guarantees

Lease payments specifically exclude the following:

a. Certain other variable lease payments

b. Any guarantee by the lessee of the lessor's debt

c. Certain amounts allocated to nonlease components

Reassessment of the lease term and purchase options, and subsequent remeasurement by either the lessee or lessor are limited to certain specified circumstances.

Lessee

Recognition and Measurement

Commencement Date

At the commencement date of the lease, a lessee should recognize a right-of-use asset and a lease liability; for short term leases, an alternative accounting policy election is available.

The lease liability should be measured at the present value of the unpaid lease payments. The right-of-use asset should consist of the following: the amount of the initial lease liability; any lease payments made to lessor at or before the commencement date minus any incentives received; and initial direct costs.

A short term lease is defined by the FASB ASC master glossary as a lease that, at the commencement date has a lease term of 12 months or less and does not include an option to purchase the underlying asset that the lessee is reasonably certain to exercise. The accounting policy election for short term leases should be made by class of underlying asset. The election provides for recognition of the lease payments in profit or loss on a straight-line basis over the lease term and variable lease payments in the period in which the obligation for those payments is incurred.

After the Commencement Date

After the commencement date, the lessee should recognize in profit or loss (unless costs are included in the carrying amount of another asset) the following:

- Finance leases:
  a. Amortization of the right-of-use asset and interest on the lease liability
  b. Variable lease payments not included in the lease liability in the period obligation incurred
  c. Any impairment

- Operating leases:
  a. A single lease cost calculated such that the remaining cost is allocated on a straight line basis over the remaining lease term (unless another allocation is more representative of the benefit from use of the asset)
  b. Variable lease payments not included in the lease liability in the period in which the obligation is incurred
  c. Any impairment

Subsequent Measurement

FASB ASC 842-20-35 provides guidance for subsequent measurement.

Presentation and Disclosure

Key presentation matters include the following:

- Statement of financial position.
  — Separate presentation of right-of-use assets and lease liabilities from finance leases and operating leases.
- Statement of comprehensive income.
  — Finance leases—interest expense on the lease liability and amortization of right-of-use asset in a manner consistent with how the entity presents other interest expense and depreciation or amortization of similar assets.
  — Operating leases—expense to be included in the lessee's income from continuing operations.

- Statement of cash flows.
  - Presentation within financing activities—the repayment of the principal portion of the lease liability arising from finance leases.
  - Presentation within operating activities—payments arising from operating leases; interest payments on the lease liability; variable lease payments and short term lease payments not included in lease liability.

Disclosure requirements include qualitative and quantitative information for leases, significant judgements, and amounts recognized in the financial statements, including certain specified information and amounts.

Lessor

Recognition and Measurement

FASB ASC 842 provides recognition guidance for sales-type leases, direct financing leases, and operating leases. The following table summarizes the guidance:

Sales-Type Leases	
At the Commencement Date	**After the Commencement Date**
Lessor should derecognize the underlying asset and recognize the following: *a.* Net investment in the lease (lease receivable and unguaranteed residual asset) *b.* Selling profit or loss arising from the lease *c.* Initial direct costs as an expense	Lessor should recognize all of the following: *a.* Interest income on the net investment in the lease *b.* Certain variable lease payments *c.* Impairment

Direct Financing Leases	
At the Commencement Date	**After the Commencement Date**
Lessor should derecognize the underlying asset and recognize the following: *a.* Net investment in the lease (lease receivable and unguaranteed residual asset reduced by selling profit) *b.* Selling loss arising from the lease, if applicable	Lessor should recognize all of the following: *a.* Interest income on the net investment in the lease *b.* Certain variable lease payments *c.* Impairment

(continued)

Operating Leases	
At the Commencement Date	**After the Commencement Date**
Lessor should defer initial direct costs.	Lessor should recognize all of the following: a. The lease payments as income in profit or loss over the lease term on a straight line basis (unless another method in more representative of the benefit received) b. Certain variable lease payments as income in profit or loss c. Initial direct costs as an expense over the lease term on the same basis as lease income

FASB ASC 842-30-35 provides guidance for subsequent measurement.

Presentation and Disclosure

Key presentation matters include the following:

For sales-type and direct financing leases:

- Statement of financial position

  — Separate presentation of lease assets (that is, aggregate of lessor's net investment in sales-type leases and direct financing leases) from other assets.

  — Classified as current or noncurrent based on same considerations as other assets.

- Statement of comprehensive income

  — Presentation of income from leases in the statement of comprehensive income or disclosure of income from leases in the notes with a reference to the corresponding line in the statement of comprehensive income.

  — Presentation of profit or loss recognized at commencement date in a manner appropriate to lessor's business model.

- Statement of cash flows

  — Presentation within operating activities—cash receipts from leases.

For operating leases:

- Statement of financial position

    — Presentation of an underlying asset subject to an operating leases in accordance with other FASB ASC topics.

- Statement of cash flows

    — Presentation within operating activities—cash receipts from leases.

Disclosure requirements include qualitative and quantitative information for leases, significant judgements, and amounts recognized in the financial statements, including certain specified information and amounts.

Sale and Leaseback Transactions

FASB ASC 842 provides guidance for both the transfer contract and the lease in a sale and leaseback transaction (a transaction in which a seller-lessee transfers an asset to a buyer-lessor and leases that asset back). Determination of whether the transfer is a sale should be based on provisions of FASB ASC 606, *Revenue from Contracts with Customers*. FASB ASC 842-40-25 provides measurement guidance for a transfer that is either determined to be a sale or determined not to be a sale.

FASB ASC 842-40 provides guidance for subsequent measurement, financial statement presentation, and disclosures.

Leveraged Lease Arrangements

The legacy accounting model for leveraged leases continues to apply to those leveraged leases that commenced before the effective date of FASB ASC 842. There is no separate accounting model for leveraged leases that commence after the effective date of FASB ASC 842.

Appendix G

Accounting for Financial Instruments

This appendix is nonauthoritative and is included for informational purposes only.

Overall Project Objective

The objective of FASB's Accounting for Financial Instruments project is to significantly improve the decision usefulness of financial instrument reporting for users of financial statements. The project was initiated to reconsider recognition and measurement of financial instruments, address issues related to impairment of financial instruments and hedge accounting, and increase convergence in accounting for financial instruments. In replacing the existing financial instruments standards, an expected outcome is the simplification of the accounting requirements for financial instruments. The project was split into three phases including classification and measurement, impairment, and hedge accounting. This appendix focusses on the latest developments in each of these phases.

Classification and Measurement

Overview

On January 5, 2016, FASB issued Accounting Standards Update (ASU) No. 2016-01, *Financial Instruments—Overall (Subtopic 825-10): Recognition and Measurement of Financial Assets and Financial Liabilities*, to enhance the reporting model for financial instruments and to provide users of financial statements with more decision-useful information. The amendments in the ASU are intended to improve certain aspects of recognition, measurement, presentation, and disclosure of financial instruments.

The new guidance will accomplish the following:

- Require equity investments (except those accounted for under the equity method of accounting or those that result in consolidation of the investee) to be measured at fair value with changes in fair value recognized in net income

- Replace the impairment model for equity investments without readily determinable fair values with a qualitative impairment assessment

- Eliminate the requirement to disclose the fair values of financial assets and financial liabilities measured at amortized cost for entities that are not public business entities

- Eliminate the requirement for public business entities to disclose the methods and significant assumptions used to estimate fair value that is required to be disclosed for financial assets and financial liabilities measured at amortized cost on the balance sheet

- Require public business entities to use the exit price notion when measuring the fair value of financial instruments for disclosure purposes

- Require an entity to present separately in other comprehensive income the portion of the total change in the fair value of a liability resulting from a change in instrument-specific credit risk when the entity has elected to measure the liability at fair value in accordance with the fair value option for financial instruments

- Require separate presentation of financial assets and financial liabilities by measurement category and form of financial asset (that is, securities or loans and receivables) on the balance sheet or the accompanying notes to the financial statements

- Clarify that an entity should evaluate the need for a valuation allowance on a deferred tax asset related to available-for-sale debt securities in combination with an entity's other deferred tax assets

- Eliminate an entity's ability to estimate the disclosed fair values of financial assets and financial liabilities on the basis of entry prices

Applicability and Effective Date

ASU No. 2016-01 affects all entities that hold financial assets or have financial liabilities and is effective as follows:

	Fiscal Years Beginning After	*Interim Periods Within Fiscal Years Beginning After*
Public business entities	December 15, 2017	December 15, 2017
All other entities, including not-for-profit entities and employee benefit plans within the scope of FASB *Accounting Standards Codification* (ASC) 960–965 on plan accounting	December 15, 2018	December 15, 2019

All entities that are not public business entities may adopt the amendments in this ASU earlier as of the fiscal years beginning after December 15, 2017, including interim periods within those fiscal years.

Early application by public business entities to financial statements of fiscal years or interim periods that have not yet been issued or, by all other entities, that have not yet been made available for issuance of the following amendments in this ASU are permitted as of the beginning of the fiscal year of adoption:

- An entity should present separately in other comprehensive income the portion of the total change in the fair value of a liability resulting from a change in the instrument-specific credit risk if the entity has elected to measure the liability at fair value in accordance with the fair value option for financial instruments.

- Entities that are not public business entities are not required to apply the fair value of financial instruments disclosure guidance in the "General" subsection of FASB ASC 825-10-50.

With the exception of this early application guidance, early adoption of the amendments in this ASU is not permitted.

Impairment

Overview

On June 16, 2016, FASB issued ASU No. 2016-13, *Financial Instruments—Credit Losses (Topic 326): Measurement of Credit Losses on Financial Instruments*, to provide financial statement users with more decision-useful information about the expected credit losses on financial instruments and other commitments to extend credit held by a reporting entity at each reporting date. Upon the effective date of this ASU, the incurred loss impairment methodology in current general accepted accounting principles (GAAP) is replaced with a methodology that reflects expected credit losses and requires consideration of a broader range of reasonable and supportable information to inform credit loss estimates.

Assets Measured at Amortized Cost

ASU No. 2016-13 eliminates the probable initial recognition threshold under current GAAP and requires entities that measure financial assets (or a group of financial assets) at amortized cost basis to present such assets at the net amount expected to be collected. The amendments in this ASU broaden the information that an entity must consider in developing its expected credit loss estimate for assets measured either collectively or individually. In addition to past events and current conditions, entities should also consider reasonable and supportable forecasts that affect the collectibility of the reported amount. However, an entity may revert to historical loss information that is reflective of the contractual term (considering the effect of prepayments) for periods that are beyond the time frame for which the entity is able to develop reasonable and supportable forecasts.

An entity may apply any method for measuring expected credit losses as long as their method reasonably reflects its expectations of the credit loss estimate.

Purchased Financial Assets With Credit Deterioration

ASU No. 2016-13 defines *purchased financial assets with credit deterioration* (PCD assets) as acquired individual financial assets (or acquired groups of financial assets with similar risk characteristics) that as of the date of acquisition have experienced a more-than-insignificant deterioration in credit quality since origination, as determined by the acquirer's assessment. The allowance for credit losses for PCD assets that are measured at amortized cost basis is determined in a similar manner to other financial assets measured at amortized cost basis. The initial allowance for credit losses is added to the purchase price, rather than being reported as a credit loss expense. Entities record only subsequent changes in the allowance for credit losses as a credit loss expense for PCD assets. Furthermore, an entity should recognize interest income for PCD assets based on the effective interest rate, excluding the discount embedded in the purchase price that is attributable to the acquirer's assessment of credit losses at acquisition.

Disclosures

In an effort to increase users' understanding of underwriting standards and credit quality trends, ASU No. 2016-13 requires the current disclosure on credit quality indicators in relation to the amortized cost of financing receivables to be further disaggregated by year of origination (or vintage). Entities that are not public business entities are not required to disclose the disaggregation by year of origination.

Available for Sale Debt Securities

Entities will now be required to present credit losses on available-for-sale debt securities as an allowance, rather than as a permanent write-down.

An entity will now be able to record reversals of credit losses on debt securities (in situations in which the estimate of credit declines) in current period net income. Thus, aligning the income statement recognition of credit losses with the reporting period in which changes occur. However, an entity may not record an allowance for credit losses exceeding the amount by which fair value is below amortized cost.

Purchased Debt Securities With Credit Deterioration

The allowance for credit losses for purchased available-for-sale debt securities with a more-than-insignificant amount of credit deterioration since origination is also determined in a similar manner to other available-for-sale debt securities. However, ASU No. 2016-13 requires an entity to add the initial allowance for credit losses to the purchase price, rather than reporting it as a credit loss expense. Entities record only subsequent changes in the allowance for credit losses as a credit loss expense. Furthermore, an entity should recognize interest income based on the effective interest rate, excluding the discount embedded in the purchase price that is attributable to the acquirer's assessment of credit losses at acquisition.

Troubled Debt Restructurings

The ASU does not change the definition or derecognition guidelines for troubled debt restructurings (TDRs), but, rather, changes the impairment recognized on restructuring. Credit losses for TDRs now will be measured using the current expected credit loss model. The ASU eliminates the current GAAP requirement to use a discounted cash flow technique. Credit losses, including concessions given to a borrower under a TDR, will be recognized through an allowance account.

Applicability and Effective Date

ASU No. 2016-13 affects entities holding financial assets and net investment in leases that are not accounted for at fair value through net income. It also affects loans, debt securities, trade receivables, net investments in leases, off-balance sheet credit exposures, reinsurance receivables, and any other financial assets not excluded from the scope that have the contractual right to receive cash.

Because there is diversity in practice in applying the incurred loss methodology, ASU No. 2016-13 will affect entities to varying degrees depending on the credit quality of the assets held by the entities, their duration, and how the entity applies current GAAP.

ASU No. 2016-13 is effective as follows:

	Fiscal Years Beginning After	Interim Periods Within Fiscal Years Beginning After
Public business entities that are SEC filers	December 15, 2019	December 15, 2019
All other public entities	December 15, 2020	December 15, 2020
All other entities, including not-for-profit entities and employee benefit plans within the scope of FASB ASC 960–965 on plan accounting	December 15, 2020	December 15, 2021

All entities may adopt the amendments in this ASU earlier as of the fiscal years beginning after December 15, 2018, including interim periods within those fiscal years.

Transition Resource Group

Due to the potential for significant changes that may result from the issuance of the new standard, FASB has formed the Transition Resource Group (TRG) for Credit Losses to

- solicit, analyze, and discuss stakeholder issues arising from implementation of the new guidance.

- inform FASB about those implementation issues, which will help FASB determine what, if any, action will be needed to address those issues.

- provide a forum for stakeholders to learn about the new guidance from others involved with implementation.

The TRG will meet to discuss and share their views on potential implementation issues raised by concerned parties and, subsequent to each meeting, FASB will determine what actions, if any, will be taken on each issue. Refer to the page "Transition Resource Group for Credit Losses" on FASB's website for more information on this group and the status of their efforts, including meeting materials and meeting summaries.

Hedge Accounting

Overview

Hedge accounting is the third phase in FASB's overall project on accounting for financial instruments. The objective of this project is to make targeted improvements to the hedge accounting model based on the feedback received from preparers, auditors, users, and other stakeholders. FASB has also noted it will consider opportunities to align with IFRS 9, *Financial Instruments*.

Latest Developments

FASB staff are drafting a proposed ASU based on the tentative decisions reached by the board. Readers are encouraged to visit the "Technical Agenda" page under "Projects" at www.fasb.org for the latest developments regarding the hedge accounting phase.

Conclusion

The extent of the effect of the new financial instruments standards will depend upon the relative significance of financial instruments to an entity's operations and financial positon as well as the entity's business strategy. To provide CPAs with guidance during this time of transition, the AICPA's Financial Reporting Center (FRC) offers invaluable resources on the topic. In addition, the FRC includes a list of conferences, webcasts, and products to keep you informed on the latest developments in accounting for financial instruments. Refer to www .aicpa.org/interestareas/frc/accountingfinancialreporting/financialinstruments/pages/default.aspx to stay updated on the latest information available on accounting for financial instruments.

Appendix H

Schedule of Changes Made to the Text From the Previous Edition

This appendix is nonauthoritative and is included for informational purposes only.

As of September 1, 2017

This schedule of changes identifies areas in the text and footnotes of this guide that have changed since the previous edition. Entries in the table of this appendix reflect current numbering, lettering (including that in appendix names), and character designations that resulted from the renumbering or reordering that occurred in the updating of this guide.

Reference	*Change*
General	Guide content included in "Guidance Update" boxes within the chapters have been updated to appropriately reflect guidance not yet effective as of the date of the guide. See the preface of this guide for more explanation to this "dual guidance" treatment.
General	"Guidance Update" boxes found in the prior year edition of the guide containing information on guidance now fully effective have been removed. Information and guidance related to these topics have been incorporated into the text of the guide.
General	References to "Pending Content" have been updated in accordance with the FASB *Accounting Standards Codification*®.
General	Editorial changes, including rephrasing, have been made in this guide to improve readability, where necessary.
Preface	Updated.
Footnote 1 to heading before paragraph 1.01	Revised to reflect the issuance of "Presidential Executive Order on Core Principles for Regulating the United States Financial System."
Paragraph 1.02	Revised for changes in industry practice or developments that are not related to an issuance of authoritative guidance.

(continued)

Reference	Change
Former paragraph 1.05	Deleted due to passage of time.
Paragraphs 1.06 and 1.10	Revised for changes in industry practice or developments that are not related to an issuance of authoritative guidance.
Paragraph 1.14	Added for changes in industry practice or developments that are not related to an issuance of authoritative guidance.
Heading before paragraph 1.16, paragraphs 1.16, 1.29, and 1.32	Revised for changes in industry practice or developments that are not related to an issuance of authoritative guidance.
Paragraph 1.47 and footnote 3 to paragraph 1.47	Revised to reflect the issuance of SEC Release No. 34-80295, *Amendment to Securities Transaction Settlement Cycle*.
Paragraphs 1.62–.65	Added to reflect the issuance of the U.S. Department of Labor's Fiduciary Rule.
Paragraph 1.80	Revised for changes in industry practice or developments that are not related to an issuance of authoritative guidance.
Footnote 4 to paragraph 1.98	Revised due to passage of time.
Paragraph 1.103	Revised to reflect the issuance of U.S. Commodity Futures Trading Commission (CFTC) regulations.
Paragraph 1.143	Added for changes in industry practice or developments that are not related to an issuance of authoritative guidance.
Paragraphs 2.02, 2.05, and 2.13	Revised for changes in industry practice or developments that are not related to an issuance of authoritative guidance.
Paragraph 2.14	Revised due to passage of time.
Paragraph 2.17	Revised to reflect the issuance of SEC Release No. 34-80295.
Paragraphs 2.28–.29	Revised for changes in industry practice or developments that are not related to an issuance of authoritative guidance.

Reference	Change
Paragraph 2.33 and footnote 2 to paragraph 2.33	Revised to reflect the issuance of SEC Release No. 34-80295.
Footnote 4 to paragraph 2.36	Added to reflect the issuance of amendments to Financial Industry Regulatory Authority (FINRA) Rule 4210, *(Margin Requirements) Interpretations.*
Paragraph 2.98	Revised due to passage of time.
Paragraphs 2.99, 2.107, and 2.163	Revised for changes in industry practice or developments that are not related to an issuance of authoritative guidance.
Footnote 1 to heading before paragraph 3.01	Added.
Paragraph 3.03	Revised to reflect the issuance of "Presidential Executive Order on Core Principles for Regulating the United States Financial System."
Footnote 3 to paragraph 3.05	Added reference to FINRA Regulatory Notice 14-39, *New Template Available on FINRA Firm Gateway for Compliance with SEA Rule 17a-5(f)(2) (Statement Regarding Independent Public Accountant).*
Paragraphs 3.08–.09 and 3.11	Revised for changes in industry practice or developments that are not related to an issuance of authoritative guidance.
Paragraph 3.13	Relocated paragraph.
Paragraphs 3.14–.15	Revised due to passage of time.
Paragraph 3.26	Revised to reflect the issuance of SEC Release No. 34-80295.
Former paragraph 3.34	Deleted due to passage of time.
Paragraph 3.36	Revised due to passage of time.
Paragraph 3.40	Revised for changes in industry practice or developments that are not related to an issuance of authoritative guidance.
Paragraph 3.58	Revised due to passage of time.

(continued)

Reference	Change
Paragraph 3.60	Revised for changes in industry practice or developments that are not related to an issuance of authoritative guidance.
Paragraph 3.66	Relocated paragraph.
Paragraph 3.71	Revised due to passage of time.
Footnote 16 to paragraph 3.79	Added to reflect the issuance of amendments to FINRA Rule 4210.
Paragraph 3.94	Revised for changes in industry practice or developments that are not related to an issuance of authoritative guidance.
Former paragraph 3.102	Deleted due to passage of time.
Paragraph 3.110	Revised due to passage of time.
Paragraphs 3.125 and 3.141	Revised for changes in industry practice or developments that are not related to an issuance of authoritative guidance.
Footnote 25 to paragraph 3.142	Revised due to passage of time.
Paragraphs 3.143 and 3.151	Revised for changes in industry practice or developments that are not related to an issuance of authoritative guidance.
Paragraph 3.162	Revised due to passage of time.
Former footnote 28 to heading before paragraph 3.172	Deleted due to passage of time.
Paragraph 3.173	Revised due to passage of time.
Paragraph 3.182	Revised for changes in industry practice or developments that are not related to an issuance of authoritative guidance.
Footnote 36 to paragraph 3.184	Revised to reflect the issuance of "Presidential Executive Order on Core Principles for Regulating the United States Financial System."
Paragraph 3.188	Revised due to passage of time.
Paragraphs 4.09, 4.20–.23, and 4.42	Revised for changes in industry practice or developments that are not related to an issuance of authoritative guidance.

Reference	Change
Paragraph 4.46	Revised to reflect the issuance of SEC Release No. 34-80295.
Paragraphs 4.47–.49 and 4.58–.59	Revised for changes in industry practice or developments that are not related to an issuance of authoritative guidance.
Footnote 1 to first update box in chapter 5 and footnote 2 to update 5-2	Added to reflect the announcement made by the SEC at the July 20, 2017, meeting of the Emerging Issues Task Force.
Paragraphs 5.02, 5.04, and 5.11	Revised for changes in industry practice or developments that are not related to an issuance of authoritative guidance.
Paragraphs 5.12–.13	Revised to reflect the issuance of FASB Accounting Standards Update (ASU) No. 2016-19, *Technical Corrections and Improvements*.
Footnote 6 to paragraph 5.59	Revised to reflect the issuance of SEC Release No. 34-80295.
Paragraph 5.63	Revised for changes in industry practice or developments that are not related to an issuance of authoritative guidance.
Paragraph 5.66	Relocated paragraph.
Paragraph 5.69	Revised for changes in industry practice or developments that are not related to an issuance of authoritative guidance.
Paragraphs 5.88–.97	Relocated paragraphs.
Footnote 4 to heading before paragraph 5.104	Relocated footnote.
Footnote 21 to update 5-2 and footnote 1 to first update box in chapter 6	Added to reflect the announcement made by the SEC at the July 20, 2017, meeting of the Emerging Issues Task Force.
Paragraphs 6.01–.02	Revised for changes in industry practice or developments that are not related to an issuance of authoritative guidance.
Paragraphs 6.06–.07	Revised due to passage of time.
Former paragraph 6.11	Deleted.

(continued)

Reference	Change
Paragraph 6.19	Revised for changes in industry practice or developments that are not related to an issuance of authoritative guidance.
Heading before paragraph 6.28	Revised.
Footnote 5 to paragraph 6.28	Revised due to passage of time.
Paragraph 6.32	Relocated paragraph.
Paragraphs 6.33, 6.36, and 6.40	Revised for changes in industry practice or developments that are not related to an issuance of authoritative guidance.
Paragraph 6.43	Revised to reflect the issuance of FASB ASU No. 2016-19.
Former footnote 4 to paragraph 6.43	Deleted to reflect the issuance of FASB ASU No. 2016-19.
Paragraphs 6.67–.68	Added to provide guidance on initial margin. This change goes beyond a conforming change and has been approved in accordance with applicable AICPA requirements.
Paragraphs 6.84 and 6.103	Revised for changes in industry practice or developments that are not related to an issuance of authoritative guidance.
Former footnote 5 to paragraph 6.117	Deleted due to passage of time.
Appendixes A, D, E, F, and G	Updated.
Glossary	Updated.
Index of Pronouncements and Other Technical Guidance	Updated.
Subject Index	Updated.

Glossary

The following terms can be found in the FASB *Accounting Standards Codification* (ASC) glossary:

box spread. A combination of long calls and short puts (identical with respect to the underlying security issue, number of shares, exercise price, and expiration date) coupled with long puts and short calls (identical with respect to the underlying security issue, number of shares, exercise price, and expiration date). In boxing (coupling), the long calls and short puts with the long puts and short calls, the underlying security issue, the number of shares, and the expiration date remain identical. However, the exercise price of each combination is at a different amount.

collateralized financing entity. A variable interest entity that holds financial assets, issues beneficial interests in those financial assets, and has no more than nominal equity. The beneficial interests have contractual recourse only to the related assets of the collateralized financing entity and are classified as financial liabilities. A collateralized financing entity may hold nonfinancial assets temporarily as a result of default by the debtor on the underlying debt instruments held as assets by the collateralized financing entity or in an effort to restructure the debt instruments held as assets by the collateralized financing entity. A collateralized financing entity also may hold other financial assets and financial liabilities that are incidental to the operations of the collateralized financing entity and have carrying values that approximate fair value (for example, cash, broker receivables, or broker payables).

fail to deliver. Securities that the selling broker-dealer has not delivered to the purchasing broker-dealer at the settlement date.

fail to receive. Securities that the purchasing broker-dealer has not received from the selling broker-dealer at the settlement date.

fair value. The price that would be received to sell an asset or paid to transfer a liability in an orderly transaction between market participants at the measurement date.

Fed Funds effective swap rate (or overnight index swap rate). The fixed rate on a U.S. dollar, constant-notional interest rate swap that has its variable-rate leg referenced to the Fed Funds effective rate with no additional spread over the Fed Funds effective rate on that variable-rate leg. That fixed rate is the derived rate that would result in the swap having a zero fair value at inception because the present value of fixed cash flows, based on that rate, equates to the present value of the variable cash flows.

FHLMC. Abbreviation for Federal Home Loan Mortgage Corporation. Often referred to as Freddie Mac, FHLMC is a private corporation authorized by Congress to assist in the development and maintenance of a secondary market in conventional residential mortgages. FHLMC purchases mortgage loans and sells mortgages principally through mortgage participation certificates representing an undivided interest in a group of conventional mortgages. FHLMC guarantees the timely payment of interest and the collection of principal on the participation certificates.

financial asset. Cash, evidence of an ownership interest in an entity, or a contract that conveys to one entity a right to do either of the following:

    a. Receive cash or another financial instrument from a second entity

    b. Exchange other financial instruments on potentially favorable terms with the second entity.

floor broker. A member of a securities exchange who executes transactions on the floor of an exchange for the account of that member's own entity or for the account of other member entities. Broker-dealers often engage floor brokers, who are responsible for executing securities transactions on the exchanges for the account of the broker-dealer. Floor brokers employed by the entity may execute trades on behalf of other broker-dealers, for which the entity is paid a brokerage fee. The purchase and sale department of the broker-dealer maintains the records of floor brokerage fees that are due to other broker-dealers who execute orders on the entity's behalf and brokerage fees due from other broker-dealers.

FNMA. Abbreviation for Federal National Mortgage Association. Often referred to as Fannie Mae, FNMA is an investor-owned corporation established by Congress to support the secondary mortgage loan market by purchasing mortgage loans when other investor funds are limited and selling mortgage loans when other investor funds are available.

GNMA. Abbreviation for Government National Mortgage Association, often referred to as Ginnie Mae. GNMA is a U.S. governmental agency that guarantees certain types of mortgage-backed securities and provides funds for and administers certain types of low-income housing assistance programs.

proprietary transactions. Transactions in financial instruments that broker-dealers execute for their own account.

public business entity. A public business entity is a business entity meeting any one of the criteria below. Neither a not-for-profit entity nor an employee benefit plan is a business entity.

    a. It is required by the U.S. Securities and Exchange Commission (SEC) to file or furnish financial statements, or does file or furnish financial statements (including voluntary filers), with the SEC (including other entities whose financial statements or financial information are required to be or are included in a filing).

    b. It is required by the Securities Exchange Act of 1934 (the Act), as amended, or rules or regulations promulgated under the Act, to file or furnish financial statements with a regulatory agency other than the SEC.

    c. It is required to file or furnish financial statements with a foreign or domestic regulatory agency in preparation for the sale of or for purposes of issuing securities that are not subject to contractual restrictions on transfer.

    d. It has issued, or is a conduit bond obligor for, securities that are traded, listed, or quoted on an exchange or an over-the-counter market.

    e. It has one or more securities that are not subject to contractual restrictions on transfer, and it is required by law, contract, or regulation to prepare U.S. GAAP financial statements (including footnotes) and make them publicly available on a periodic basis (for example, interim or annual periods). An entity must meet both of these conditions to meet this criterion.

An entity may meet the definition of a public business entity solely because its financial statements or financial information is included in another entity's filing with the SEC. In that case, the entity is only a public business entity for purposes of financial statements that are filed or furnished with the SEC.

regular-way trades. Include both of the following: (*a*) all transactions in exchange-traded financial instruments that are expected to settle within the standard settlement cycle of that exchange (for example, three days for U.S. securities exchanges);[1] and (*b*) all transactions in cash-market-traded financial instruments that are expected to settle within the time frame prevalent or traditional for each specific instrument (for example, for U.S. government securities, one or two days).

repurchase agreement (repo agreement). An agreement under which the transferor (repo party) transfers a financial asset to a transferee (repo counterparty or reverse party) in exchange for cash and concurrently agrees to reacquire that financial asset at a future date for an amount equal to the cash exchanged plus or minus a stipulated interest factor. Instead of cash, other securities or letters of credit sometimes are exchanged. Some repurchase agreements call for repurchase of financial assets that need not be identical to the financial assets transferred.

repurchase agreement accounted for as a collateralized borrowing (repo agreement). A transaction in which a seller-borrower of securities sells those securities to a buyer-lender with an agreement to repurchase them at a stated price plus interest at a specified date or in specified circumstances. A repurchase agreement accounted for as a collateralized borrowing is a repo that does not qualify for sale accounting under FASB ASC 860, *Transfers and Servicing*. The payable under a repurchase agreement accounted for as a collateralized borrowing refers to the amount of the seller-borrower's obligation recognized for the future repurchase of the securities from the buyer-lender. In certain industries, the terminology is reversed; that is, entities in those industries refer to this type of agreement as a reverse repo (see **reverse repurchase agreement accounted for as a collateralized borrowing**).

repurchase-to-maturity transaction. A repurchase agreement in which the settlement date of the agreement to repurchase a transferred financial asset is at the maturity date of that financial as-set and the agreement would not require the transferor to reacquire the financial asset.

reverse repurchase agreement accounted for as a collateralized borrowing (reverse repo or resale agreement). A transaction that is accounted for as a collateralized lending in which a buyer-lender buys securities with an agreement to resell them to the seller-borrower at a stated price plus interest at a specified date or in specified circumstances. The receivable under a reverse repurchase agreement accounted for as a collateralized borrowing refers to the amount due from the seller-borrower for the repurchase of the securities from the buyer-lender. In certain industries, the terminology is reversed; that is, entities in those industries

---

[1] Under SEC Release No. 34-80295, "Amendment to Securities Transaction Settlement Cycle," the SEC amended Rule 15c6-1(a), *Settlement Cycle Rule*, to shorten the standard settlement cycle for most broker-dealer transactions from three business days after the trade date ("T+3") to two business days after the trade date ("T+2").

refer to this type of agreement as a repo (see **repurchase agreement accounted for as a collateralized borrowing**).

soft-dollar arrangements. Arrangements in which a broker-dealer provides research to a customer in return for trade order flow (a certain volume of trades) from that customer.

substantial doubt about an entity's ability to continue as a going concern. Substantial doubt about an entity's ability to continue as a going concern exists when conditions and events, considered in the aggregate, indicate that it is probable that the entity will be unable to meet its obligations as they become due within one year after the date that the financial statements are issued (or within one year after the date that the financial statements are available to be issued when applicable). The term probable is used consistently with its use in FASB ASC 450 on contingencies.

The following is a list of additional terms that have been used in this guide:

account executive. See **registered representative**.

active box. A position on the stock record (street side) indicating securities under the control of the broker-dealer that are normally available for the broker-dealer's general use.

adequately collateralized. Indebtedness for which the difference between the amount of the indebtedness and the fair value of the collateral is sufficient to make the loan acceptable as a fully secured loan to banks that regularly make comparable loans to broker-dealers in the community.

ADR. Abbreviation for American Depository Receipt, a certificate issued by a U.S. bank that serves as evidence of ownership of original foreign shares. These certificates are transferable and can be traded. The original foreign stock certificates are deposited with a foreign branch or foreign correspondent bank of the issuing U.S. bank.

agency transactions. Transactions in financial instruments that broker-dealers execute on behalf of customers to earn commission income.

aggregate indebtedness. The total of certain liabilities of a broker-dealer that are set forth in SEC Rule 15c3-1. The rule states that a broker-dealer shall not permit its aggregate indebtedness to exceed a specified percentage of its net capital as defined in the rule.

allied member. Any general partner, qualified voting stockholder, or officer of a FINRA (former NYSE) member firm, who is deemed to be a control person of a member organization and who is not himself or herself a member of a stock exchange.

AMEX. Popular name for the American Stock Exchange. AMEX was acquired by NYSE Euronext in 2008. In 2009, NYSE Amex was formed for trading small and mid-cap growth companies.

arbitrage. The act of buying a security in one market and simultaneously selling it in another in order to profit from price discrepancies. Also, buying a security subject to exchange, conversion, or reorganization and selling the security or securities to be received upon completion of the exchange, conversion, or reorganization.

ask. The lowest price a seller is willing to accept for a security at a particular time, also known as *offer* by exchanges.

asset-backed commercial paper (ABCP). Short-term promissory notes issued in bearer form by large corporations with similar features to the standard commercial paper, with the exception that the note is secured against specific assets, usually short-term trade receivables from a company (or companies). ABCP may also have liquidity support from a sponsoring bank to allow timely repayment at maturity (see **commercial paper**).

auction rate securities. Long-term debt securities with legal maturities typically of at least 20 years, with interest rates that are reset periodically (typically every week or month, but in some cases every 49, 60, or 90 days) in blind auctions held by investment banks. Most auction rate securities are guaranteed by a third party, typically known as a *bond insurer*, and the bond insurer's rating typically affects the rating of the bond.

back office. The operations area of a brokerage office, containing the bookkeeping, margin, purchase and sales, cashier's, and dividend departments. The back office function generally supports trading thorough trade reconciliations, confirmations, settlement, and recordkeeping.

bad delivery. A delivery of securities that does not fulfill the requirements for delivery, including the standards required to transfer title to the buyer.

balance order. The net balance instructions, issued by a clearing organization, to receive or deliver securities based on a netting of all trades in a given security settling on the date of netting. The instructions give all the information needed by the member firm to clear its transactions on a given settlement date.

basis point. A measurement of changes in price or yields for fixed-income securities. One basis point equals 0.01 percent, or 10 cents per $1,000 per annum.

best efforts. Refers to an agreement by an underwriter to buy from the issuing corporation only those securities it is able to sell to the public.

bid. The price a buyer is willing to pay for a security at a particular time.

Big Board. Popular name for the New York Stock Exchange.

block trading. The acquisition or disposition of large quantities (10,000 shares or more) or blocks of stock by a broker-dealer in order to facilitate the execution of buy and sell orders of customers, usually institutions. Often, a broker-dealer absorbs a portion of the order for its own account and risk.

blotter. A record of original entry. A book or individual unit used as a record of original entry to record transactions as they occur. It covers purchases, sales, cash receipts and disbursements, and securities received and delivered.

blue list. Daily publication, either or both print and electronic, listing primarily municipal bonds offered for sale.

book entry system. A system in which securities are not represented by physical certificates, but are maintained in computerized records at the custodian (such as the Depository Trust Company) in the name of registered owners.

books closed. The cutoff time that determines the stockholders of record for a prescribed period. Any entries affecting the registration or ownership of securities for dividend disbursements or proxy purposes must be made before this time.

borrowed. The act of borrowing a security for delivery. The equivalent value in money is usually deposited with the lender.

box. A term used for a "short" position in the stock record representing securities under the control of or in the possession of the broker-dealer. It indicates a place where securities are kept, such as a vault, file cabinet, and so forth. A box is also identified as a safekeeping box, segregation box, name-of box, active box, and so forth.

box count. An actual count of securities either in connection with an audit or with periodic checking.

break. The term applied to that position in the stock record to designate an out-of-balance position between the stock record long and short positions.

broker loans. Money borrowed by broker-dealers from banks. Typically loans are collateralized by DTC eligible stocks with a fair value of more than five dollars, subject to concentration limitations.

broker's transfer account. An account kept by the transfer clerk of a broker-dealer giving details of securities transferred for the account of other broker-dealers. The need for the account arises when delivery is made by transfer as directed (TAD) instead of by delivery of the actual certificates.

bulk segregation. Securities (usually constituting excess collateral in margin accounts) that are filed in alphabetical order in special boxes in the vault but that are not specifically identified by owner. The securities are usually in the name of the broker-dealer, who maintains collateral records that indicate the owners.

buy in. The procedure followed by a broker-dealer desiring to settle a buy contract that is past due. The broker-dealer may file a notice termed a buy in with a stock exchange or the National Association of Security Dealers (NASD), as appropriate. A copy of the notice is also served on the broker-dealer from whom the securities were to be received. If the securities are not delivered, the stock or bond may be bought in for cash for the account of the broker-dealer from whom the securities are to be received. The difference in price between the buy in and the contract price is adjusted by check from one broker-dealer to another.

buying power. The equity remaining in a margin account after providing for the margining of existing securities in the account in accordance with federal and house margin requirements.

cage. The term given to the area of the broker or dealer's office where the cashier, stock clerks, loan clerks, transfer clerks, blotter clerks, and others have, as a part of their duties, responsibility for receiving and delivering securities.

call (margin). A request, usually in writing, for a margin customer to put up additional collateral (cash or securities).

call loan. A loan that has no definite maturity or rate of interest. The loan may be either called by the lender or paid off by the borrower at any time.

call option. A contract that entitles the holder to buy (call), entirely at his or her option, a specified number of underlying units of a particular security at a specified price at any time until the stated expiration date of the contract. (This is an American-style option; a European-style option is exercisable only at a specific date.) Such an option (which is always for a transferable, round-lot amount) is bought with the expectation that the price will rise above the contract price. If the price rises as anticipated, the purchaser will exercise the option; if it does not, he or she will let the option expire and will lose only the cost of the option. There is both a listed and over-the-counter market in options. (During the existence of an OTC option, the exercise price and number of underlying units are adjusted on the expiration date for cash dividends, rights, and stock dividends or splits.)

carry. The cost of financing (borrowing to buy) a position in financial instruments. Positive carry is a condition that arises if the cost of financing (the short-term rate of interest) is less than the current return of the instrument. Negative carry is a condition that arises if the cost of financing is above the current return of the instrument.

cash account. The account of a customer of a broker-dealer who purchases and sells securities strictly on a cash basis. No credit margin is allowed.

cash sale. A sale with the same trade and settlement dates. The selling broker-dealer must be able to make delivery of the security sold on the trade date. The customer who is selling usually receives a discounted price on the sale for this special service.

cash transaction. A transaction that is expected to clear within the time prescribed by Federal Reserve Regulation T of the Board of Governors of the Federal Reserve System.

cashier's department. A division of the operations department of a broker-dealer that handles the securities and money that are received or delivered by the broker-dealer (see **cage**).

CBOE. Abbreviation for Chicago Board Options Exchange, a national securities exchange based in Chicago that provides a continuous market for trading in put and call options. Various other exchanges (such as NYSE Arca Options and Philadelphia [now NASDAQ OMX PHLX]) also provide such markets.

CFTC. Abbreviation for Commodity Futures Trading Commission, an agency established by Congress to regulate U.S. commodity futures markets and futures commission merchants. Among other things, this agency establishes rules governing the minimum financial, reporting, and audit requirements of its members. Its function is similar to that performed by the SEC in regulating broker-dealers in securities and various securities markets.

churning. The process of excessive purchases and sales in customers' accounts for the purpose of generating commissions.

circuit breaker. A system of trading halts and price limits on equities, options, and futures markets designed to provide a cooling-off period during large, intraday market declines. The breakers are triggered when a market has fallen by a specific amount within a specified period.

cleanup call. A provision of an asset-backed security that permits the issuer to call it at par when the collateral has been paid down to a specified level.

clearance. The act of clearing securities transactions between buyers and sellers; receipt or delivery of securities against payment.

clearing broker. Usually, a broker-dealer who clears the transactions of another broker-dealer (see **correspondent**).

clearinghouse. The central location for matching and settling commodity transactions, collecting and maintaining margin, regulating delivery, and reporting trade information of members. The clearinghouse is responsible to all members for the fulfillment of the contracts and maintains sufficient funds by calling for margin deposits from members.

clearing member. A broker-dealer entitled to use the services of the clearing organization.

clearing number. A number assigned to a member by a clearing organization in order to identify that clearing member.

clearing organization. The central location for matching the security transactions of members (see **clearinghouse**).

commercial paper (CP). Short-term promissory notes issued in bearer form by large corporations, with maturities ranging from overnight to 270 days. However, most paper issued matures in less than 40 days. Standard CP is unsecured and subject to counterparty risk (see **asset-backed commercial paper**).

commodity holdout. Commodity transactions on the broker or dealer's records that are not reported on the clearinghouse sheets.

commodity spreading. Implies open purchase (long) and sale (short) contracts in the same commodity or in different commodities.

comparison. A formal notice that details the terms of the contract between broker-dealers that are parties to nonexchange trades. If the details of the trade are correct, the comparison is stamped (acknowledged) and returned; if they are incorrect, the broker-dealer indicates the differences and returns the comparison (see **DK**).

compliance department. The department of a broker-dealer that enforces adherence to policies established by the broker-dealer, plus all rules and regulations promulgated by the various regulatory agencies.

confirmation. A notice that sets forth the terms of a contract between a broker-dealer and its customer for the purchase or sale of securities. Details shown on a confirmation are the trade date, settlement date, number of shares or par value of bonds, security description, contract price, commission, account number and type of account, and customer's name and address, as well as any other information required.

contract difference. The difference between the contract and the fair values of commodities.

contract sheet. A listing of compared and uncompared transactions sent to each member firm by a stock-clearing corporation.

control stock. Securities of an issuer that are owned by an affiliate of that issuer. An affiliate of that issuer is a person who, directly or indirectly through one or more intermediaries, controls or is controlled by or is under common control with the issuer. Control is likely to be found if the person is a director, officer, or owner of a relatively large number of the issuing company's voting securities. However, the notion of control is a factual matter that is determined on a case-by-case basis.

correspondent. One of the parties to an agreement between two broker-dealers who perform services for each other, such as the execution and the clearance of trades or the maintenance of customer accounts.

cover value. The amount necessary to buy-in a short security position at the fair value.

CRD. Abbreviation for Centralized Registration Depository; a computerized filing and data processing system, operated by FINRA, that maintains registration information regarding broker-dealers and their registered personnel.

credit department. See **margin department**.

CUSIP number. A means of uniformly describing and identifying all stocks and registered bonds in numeric form developed by the Committee on Uniform Security Identification Procedures.

DAP. Abbreviation for delivery against payment; a type of settlement in which the security is paid for when the selling broker-dealer delivers it to the purchaser or their agent. Also referred to as COD (cash on delivery), POD (payment on delivery), and DVP (delivery versus payment).

day loan. A loan made for only one day, generally on an unsecured basis, for the convenience of the broker-dealer.

day traders. Speculators or exchange members on the trading floor who take positions in securities or commodities for a very short period of time and generally liquidate them prior to the close of the same trading day.

definitive certificates. Actual and permanent certificates of bonds or stock given in exchange for temporary receipts. These temporary receipts are usually issued at the time of a new offering, before the engraved certificates are available.

delayed delivery. A transaction involving deferral of the settlement date (which is normally three business days for securities and one business day for options) to some point further in the future as agreed on by both buyer and seller (see **seller's option**).

derivative. A financial instrument, traded on or off an exchange, the price of which is directly dependent upon (that is, derived from) the value of one or more underlying securities, equity indices, debt instruments, commodities, other derivative instruments, or any agreed upon pricing index or arrangement (for example, the movement over time of the Consumer Price Index or freight rates). Derivatives involve the trading of rights or obligations based on the underlying product but do not directly transfer property.

directed sale. Sale by the manager of a syndicate to a customer, usually an institution, of a syndicate member.

discretionary account. An account over which a broker-dealer or some other person has been given authority by the customer to make decisions (including the kind of securities to buy or sell, as well as the date and prices to be paid or received) concerning purchases and sales of securities. The discretion may be complete or limited.

distribution. The sale of a large block of securities to the investing public.

divided liability. Liability in a syndicate or underwriting that is fixed or definite in the amount of shares or principal value for each participant (see **undivided liability**).

dividend department. A division of the operations department that is charged with the collection of dividends and the crediting of these dividends to the accounts of customers.

DK. Abbreviation for "don't know;" an expression used by a broker-dealer to indicate that a transaction another broker-dealer is attempting to confirm or compare is unknown or is questioned (meaning that it is a questioned trade or a QT). When mutual understanding is reached, the transaction is properly compared or canceled.

DTC. Abbreviation for Depository Trust Company, a depository for eligible securities that facilitates clearance between member organizations and banks without the necessity of receiving or delivering actual certificates. DTC is a subsidiary of DTCC.

DTCC. The Depository Trust & Clearing Corporation, a holding company for DTC and NSCC.

due bill. A document, used to adjust security transactions, passed between broker-dealers stating that dividends, rights to subscribe, stock dividends, and so forth, are the property of the holder of the due bill.

DVP. Abbreviation for delivery versus payment; a type of settlement in which the security is paid for when the selling broker-dealer delivers the security to the purchaser or their agent.

ECN. Electronic Communication Network, an alternative trading system that facilitates trading of financial products outside of stock exchanges by directly connecting equity traders, agency brokers, market makers, and investors. ECNs must register with the SEC as a broker-dealer or an exchange and are subject to Regulation ATS.

equity. The net worth in an account carried by a broker-dealer, computed by subtracting the total of the short security values and the debit balance from the total of the long security values and the credit balance. If the result is a net credit, the account is said to liquidate to an equity.

equity securities. Term applied to common and preferred stocks.

equity statements (runs). Statements showing details of an account with security valuations.

exchange tickets. The tickets in a clearing corporation format, prepared by a broker-dealer for each transaction made on an exchange. These tickets list all pertinent details of the trade and are sent, along with a daily summary listing, to the clearing corporation for comparison and confirmation.

ex-clearinghouse. Transactions that are not settled through the clearinghouse.

ex-dividend. Synonym for without dividend. The buyer of a stock selling ex-dividend does not receive the recently declared dividend. Open buy and sell stop orders and sell stop limit orders in a stock on the ex-dividend date are ordinarily reduced by the value of the particular dividend. In the case of open stop limit orders to sell, both the stop price and the limit price are reduced. Every dividend is payable on a fixed date to all shareholders recorded on the books of the disbursing company as of a previous date of record. For example, a dividend may be declared as payable to holders of record on the books of the disbursing company on a given Friday. Because three business days are allowed for delivering the security via regular-way delivery in transactions on a stock exchange, the exchange would declare the stock ex-dividend as of the opening of the market on the preceding Wednesday. This means that anyone buying the stock on and after Wednesday would not be entitled to the dividend.

execution report. A confirmation notice of the completion of a trade that is sent from the floor of an exchange (for listed securities) or trading desk (for over-the-counter securities) back to the point of origin of the order.

exempt securities. Securities exempted from registration under the Securities Exchange Act of 1934, rather than by action of the SEC. Such securities include U.S. government and agency securities, and municipal bonds.

ex-rights. Same principle as ex-dividend. The buyer of stock selling ex-rights is not entitled to the rights distribution.

extension. Permission to extend credit beyond the time prescribed by Federal Reserve Regulation T of the Board of Governors of the Federal Reserve System.

ex-warrants. On occasion, stocks or bonds have warrants attached entitling the holder to subscribe to additional shares within specified periods of time and at specified prices. If these warrants are detached, the security is traded ex-warrants—or without warrants.

fails. Uncompleted securities transactions between two broker-dealers (see **fail-to-deliver** and **fail-to-receive** in the FASB ASC section of the glossary).

fair value. As used in connection with margin trading, generally the closing price of a security as of the preceding business day.

financial consultant. See **registered representative**.

FINRA. Financial Industry Regulatory Authority was created in July 2007 through the consolidation of the National Association of Securities Dealers (NASD) and the member regulation, enforcement, and arbitration functions of the New York Stock Exchange (NYSE).

fire wall. (Also referred to as *systems security*.) An intangible barrier between the trading side of a broker-dealer and the corporate finance and research side that prevents broker-dealers from taking advantage of the corporate finance department's inside information.

firm account. An account consisting of securities in which the broker-dealer has taken a position for investment purposes, is making a market (principal wholesaler), or has an interest with another party (joint account).

firm commitment. The agreement of an underwriter to buy the entire issue of a security from the issuing corporation at a specified price.

firm price. The price at which a security can be bought or sold in the over-the-counter market for such period of time as the seller may specify.

flat. A method of trading in certain kinds of bonds. Usually used in trading income bonds that do not pay interest unless it has been earned and declared payable, or in bonds on which the issuer has defaulted in the payment of interest. When bonds are traded "flat," the seller is not entitled to the interest that has accumulated since the date of the last interest payment. The seller of a bond that is traded flat must deliver the bond with all unpaid coupons attached or a due bill authorizing the buyer to collect any payments of interest that may be made by the issuer in the future.

flat statement. A statement with no money or security balance.

floating rate notes (FRN). Notes issued by banks and corporations, typically with maturities of one year or more, that pay a regular coupon with the promise of return of the face value at maturity. The coupon rate is generally pegged to a benchmark rate such as the LIBOR or Euribor. Notes without maturities are known as perpetual FRNs whereby investors can only regain capital by selling the instrument in the secondary market.

floor. Popular name for the area where securities are bought or sold at an exchange.

floor brokerage. The commission charged by one broker-dealer to another for executions of transactions at exchanges.

floor clerk. An employee of a broker-dealer who maintains a liaison between the order room and the floor broker.

floor report. A report of an executed trade given to the floor clerk by the floor broker and containing the number of shares, the price, and the identity of the other broker on the trade.

FOCUS report. Acronym for Financial and Operational Combined Uniform Single report. The uniform regulatory report (Form X-17A-5) filed periodically by all broker-dealers pursuant to Rule 17a-5 of the SEC.

forward market. Reference made to nonexchange trading of commodities and securities for settlement at a future date. Contracts of this nature are designed by both the buyer and seller about the delivery time, the amount, and so on.

free securities. Securities that are fully paid for.

free shipment. Shipments of securities, usually to out-of-town broker-dealers, without a draft attached, in order to avoid payment of collection charges.

fully disclosed basis. Situation in which a nonclearing broker introduces a customer to a clearing broker and the customer's name and statement are carried by, and disclosed to, that clearing broker.

fully paid accounts. Customer accounts in which the contract price to purchase securities has been paid. These securities should be locked up in the segregation or safekeeping box.

fungibility. Similar securities that are interchangeable, such as GNMA securities transactions that are interchangeable about interest rate and pool and are traded and settled at an equivalent yield basis.

futures contract. An exchange-traded contract for the purchase or sale of commodities at some time in the future.

give-up. Type of order that is given by a customer to a member firm on whose books the customer does not have an account.

good delivery. Certain basic qualifications that must be met before a security sold may be delivered. The security must be in proper form to comply with the contract of sale and to transfer title by delivery to the purchaser.

good-faith deposit. Deposit to guarantee performance, usually with respect to new issues of securities.

group account. A syndicate or joint account.

GTC. Abbreviation for good 'til canceled. Also called an open order. If this term appears on an order to buy or sell a security, it means that the order is to remain in effect until it is either executed or canceled.

haircut. Deductions from the net capital of certain specified percentages of the fair value of securities and commodity futures contracts that are long and short in the capital and proprietary accounts of a broker-dealer and in the accounts of partners. These deductions are solely for the purpose of computing net capital and are not entered on the books.

holder of record. The party listed as the owner on the transfer records of a corporation.

holder's file. A subsidiary file (punched cards, discs, or tapes) in account sequence showing securities owned or carried in such accounts.

house account. An account used by a broker-dealer to maintain a trading or investment position in a security for itself or its officers or partners. Also, a name given to a customer's account to which no registered representative has been assigned.

house rules. Rules promulgated by the broker-dealer. Usually refers to the maintenance margin required by the broker-dealer over and above the requirements of regulatory bodies.

hypothecation agreement. An agreement signed by a customer that permits his or her broker to use securities in the customer's margin account as collateral for loans made to the broker.

in-house. Within the broker or dealer's firm.

initial margin. The amount of money or its equivalent, specified by the Board of Governors of the Federal Reserve System, that a customer must deposit with his or her broker when the customer buys a security on margin.

interest trades. These transactions, as defined, involve (1) a purchase of GNMA securities for current settlement; (2) a delayed settlement sale of these securities or the possession of a long standby; and (3) a financing of the long GNMA position by a sale under an agreement to repurchase on or before the future delivery date.

international arbitrage. Same as arbitrage, except the markets are in different countries.

investment banker. One who underwrites securities on an initial or secondary basis. This type of underwriting often involves private placements for which the investment banker may act as both a broker and a dealer.

joint account. An account in which two or more persons have an interest.

legal list. A list of securities in which insurance companies, banks, and fiduciaries are permitted by law to invest.

legal transfer. A stock certificate having an assignment executed by an executor, administrator, trustee, guardian, and so forth, and requiring certain legal documents indicating the authority of the party signing the securities.

letter of credit. An unqualified commitment issued by banks or trust companies to pay a specified sum of money immediately upon demand at any time prior to the expiration of the letter of credit. Most commonly used by broker-dealers to satisfy margin requirements at the Options Clearing Corporation or commodity-clearing organizations or in stock-borrowed transactions.

limit order. Also called a limited order or limited price order, an order to buy or sell a security at a price specified by the customer or at a better price, if such a price can be obtained.

liquidity rebate. ECN's credit fee structure that pays a rebate or charges a fee based on whether the trade adds or removes liquidity. Under this credit structure, the ECN makes a profit from the difference between what they rebate and charge for the trade. This differs from the classic exchange-like fee structure that charges an exchange fee to all market participants regardless of whether they add or remove liquidity.

listed security. A security that is traded on an exchange.

loan consent. An agreement signed by a customer that permits the broker-dealer to lend securities owned by the customer to other broker-dealers.

loaned. The act of lending a security, usually for delivery against a short sale. The equivalent value in money is usually deposited by the borrower. This term is the opposite of *borrowed*.

Loanet. A privately owned and operated online real-time accounting service used by brokers and institutions in support of their domestic and international securities borrowing and lending activities. The system, part of SunGard Data Systems, Inc., provides interfaces to the Depository Trust Company for both receipt and delivery of securities, including fair values of the securities, and to clients' internal recordkeeping systems or outside accounting services. In addition, Loanet also provides daily contract comparison for all subscribers engaged in the borrowing and lending of securities and portfolio availability of most major lending institutions.

loan value. The value at which a security is accepted for margin. This value is usually less than, or at a discount from, the fair value.

lock-up. The act of placing securities in safekeeping or segregation.

long. Denotes ownership, or the right to possession, of securities.

long and short record. See **stock record**.

long securities differences. The excess of securities positions accounted for over the broker-dealer's long positions on the stock record. When recorded in a difference account, the excess would be recorded long on the stock record (see **short securities differences**).

maintenance margin. The amount of equity required to be maintained in a margin account in accordance with exchange regulations or house rules.

margin. The equity in an account. The requirements for the amount of margin vary between initial margin and maintenance margin and also according to the type of collateral used in computing the equity.

margin call. A request for additional margin.

margin department. A division of the operations department. Its functions include keeping an up-to-date record of each customer's purchases and sales of securities, carefully monitoring extensions of credit to customers, and the segregation of fully paid for or excess-margin securities.

margin transaction. A transaction in which the broker-dealer advances credit to the customer for a portion of the purchase price.

market maker. A broker-dealer that stands ready to buy or sell a particular security in the over-the-counter market at prices the broker-dealer has quoted. Also, an options trader on the floor of a registered exchange who stands ready to buy or sell a particular option.

market price. Usually means the last reported price at which a security has been sold.

mark up. The difference between what a broker-dealer has paid for a security and the price at which it offers the security to another person.

master file. A file that contains the official account numbers and descriptions of securities and customers' names and addresses.

material associated person (MAP). The determination of whether an affiliated person of a broker or dealer is a material associated person involves consideration of all aspects of the activities of, and the relationship between, both entities, including the factors enumerated in SEC Rule 17h-1T.

matrix pricing. A mathematical technique used to value normal institutional-size trading units of debt securities without relying exclusively on quoted prices of the specific security. Factors such as the issue's coupon or stated interest rate, maturity, and rating and quoted prices of similar issues are considered in developing the issue's current market yield.

maximum loan value. The percentage of the purchase price of a security that a broker-dealer may lend to a customer who is buying a security on margin.

member corporation. A broker-dealer that is organized as a corporation and that has at least one director-holder of voting stock who is a member of an organized stock exchange.

member firm. A broker-dealer that is organized as a partnership and that has at least one general partner who is a member of an organized stock exchange.

mixed account. An account containing both long and short securities.

money market deposit account. Not to be confused with a money market mutual fund, this account is a type of savings account offered by banks and credit unions under Regulation D. A money market deposit account generally requires a higher minimum balance and a limited number of transactions and pays a higher interest rate. Assets in this account are Federal Deposit Insurance Corporation (FDIC) insured. The interest rate is either negotiated or determined by the bank and is based on a benchmark rate. These accounts are not subject to regulatory haircuts.

money market mutual fund. A type of mutual fund subject to the SEC Rule 2a-7, with an objective to preserve capital and maintain liquidity. Assets in this account are not FDIC insured. Although possible, investments in money market mutual funds have a low likelihood of loss of capital. The haircut on this type of investment is 2 percent (see SEC Rule 15c3-1).

Municipal Securities Rulemaking Board (MSRB). Agency established by Congress to establish rules for broker-dealers effecting transactions in obligations of, or guaranteed by, state or local governments or any agency or instrumentality thereof.

name-of securities. Securities registered in the name of customers of the broker-dealer (see **safekeeping**).

NASD. Abbreviation for National Association of Securities Dealers, Inc., formerly an association of broker-dealers doing business in the over-the-counter market. Prior to its incorporation into FINRA, the association supervised and regulated the trading conduct and sales practices of its members. See **FINRA**.

NASDAQ. Abbreviation for the NASDAQ Stock Market, an electronic stock market (formerly known as the National Association of Securities Dealers Automated Quotation System).

net capital. Net worth of a broker-dealer, less certain items such as exchange memberships, the carrying value of securities that are not readily marketable, haircuts on marketable securities in proprietary accounts, furniture and equipment, and other illiquid assets, as defined in the net capital rules.

new issue. A security that is sold by an issuing corporation for the first time. It may be referred to as an initial public offering or IPO.

no-action letter. A letter issued to a broker-dealer by the SEC staff of the Securities and Exchange Commission (SEC) in response to a request filed by the broker-dealer describing a proposed business activity that may or may not conform to SEC rules and regulations. In a no-action letter, the SEC staff indicates that, based on the facts presented by the broker-dealer, the SEC staff will recommend no action be taken against the broker-dealer for engaging in the proposed activity. A no-action letter does not have the force of law; however, it represents an interpretation of the SEC staff that may be applied in a situation where the broker-dealer is engaging in an activity not addressed by existing SEC rules and regulations.

NSCC. Abbreviation for National Securities Clearing Corporation, a subsidiary of DTCC, that provides trade processing, clearance, delivery, and settlement services to its members. It deals with brokers, dealers, and banks in the United States and Canada.

NYSE. Abbreviation for New York Stock Exchange, a not-for-profit corporation that is the largest securities exchange in the United States, and now a part of NYSE Euronext. It furnishes facilities for its members, allied members, member firms, and member corporations to aid them in conducting securities business.

odd lot. A quantity of securities that is less than the trading unit or round lot, usually a quantity less than an even 100 shares.

off-board. Used to describe transactions in listed securities that are not executed on a stock exchange.

offer. The lowest price at which a seller is willing to sell a security.

omnibus account. An open account carried and cleared by another broker-dealer and containing accounts of undisclosed customers on a commingled basis that are carried individually on the books of the broker-dealer introducing the trades.

operations department. The name associated with the overall clerical functions of a broker-dealer. Sometimes referred to as the back office.

option conversion accounts. Accounts consisting of long option and short option positions and a related underlying securities position.

optional commitment. A call exercisable at a future date. A long optional commitment is an option to purchase GNMA securities; a short optional commitment is an option to sell.

optional commitment fee. The amount received or paid for the sale or purchase of an optional commitment.

optional dividend. A dividend that is payable in either stock or cash at the option of the holder of record.

order department. A division of the operations department that receives customers' orders and transmits them either to the floor of a stock exchange or to the trading department for execution. The order department also receives notices of executed trades and transmits such notices to the purchases and sales department and to the registered representatives.

order room. Another name for the order department.

OTC. Abbreviation for over-the-counter. A securities trading market made up of broker-dealers that may or may not be members of a securities exchange. Thousands of companies either have insufficient shares outstanding, stockholders, or earnings to warrant application for or maintaining a listing on a stock exchange, or choose not to be listed on a stock exchange for other business or economic reasons. Securities of these and other companies are traded in the OTC market between broker-dealers that act as either principals (dealers) or agents (brokers) for customers. The OTC market is the principal market for U.S. government and corporate bonds and municipal securities. In the United States, over-the-counter trading in securities is carried out by market makers using interdealer quotation services such as OTC Pink (operated by OTC Markets Group) and OTC Bulletin Board (operated by FINRA).

overdelivery. Delivering a greater amount of securities than called for, the surplus amount being returned by transferring it to the name of the delivering broker-dealer. An overdelivery can also occur if excess securities are delivered in error.

over the window. The direct delivery of securities between two brokerage concerns, rather than by use of the clearinghouse facilities. Delivery is made by hand to the receive window of the broker and is said to be "over the window."

pair off. This can occur if two broker-dealers owe each other the same number of shares of the same security. Instead of actually receiving the security and delivering it back again, they will "pair off" the transaction by giving or receiving a check for the difference in price or exchanging checks for the full amount of each side of the transaction.

papers. A term sometimes given to put and call options.

payable date. The date on which a dividend is payable to holders of record as of some previous date.

pink sheets. Pink sheets got their name because they were formerly a listing of over-the-counter securities published on pink paper by the National Quotation Bureau (now Pink OTC Markets). Yellow sheets are to bonds what pink sheets are to corporate equity securities traded in the OTC market (see **OTC**).

point. If used in connection with the purchase or sale of stocks, point means a rise or decline of $1 per share. If used in connection with the purchase or sale of bonds, it means a rise or decline of $10 per $1,000 principal amount.

point balance. A daily summary by commodity for exchange-traded futures and options on futures contracts that contains all open long and short positions and the original transaction price valued at the closing settlement prices. Separate summaries are prepared for customer transactions and proprietary and noncustomer transactions.

position. This term is used in referring to the securities "long" or "short" in an account or in the stock record.

post. A designated place on an exchange floor where specific securities must be traded.

private placement. The direct sale of a block of securities, either a new issue or a secondary issue, to a single investor or a group of investors. This is usually accomplished through an investment banker.

proxy department. A division of the operations department that helps corporations communicate with their stockholders in cases in which stock certificates are in street name.

purchase and sales department. A division of the operations department that is concerned with the preparation of customers' confirmations of security transactions and the comparison of such transactions with other brokerage concerns.

put option. A contract that entitles the holder to sell (put), entirely at his or her option, a specified number of underlying units of a particular security at a specified price anytime until the stated expiration date of the contract. (This is an American-style option; a European-style option is exercisable only at a specific date.) Such an option, which is always for a round-lot amount and which is transferable, is bought with the expectation of a price decline below the contract price. If the price decline occurs, the purchaser will exercise or sell the option. If the decline does not occur, he or she will let the option expire and will lose only the cost of the option. There are both listed and OTC markets in options. During the existence of an OTC option, the exercise price and number of underlying units are adjusted on the ex-date for cash dividends, rights, and stock dividends or splits.

puts and calls. Options to sell (put) or buy (call) securities within a specified period of time at specified prices (see **put option; call option; straddle**).

quote. The price of a security. It may be the price of the last sale made on an exchange or the current bid and ask price.

receive-and-deliver department. A division of the operations department responsible for the physical receipt and delivery of incoming and outgoing securities. Often, it is also responsible for the daily balancing of cash entries made by the various operations department divisions.

record date. The date on which the stockholder's name must be registered on the books of a company in order to receive a declared dividend or among other things to vote on company affairs.

registered owner. The owner of a security, whose name is recorded on the face of the certificate and on the books of the issuing corporation or its agent.

registered representative. Salesperson (often referred to as an account executive) of the broker-dealer. Salespeople are registered with the CRD (see **CRD**).

registered trader. Individuals or entities who have obtained approval to trade for their own account on the floor of a national securities exchange. Such individuals or entities have certain obligations with regard to the stabilization of the market in securities for which they are registered. They also have less stringent financial responsibilities and reporting requirements than do full-service broker-dealers.

registrar. Usually a trust company or bank charged with the responsibility of preventing the issuance of more stock than that authorized by the issuing company.

regular way delivery. Unless otherwise specified, the delivery of securities (other than those of the U.S. government) to the buying broker-dealer by the selling broker-dealer, with payments received on the third business day after the transaction. The regular-way delivery day for government bonds is the business day following the transaction.

Regulation G. The Federal Reserve Board regulation governing the amount of credit that persons other than banks or broker-dealers may extend to investors who borrow money to buy securities on margin.

Regulation T. The Federal Reserve Board regulation governing the amount of credit that broker-dealers may extend to customers who buy securities.

Regulation U. The Federal Reserve Board regulation governing the amount of credit that banks may extend to customers, including broker-dealers, who borrow money to buy securities on margin.

Regulation X. The Federal Reserve Board regulation specifying conditions with which a U.S. borrower, and foreign persons controlled by or acting on behalf of or in conjunction with a U.S. borrower, must comply when obtaining credit outside the United States for the purpose of purchasing or carrying U.S. securities or when obtaining credit within the United States to purchase or carry any securities.

reorganization department. A division of the operations department that processes securities involving corporate reorganizations, mergers, consolidations, subscriptions, and the exchange of convertible securities into common stocks.

restricted account. This means that a broker may not buy securities for a particular customer for a specified period of time unless the customer has deposited enough money in his or her account to pay for the securities before the customer's orders are executed.

reverse split. Opposite of stock split.

rights. The privilege offered by a corporation to its stockholders to subscribe to certain securities, usually at a advantageous price.

riskless principal transaction. A transaction in which, after having received an order to buy from a customer, the bank purchased the security from another person to offset a contemporaneous sale to such customer or, after having received an order to sell from a customer, the bank sold the security to another person to offset a contemporaneous purchase from such customer.

round lot. A unit of trading or a multiple thereof. On the NYSE, the unit of trading is generally 100 shares in stocks and $1,000 par value in bonds.

RVP. Abbreviation for receive versus payment.

safekeeping. A position on the stock record (street side) indicating securities that have been fully paid for by customers and that are being held by the broker-dealer under custody arrangements. These securities are generally registered in the name of the customer.

safekeeping box. Location in which customers' fully paid-for securities are kept.

SCA. Abbreviation for subsequent coupons attached.

scrip. A certificate issued to stockholders of a corporation that may be exchanged for fractional shares of stock or the equivalent in cash by a fixed date. Scrip is usually issued in connection with a stock dividend or a stock split.

seat. Popular name for a membership on a stock exchange.

SEC. Abbreviation for Securities and Exchange Commission. An agency established by the U.S. Congress to administer federal securities laws.

secondary distribution. The sale of a large block of listed securities (other than an initial issue of a corporation) outside of the exchange on which they are listed. It is usually the holdings of a large individual stockholder or an estate that are being liquidated.

securities borrowed. See **borrowed**.

securities loaned. See **loaned.**

securities not readily marketable. This term refers to (1) securities, except exempted securities, for which there is no market on a securities exchange or no independent publicly quoted market; (2) securities that cannot be publicly offered or sold unless registration has been effected under the Securities Act of 1933 (or the conditions of an exemption, such as Regulation A under Section 3(b) of this act, have been complied with); or (3) securities that cannot be offered or sold because of other arrangements, restrictions, or conditions applicable to the securities or the broker-dealer.

segregation. A position on the stock record (street side) indicating customers' fully paid-for or excess-margin securities that are subject to the customers' instructions and that have been set aside. These securities are generally in the name of the broker-dealer (see **bulk segregation**).

segregation box. Location in which segregated securities are kept.

sell out. Action taken by a broker-dealer to liquidate an account or transaction for failure to maintain proper margin or make timely payment.

seller's option. Transaction that, by agreement, is to be settled at a date later than the usual regular-way transaction.

selling against the box. This is similar to a short sale except that the seller already owns the stock being sold but keeps possession of it and so has to borrow the equivalent stock with which to make delivery to the purchaser.

selling concession. A discount in the public offering price offered by the issuer to members of its underwriting group.

selling group. A group of broker-dealers that has formed a joint account for the sale of securities, usually in connection with an underwriting.

service bureau. A data processing center that processes the transactions of broker-dealers. These centers are located away from the broker-dealer's office.

settlement date. The date on which a securities transaction is to be settled by the delivery or receipt of securities and the receipt or payment of cash.

settlement price. The price at which a security or commodity is to be settled. Used primarily in connection with clearing organization operations.

short. A stock record position (street side) that represents location (such as box, transfer, and so forth) or due from (such as failed to receive or owed to the brokerage concern by a customer.)

short against the box. See **selling against the box**.

short covering. The purchase of securities so that stock previously borrowed to make delivery on a short sale may be returned.

short sale. A sale of securities that requires borrowing equivalent securities to make delivery to the purchaser.

short securities differences. The excess of securities positions for which the broker-dealer is accountable on its stock record (longs) over those whose locations have been accounted for (shorts) after a securities verification. When recorded in a difference account, the excess would be recorded short on the stock record. See **long securities differences**.

SIAC. Abbreviation for Securities Industry Automation Corporation. Formerly owned and operated by AMEX and NYSE, this organization has been absorbed into the operations of NYSE Euronext.

signature guarantee. In order that a registered security may be a good delivery on the exchange or a good transfer, the signature of the registered owner must be properly guaranteed. The guarantee of a stock exchange member or a bank is usually considered sufficient guarantee.

single stock future. A contract for the sale or future delivery of a single security.

SIPC. Abbreviation for Securities Investor Protection Corporation, a corporation established for the purpose of protecting customers of broker-dealers in financial difficulty.

specialist. A broker who is a member of an exchange and who operates on the floor of the exchange to execute transactions and to maintain an orderly market in certain specified securities.

special offering. The sale of a large block of securities on the floor of a stock exchange. The sale is made in accordance with special procedures worked out by officials of the exchange.

split. The action of increasing the number of outstanding shares of stock of a company in order to decrease the market price and afford a greater distribution of the shares. For example, two shares for each share held will have the effect of reducing the price of the shares by approximately one-half.

spot (commodity). (1) The actual commodity as distinguished from a futures contract. (2) An outgrowth of the phrase "on the spot," it usually refers to a cash market price for stocks of the physical commodity that are available for immediate delivery. (3) This term is also used when referring to the futures contract of the current month, in which case trading is still "futures" trading but delivery is possible at any time.

spread. A combination of a put and call option at different prices—one below and the other above the current market price. Also refers to the difference between the bid and asked prices of a security.

SRO. Abbreviation for self-regulatory organization. An SRO, of which a broker-dealer is a member, assumes responsibility for monitoring the broker-dealer's compliance with minimum financial and related reporting requirements.

standby. A put exercisable at a future date. A long standby is an option to sell GNMA securities; a short standby is a commitment to buy.

standby fee. A negotiated amount received or paid for the sale or purchase of a standby.

stock dividend. A dividend payable in the stock of the issuing corporation.

stock power. A legal document used in lieu of the assignment section of a stock certificate.

stock record (or position record). The record of individual securities on which both the long and short positions are shown. For each security, the total of the long positions and the total of the short positions should be in balance.

stock record department. A division of the operations department that keeps up-to-date records of all securities positions, and is usually responsible for reconciling out-of-balance conditions.

stock split. See **split**.

stockholder of record. A stockholder whose name is registered on the books of the issuing corporation.

stop order. Also called a stop loss order, this is an order used by a customer to protect a paper profit in a security or to keep down a possible loss in a security. The stop order becomes a market order if the price of the security reaches or sells through the price specified by the customer.

straddle. A combination of one put and one call, identical with respect to the security issue, number of shares, exercise price, and expiration date.

street. A shortened term for Wall Street that refers to brokers, dealers, and other financial business concerns.

street item. A transaction or account between broker-dealers (for example, fail-to-receive, fail-to-deliver, stock loaned, and stock borrowed).

street name. Securities held in the name of a broker-dealer or a nominee instead of in customers' names are said to be carried in street name.

striking price. The price at which GNMA securities can be purchased or sold upon the exercise of a standby or optional commitment. The price at which an option (put or call) can be exercised (sometimes called the exercise price).

subscription. The offer to purchase a certain offering, such as a certain number of shares of the stipulated stock or principal amount of bonds, for a stipulated amount of money. The offer is not binding unless accepted by the proper authorized representatives of the issuing corporation.

subsequently measured at fair value. Term used to describe the process of valuing security positions for purposes of determining profit or loss on security positions in proprietary trading and investment accounts. The term also is applied to open contracts between broker-dealers and clearing corporations for determining the adjustments to be made for funds owed or receivable as a result of adjusting those contracts to fair values.

substitution. The act of withdrawing securities from a bank loan and substituting other securities of approximately equal value.

suspense account. An account used to record securities or monies that cannot be immediately identified and cleared (for example, reclamations, DK items, and bad deliveries).

syndicate. A group of broker-dealers that underwrites and distributes new issues of securities or large blocks of an outstanding issue.

TAD. An acronym for transfer as directed.

takeoff. Sometimes referred to as a daily activity list, this is a daily record showing the net changes in each security. A separate record is prepared for each security, and the information is used to post (update) the stock record. Also, a record of the long and short positions in a security on the record date, used by the dividend department to make the appropriate dividend entries.

tax stamp. A rubber-stamp facsimile (in some instances, a documentary stamp) affixed to a certificate to indicate that all applicable transfer taxes for the item have been paid.

TBA. Abbreviation for to be announced future government sponsored enterprises' pools that are bought and sold for future settlement. TBA refers to the announcement of the specific pools to be delivered or received.

ticker. An instrument that prints the price at which a security has been traded on an exchange after the trade has been executed.

time loan. A loan having a definite date of maturity and a specified rate of interest for the entire period.

trade. A term that indicates the consummation of a securities transaction, either a purchase or a sale.

trade date. The date on which a securities transaction is actually executed.

trader. An employee of a broker-dealer who executes orders in the OTC market for customers. Also, a person who buys or sells securities for his or her own or his or her company's account for short-term profit.

trading post. Another name for post.

trading unit. The unit by which the security is traded on an exchange, usually 100 shares of stock or $1,000 principal amount of bonds (see **round lot**).

transfer. Usually refers to the act of changing the ownership of registered securities on the books of the issuing corporation.

transfer agent. A transfer agent keeps a record of the name and address of each registered shareholder and the number of shares each owns. The agent sees that certificates presented to his or her office for transfer are properly canceled and that new certificates are issued in the name of the transferee.

transfer department. A division of the operations department that matches, processes, and controls securities being transferred.

two-dollar broker. A name given to a member of an exchange who executes orders for other brokers on that exchange.

underwriting. The act of distributing a new issue of securities or a large block of issued securities, that is, a secondary offering.

undivided liability. An arrangement whereby each member of an underwriting syndicate is liable for his or her proportionate share of unsold securities in the underwriting account regardless of the number of securities the member has previously sold.

undue concentration. The additional haircut from net capital (see SEC Rule 15c3-1) on the fair value of certain proprietary security positions of a single class or series of the same issuer that exceeds 10 percent of a broker or dealer's net capital before haircuts.

unlisted security. A security that is not listed on an exchange.

up-front fee. The amount of cash paid to a delayed-settlement to-be-announced securities or GNMA purchaser that is offset by an increase in the sales price.

value date. See **settlement date**.

valued stock record. The stock record at the examination date, with each security position other than those in segregation and safekeeping assigned a price. Remaining quantities within the position are valued at the assigned price.

variable rate demand obligations. Short-term obligations that are characterized by a "put" or demand feature that gives the bondholder the ability to "put" the bonds back to the issuer. If the "put" bonds cannot be remarketed to another investor, a liquidity facility issued by a financial institution, such as a standby bond purchase agreement, letter of credit, or line of credit, typically provides the issuer's funding to cover the put.

variation margin. A term, used in commodity operations, that refers to the last-day point fluctuation (the difference between the prior day's settling price and the last day's settling price) on net positions long and short.

warrants. Rights to purchase additional securities. Usually affixed to the certificate at the time securities are originally issued. Also, a document evidencing rights, for instance, a warrant for 125 rights.

when-distributed. Refers to the distribution of new securities. Transactions are sometimes entered into on a when-distributed basis before the distribution takes place.

when-issued. A short form of *when, as, and if issued*. The term indicates a conditional transaction in a security authorized for issuance but not yet actually issued. All when-issued transactions are on an "if" basis, to be settled if and when the actual security is issued.

window. A term applied to a place in the office of a broker-dealer where securities are actually received or delivered.

window ticket. A term applied to a document given to the broker-dealer by a transfer agent as a receipt. Also applies to a transfer document originating with the brokerage concern (broker-originated window ticket).

wire house. A brokerage concern that has a network of communications (telephone or teletype) that links the main office to branch offices and to offices of correspondent brokerage concerns.

wire room. See **order department; order room**.

yield. The return on investment that an investor will receive from dividends or interest. The return is expressed as a percentage of the current market price of the security or, if the investor already owns the security, of the price he or she paid. The return on stocks is computed by dividing the total dividends paid in the past calendar year by the price of the stock. The return on bonds is computed by dividing the interest by the price of the bid and is computed as yield to maturity or as yield to earliest call.

Index of Pronouncements and Other Technical Guidance

A

Title	Paragraphs
AICPA Member Alert on SEC and PCAOB independence considerations	3.117
AT-C Section	
315, *Compliance Attestation*	3.173
320, *Reporting on an Examination of Controls at a Service Organization Relevant to User Entities' Internal Control Over Financial Reporting*	3.180
Audit And Accounting Guides	
Investment Companies	1.135, 3.180
Revenue Recognition	5.01. 6.01

C

Title	Paragraphs
CFR Title	
17 CFR Ch 1 Part 1	3.182
17 CFR Ch 1 Part 22	3.182
17 CFR Ch 1 Part 23	3.182
17 CFR Ch 1 Part 30	3.182
17 CFR Ch 1 Part 32	3.182
17 CFR Ch 1 Part 140	3.182
17 CFR Ch IV Part 402	3.183
17 CFR Ch IV Part 403	3.183
17 CFR Ch IV Part 404	3.183
17 CFR Ch IV Part 405	3.183
CFTC Regulation	
1.10	3.182, 6.24
1.10–1.32, 5.6–5.14, 22.2–22.7, and 30.7	3.07
1.10(d)(2)	3.141

F

Title	Paragraphs
210-20	4.60, 5.62, 5.65, 5.70, 5.85, 6.49–.50, 6.52, 6.59, 6.127, 6.154–.155, 6.155, 6.157–.159
230, *Statement of Cash Flows*	
230-10	6.20
250, *Accounting Changes and Error Corrections*	5.14
275, *Risks and Uncertainties*	6.128–.129
275-10	6.130–.131, 6.134, 6.136–.138
350, *Intangibles—Goodwill and Other*	
350-10	5.86
420, *Exit or Disposal Cost Obligations*	5.124
420-10	5.124
440, *Commitments*	6.94
450, *Contingencies*	
450-20	6.132
460, *Guarantees*	6.95, 6.139, 6.144
460-10	6.95, 6.143
470, *Debt*	
470-10	6.88
480, *Distinguishing Liabilities From Equity*	5.110, 5.112
480-10	5.110, 5.112, 6.23
505, *Equity*	
505-10	6.96
605, *Revenue Recognition*	
605-10	6.108
605-45	6.19, 6.100, 6.111
606, *Revenue From Contracts With Customers*	
606-10	5.01
718, *Compensation—Stock Compensation*	6.117
740, *Income Taxes*	
740-10	6.147

Title	Paragraphs
805, *Business Combinations*	6.25
810, *Consolidation*	5.103, 5.104, 6.25
810-10	5.99, 5.104, 6.15, 6.27
815, *Derivatives and Hedging*	2.50, 2.101, 2.104, 2.110, 5.62, 5.88, 5.98, 6.139, 6.141–.142, 6.144, 6.155
815-10	5.89, 5.92–.93, 5.97, 5.98, 6.125, 6.140–.142, 6.155
815-15	5.96
815-20	5.93
815-30	6.141
820, *Fair Value Measurement*	5.04–.05, 5.35, 5.41, 5.49, 5.54, 5.62, 6.82, 6.139
820-10	5.06–.38, 5.42–.43, 5.45, 5.48, 5.50, 5.53, 6.121–.124
825, *Financial Instruments*	5.38, 6.139
825-10	5.38–.40, 6.87, 6.139, 6.145
845, *Nonmonetary Transactions*	
845-10	5.62
850, *Related Party Disclosures*	6.147
850-10	6.145–.146, 6.150
855, *Subsequent Events*	6.151–.153
855-10	6.152–.153
860, *Transfers And Servicing*	2.152, 5.71, 5.103, 6.25, 6.47, 6.60
860-10	1.132, 5.71, 5.76–.77, 5.79–.82, 6.46–.47
860-20	5.78, 6.125–.126
860-30	5.79, 5.81, 5.83–.84, 6.56, 6.62, 6.84, 6.127
860-50	5.101

Title	Paragraphs
940, *Financial Services—Brokers and Dealers*	5.01, 6.27
940-20	2.65, 2.80–.81, 2.142, 5.03, 5.61, 5.67–.58, 5.87, 5.98, 5.105, 5.108, 5.113, 5.117–.118, 6.69–.70, 6.85, 6.99, 6.101
940-320	2.63, 5.58–.59, 5.61, 5.64, 5.123, 6.21, 6.78, 6.80, 6.105
940-325	5.99
940-340	5.86, 5.114, 5.116, 6.41, 6.43–.44, 6.107
940-405	5.122, 6.59
940-605	2.60, 5.115, 5.119–.120, 6.106
940-810	5.99, 6.27
940-820	5.52, 6.124
946, *Financial Services—Investment Companies*	5.29, 5.30
FASB ASU	
No. 2014-09, *Revenue From Contracts With Customers (Topic 606): Summary and Amendments That Create Revenue From Contracts With Customers*	Appendix E
No. 2016-02, *Leases (Topic 842)*	Appendix F
Federal Deposit Insurance Act Section 3(B)(1)	3.177
Federal Reserve	
Regulation G	1.122
Regulation T	1.67–.68, 1.70–.72, 1.122, 1.123, 2.31, 2.32, 2.33, 2.35–.37, 3.07, 3.19, 3.20–.21, 3.73–.79, 4.48, 4.59, 6.53, 6.55, 6.73
Section 220.10(A)	2.151
Regulation U	1.122
Regulation X	1.122

Title	Paragraphs
FINCEN Form	
101, *Suspicious Activity Report by the Securities and Futures Industries*	2.176
104, *Currency Transaction Report*	2.176
FINRA Notice To Members 03-63	6.120
FINRA Regulatory Notice	
09-71	3.65
13-19	2.29
FINRA Rule	
2340, *Customer Account Statements*	3.07, 3.80
3130, *Annual Certification Of Compliance and Supervisory Processes*	3.187
3310, *Anti-Money Laundering Compliance Program*	3.125
4110, *Capital Compliance*	3.65
4120, *Regulatory Notification And Business Curtailment*	3.60
4210, *Margin Requirements*	2.36, 3.79, 4.48
4522, *Periodic Security Counts, Verifications And Comparisons*	3.69

Title	Paragraphs
Investment Advisers Act of 1940	
Rule 206(4)-2	3.173, 3.174, 3.178
Rule 206(4)-2(a)(4)(ii)	3.174
Rule 206(4)-2(a)(6)	3.179
Rule 206(4)-2(b)	3.174, 3.178
Rule 206(4)-2(d)(2)	3.176
Section 202(a)(2)	3.177
Investment Company Act of 1940 (the 1940 Act)	
Rule 10b-10	2.41
Section 2(a)(20)	3.172

Title	Paragraphs
IRC Form	
1099-B	2.173
1099-DIV	2.173
1099-INT	2.173
1099-MISC	2.173
1099-OID	2.173
1099-R	2.173
W-8	4.41
W-9	2.174, 4.41
IRS Publication 1281, *Backup Withholding for Missing and Incorrect Name/TIN(s)*	2.175

N

Title	Paragraphs
National Association of Securities Dealers (NASD) Notice to Members 03-63	3.57–.58

P

Title	Paragraphs
PCAOB AS 2701, *Auditing Supplemental Information Accompanying Audited Financial Statements*	1.05
PCAOB Attestation Standard	
No. 1, *Examination Engagements Regarding Compliance Reports of Brokers and Dealers*	1.05
No. 2, *Review Engagements Regarding Exemption Reports of Brokers and Dealers*	1.05

S

Title	Paragraphs
Sarbanes-Oxley Act of 2002 (SOX)	
Section 404	4.64
Section 404(b)	4.66

Title	Paragraphs
SEC	
Attestation Report of the Registered Public Accounting Firm	4.67
Changes in Internal Control Over Financial Reporting	4.67
Customer fund handling	1.66
Division of Trading and Markets	3.56–.57
Management's Annual Report on Internal Control Over Financial Reporting	4.63–.70
Notification of accountant replacement	3.119–.121
Recordkeeping requirements	2.13–.14
Registration, private placement exemption	1.119
Swaps regulation	1.21
SEC SAB No. 109, Written Loan Commitments Recorded at Fair Value Through Earnings	5.90
SEC FAQ	
Responses to Frequently Asked Questions Concerning Risk Management Controls for Brokers or Dealers With Market Access	3.06, 3.101
Responses to Frequently Asked Questions Concerning the Amendments to Certain Broker-Dealer Financial Responsibility Rules	3.110
Responses to Frequently Asked Questions Concerning the July 30, 2013 Amendments to the Broker-Dealer Financial Reporting Rules	3.110
SEC Final Rule Release	
No. 34-54165, Commission Guidance Regarding Client Commission Practices Under Section 28[E] of the Securities Exchange Act Of 1934	5.107
No. 34-68668, Lost Securityholders And Unresponsive Payees	3.88
No. 34-70072, Financial Responsibility Rules for Broker-Dealers	3.36
No. 34-70073, Broker-Dealer Reports	3.04
No. 34-80295, "Amendment to Securities Transaction Settlement Cycle"	1.47
SEC Form	
10-K	4.67

Title	Paragraphs
17-H	3.85
ADV-E	3.174
X-17A-5 (Focus Report)	3.127, 3.135, 3.185, 6.01, 6.03, 6.13, 6.16, 6.22, 6.32–.38, 6.83, 6.161, *Exhibit 6-1* at 6.163
SEC Interpretation No. 99-5	3.32
SEC Regulation D Rule 506	3.07, 3.96–.97
SEC Regulation S-ID 17-248–Subpart C	3.07, 3.95
SEC Regulation S-X	3.94, 3.117, 6.04
SEC Regulation SHO	2.37–.38, 2.151
SEC Rules and Regulations	
3b-12	3.185
3b-13	3.184, 3.185
3b-14	3.184, 3.185
3b-15	3.184, 3.185
8c-1	2.158, 3.07
11a1-6	3.185
12b-2	4.66
13a-15(d)	4.69
13a-15(f)	4.63
13h-1	3.131
15a-1	3.185
15a-6	3.07
15b9-2	3.185
15c2-1	2.158, 3.07
15c3-1	2.14, 2.55, 2.84, 2.113, 2.119, 2.144, 2.169, 2.172, 3.07, 3.15, 3.35, 3.41–.60, 3.71, 3.102, 3.104–.106, 3.108, 3.111, 3.132–.133, 3.141, 3.156, 6.07, 6.26, 6.33
15c3-1(a)	5.112
15c3-1(c)(2)(X)	2.119

Title	Paragraphs
15c3-1(c)(15)	3.170
15c3-1(d)	5.112
15c3-1(e)	3.07, 3.61–.65
15c3-3	1.18, 1.66, 1.69, 1.122–.123, 2.39, 2.83, 2.87, 2.113, 2.123, 2.125, 2.128, 2.144, 2.158, 2.172, 3.07, 3.11–.40, 3.59, 3.70, 3.81, 3.83, 3.102–.106, 3.108–.109, 3.111, 3.141, 3.152–.153, 4.49, 4.59, 4.61, 6.07, 6.09, 6.36–.37, 6.40, 6.53
15c3-3a	2.14, 3.71
15c3-3(a)(16)	3.14
15c3-3(b)(5)	2.129
15c3-3(c)(7)	3.19
15c3-4	3.185
15c3-5	3.06, 3.07, 3.98–.101
15c6-1(a)	1.47, 2.17
17a-1	3.94
17a-3	2.13, 2.25, 2.28, 2.30, 2.114, 2.165, 2.166, 2.170, 3.07, 3.71, 3.72
17a-3(a)(17)	2.30
17a-3(a)(23)	2.14
17a-4	2.13, 2.41, 2.114, 2.166, 2.168, 3.07, 3.72
17a-4(e)(7)	3.100
17a-4(e)(9)	2.14
17a-5	1.05, 3.02, 3.04, 3.07, 3.60, 3.102–.122, 3.120, 3.129, 3.137, 3.141, 3.152–.154, 3.157, 3.160–.161, 3.164, 3.179, 6.01–.07, 6.12, 6.26, 6.160, Appendix B, Appendix C
17a-5(a)(5)	3.135

Title	Paragraphs
17a-5(c)(3)	6.02
17a-5(c)(5)	6.02
17a-5(d)	6.03
17a-5(f)(2)	3.05
17a-11	2.170, 3.07, 3.60, 3.106, 3.111
17a-12	3.137, 3.185
17a-13	2.171, 3.07, 3.66–.70, 3.104, 3.106, 3.108, 3.111, 4.47, 4.49, 4.59, 4.61, 6.07
17Ad-17	3.07, 3.87–.92
17Ad-22	3.07, 3.93–.94
17f-4	2.113
17h-1T	3.07, 3.83–.86
17h-2T	3.07, 3.83–.86
19c-3	1.40
36a1-1	3.185
36a1-2	3.185
144A	1.119
400-406	2.35, 3.82, 4.48
Securities Act of 1933 (the 1933 Act)	1.114, 1.119, 4.44
Rule 144A	3.96
Securities Exchange Act of 1934 (the 1934 Act)	
Section 3(a)(6)	3.28
Section 12(b)	6.04
Section 12(g)	6.04
Section 12(i)	6.153
Section 15(b)(1)	3.177
Section 15C	3.02
Section 28(e)	1.141, 5.106
SIPC Rule 600	3.164

Subject Index